IT WILL BE
MORE
BEAUTIFUL
THAN YOU
COULD EVER
IMAGINE

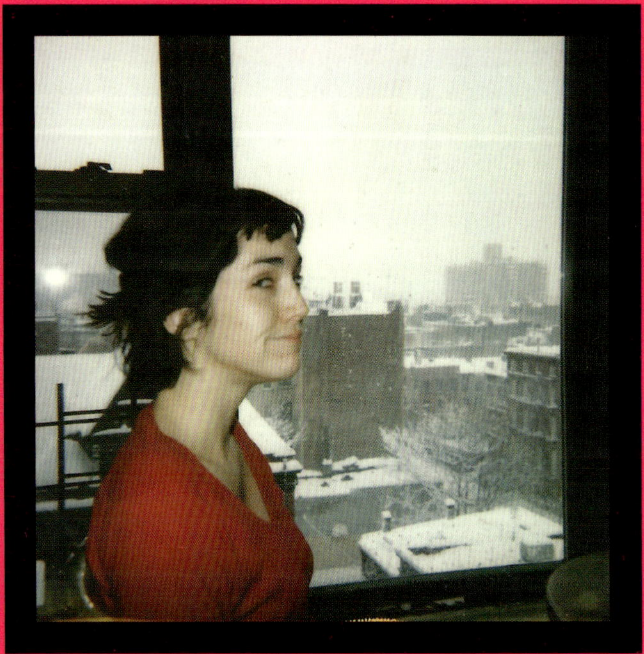

IT WILL BE MORE BEAUTIFUL THAN YOU COULD EVER IMAGINE

The Art of Susan O'Malley

By Christina Amini

CHRONICLE BOOKS
SAN FRANCISCO

Previous spread: Susan O'Malley, circa 2000

Library of Congress Cataloging-in-Publication Data
Names: Amini, Christina Maheen author
Title: It will be more beautiful than you could ever imagine : the art of Susan O'Malley / by Christina Amini.
Description: San Francisco : Chronicle Books, [2026]
Identifiers: LCCN 2025052162 | ISBN 9781797230627 hardcover
Subjects: LCSH: O'Malley, Susan, 1976-2015—Criticism and interpretation
Classification: LCC N6537.049 A86 2026
LC record available at https://lccn.loc.gov/2025052162

Manufactured in China.

FSC MIX Paper | Supporting responsible forestry FSC™ C169962 www.fsc.org

Design by Kristen Hewitt.
Typeset in Galaxie Polaris and Galaxie Copernicus.

10 9 8 7 6 5 4 3 2 1

Chronicle Books is represented in the UK and Europe by Abrams & Chronicle Books, 22 Ely Place, London EC1N 6TE, abramsandchronicle.co.uk, and Média-Participations, 57 rue Gaston Tessier, 75166 Paris CEDEX 19, media-participations.com.

Chronicle Books LLC
680 Second Street
San Francisco, California 94107
chroniclebooks.com

FOR SUSAN.

AND FOR ALL THE ARTISTS,

WHICH INCLUDES YOU.

Contents

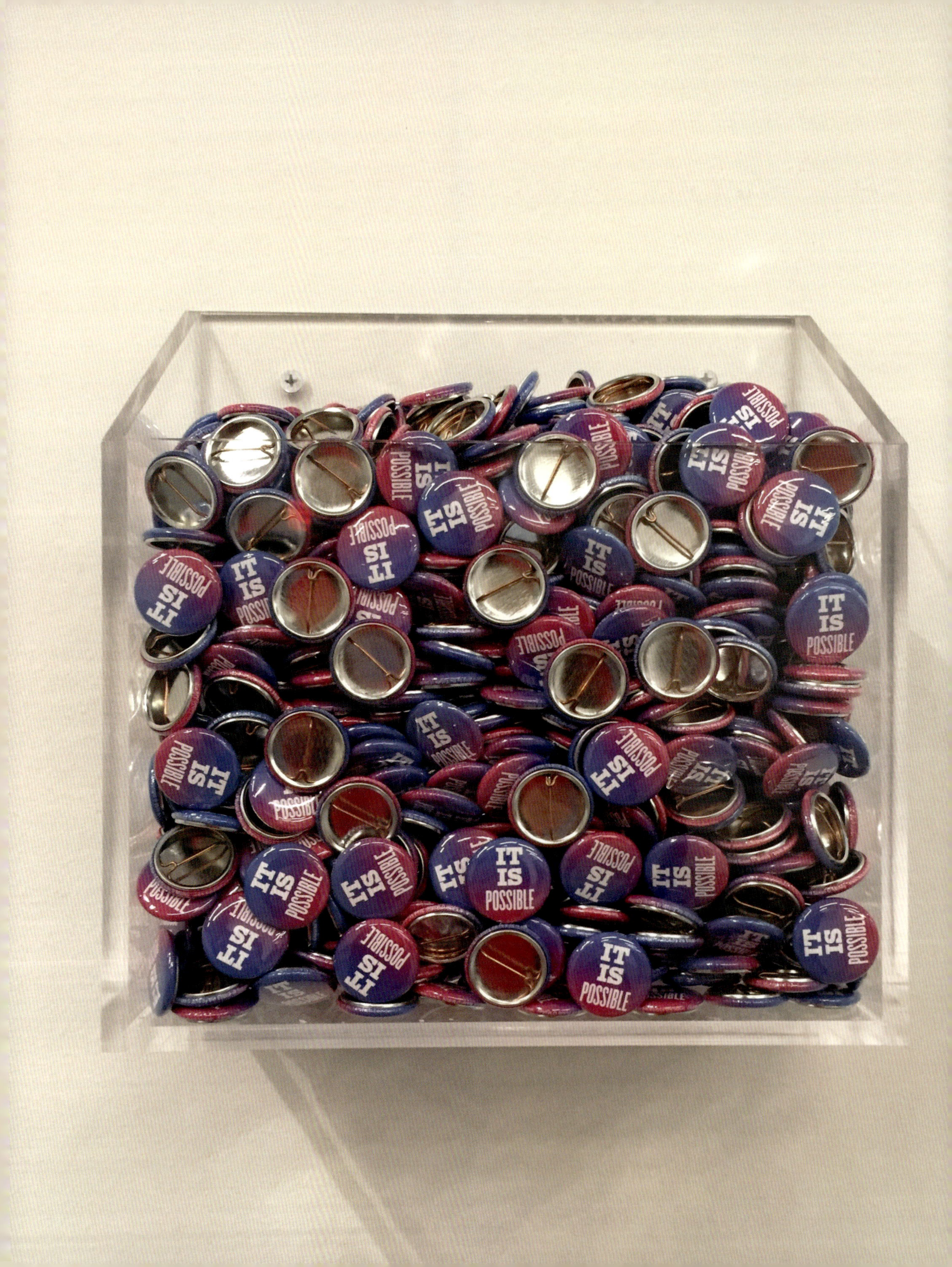
IT IS POSSIBLE

INTRODUCTION

You Are Here Awake and Alive

Christina Amini

Susan O'Malley was born in San Jose, California, in 1976. One of six children of a Mexican American mother, Guadalupe "Lupe" Reyna O'Malley, and an Irish American father, Patrick O'Malley, she always knew what it was to be in relation to others. The family lived in Willow Glen, a suburb of San Jose, to which O'Malley would return as an adult to make art.

As an undergraduate, O'Malley attended Stanford University and majored in urban studies. She was intrigued by the ideas of how and where we live, how we relate to one another, and how our physical environment plays a role in that engagement. After college O'Malley moved to New York City and worked at an advertising agency during the first dot-com boom, teaching herself design and absorbing the language of commerce.

Ready to forge a new path and curious about pursuing art, O'Malley returned to the San Francisco Bay Area. She took printmaking courses at Foothill College, turned her mother's garage into a studio space, and worked at a gallery in Palo Alto before beginning a graduate program at California College of the Arts (CCA) in 2003. One of O'Malley's professors at CCA was the artist Ted Purves, who would soon start a pioneering new program—the first of its kind in the United States—in Social Practice, artwork for which the theory and practice of social engagement is central. Fortuitously, this program and its teachers perfectly matched where O'Malley wanted to go with her own artistic practice—toward art that pushed what art might be.

Projects like Purves's *Temescal Amity Works*—in which artists collected and redistributed surplus neighborhood fruit—inspired her. Her teachers Jon Rubin and Jonn Herschend created the Independent School of Art, which explored what a new (entirely free) art school might look like, and O'Malley was an active participant. She was curious about artists who crossed boundaries between media and those who made their daily life and relationships part of the work. O'Malley gravitated toward art that was generous, art that engaged the viewer in participatory experiences, and art with a sense of humor and warmth (both of which she possessed in abundance).

Opposite: *It Is Possible* buttons presented alongside the *Advice from My 80-Year-Old Self* series, San Francisco Museum of Modern Art, 2016. More than 50,000 of these buttons were distributed for free during the exhibition.

As a graduate student, O'Malley ventured into new territory, both discovering new avenues for her own creative expression and good-humoredly pushing up against the collective understanding of what art could be. Social Practice was in its infancy, and O'Malley was—at times very intentionally and at other times more unwittingly—at the vanguard of the movement. When she started the *Pep Talk Squad*—a project of listening to and then cheering on anyone who wanted encouragement—her teachers asked why this project was art and not social work. Susan wondered if she could make work that was both, or more. With relentless spirit, she persisted with pep, writing the *Pep Talk Squad Manual* for her thesis.

O'Malley offered *Bubble Gum Therapy* in her studio space, creating a moment in time for folks to chew, reflect, and analyze the chewed outcome for its meaning. Later on in her grad school career, she staged the *MFA Debate* between Bay Area art schools—part comedy, part performance art. She created vending machines that distributed buttons featuring the names of every person she had ever met. She appointed herself the artist-in-residence in her hometown of Willow Glen, and she traveled the neighborhood rearranging the hoses and rock gardens like an off-kilter Andy Goldsworthy.

In 2006, just as Social Practice was being defined, O'Malley was one of the first people to graduate with an MFA in the field. Upon graduation, she brought her keen sense of audience and talent for collaboration to the curatorial sphere, working first in a gallery and then as curator and print center director at the Institute of Contemporary Art San José, where she would curate over fifty exhibitions.

Widely connected in the Bay Area art community, O'Malley was known as both a curator and an artist. She exhibited her own work at the Montalvo Arts Center in Saratoga, California, the Contemporary Arts Museum Houston, the Parthenon in Nashville, Tennessee, and various other locations. She also completed public art projects in San Francisco, New York, London, Poland, and Denmark.

In one of her most personal projects, *My Healing Garden is Green*, she asked her mother, Lupe O'Malley, who was ailing with a progressive neurogenerative disease, to write down messages she wanted to remember. O'Malley blew up images of the words—written in a shaky but determined hand—to large scale, allowing viewers to appreciate her mother's love at full volume.

At the San José Museum of Art, O'Malley participated in a show called *Now Serving: Love*. She set up a small food stall, lit a candle on a cupcake, and asked the viewer to make a wish. With a twinkle in her eye, wholehearted warmth, whip-smart sensibility, and daring openness, Susan made an offering to the viewer—an invitation to connect to themselves, to each other, and to her.

In 2014 O'Malley quit her job as a curator to make art full-time. That same year she created what would become her best-known work, *Advice from My 80-Year-Old Self*.

"What advice would your eighty-year-old self give you?" O'Malley posed this question to strangers at farmers' markets, in senior centers, and on the street around the Bay Area. Altogether she approached and spoke to more than a hundred ordinary people of all ages. Next she transformed their responses into vibrant text-based images, reminders to do things that matter to your heart. Permission to have sugar in your tea.

The resulting art pieces became a book, a series of posters lining San Francisco's Market Street, and numerous murals and installations on public buildings and at art institutions, including the San Francisco Museum of Modern Art (SFMOMA).

Throughout her career, one of the guiding principles of O'Malley's socially based art practice was using simple and recognizable tools of engagement: giving a pep talk, asking for advice, taking a walk, distributing flyers, doodling, sharing food. These easily understood and sometimes humorous actions and interactions of everyday life offered entry points into her work. O'Malley shifted otherwise mundane exchanges into heightened experiences.

Tragically, Susan O'Malley died unexpectedly in 2015 due to an undiagnosed heart condition. She was thirty-eight years old. She and her husband were expecting twin girls, Reyna and Lucy, who did not survive O'Malley's collapse. It was an unimaginable loss.

The Bay Area mourned her. The Montalvo Arts Center and the Yerba Buena Center for the Arts both held memorials. One of O'Malley's signature pieces, *It Will Be More Beautiful Than You Could Ever Imagine*, was printed as a memorial broadside. That colorful poster became something of a talisman for O'Malley's friends, family, and fans—cropping up around the Bay Area, in windows, on walls, and in local businesses, offices, and homes—for years after her death, always a vibrant reminder of her inimitable spirit.

More than a decade later, Susan O'Malley's impact—on art, on the world, and on the art world—continues to grow and expand. Just days before her death, she had turned in the final artwork for her book *Advice from My 80-Year-Old Self*. The book was published by Chronicle Books one year later. Chief curator at large and publisher at the Museum of Modern Art (MoMA) Michelle Kuo called the book "a brilliant and winsome inversion of that quintessentially twenty-first-century genre, the self-help book. Rather than looking inward, O'Malley reaches outward—to others, strangers, friends. She turns introspective reflection into a resolutely collective and communitarian experience."

In the years since her death, O'Malley's artwork has been acquired and shown by SFMOMA, the Oakland Museum of California, and the Berkeley Art Museum and Pacific Film Archive. It has been installed in public places in San Francisco, Berkeley, San Diego, Cincinnati, and more. O'Malley's work is resonant and lasting because our connection to one another is resonant and lasting. She knew this, and she was always showing it to us. O'Malley's legacy and works ask us to be open to the possibilities of art, and of one another, at once seriously and playfully.

Writing about her work on the project *Moment to Moment*, O'Malley said that she wanted to "open the possibility of a flash of introspection in the hamster-wheel of life. . . . In these works I'm suggesting my wish for how things could be: if we paid closer attention to our being, to our grieving, to the way the sun makes a spectacular reflection on the buildings at that certain time of the day. It has to begin somewhere, why not here?"

Opposite: *It Will Be More Beautiful Than You Could Ever Imagine* print, 2009

IT WILL BE
MORE
BEAUTIFUL
THAN YOU
COULD EVER
IMAGINE

Dear Young-ish artist,

I noticed that you needed to be reminded of a few things – many of which I'm sure you already know. But it doesn't hurt to be reminded. So here it goes.

Taking the path of an artist is a radical one. There is no steady paycheck, 401K or linear trajectory. You do it because it's either art or insanity; or because you have a gift that needs to be shared with the world; or because you want to be famous. But here's the deal: it takes time to cultivate it. Very few of us can jump out of undergrad and earn a living as a novelist. Sometimes you have to take a job writing copy at an internet company to prove that you can take care of yourself; or you have to take several jobs so you can buy the materials for your giant octopus sculpture; or you have to experience the darkest grief of your life in order to find your voice. And there will be lots of bad poems and terrible paintings and bad decisions before anything comes of it. It takes time and it takes space and sometimes it takes doing very little alone or in the company of other like-minded people for these things to happen. Everything is part of it. So be patient, pay attention, and be kind to yourself.

Maybe it will take 15 years, so in the year 2028, when you quit your day job writing ad copy for Hologram Space to begin. Maybe then you'll decide to finish the novel you've been plugging away at in your free evenings. You decide to do it because it's been nagging at you for years, sometimes making you feel so empty inside that you don't recognize yourself, your spouse, or your children. And as you finally jump into this adventure it dawns on you: it's always been here. You've always had everything you needed to do it. It just took you this long to accept this and the uncertainty of the process. And, now finally, you've said yes and things are happening. Don't scold yourself for taking so long, just appreciate that you've finally made it here.

Sincerely,
Your friend

Above: *An Unsolicited Open Letter to the Young-ish Artist (this means all of us, right?)*, 2013

Opposite: *Now Serving: Love*, San José Museum of Art, California, February 14, 2014. As part of the exhibition *Around the Table: Food, Creativity, Community*, O'Malley set up a stand where participants each made a wish and blew out a candle on a cupcake.

Pages 18-19: Self-portrait in Susan O'Malley's Berkeley, California, studio with *You Are Here Awake and Alive* etched mirror, 2013

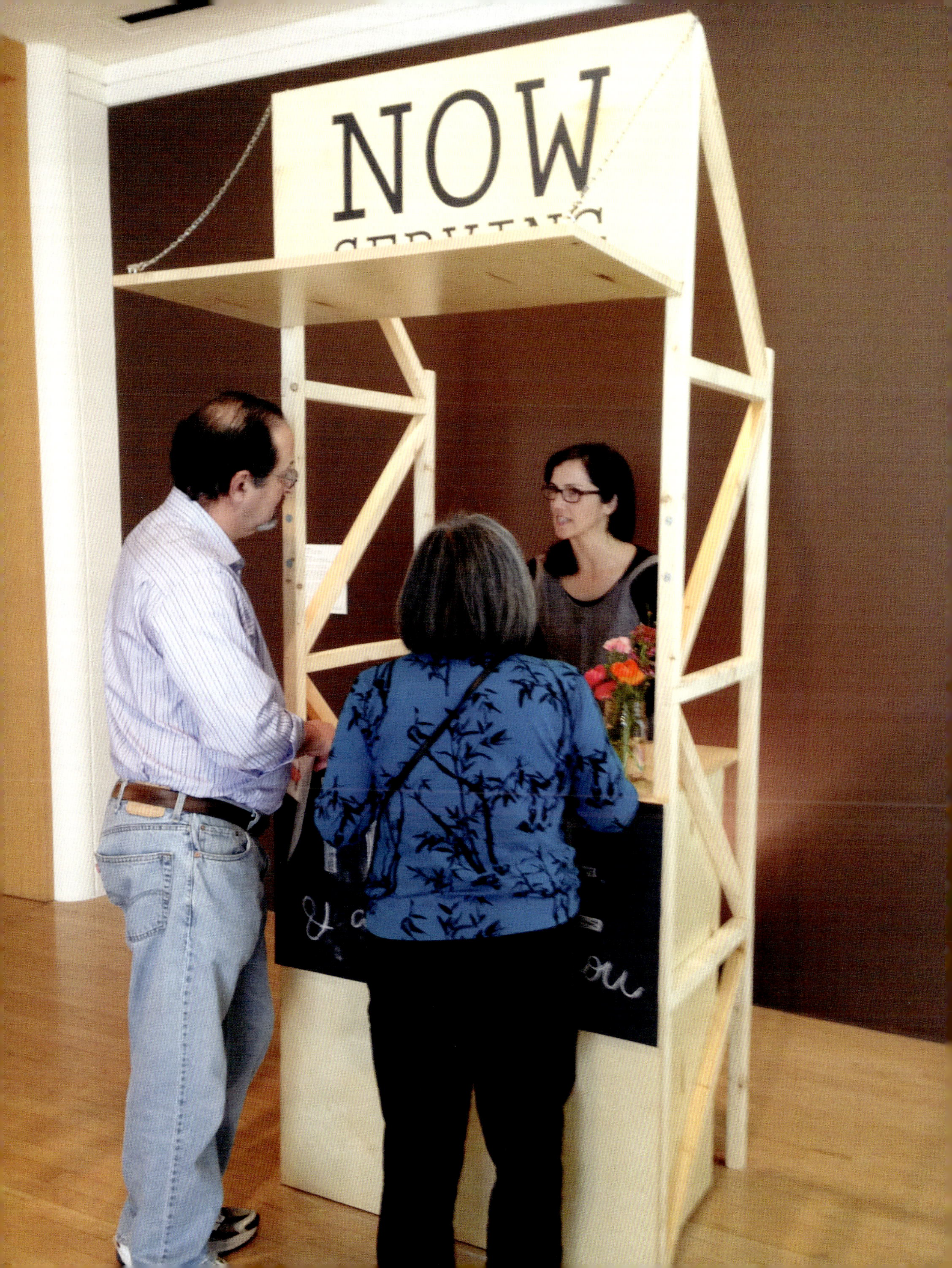
NOW

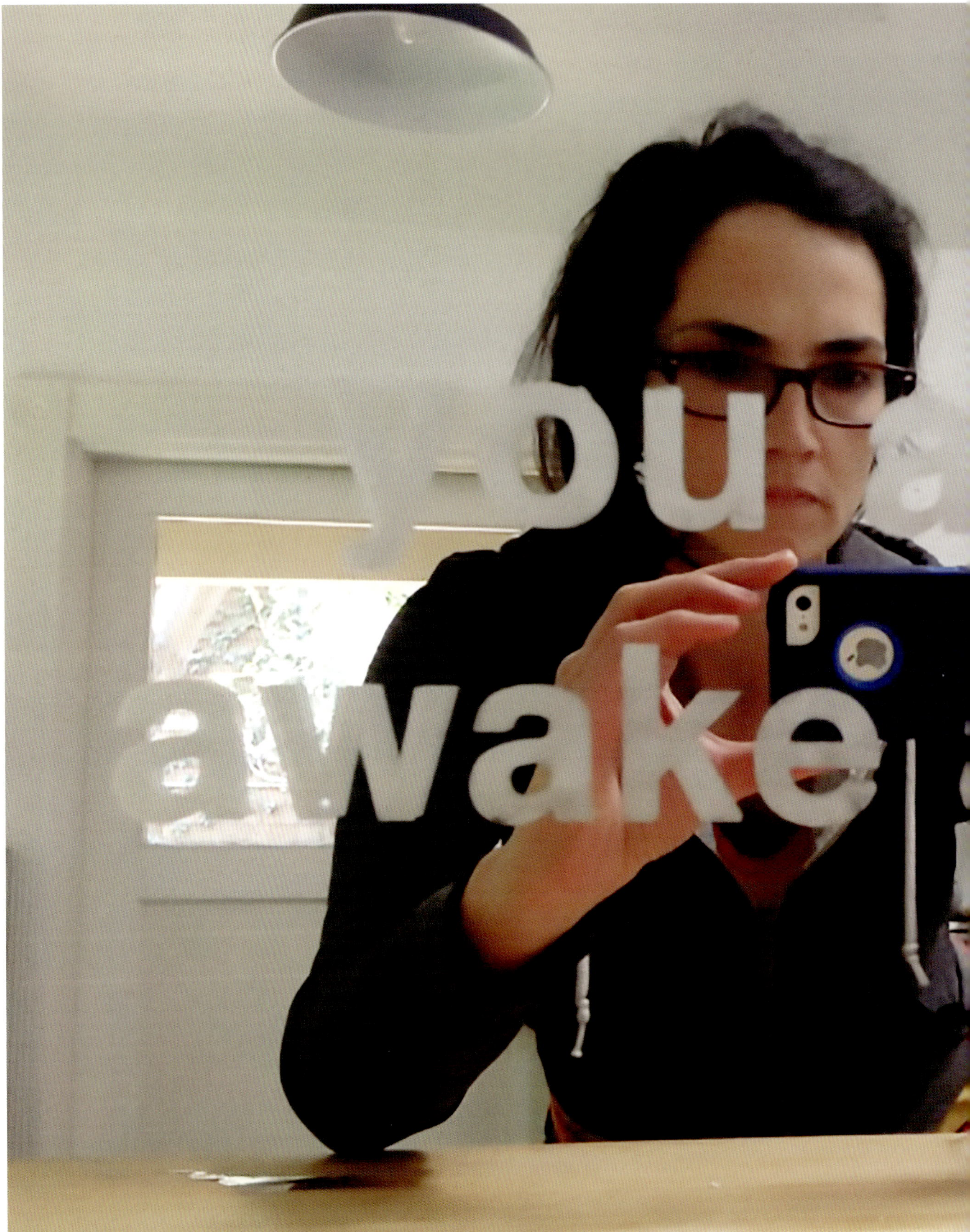
ou
awake

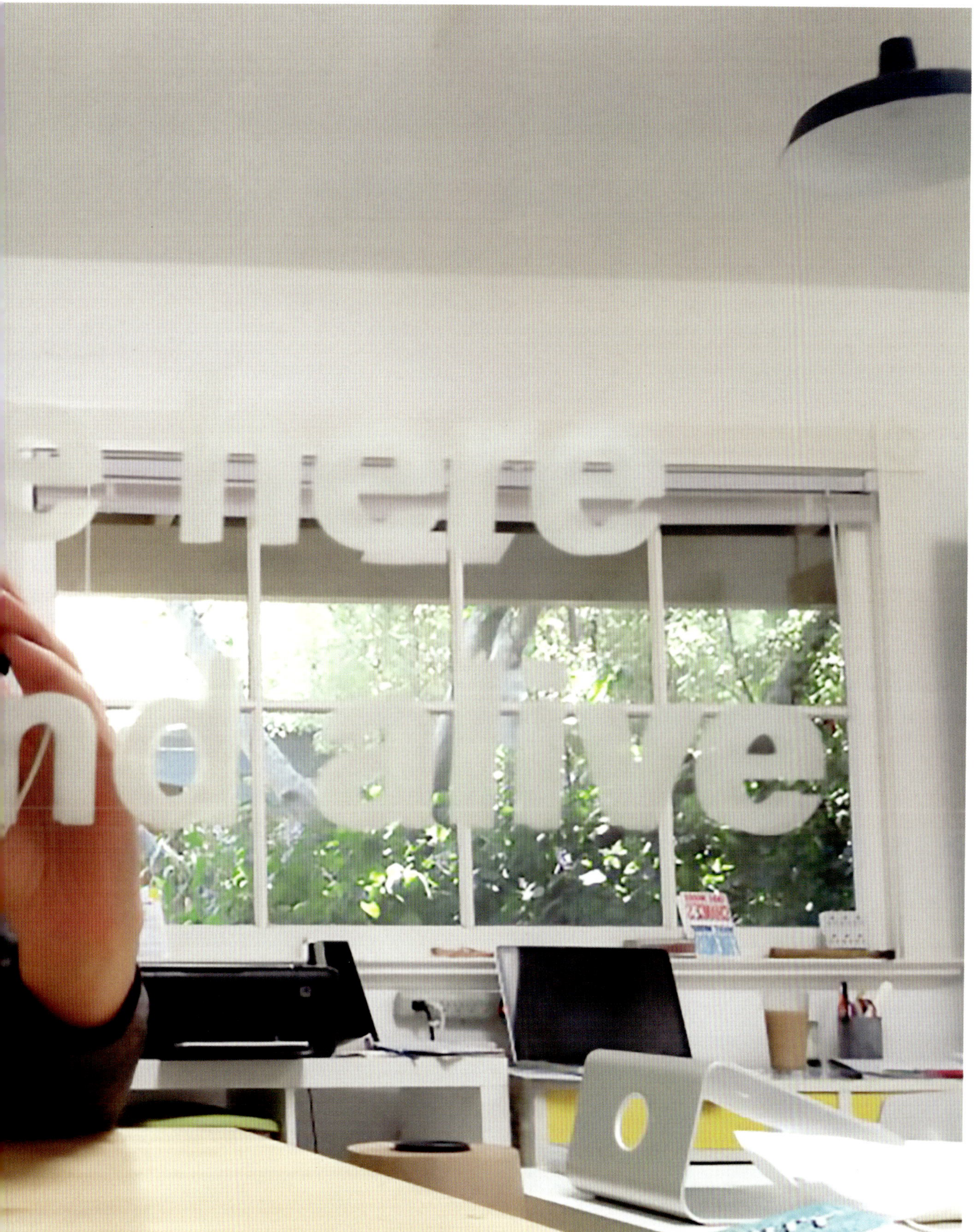

Art and Social Practice: An Introduction

Harrell Fletcher

What is Art and Social Practice? Well, let me start by saying that there are a lot of different perspectives on that question. I actually think it's much better that socially engaged art exists as a diverse, messy mix of definitions rather than one absolute denotation, even though that can be frustrating for people trying to understand what it is. I prefer that no single person or institution owns the concept, that there are differences of opinion about what qualifies as socially engaged art, and that there's room for variation and evolution. I can say that, generally, the methods and values related to Art and Social Practice tend to include collaboration and participation, site and situation specificity, interdisciplinarity and variable forms, and sometimes presenting work in everyday contexts.

There is a long list of precedents for Art and Social Practice. Participatory projects have existed throughout the history of art and of other, diverse fields, from farming to documentary filmmaking, from alternative education to church choirs. Some notable artists who employed social engagement before the term *Art and Social Practice* was put into use include Mierle Laderman Ukeles, the members of Group Material, John Malpede, Wendy Ewald, and John Ahern.

My own practice of working with participants and collaborators on site-specific projects goes back at least three decades, to before the first Social Practice MFA program was developed at California College of the Arts in 2005. Susan O'Malley was in that first MFA class. I started another Social Practice MFA program at Portland State University in 2007, and around that same time and in the following years other MFA programs popped up around the country and internationally. Sometimes they used slightly different terms, such as *Public Practice*, *Contextual Practice*, and *Art and Social Engagement*. Not long after that, Social Practice started being included as a category in artist residency programs, public art commissions, conferences, books, grants, and even museums.

My own take is that Art and Social Practice is in some ways the opposite (or maybe the reverse) of what most people assume art to be—the status quo version, what I call the studio/gallery paradigm. The typical concept of artists is that they work in studios, whereas artists working in socially engaged ways usually operate out in the world in one way or another. We usually think of artists working alone in those studios, expressing their personal feelings in the form of objects like paintings and sculptures, and we assume that those objects later get presented in galleries and museums for art-going audiences to view and appreciate. Social Practice artists usually work with other people, often basing their art on the interests and lives of others rather than themselves, and the products of their work might not be objects at all. Instead, the product could take the form of an event or activity in a nonart context, or it might be ephemeral, like a set of posters on the street (a form that some of Susan's work took), or it could be so permanent and particular to a place that it only makes sense in a specific neighborhood front yard.

These differences between the two approaches—studio and social—have other implications as well. Normally when an artist makes art in the isolation of a studio, it is necessary for gallerists or curators to find and relocate it to a context where an audience can view the work (which, in reality, rarely happens). In the case of socially engaged art, the work can be made available to the public directly, without an intermediary validating and presenting it. With Social Practice there is no need to rent a studio, purchase art materials, or pay to store any work that goes unexhibited or unsold. Artists working in socially engaged ways don't need to rely on the commercial gallery system for support and exposure. They can make work anywhere—in a park, in a library, at the beach, on the radio, in a prison, or on a T-shirt. They don't need to use traditional art materials or any physical materials at all if the work is conceptual in nature. There is no need to reach an art audience or to sell work, and instead the public can function as both participants and audience, and funding can come from commissions or even be built into the project itself if it takes the form of a small business or nonprofit organization.

At the same time, socially engaged artists can participate in any status quo art approaches they want, as long as they have access to them and find them useful or interesting. Some artists who work in the realm of Social Practice do have studios or offices, make objects as part of their projects, present work in art contexts, and in a few cases even work within the commercial gallery system to some extent. For example, Susan's work was sometimes self-initiated and occurred in everyday environments, but at other times she curated, programmed, and exhibited within galleries and museums.

For artists, having options to work in a variety of ways, and not just within art world conventions, is liberatory. It brings us closer to realizing the assumed, but not always true, idea that artists have special freedoms to act outside of societal strictures and to make whatever kind of work they want. If artists are trained to think that the only valid platform for showing their work is a gallery, then they will limit themselves to making art that is designed for a gallery. If artists realize they have the agency to validate themselves, to make art and present it in any way that they want to, and to even think of the process (which can be participatory and collaborative), the systems of presentation, and the means of distribution as the work itself or at least part of it, they expand their own set of possibilities while creating liberating precedents for other artists to build on.

Susan was one of a handful of people leading the way toward this alternative paradigm for art and artists. There had been many examples of socially engaged art, but until the formalization of Art and Social Practice (and its variants), those historical works were scattered and often marginalized within the larger context of studio/gallery art. By giving socially engaged art a name and actively working within that framework, Susan and other boundary-breaking artists helped establish and legitimize a way for artists to prioritize direct connections with the public, appreciate and respond to people and places often left out of the art world, and be self-realized and self-reliant as they navigate their own way of creatively engaging with the world.

Pages 23–27: *What Is Your Secret Hope and Dream?*, San Francisco Bay Area, 2004–5. As part of her Susan O'Malley Research Team project, O'Malley asked participants to write down their secret hopes and dreams and photograph her holding them up.

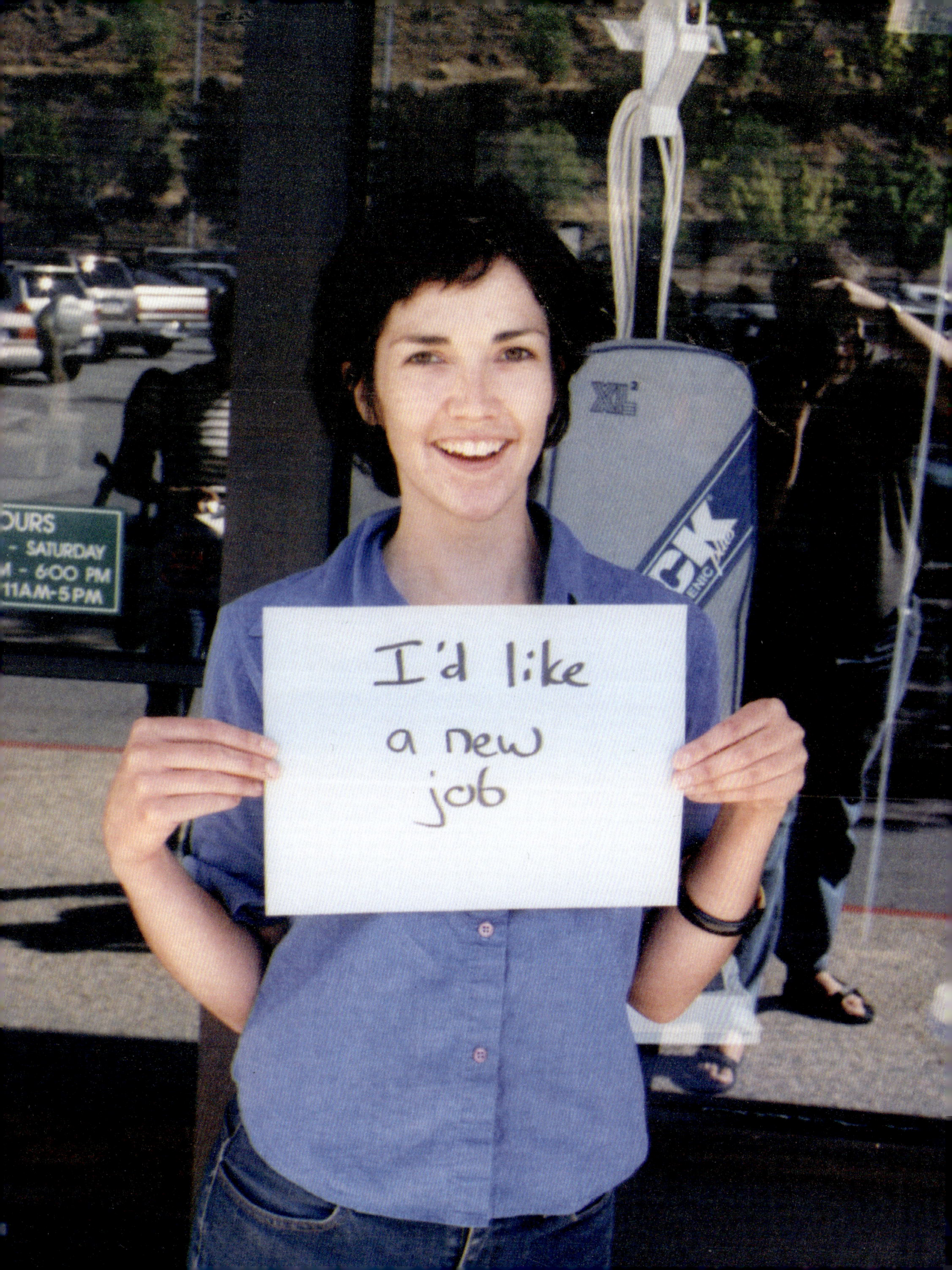
I'd like
a new
job

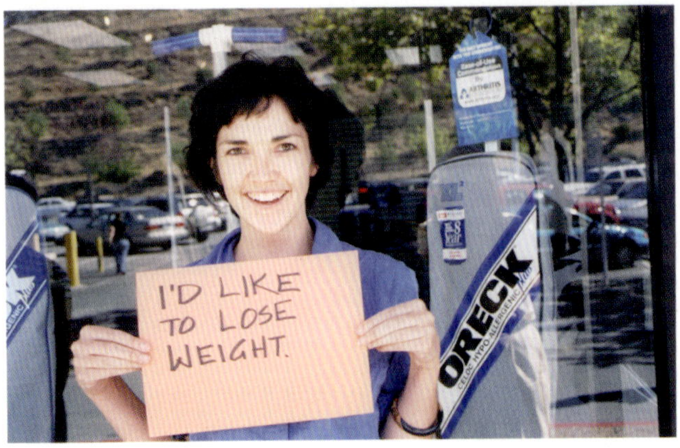
I'D LIKE
TO LOSE
WEIGHT.

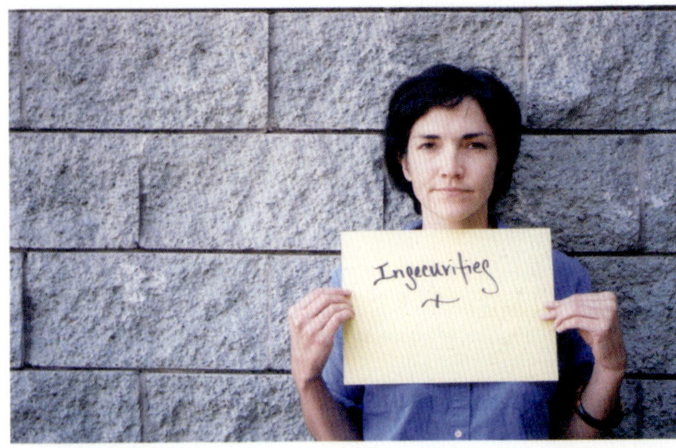
Insecurities

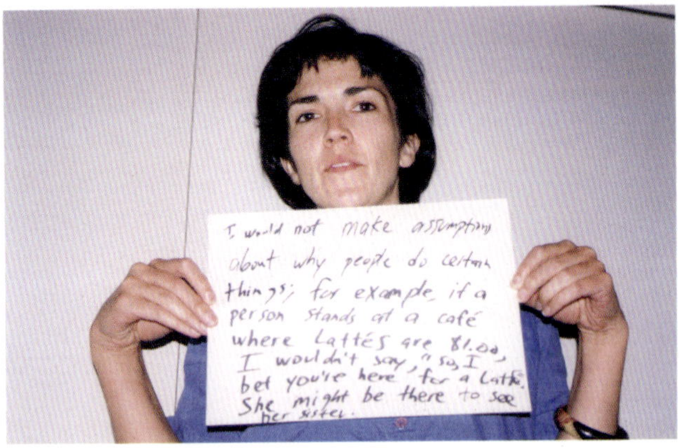
I would not make assumptions
about why people do certain
things; for example if a
person stands at a café
where Lattés are $1.00,
I wouldn't say, "so, I
bet you're here for a Latté.
She might be there to see
her sister.

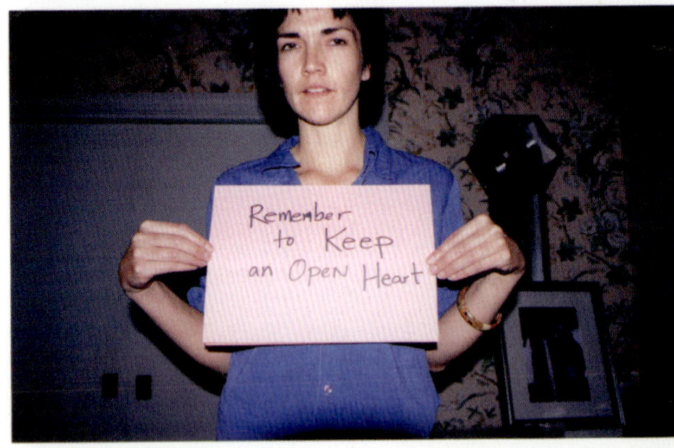
Remember
to Keep
an Open Heart

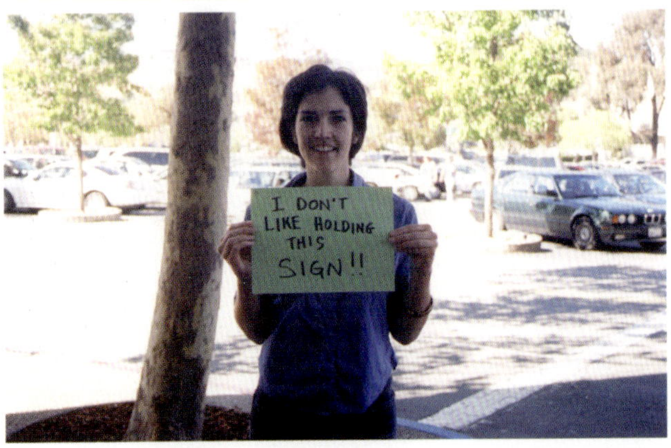
I DON'T
LIKE HOLDING
THIS
SIGN!!

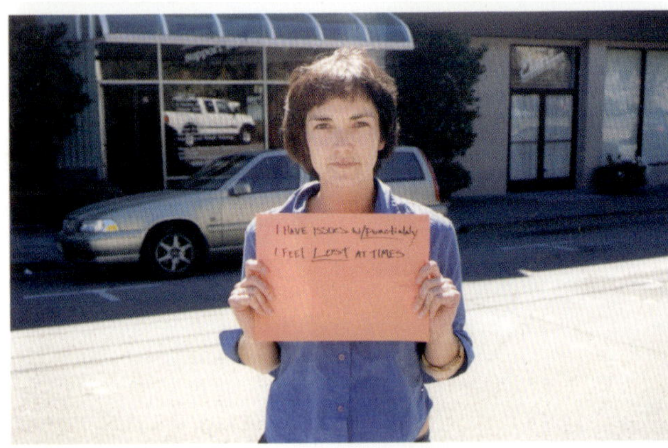
I HAVE ISSUES w/punctuality
I FEEL LOST AT TIMES

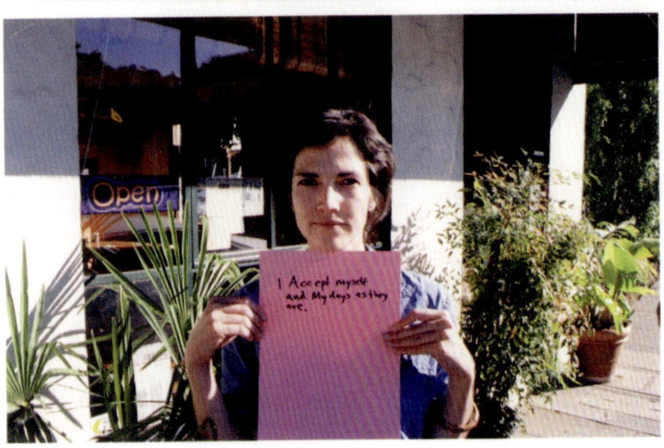
I Accept myself
and My days as they
are.
Open

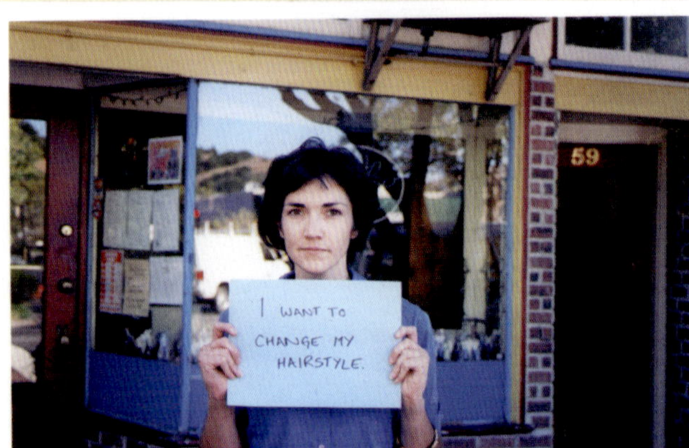
I WANT TO
CHANGE MY
HAIRSTYLE.
59

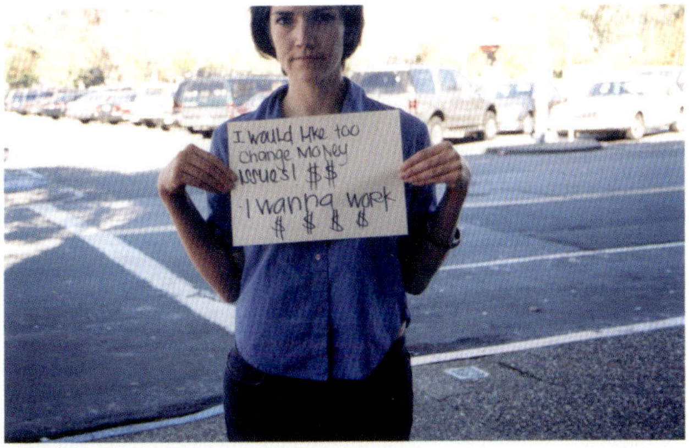
I would like too
change Money
issue's! $$
I wanna work
$ $ $ $

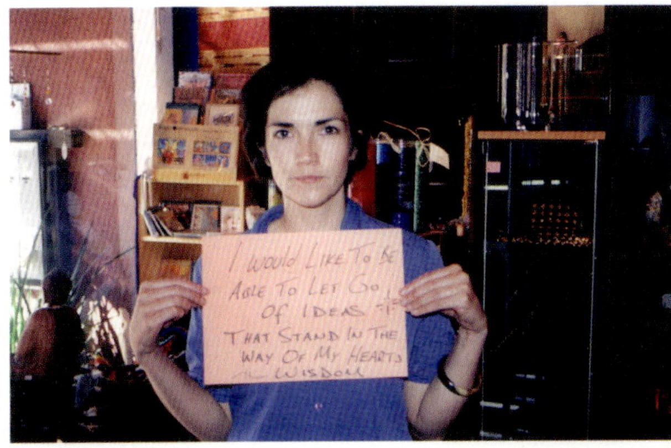
I WOULD LIKE TO BE
ABLE TO LET GO
OF IDEAS
THAT STAND IN THE
WAY OF MY HEARTS
WISDOM

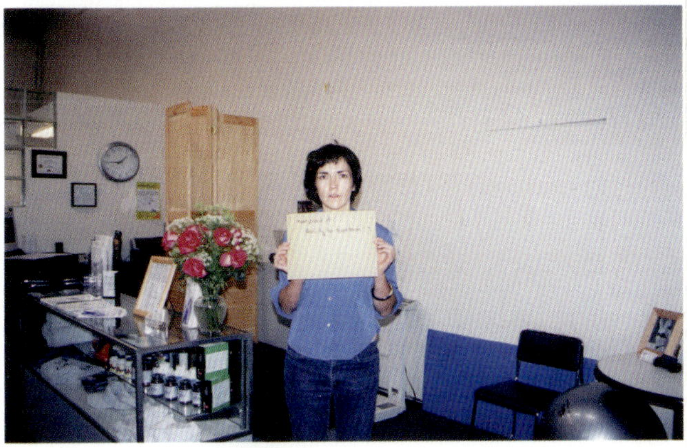

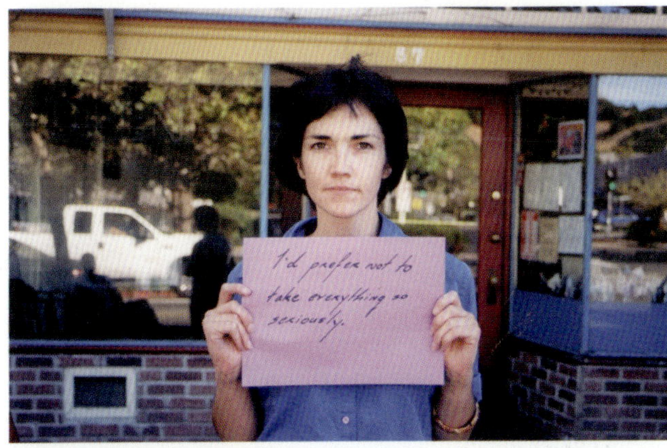
I'd prefer not to
take everything so
seriously.

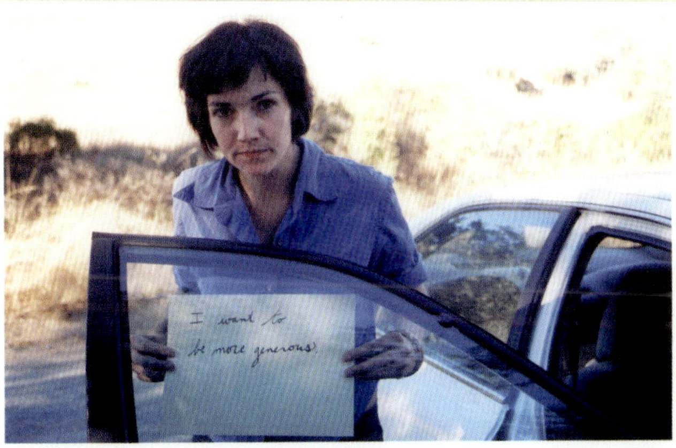
I want to
be more generous.

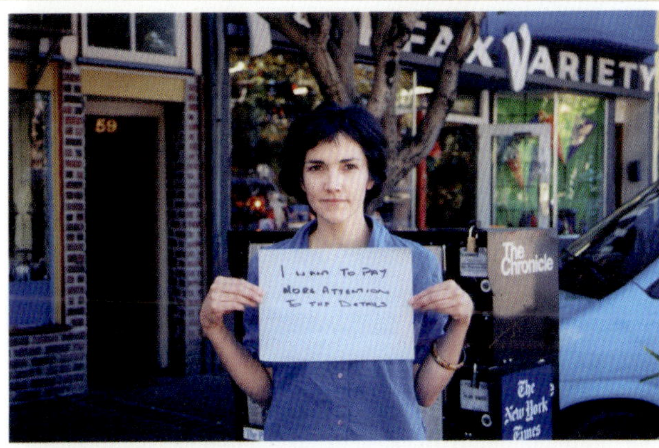
FAX VARIETY
59
The Chronicle
The New York Times
I WANT TO PAY
MORE ATTENTION
TO THE DETAILS

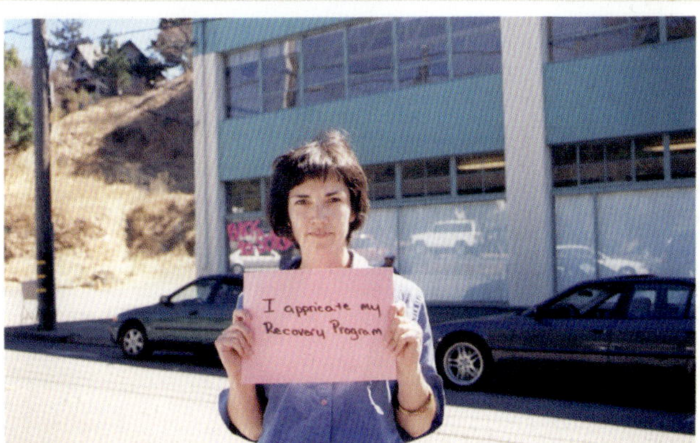
I appriciate my
Recovery Program

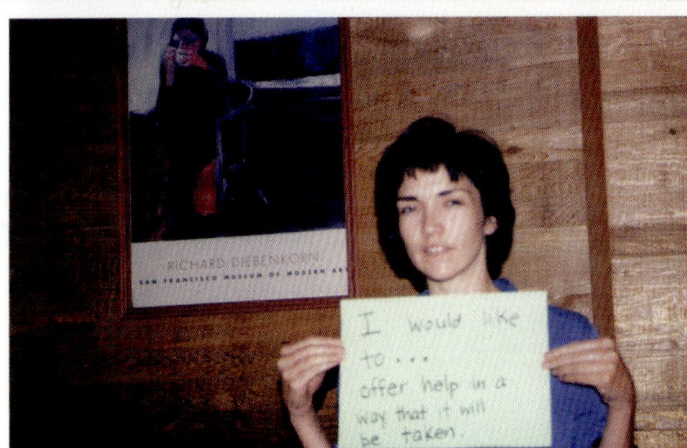
RICHARD DIEBENKORN
SAN FRANCISCO MUSEUM OF MODERN ART
I would like
to ...
offer help in a
way that it will
be taken.

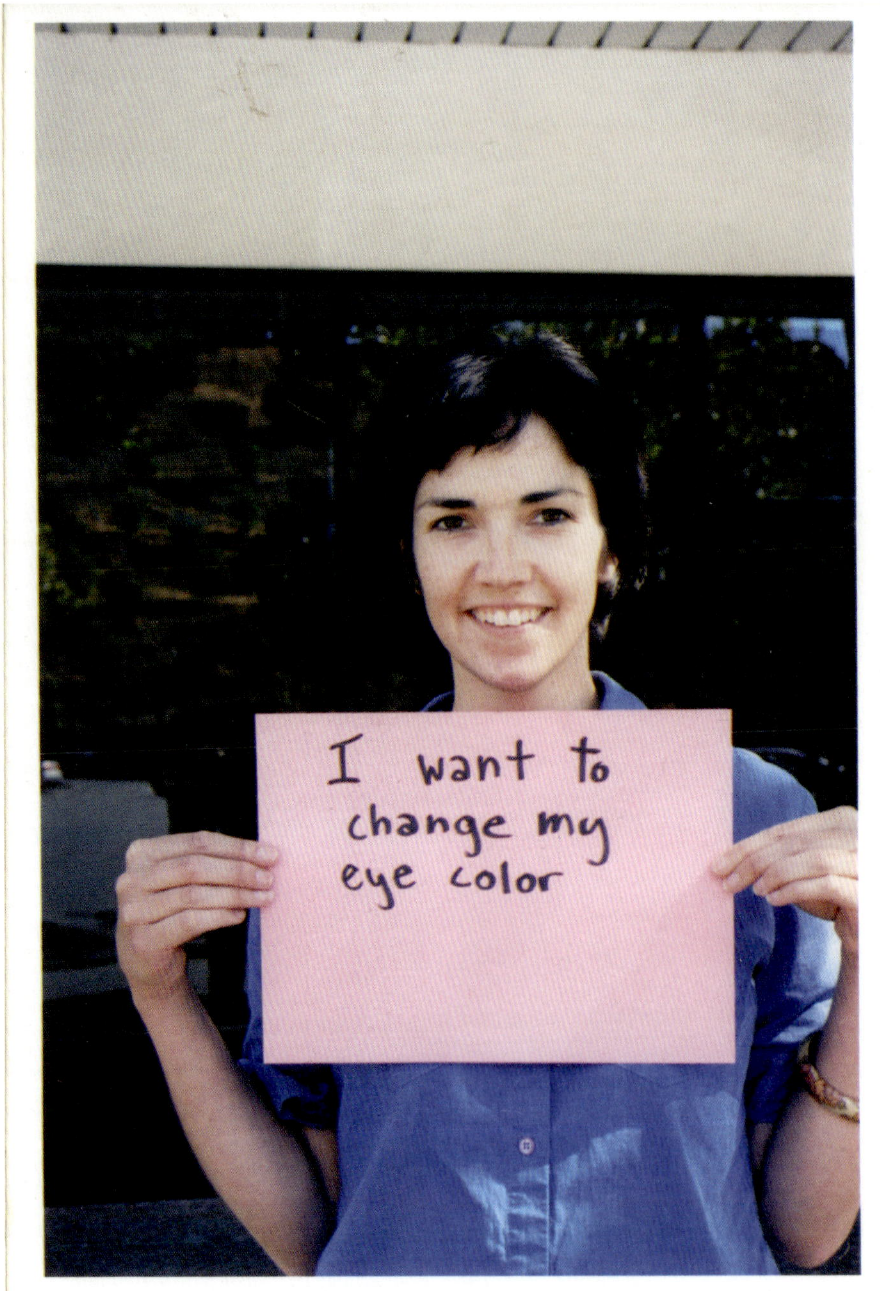
I want to
change my
eye color

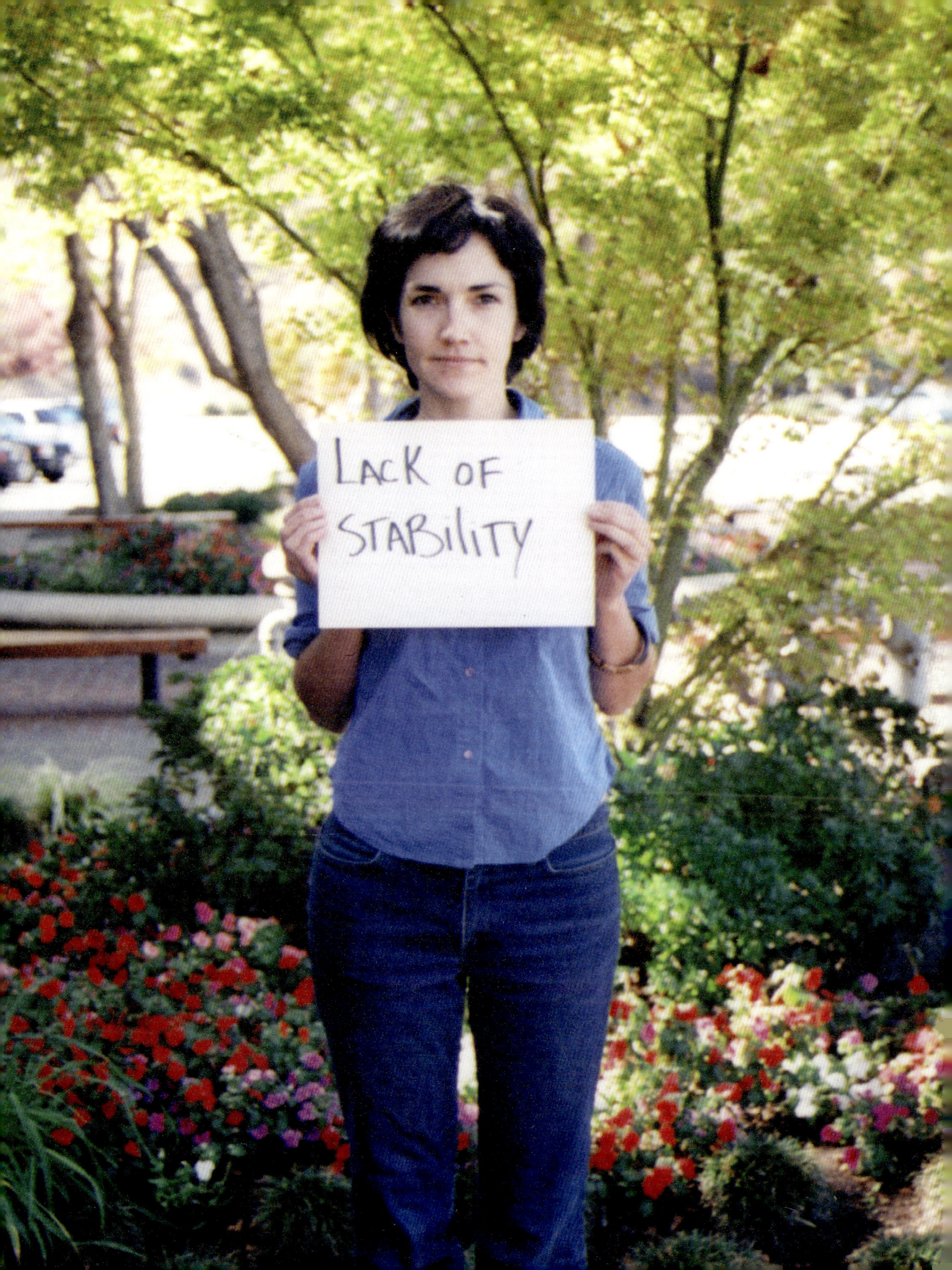
LACK OF
STABILITY

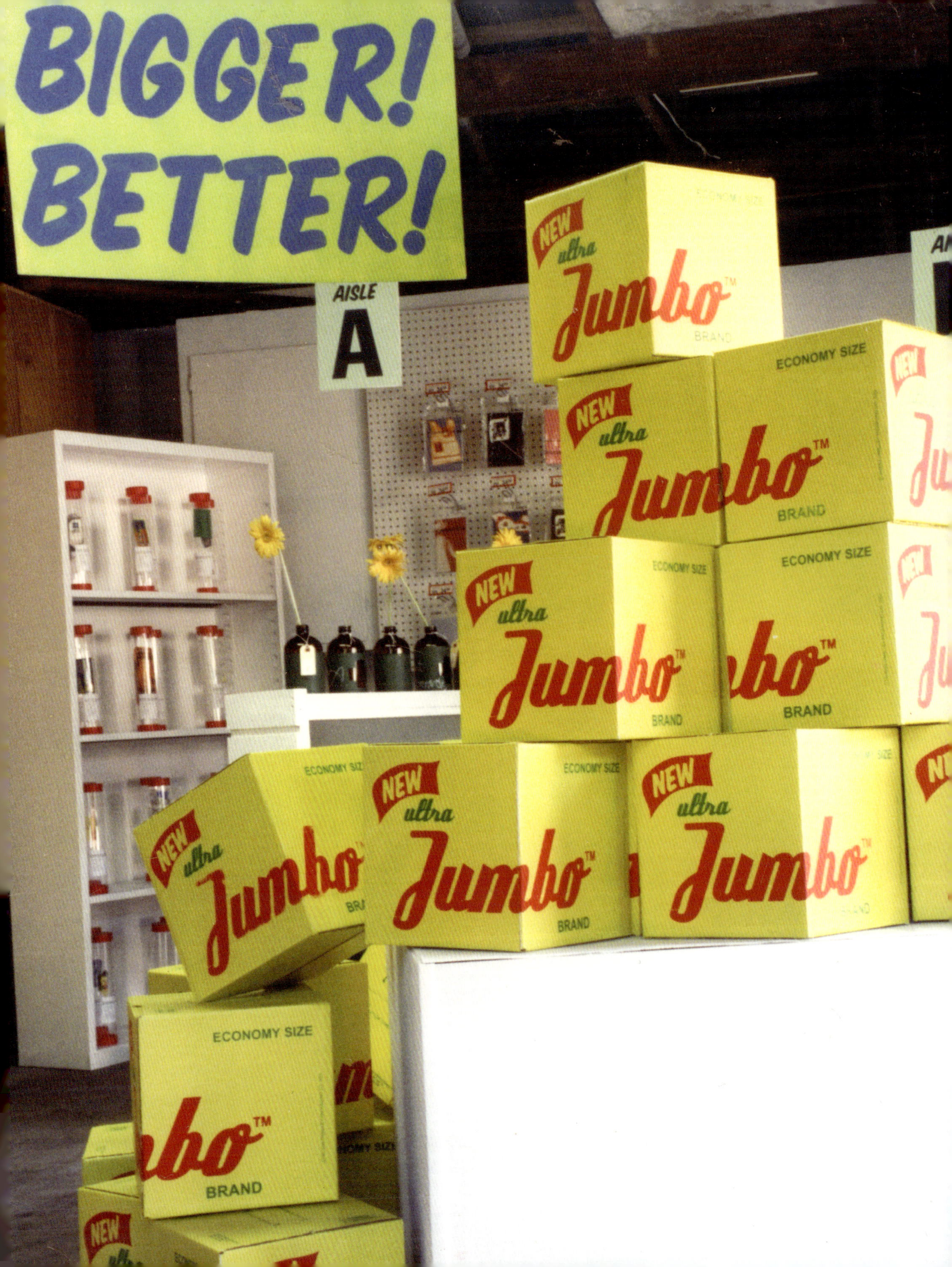
BIGGER!
BETTER!
AISLE
A
ECONOMY SIZE
NEW
ultra
Jumbo™
BRAND

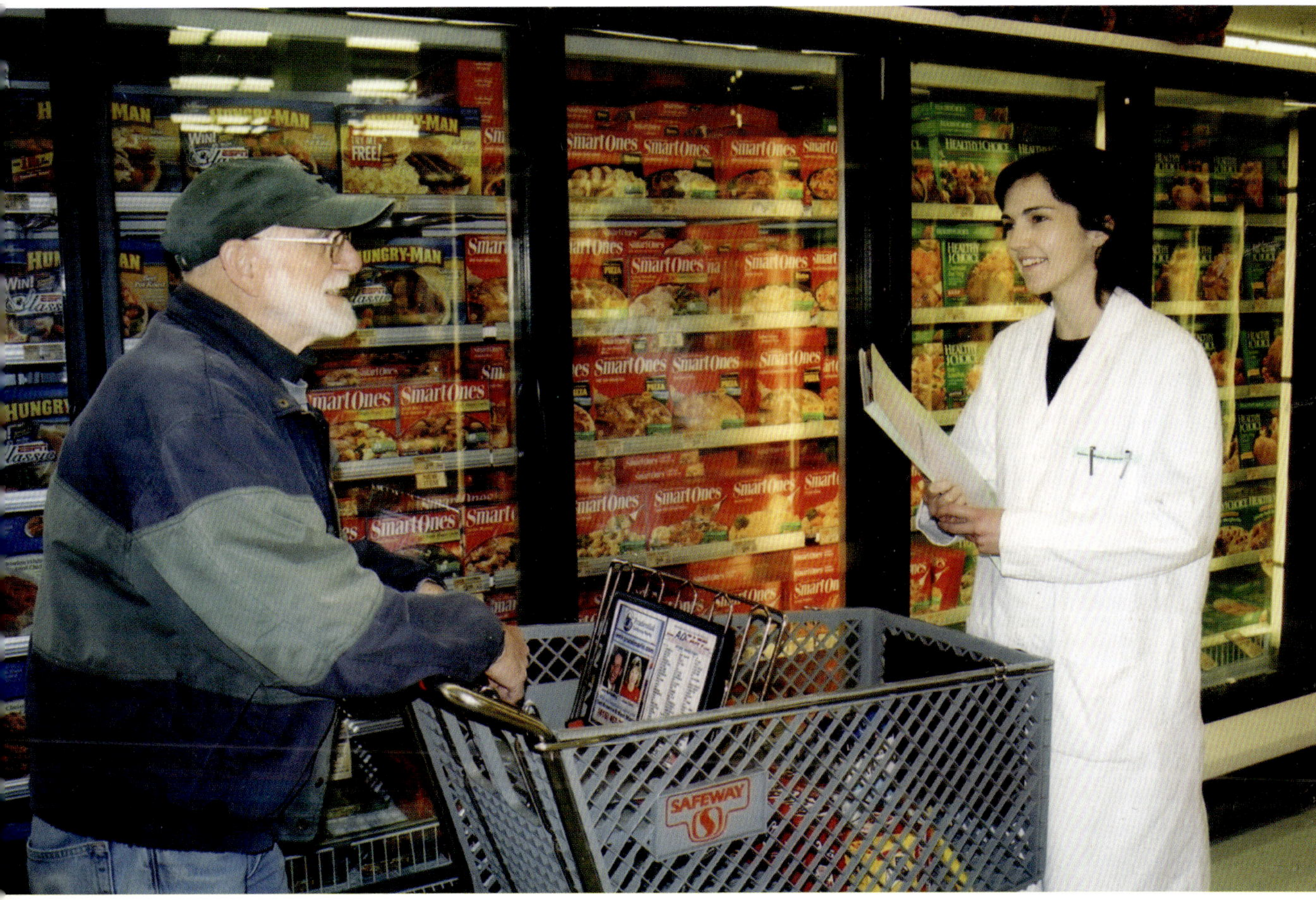

Opposite: Items from the Susan O'Malley Packaging Company, *The Garage Show: A Fake Art Store Installation*, San Jose, California, 2002

Above: O'Malley interviewing grocery patrons in San Jose as part of the Susan O'Malley Research Team, circa 2003–4

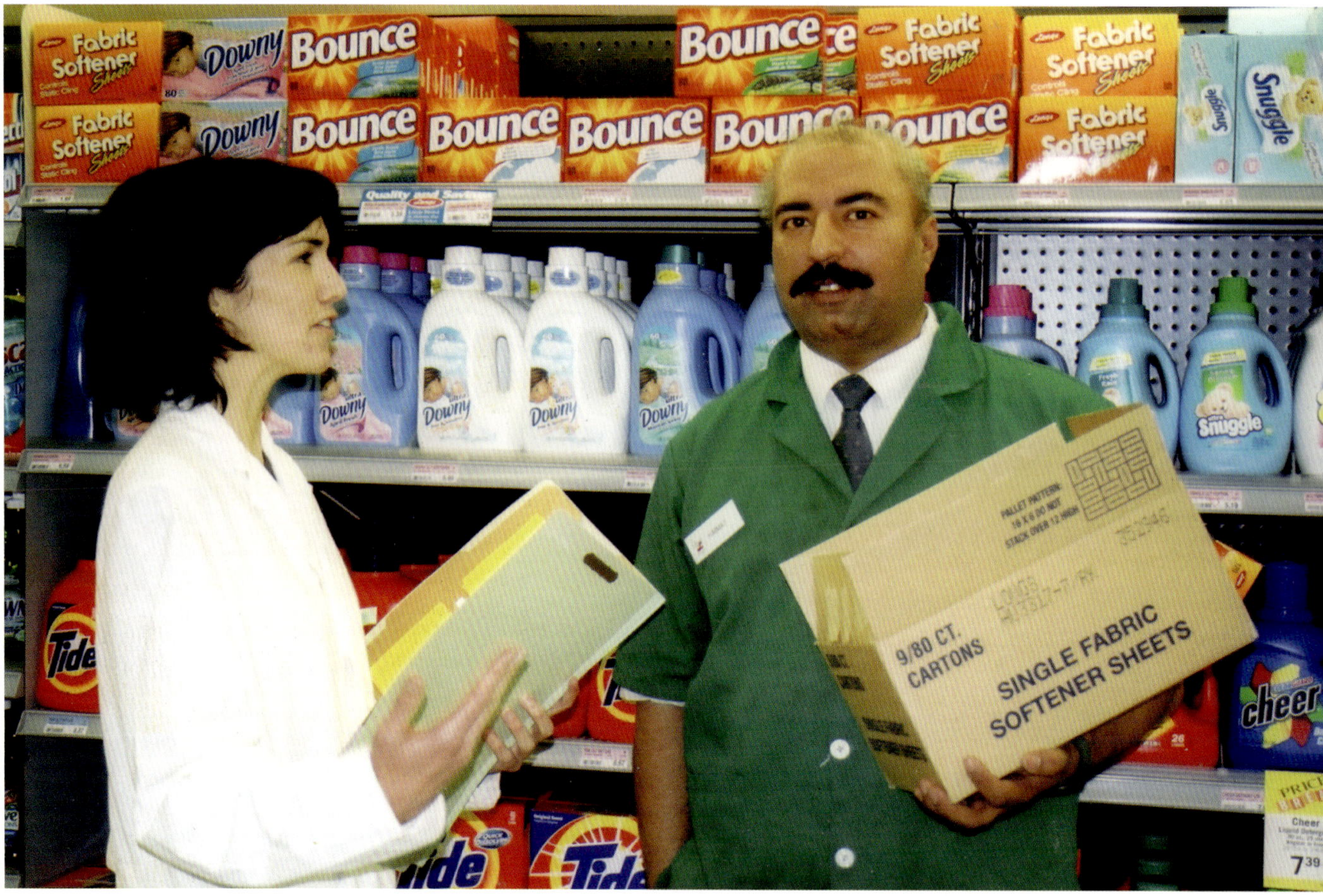

Above: O'Malley interviewing a grocery store employee in San Jose as part of the Susan O'Malley Research Team, circa 2003–4

Opposite: Items from the Susan O'Malley Packaging Company, *The Garage Show: A Fake Art Store Installation*, San Jose, California, 2002

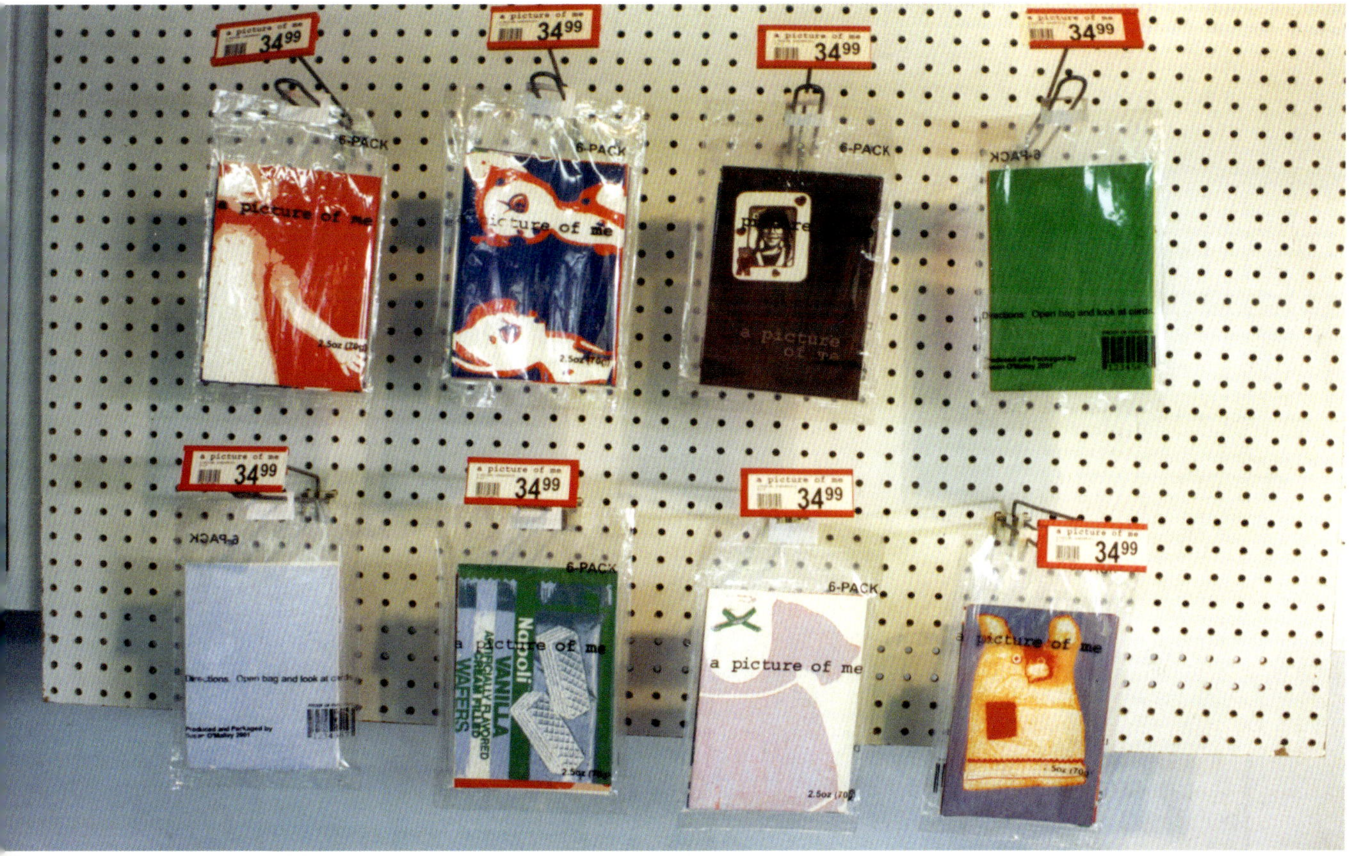
a picture of me
34.99
6-PACK
Directions: Open bag and look at cards
Produced and Packaged by
2.5oz (70g)
VANILLA
WAFERS

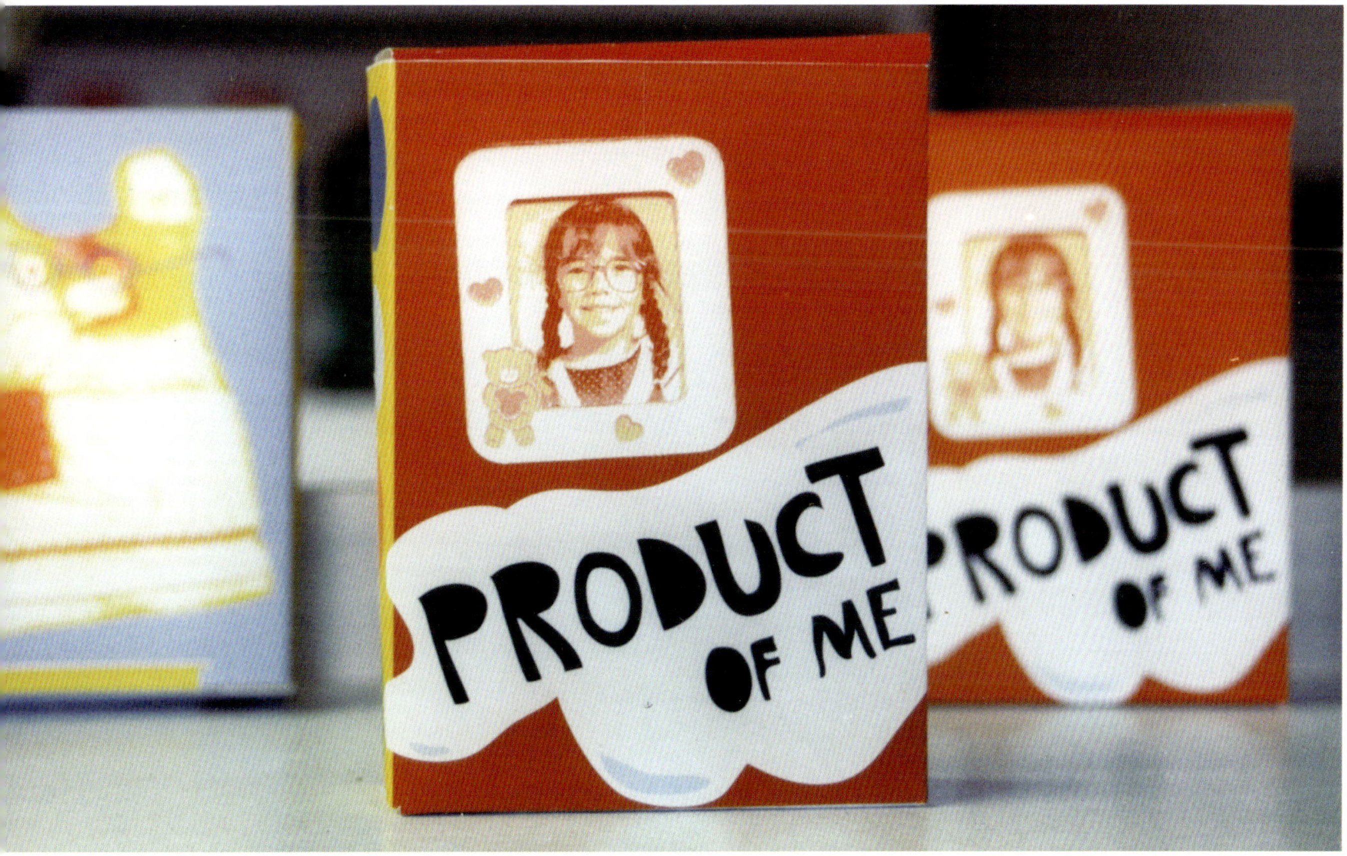
PRODUCT OF ME
PRODUCT OF ME

The Tender Predicament

Griff Williams

Is optimism a political act?

What happens when art becomes so enmeshed in life that it isn't seen as art?

I have no idea whether Susan O'Malley asked herself these questions, but I think about them when I encounter her work, which originally existed in places where art wasn't supposed to exist. You might find her work on fences, vending machines, and bus stops, in subway stations or distributed in neighborhood mailboxes. O'Malley's work camouflaged itself within our day-to-day lived environments. It was inserted into the places where we all coexist, purposely disconnected from the elevated realms of contemporary art. Let's face it: The world of contemporary art is often alienating, elitist, and detached from our lived experiences. O'Malley's work is none of those things. She, like many of us in the arts, found herself discontented with the exclusionary and consumerist aspects of the field. So she went about creating around her a world that she wanted to live in.

Susan O'Malley was born, raised, and educated in the San Francisco Bay Area, a place with an outsize reputation for dissent and a rich history of activism and social justice organizing—from mass movements like the Free Speech Movement, the Black Panther Party, the disability rights movement, the LGBTQ rights movements, and the environmental movement to historic individuals like Angela Davis, Cesar Chavez, Harvey Milk, Fred Korematsu, Elaine Brown, Dolores Huerta, Yuri Kochiyama, and countless others. It's not surprising that this spirit of resistance produced a fertile ground for artists who create socially engaged, market-averse artwork. This concept is now frequently described by art world terms such as *Social Practice* or *Relational Aesthetics*. But at its root, it is a desire to make art more humane, more integrated into our lived experiences, and less bound by the limitations of capitalism.

A great many Bay Area artists believe that social behavior and cultural expression are soulmates. And in the 1970s and '80s, the region was awash with creators inspired by the protest movements. Artists like Emory Douglas, Mildred Howard, Lynn Hershman Leeson, Bruce Conner, Rupert García, Carlos Villa, Terry Fox, Tony Labat, Ant Farm, and Bonnie Ora Sherk all used their practice to respond to cultural and political issues.

Bonnie Sherk, in particular, should be considered in this regard. Sherk was a pioneering ecological artist. In 1974 she founded the Crossroads Community, affectionately known as The Farm, a now-legendary urban farm, community center, and performance space. It was located on seven acres in San Francisco, underneath a highway overpass and at the intersection of four low-income, multicultural communities. The Farm was an alternative to alternative art spaces. It included a state-run preschool, a library, several performance spaces, a farmhouse, and a kitchen. It hosted events, dances, community meetings, classes, and concerts. People from all over the world came to visit The Farm; it was a prototype for urban agriculture before it became a burgeoning field.

By the late 1990s and early 2000s, a range of influential Bay Area artists had begun making art that wasn't just about the world but *of* the world. Much of what they were creating involved acts of honoring and existed in locations that were inextricable from their making. Some of these artists had a profound effect on O'Malley.

Especially significant among those were Jon Rubin and Harrell Fletcher. Between 1993 and 1994, Rubin and Fletcher worked together to create a gallery-as-art-project called Gallery HERE in an unused storefront in a strip mall in Oakland, California. For two years this project presented exhibitions, events, and actions based on the lives and everyday activities of people in the neighborhood surrounding the gallery. Fletcher and Rubin visited homes in the area. Each week a different household was invited to bring items from their home to be exhibited. These "garage sale" items were cataloged with stories of their use and the reasons why they were being sold.

Rubin later founded the Independent School of Art, an experimental art school that operated without grant funding and asked the question "What would an arts education look like if you removed all of the institutional trappings and economic burdens from it?" It was run solely through the labor of its participants; one of them was Susan O'Malley.

Fletcher, Miranda July, and Yuri Ono—who also lived and worked in the Bay Area—are credited with bringing Social Practice to an international stage through their project *Learning to Love You More*. For me, this is still one of the most beautiful artistic uses of the internet. It was made up of seventy instructional assignments for anyone to complete. Lesson prompts included "Assignment #2: Make a neighborhood field recording," "#39: Take a picture of your parents kissing," and "#53: Give advice to yourself in the past"—a prompt that likely inspired O'Malley's project *Advice from My 80-Year-Old Self*. Fletcher remarked, "There is a built-in selfishness to the art world, but very little support for behaving generously. Regardless of our station in life, and regardless of our perception of our achievements, generosity is a way of living that can ground us and give us a sense of purpose."

The notion of generosity was at the root of Ted Purves's work as well. Purves (1964–2017) was a professor at California College of the Arts, where, in the mid-2000s, O'Malley was one of his first MFA students in the Social Practice curriculum. For three years, Purves and Susanne Cockrell operated *Temescal Amity Works*, a project that served the local Oakland community by collecting and redistributing surplus fruit from neighborhood trees. They moved through the streets, collecting both fruit and oral histories from the neighbors. The "preserves," in the form of marmalade and history-filled postcards, were free to all.

I don't know what it is about the Bay Area that nurtures less careerist and more civic-minded artists, but they seem to abound. They give more than they take. It could be said that optimism is required to make any work of art, literature, or music. Art depends upon a belief in the future. Civilization itself depends on optimism. It requires cooperation among strangers, which requires both trust and optimism. O'Malley once described her work as "making art that connects us to each other."

Another Bay Area artist, Ann Chamberlain (1951–2008), created poetic public projects by collaborating with ordinary people to bring art to unexpected places. For the Healing Garden at UCSF Mount Zion's Women's Health Center, she worked with patients to turn a bleak hospital courtyard into an inviting lush garden where they could share stories while recovering from illness. Conceived while Chamberlain was herself a patient there, the garden features a wall composed of over five hundred ceramic tiles, each containing an impression of a plant and a personal story or thought written by a patient, family member, friend, or doctor.

Amy Franceschini is the founder of Futurefarmers, an artists' collective designed to raise awareness about sustainable living and inspire inquiry and innovation. Franceschini read that between 1941 and 1943, a staggering 41 percent of the total food production in the United States was being grown in victory gardens. So, she reimagined the wartime victory garden program for the city of San Francisco, partnering with the San Francisco Environment Department to support the transition of backyards, front yards, window boxes, rooftops, and unused land into food production areas.

The concept of an art that connects is at the root of tradition for Indigenous communities—the Bay Area's first inhabitants. Before colonization, the Bay Area was home to nearly sixty small Indigenous tribes. Those groups organized themselves into equanimity and social equity, based on how Tribal members could access resources. Seen through a Eurocentric lens, art is mostly ornamental. The idea of art being a presentation or performance is tied to the Eurocentric notion of culture as entertainment, something to be admired from a distance. From a Native perspective, art is woven into the central principles of Indigenous identity, such as land use, family, spirituality, oral traditions, and ceremony.

When we view Susan O'Malley's work in the context of Bay Area art—that which existed both before and during her career—it deepens our understanding of her ethos: integrating acts of creative kindness into our daily lives. Her work reminds us that creativity is fundamental to the health of communities. It serves as a public service announcement for our emotional lives. Her pep talks and inspirational posters are expressions of her optimism about the heights each one of us can achieve. She wrote, "My hope is that these community-authored public service announcements will reflect back our inner brilliance and perhaps allow a brief space to gently listen to our own advice."

The Pep Talk Squad

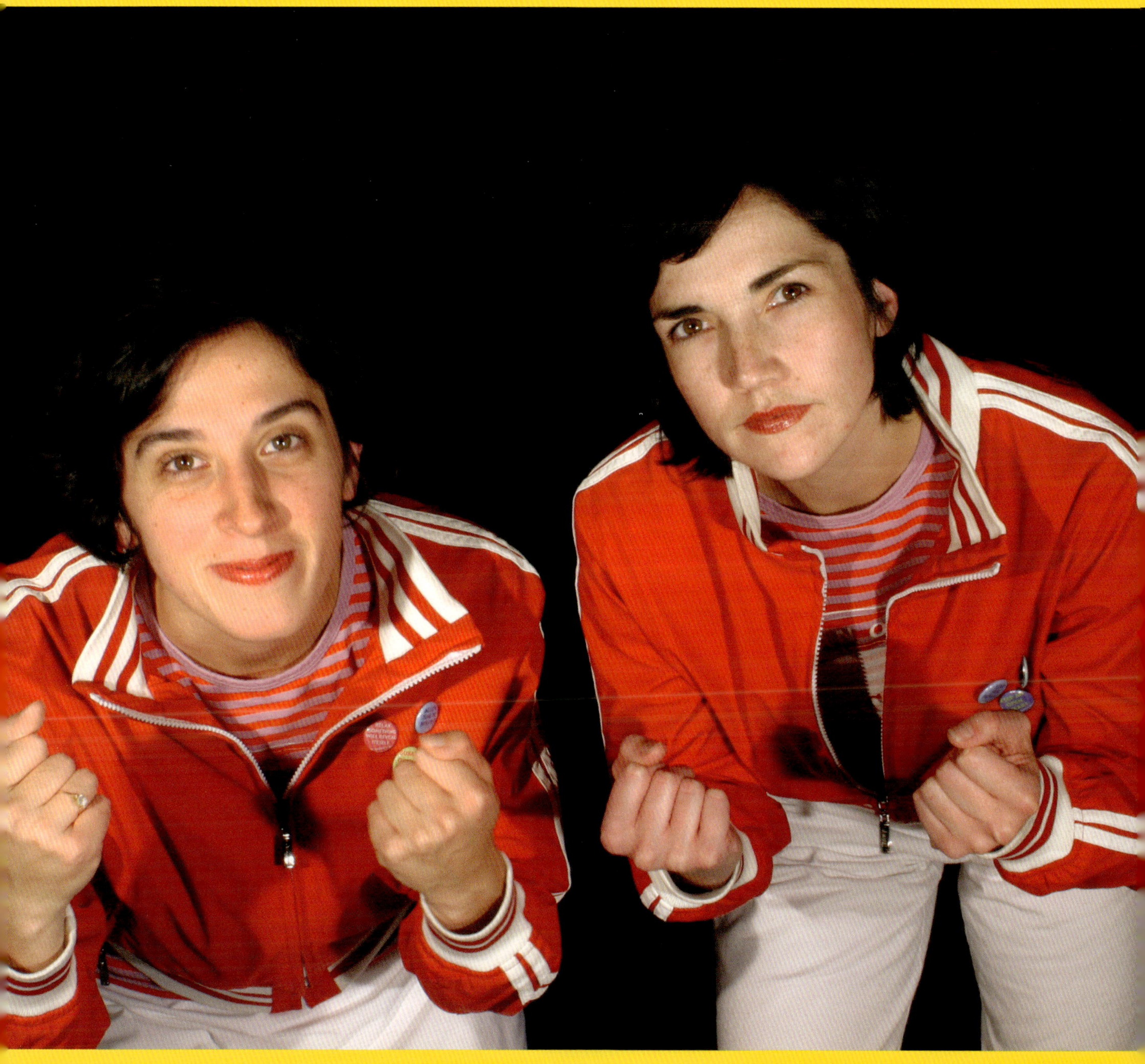

Goofy and Deeply Committed

Lori Gordon

Susan O'Malley's impact on the Bay Area art scene, the sphere of Social Practice, and beyond transcends the boundaries of traditional creative practice. As a fellow artist who had the privilege of knowing Susan during our graduate work at California College of the Arts (CCA), I reflect on her work, particularly the *Pep Talk Squad*, through the unique lenses of a classmate, friend, and recipient of her uplifting messages.

In the dynamic landscape of contemporary art, Susan O'Malley stood out for her commitment to genuine human connection. Our graduate school days at CCA were marked by collaborative efforts and impassioned discussions about the essence of art. Susan and I shared a camaraderie that went beyond the confines of the studio; we were goofy and uninhibited, yet also deeply committed to the profound exploration of love and interconnectedness in our work. Her infectious enthusiasm for life and art made her a constant source of inspiration, pushing the rest of us to break free from conventional norms and embrace the beauty in human relationships.

The *Pep Talk Squad*, one of Susan's notable Social Practice projects, which she created in collaboration with Christina Amini, encapsulates her commitment to uplifting others. As a recipient of one of Susan and Christina's pep talks, I experienced firsthand the impact of these encouraging messages. My *Pep Talk Squad* experience emphasized the importance of self-compassion and flexibility. The supportive tone and cheer-squad-style encouragement were powerful, to say the least. The typed document I took home was a great reminder to be kind to myself and keep moving forward. The squad was a conceptual art piece, but it was also a genuine extension of Susan's belief in the power of positivity. Her messages transcended mere pep talks; they were affirmations of our worth and potential, conveying the sentiment that she believed in each of us 1,000 percent.

One memorable day encapsulates Susan's adventurous spirit and her ability to infuse awe and wonder into everyday moments. We had embarked on a spontaneous journey through San Jose, exploring her favorite spots, laughing at quirky garden ornaments, and reveling in the treasures hidden in her mom's garage. While we were exploring the city, a chance encounter with a life-size plastic horse tethered to a sidewalk led to an impromptu act of courage. Susan, undeterred by the setting

---

Page 37: *Pep Talk Squad* promotional photo of Christina Amini (left) and Susan O'Malley (right), circa 2003–4

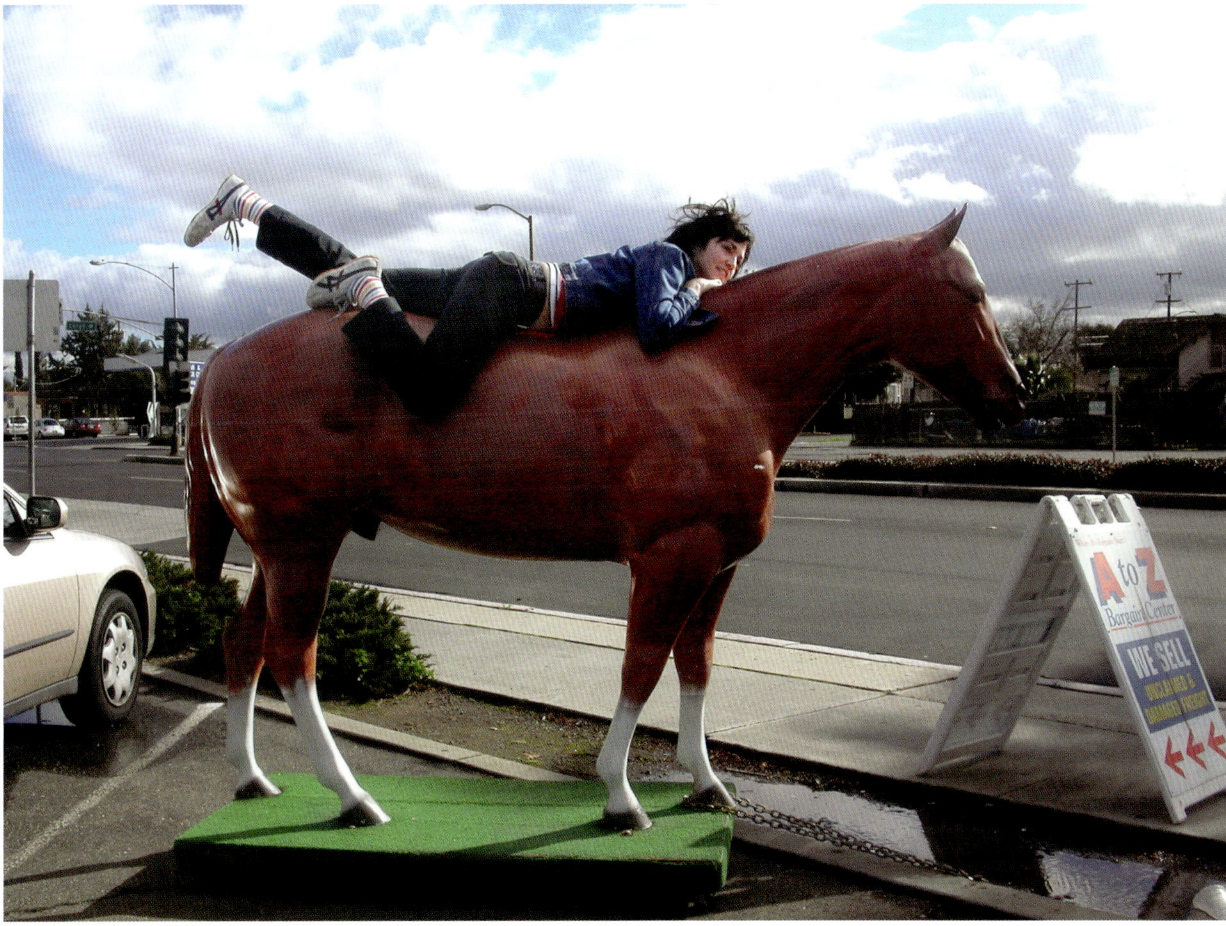

Above: O'Malley giving a tour of her favorite spots in San Jose, California, circa 2004-5

sun and the chill in the air, climbed onto the horse, proudly waving to passing cars as they honked in response. It was a moment of sheer bravery and moxie, a testament to the kind of friend we all need—someone to push us forward and remind us that magic exists in the ordinary.

Though Susan's untimely passing left a void that will never completely heal, I take comfort in my memories and in her enduring artistic legacy. Her work serves as an eternal reminder that she believed in each of us with unwavering certainty, that there is magic to be found in the world, and that I can honor the *Pep Talk Squad* legacy by continuing to believe in myself just as she believed in me—without hesitation.

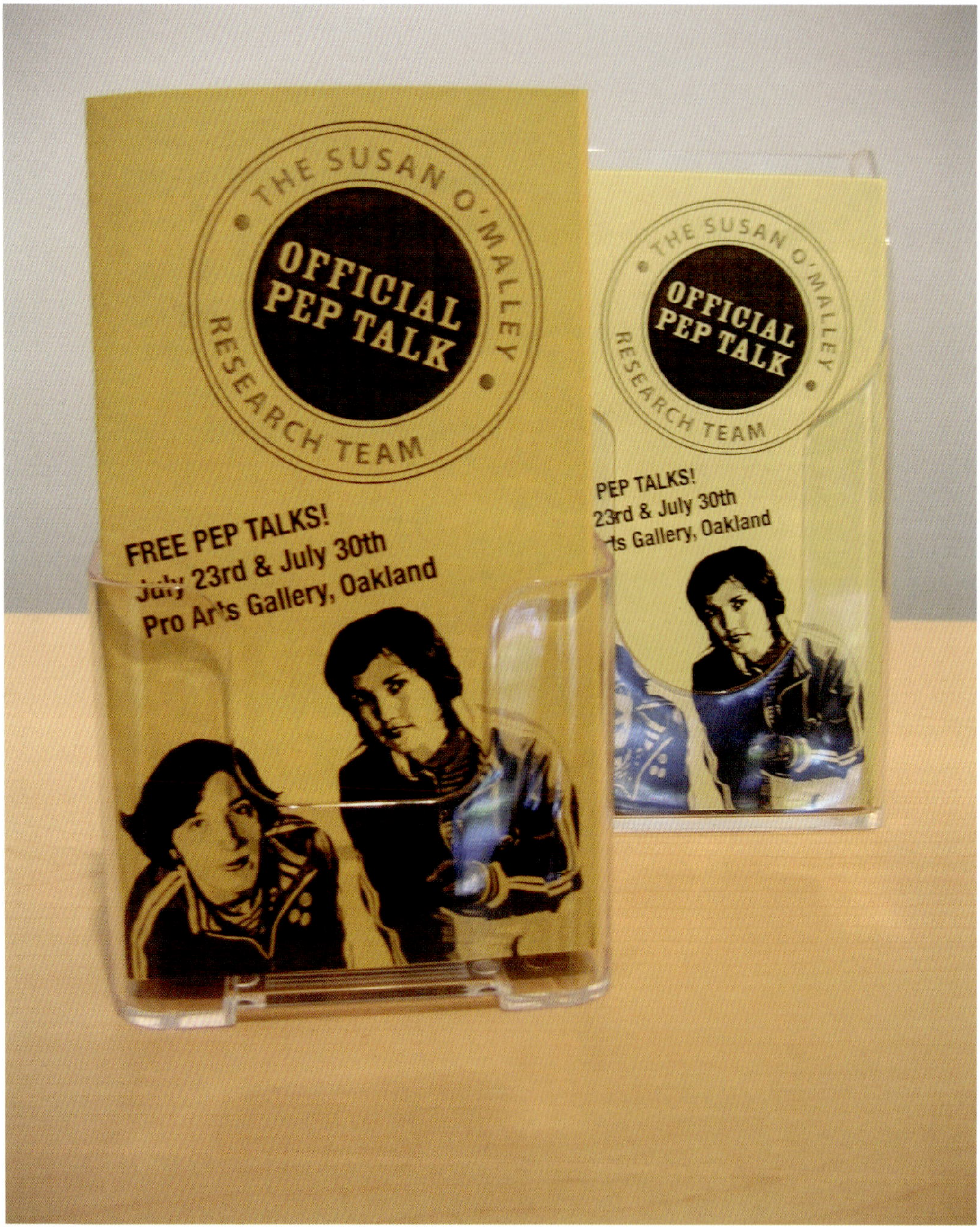
THE SUSAN O'MALLEY
OFFICIAL PEP TALK
RESEARCH TEAM
FREE PEP TALKS!
July 23rd & July 30th
Pro Arts Gallery, Oakland

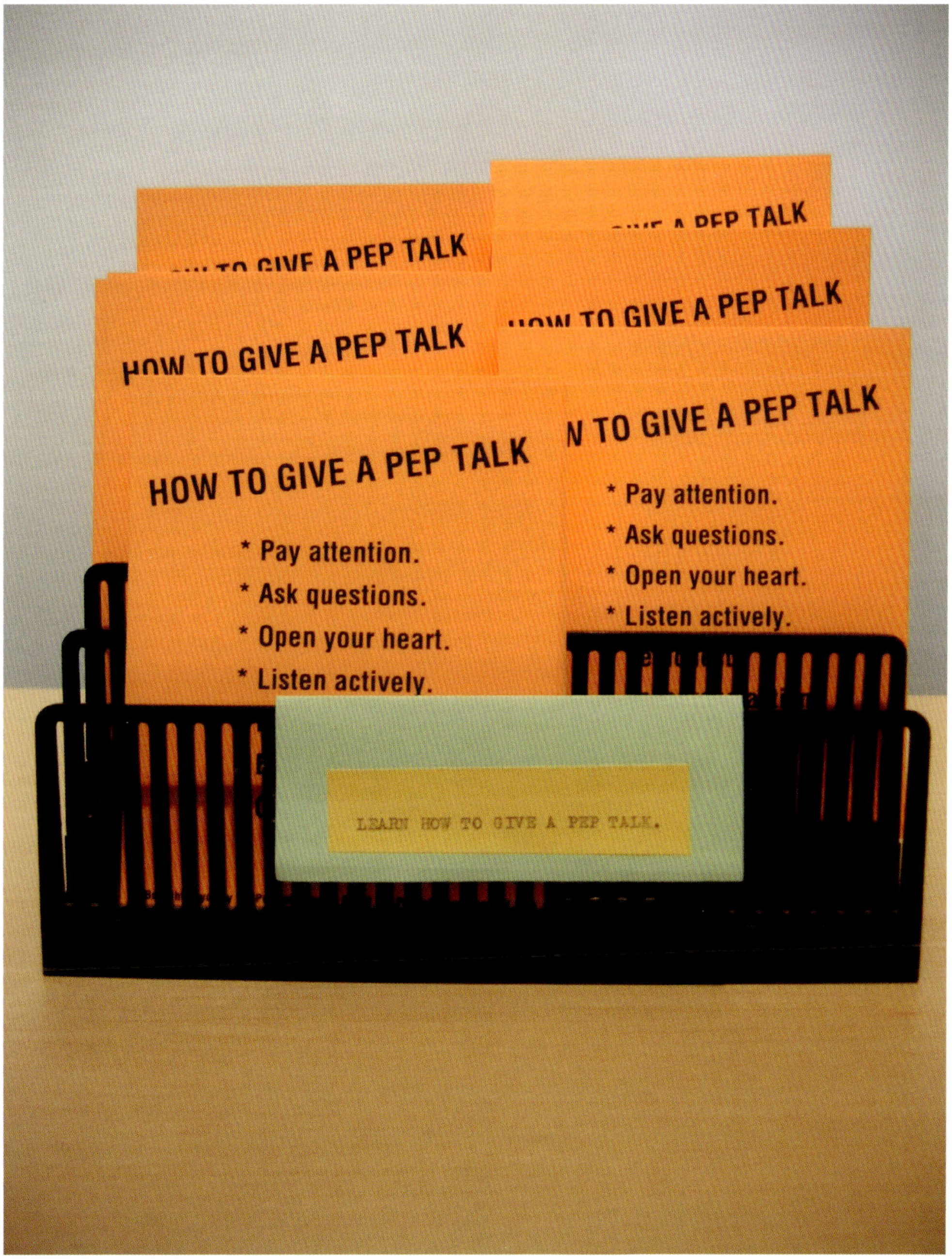

Opposite and above: Materials from *Official Pep Talk* from the Susan O'Malley Research Team, Pro Arts Gallery, Oakland, California, 2005

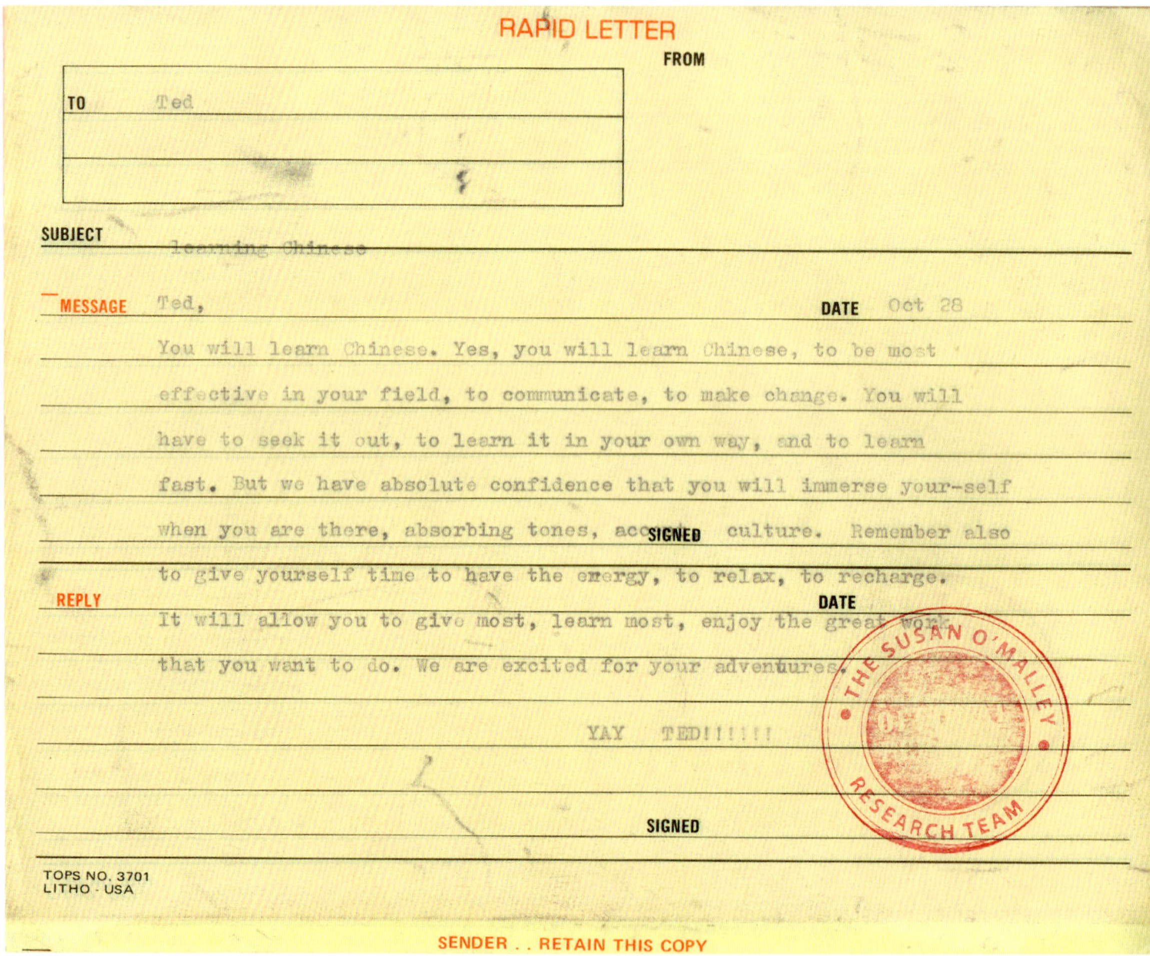

RAPID LETTER

FROM

TO Ted

SUBJECT learning Chinese

MESSAGE Ted,

DATE Oct 28

You will learn Chinese. Yes, you will learn Chinese, to be most
effective in your field, to communicate, to make change. You will
have to seek it out, to learn it in your own way, and to learn
fast. But we have absolute confidence that you will immerse your-self
when you are there, absorbing tones, acc[illegible] culture. Remember also
to give yourself time to have the energy, to relax, to recharge.
It will allow you to give most, learn most, enjoy the great work
that you want to do. We are excited for your adventures.

YAY TED!!!!!!

SIGNED

REPLY

DATE

SIGNED

THE SUSAN O'MALLEY RESEARCH TEAM

TOPS NO. 3701
LITHO · USA

SENDER . . RETAIN THIS COPY

Above and opposite: Pep Talk carbon copies, Duke University, Durham, North Carolina, 2005. The Pep Talk Squad, part of the Susan O'Malley Research Team, gave Pep Talks at public parks, galleries, universities, and fairs and on buses and walks for anyone in need of pep or encouragement during the years 2003–13.

TOPS Snap-off **CARBONLESS FORM 3701**

NO CARBON REQUIRED

RAPID LETTER
NOTE: Send White and Pink copies. Sender retains Canary copy.
TRIPLICATE

RAPID LETTER

FROM

TO Grant

SUBJECT

MESSAGE

DATE

Grant,

A rich, and varied, fulfilling, and yes, superhuman life is the most -- the most wonderful undertaking possible. Your curiosity, generosity, and intereats in people will help you find that rich life that you seek. It IS your responsibility , not only to the world, but to yourself to follow what reealy inspires you, brings you joy, and brings your joy to those around you. And remember that life can change, you can change it to make it yours--to [illegible] your way to a full family life, a full career, -- most of all a full life. We are thankful for your honesty and pursuit of finding it all.

YAY GRANT!!!

SIGNED

REPLY

DATE

THE SUSAN O'MALLEY RESEARCH TEAM

SIGNED

TOPS NO. 3701
LITHO · USA

SENDER . . RETAIN THIS COPY

FORM 3701 REQUIRED TRIPLICATE

RAPID LETTER

FROM

TO Andrew

SUBJECT Andrew, your experiences in Ghana & Atlanta have shaped your per-

MESSAGE spective to be a Doctor, commit to making meaningful DATE

interactions, changing & helping lives. You have found medicine as a path & we are lucky to have you -- a caring, intelligent person to be a doctor. You are compelled in this direction which will bring a fuller vision of what you are doing. Prepare yourself for Harvard because you not SIGNED

REPLY DATE only owe it to yourself but you owe it to the individuals that do not even know you yet, who you will provide care, education and share your unique personality with.

Thank you for finding your path at your own Andrew time line.

Your assets to what you will bring to this field aer obvious and we know you will convey this tô your interviewers at Harvard. SIGNED

YAY ANDREW!!!!

THE SUSAN O'MALLEY RESEARCH TEAM

TOPS NO. 3701 LITHO · USA

FORM 3701 REQUIRED TRIPLICATE

RAPID LETTER

FROM

TO T. Lee

SUBJECT 3 finals, a paper & qualifying exam

separation anxiety

MESSAGE T. DATE

There is alot happening in your life right now, you are finishing 2 degr
ypu are away from your friends, you are soon moving tô D.C. There will
so much to celebrate. Right now you are on a different study universe f
your friendse on the other coast, but in time you willbe on the party-pl
committee, you will be able to reconnect with your core Princeton peeps, SIGNED
will have Breakfast all day with them and celebrate your transition

REPLY So much can happen in the space between-- enjoy this time-- DATE endure yo
finals stretch so that you can enjoy your completion with your friends.

Sounds like an awesome time to look forward to..... YAY THERESA!!!!!

SIGNED

TOPS NO. 3701 LITHO · USA

SENDER . . RETAIN THIS COPY

CARBONLESS FORM 3701 CARBON REQUIRED

NOTE: Send White and Pink copies. Sender retains Canary copy. TRIPLICATE

RAPID LETTER

FROM

TO Martin

SUBJECT

MESSAGE Martin, writing is a process. And it requires DATE time.

It requires a love for theatre, ideas, collaboration with your vision. Every moment is a crestive one -- listening to the way people tàlk, howthey move, where there is drama and beauty in every-thing. Th ngs can happen when you allow yourself to wander. Pay attention to these moments. SIGNED

REPLY Writing and being a p laywright will be a trickier DATE path. There is no steady course, like being a lawyer or economist. Finding your voice, learning how you work are areas that you are learning and this is both the most exciting and most challenging parts of the process. YAY Martin !!

SIGNED

THE SUSAN O'MALLEY RESEARCH TEAM

TOPS NO. 3701 LITHO · USA

CARBONLESS FORM 3701 NO CARBON REQUIRED

RAPID LETTER

NOTE: Send White and ... Sender retains ... TRIPLICATE

RAPID LETTER

FROM

TO Jonathan

SUBJECT

MESSAGE DATE

Jonathan, You want to learn âbout & practice law and you are on your way
to achieve this goal. This will open opportunities and ideas as to how
your practice as a lawywe will shape in the future.

Your applications are part of the process and you have a healthy attitude
of what life has to offer and your belief in yourself, SIGNED your way of navigat
it will provide you with what you need.

REPLY DATE

Congratulate yourself for moving forward and being grateful for what you h

You will bring this in allavenues of your life and it will ...
to yòu. YAY Jonathan!!

SIGNED

THE SUSAN O'MALLEY OFFICIAL PEP TALK RESEARCH TEAM

TOPS NO. 3701 LITHO · USA

CARBONLESS FORM 3701 NO CARBON REQUIRED

RAPID LETTER

NOTE: Send White and Pink copies. Sender retains Canary copy. TRIPLICATE

RAPID LETTER

FROM

TO Kelsey & Rusty

SUBJECT general encouragement

MESSAGE DATE /15/06

Kelsey & Rusty,

You are gaining more physical space, but the good news is-- you both like being in each others8' space -- emotionally and physically.

Keep up the momentum, you can, the relationship willresist and be shaped by your new tenminute walk. Heck, you SIGNED might even get some more

REPLY wosk done. You can make this change mean whatever you want DATE it to mean.

And you can always change again as the relationship demands. Your relation-sip can grow andgrow enough to fill two houses with your office space, ur lunch time hangouts, and your dinne r parties and crash pads. Congrats on the new house, and spend lotsof time together.

SENDER . . RETAIN THIS COPY

FORM 3701 REQUIRED

Sender retains ... TRIPLICATE

RAPID LETTER

FROM

TO David

SUBJECT computer takes over my life

MESSAGE David, DATE

Your curiosity is brilliant. And a real joy and relief to be around.
The world needs peopàe who think critically and who know what the fuc
is going on -- maybe not linux, but, well maybe. Continue yöu to
connect your knowledges, to read, to thìnk, to discuss your thoughts
with people. Allow yourself to stop, to SIGNED ect, to walk away from

REPLY the computer. it will still be there when you get back DATE om studying
inese, hangìng out with friendsm, reading your coursework. Your time
is abso.utely precious, be sure that you8re spending it, enjoying it
just the way you want. ### Your inquisitiveness, humor, and self
awareness, will always guide you. YAY DAVID!!!!!

FORM 3701 REQUIRED TRIPLICATE

RAPID LETTER

FROM

Andy, Your Mind can hold many ideas and so will your major.
have a vision of social justice, collaboration, and the media. t
ust this. You said yourself that this is only a
four year stint and learning, growing, and experience will
go beyond your major, beyond Duke. You will always face
critism, so you have to believe in these intersections as
your foundation. Where you bring your energy & intellect
your ideasw will coelesce.

Write your prposal because you need to
design a major specific to these ideas that holds all
of your interests. Write it because
it will prove to you WHY it is impotant to you.
lso, thank you for thinking the way you do. You thi
eeply and critically & care. YAY, ANDY!!!!

THE SUSAN O'MALLEY · OFFICIAL PEP TALK · RESEARCH TEAM

SIGNED

FORM 3701 REQUIRED TRIPLICATE

RAPID LETTER

FROM

TO Jason

SUBJECT

MESSAGE Focus. Focus. Focus. But also, rest, relax, unwind.

You said it yourself -- you know how much time it will take you to prepare
for Orgo. So take that time, and then ace the heck out of that test. We'll
be thinking of you Tuesday. Keep up the interactions, the balance of
work life and friend life--it's why you're here, at Duke, on earth.
Your enjoyment of spontaneity and social good f

REPLY will buoy you and keep you energized and thoughtful.
You've got a lot of good fun, good work, memory-making ahead.

YAY JASON!!!!

THE SUSAN O'MALLEY · OFFICIAL PEP TALK · RESEARCH TEAM

SIGNED

TOPS NO. 3701
LITHO · USA

SENDER . . RETAIN THIS COPY

CARBONLESS FORM 3701 NO CARBON REQUIRED
NOTE: Send White and Pink copies. Sender retains Canary copy. TRIPLICATE

RAPID LETTER

FROM

tte

roposal // skin care product

aurette, DATE /15/06

u have vision beyond the individual, beyond just yourself -- and
you are a leadrer. There is power in a group, in a strong group
ed, generous women. Take this program to the next step, you can.
your ideas, present them, research others, and give your vision
your voice.Then follow-up and proceed. Many women, their familie
and YOU, will all benefit and gain from it. This program, these
need you. Persist and it will happen.
ur business plan, and your class, recognize what is available for
e, and how it will feed you, and then how you will find the rest of
ou need to lea rn.You are fantastically driven to learn more, to
your business plan, to contact your classmates, and to continue
lenging yourse f. Congratulations+! And keep pushing to make
e organizations. You can do it!

YATY LAURETTE!!

TOPS Snap-off CARBONLESS FORM 3701 NO CARBON REQUIRED
RAPID LETTER
NOTE: Send White and Pink copies. Sender retains Canary copy. TRIPLICATE

RAPID LETTER

FROM

TO Jimmy

SUBJECT

MESSAGE

Thank you for driving Duke Students around campus.

You are appreciated,

YAY YOU

From, THE PEP TALK SQ

REPLY DATE

SIGNED

TOPS NO. 3701
LITHO · USA

Snap-off CARBONLESS FORM 3701 NO CARBON REQUIRED
RAPID LETTER
NOTE: Send White and Pink copies. Sender retains Canary copy. TRIPLICATE

RAPID LETTER

FROM

nda

HANGE!

DATE April 15

all -- CONGRATULATIONS! on many fronts: on the celebration of your
trying a new city, & a new adventure! As the wise old Goethe said,
s has genius, magic, and power in it." You as well as you and Paul
e bold, and can begin anew now.
and will have its joys and its challenges--and I trust that you will
people, the farmer's markets, and the car shares, just like you always
yourself the space to walk, to think to alone and to seek out
when you need them. Brenda, the sky is the limit for you. It's
angle from your old title (assox. managing ed--goodbye!)and to try
ny new titles (garden center exptert, interior de sign even, you name it
s you like.

Brenda, I am so freaking excited for you.
Ready, set, begin!

YAY BRENDA!!!!

TOPS Snap-off CARBONLESS FORM 3701 NO CARBON REQUIRED
RAPID LETTER
NOTE: Send White and Pink copies. Sender retains Canary copy. TRIPLICATE

RAPID LETTER

FROM

TO Abbey

SUBJECT

MESSAGE Abbey,

As long as you are you, you'll have your options open to try and do whatever
itis that you want to do. And now you've chosen a path -- medicine -- that will
allow you to find new research, aid more people, to set up community clinics
here or abroad. As you said, the end point is not the gãol -- but the process.
o use your aplplications to help you suss out

REPLY and articulate your go vision,. And you can do it on your
own time, in your own way. Your path has taken you this far, and
the research, the writing, the pra ctice of your life h##
to places we haven't even dreamed of yet. Congratulations!

THE SUSAN O'MALLEY · OFFICIAL PEP TALK

Pages 44–45: Pep Talks, various locations in the San Francisco Bay Area, 2004–6

Opposite: Pep Talks on dreams, Montalvo Arts Center, Saratoga, California, 2013

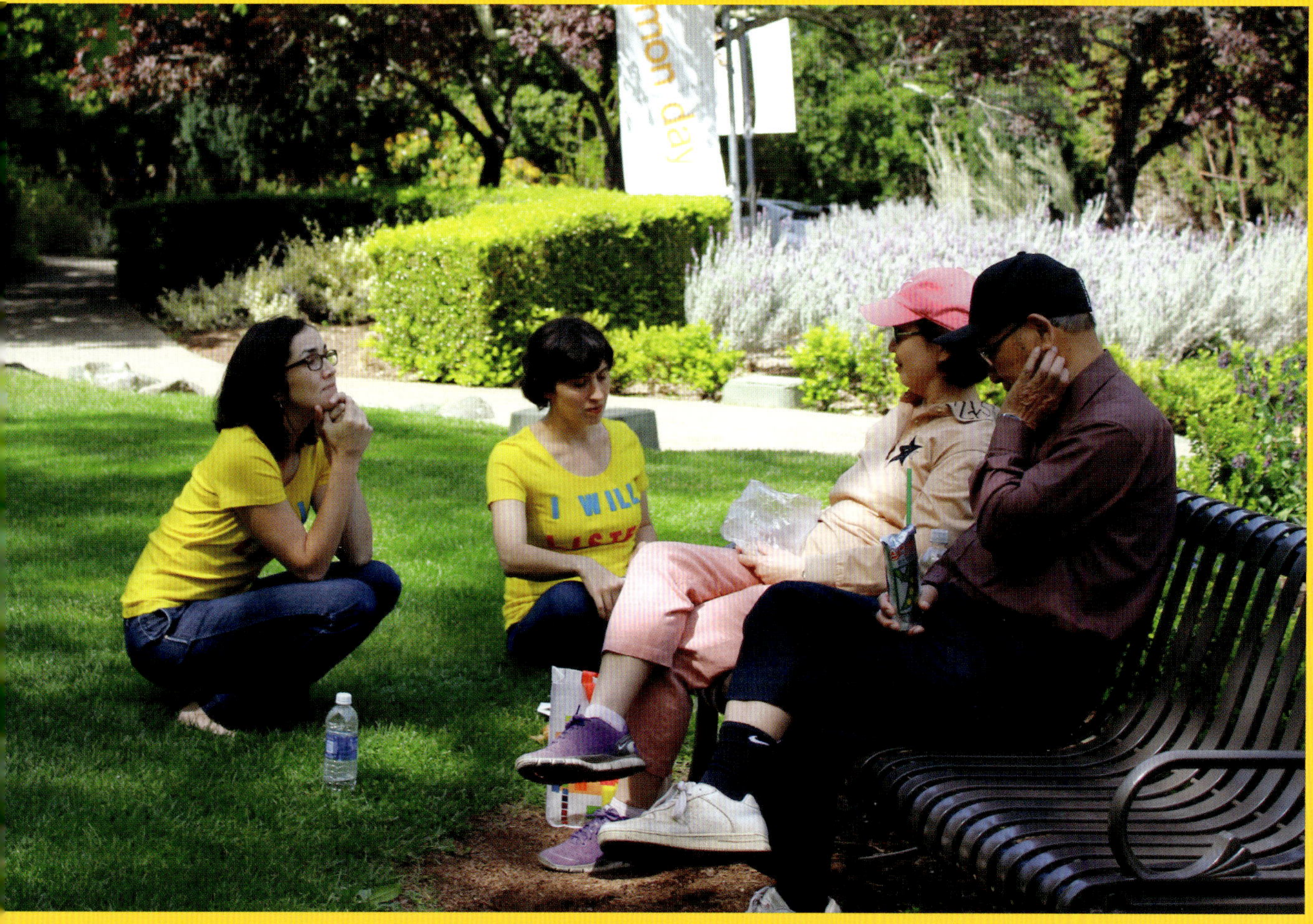

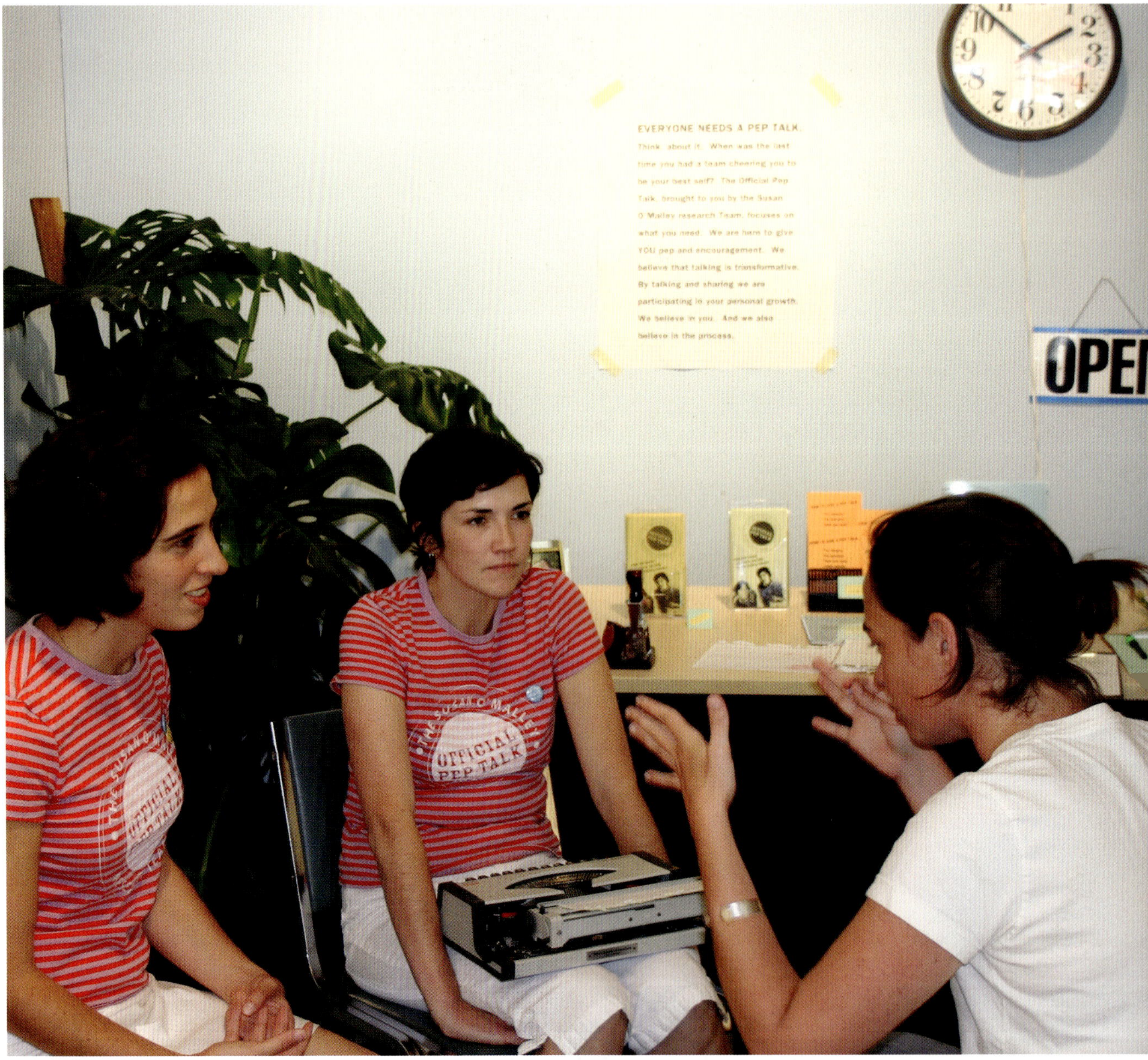

Above and opposite: Pep Talk Squad active listening, Pro Arts Gallery, Oakland, California, 2005

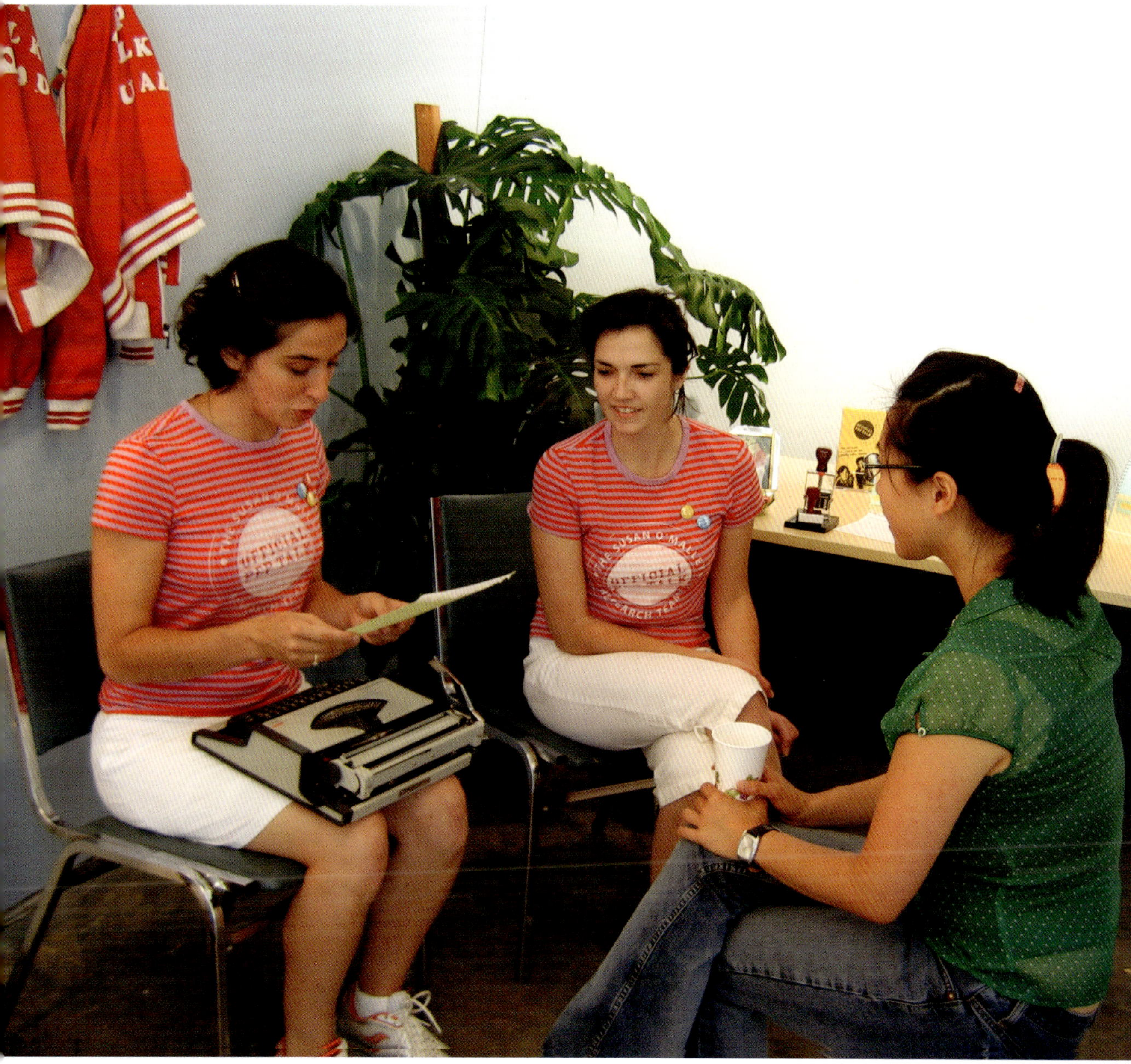

EVERYONE NEEDS A PEP TALK
Think about it. When was the last time you had a team cheering you on to be your best self? The Official Pep Talk, brought to you by the Pep Talk Squad and The Susan O'Malley Research Team, focuses on what you need. We are here to listen to YOU and give YOU pep and encouragement. We believe that talking is transformative. By talking and sharing we are participating in your personal growth. We believe in you. And we also believe in the process.

WHAT IS AN OFFICIAL PEP TALK?

The Official Pep Talk is a free service open to anyone who wants words of inspiration. A hybrid of life coaching, cheerleading, pop-psychology and intuition, the pep talk is a 10-15 minute session where you may express concerns and questions to the Pep Talk Squad (PTS). In response, the PTS will write, read and give you an "Official Pep Talk." Quick, easy, and fun with proven results!

"I am more encouraged to talk to strangers, especially counter people, to give them a quick 'good job' comment. It's simple and free."

WHO IS ON THE PEP TALK SQUAD

Christina Amini
Senior Creative Maximizer Associate
A leader in the field of Pep Talk Technology, Christina is fascinated with the intersections of psychoanalysis and life coaching. Currently, Christina is working on her second bo "Finding the Pep from Within."

Susan O'Malley
Head Research Point Person
At the age of eleven, Susan won the fifth grade "Pep Award" for her cheers at basketball games and for her positive attitude. Today, she realizes her passion for talking, cheering, social research with the Pep Talk Squad.

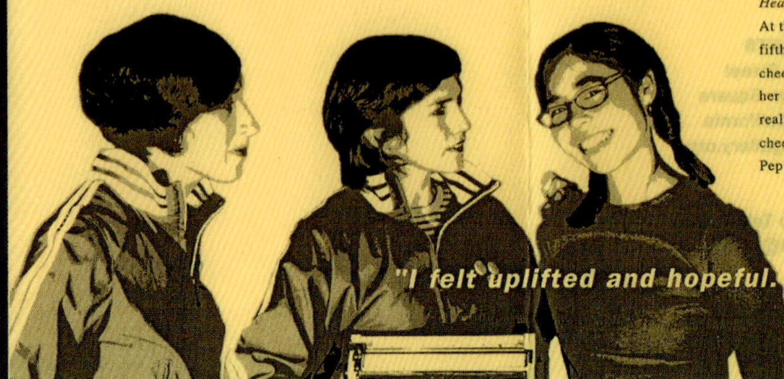

"I felt uplifted and hopeful. It worked!"

Excerpt on the Pep Talks and *Pep Talk Squad* from the self-published book *Recent Projects, Products, and Services: Volume 1* by the Susan O'Malley Research Team, 2005

The Official Pep Talk is a free service open to anyone who wants words of inspiration. A hybrid life coaching, cheerleading, pop-psychology and personal intuition, the pep talk is a 10-15 minute session where you may express concerns and questions to the Pep Talk Squad (PTS). In response, the PTS will write, read and give you an "Official Pep Talk."

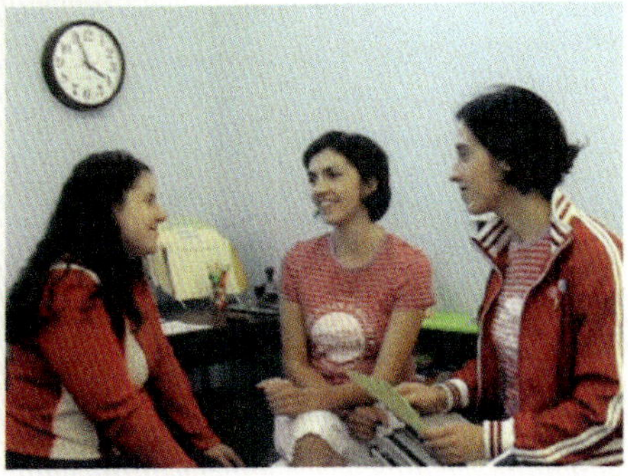

Lori needed a Pep Talk because she had difficulties saying "no" when asked for favors by friends and collegues. As a result, she did not focus on her own needs. The Pep Talk Squad reminded her that she needed to fuel herself in order to give to others. Please read her official pep talk below.

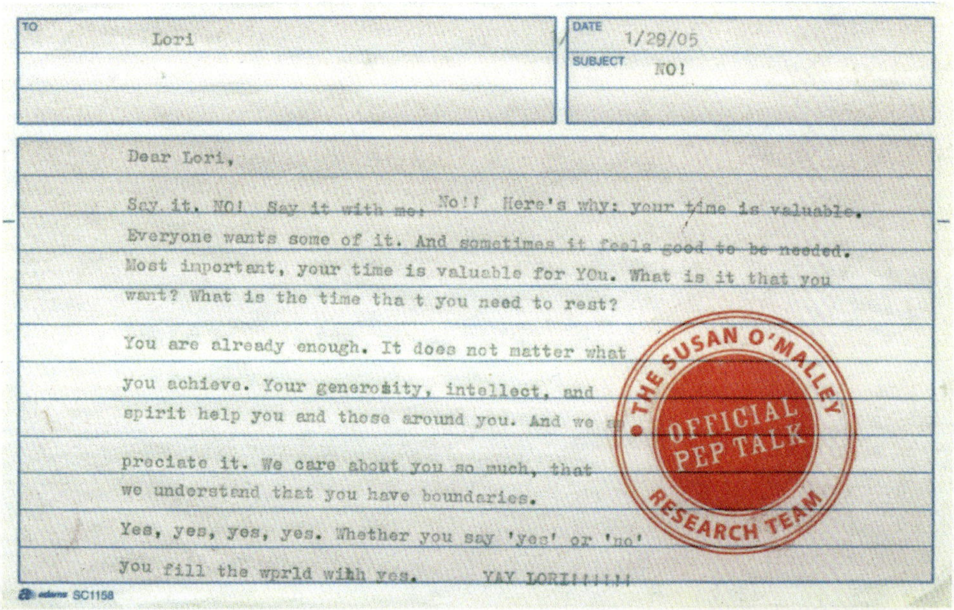

TO Lori

DATE 1/29/05

SUBJECT NO!

Dear Lori,

Say it. NO! Say it with me: No!! Here's why: your time is valuable. Everyone wants some of it. And sometimes it feels good to be needed. Most important, your time is valuable for YOu. What is it that you want? What is the time tha t you need to rest?

You are already enough. It does not matter what you achieve. Your generosity, intellect, and spirit help you and those around you. And we a- preciate it. We care about you so much, that we understand that you have boundaries.

Yes, yes, yes, yes. Whether you say 'yes' or 'no' you fill the wprld wihh yes. YAY LORI!!!!!!

adams SC1158

Teamwork Is the Dream Work

Christina Amini

My best friend Susan O'Malley and I were wearing matching red sports jackets and sitting at our booth at the San Jose Book Arts Jam when we noticed him: a short, middle-aged man in baggy jeans. It was our first day of giving Official Pep Talks.

Robert looked up with these kind eyes. He seemed like maybe he needed something. Susan and I introduced ourselves and asked him if he needed a Pep Talk. Robert said he did. When he started speaking, he had this *voice*—it was smooth and low and beautiful. He started to explain, in his deep voice, that the reason he needed a Pep Talk was this: He was a radio DJ, and a pretty well-known one, but every time he met someone in person for the first time, he saw a slight look of disappointment cross their face. He didn't look like what they *thought* he'd look like. He shrugged and said, "You know, I'm not Julio Iglesias."

We sat with Robert and listened carefully. Susan asked him questions while I typed up a Pep Talk on our typewriter. After about fifteen minutes together, I pulled the Pep Talk from the typewriter and read it to him. It went something like this:

"Robert, your voice brings people joy. *You* bring people joy. Your voice is just one of the beautiful parts of you. No, you are not Julio Iglesias. You are more than that; you are the *perfect* Robert."

Then we cheered for him: "*Yay* Robert!" And we gave him a button that read, "I had a Pep Talk today."

The sweetest smile came across Robert's face. You could almost see the weight of Julio Iglesias lift off his back. I like to think that he walked away with a little extra pep in his step.

***

The Pep Talks began with Susan's seemingly ridiculous question: "Do you want to start a Pep Talk Squad?" My answer was immediate: "Sure." Susan was my dearest friend. I would do anything with Susan.

Neither of us knew where this Pep Talk thing would go, but there were three things we did know: 1) Everyone—yes, everyone—needs someone to cheer for them. 2) There is value in connecting with strangers. 3) We trusted each other to try something goofy.

And, of course: We needed to wear matching red sports jackets.

That first day at the Books Arts Jam something special happened—for Robert, for others who stopped by our booth, and for us. Our ridiculous matching outfits allowed people to say *yes* to an unexpected possibility. We asked questions. We listened wholeheartedly. We didn't interrupt. We reflected their questions and their own answers back to them. In real time, one of us typed up an Official Pep Talk and gave the recipient a tangible reminder of being cheered for. Was this art? Was it an off-kilter lemonade stand? Was it a performance piece? Was it real?

Over many years, we put on our matching red sports jackets and picked up our typewriter to try out new locations and connect with new people. We gave Pep Talks at arty spaces and non-arty spaces. We gave Pep Talks in the park at Yerba Buena Center for the Arts on the day George W. Bush was elected. We gave Pep Talks in galleries in San Francisco and Oakland. We gave Pep Talks to the honors dorm at Duke University, where we iterated from Pep Talks in dorm rooms to Pep Walks on campus so that students could get some fresh air. We even brought the students on a campus bus for a Pep Bus Ride, where we cheered for the driver at the end of our route.

The toughest Pep Talks to give were for art students. There was so much self-doubt, competition, and vulnerability in what they shared with us. Those students really needed some pep, which is probably what had inspired Susan to ask me about starting the *Pep Talk Squad* in the first place since she was a new graduate art student herself.

Susan had just become one of the participants in the first year of California College of the Arts's Social Practice master's program. She was helping push the definition of what Social Practice could mean. At her critiques, she was asked why what she was doing was art and not social work. What could art hold? Was this *Art* with a capital *A*? Despite the questions and skepticism, she kept at it. *We* kept at it.

We carried on giving Pep Talks because our question—"Is there anything you need pep or encouragement on?"—turned out to be a shortcut to the heart of things. It turned out to be a way to ask, "What are you *vulnerable* about?" In the space of fifteen minutes, we had real conversations with people. Strangers told us about how they were worried they wouldn't find "the one" and how they didn't know if their work was important. One person just needed encouragement to do the dishes. All of a sudden, a stranger was now a confidant. It was almost unbelievable how it would happen over and over again. The Pep Talks were both completely silly and completely deep. Strangers shared their vulnerabilities with us, and we gave them our full attention and energy.

What was the magic?

Of course, Susan was magic. Her curiosity, her warmth, her willingness to try something. Our friendship was magic too—her trust in me and mine in her. The Pep Talk attire added sparkle to the whole situation.

For the record, this was *not* something I would have done on my own: I am really not the performing type. Susan and I met in college, where she was in the sketch comedy troupe. I was not. Like Susan, I grew up with five siblings in the Bay Area. Susan was number four; I was number five. Born into big families with an abundance of sisters, we found ease and humor in working together, being part of a team where the dynamics of the whole were as important as the roles of the individuals.

Susan and I became friends while living in the hippie co-ops at Stanford University. I met her at a party during the first week of school, where she wore big glasses and showed off even bigger dance moves. She studied urban planning. I studied creative writing. When I took a printmaking class as a senior, I invited her to join me and layer her work with mine. For her twenty-first birthday party, we invited friends to our off-campus house, broke into groups, and made short videos based on prompts pulled out of a paper bag. One night we spoke only in a made-up language that used only the letters of another friend's name. Susan was a perfect friend and accomplice: weird, entertaining, and loving.

After college, we didn't know what we wanted to do when we grew up, but we knew we wanted to figure it out together. We moved to Brooklyn with our friends, found jobs, quit jobs. I escorted her to get LASIK eye surgery. She was there the night I broke my leg ice skating in Central Park—we were playing follow the leader. She was there the night I first met my wife. After a couple of years, we both ended up back home in the Bay Area, living within a thirty-mile radius of each other. I attended her Garage Show, a fake store stocked with Susan's fake products in her mom's garage. We had art days at her mom's house, playing with spray paint and silk screens. There were escapades and experiments. We would meet in San Francisco, the midpoint between our childhood homes, and ask people to pose us in any way they wanted and take Polaroids. Susan created the cover art for a zine that another friend and I were starting.

We were friends before anything else. Just as Susan pushed the definition of what art could include, she also pushed the definition of what friendship could include. We were friends, we had been roommates, *and* we were members of a two-person team: the Pep Talk Squad. It made me feel both nervous and expanded. For me, it was easier to take risks with my best friend beside me. For Susan, I was a solid sounding board, a conceptual counterpart. We created something that neither of us would have on our own. The work came into being because of trust and humor and our friendship. We used to say that our credentials were that Susan was an artist and my father was a psychoanalyst. Now I would add that our credentials included deep friendship.

And then Susan died. I remember wondering if the art part of me would die, had already died, alongside her. A gallery asked if I would do a *Pep Talk Squad* in her honor. *No, thank you.* That seemed impossible. It was a Pep Talk *Squad*. Not a Pep Talk *Solo*. Our artwork was about connection to strangers, and—only now do I fully realize—to each other.

But even in her death, Susan kept connecting me to her people, to all the people who loved her. Being witness to all this love gave me the energy to do one thing I knew how to do: form a team.

I assembled Team Susan Art—two curators, a collaborator, her gallerist, a writer, her husband, and me—to make decisions about the future of her work. Team Susan Art secured Susan's pieces for the Art on Market Street Poster Series in San Francisco. It was amazing—but also so heavy with grief and so overwhelming—to choose the pieces. One of my friends said, "You know, this is crazy to say, but it's like you and Susan are still collaborating."

Something lifted in me then, because I knew that Susan would trust me in this collaboration, as an editor and as a friend. I chose a piece with a quote from Susan's mom, Lupe ("Trick Your Brain and Smile") and a piece with a quote from my dad ("You Can Never Catch Up on Having Fun"). In one of the bus shelters on Market Street, they were back-to-back. I knew that she would have enjoyed that.

Creative work requires risk-taking and optimism and endurance. It benefits from a team that has built up collaborative capital, that trusts each other to problem-solve, listen, bring out the best in each other's work, and celebrate when they've arrived. My teamwork with Susan continues in a way I had never imagined.

What if instead of a part of me dying, a part of her lives on with me in all the creative work I do?

Recently I was driving to an opening of a show of Susan's work, and it occurred to me: I would always go to Susan's openings. Whether she was there or not.

And so here we are. This new relationship with Susan. This new phase of our friendship. We will always be a team, whether she is here or not.

As the steward of Susan's artwork, I proofread her press releases and proposals, contracts and captions. When the San Francisco Museum of Modern Art acquired some of the Official Pep Talks, including our Pep Talk brochure (printed at Kinko's), I still had the instinct to call her and congratulate her.

Can you believe it, Su?

She laughs, and says, *YES.*

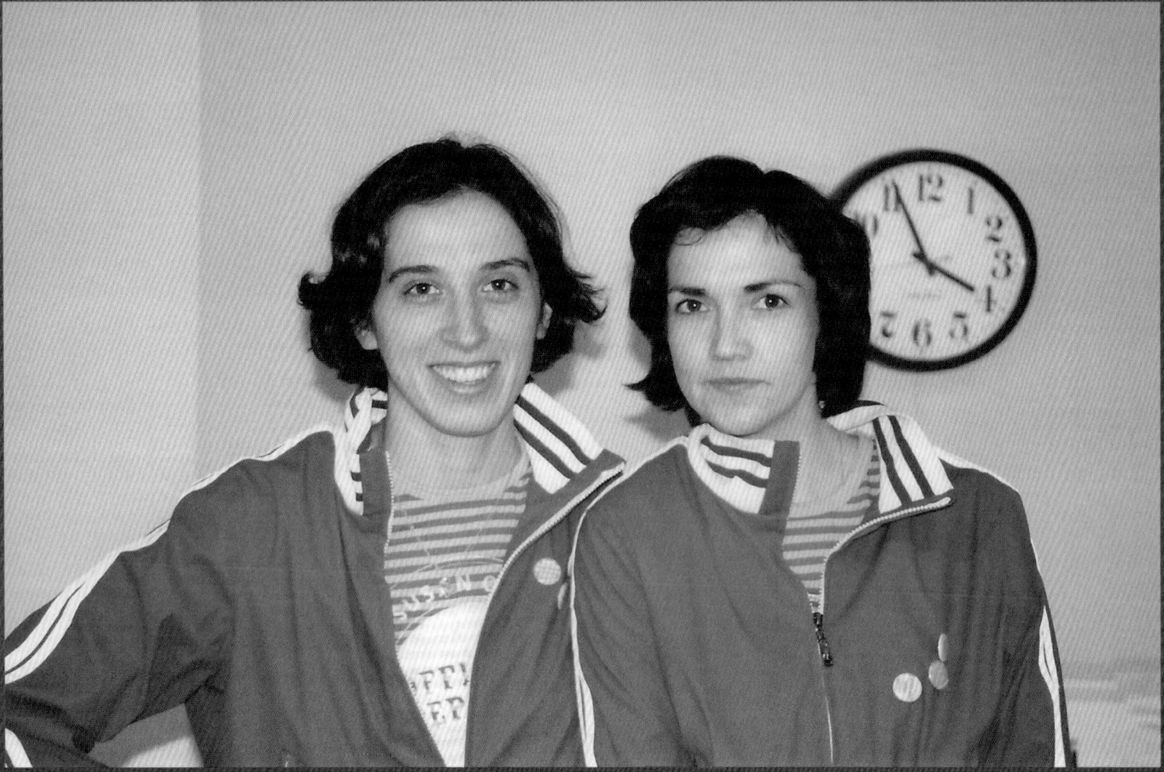

Above: Pep Talk Squad, Christina Amini (left) and Susan O'Malley (right), circa 2003–4
Opposite: Pep Talks, various locations in the San Francisco Bay Area, 2004–5

YOUR PEP-TALK

First Name: Jood RUSH

Reason for Pep-Talk:

- ☐ FINANCE
- ☐ LOVE
- ☐ WORK
- ☐ RELATIONSHIPS
- ☐ BODY IMAGE
- ☒ OTHER surgery

Pep-Talk:

Jood, your body wants to heal, and you can help it on its way. While surgery might frighten you, think of your body moving freely, dancing, walking outside. Recovery takes determination-- you are full of energy. to do it. Congratulations on beginning.

yay Jood!

Signed by: Date: OCT 2 2004

Susan O'Malley Research Team 2004

YOUR PEP-TALK

First Name: Terry

Reason for Pep-Talk:

- ☐ FINANCE
- ☐ LOVE
- ☐ WORK
- ☐ RELATIONSHIPS
- ☐ BODY IMAGE
- ☒ OTHER The world situation

Pep-Talk:

Terry, please dont give up. YOU, yes YOU are the answer. The world needs you, the envaironment needs you, people need you. And you are appreciated. Your strength and inspiration will help others find their strength. And then, the world will be a stronger and more hospitable place. Thank you for being here.

yay Terry!

Signed by: Date: OCT 2 2004

Susan O'Malley Research Team 2004

YOUR PEP-TALK

First Name: Cindy

Reason for Pep-Talk:

PICK ONE:

- ☐ FINANCE
- ☐ LOVE
- ☐ WORK
- 1. ☒ RELATIONSHIPS
- ☐ BODY IMAGE
- 2. ☒ OTHER SADNESS ABOUT THE STATE OF THE WORLD

Pep-Talk:

...y, allow yourself to feel during the holidays. This can be difficult ... everything is supposed to be happy. But remember that the people ... are absent during this time love you and are thinking of you and it ...mportant that you thin of them, talk about them and include them -- ...w their spirit to be present. Be kind to yourself during this time.

YEA CINDY!

Signed by: Date: OCT 2 2004

Susan O'Malley Research Team 2004

YOUR PEP-TALK

First Name: Judith

Reason for Pep-Talk:

- ☐ FINANCE
- ☐ LOVE
- ☐ WORK
- ☐ RELATIONSHIPS
- ☐ BODY IMAGE
- ☐ OTHER Desperate state of Things in Iraq & the upcoming US electi...

Pep-Talk:

Judith, you have what it takes to effect change. Your perseverance is needed more than ever now. Continue to educate, engage, and remain hopeful. Your spirit will create change in and of itself.

Yay Judith!

Signed by: Date: OCT 2 2004

Susan O'Malley Research Team 2004

The Independent School of Art: A Photo Essay

Jon Rubin

We had just started the Social Practice focus at California College of the Arts, where I taught, and Susan O'Malley was in one of the earliest cohorts of students. I remember that during my first studio visit with Susan, she explained a project she was developing with a collaborator where they would set themselves up in public spaces and give free pep talks to the general public. I recall thinking, perhaps because of my own cynicism or perhaps because of the general vibe of the students at the time, that this must be ironic. It was the same suspicious feeling I had as a kid when watching *Mister Rogers' Neighborhood*: Is this real, or is there an angry mess of a human just behind this facade, because this can't be real? After moving to Pittsburgh, where Fred Rogers lived in real life and filmed his show, I learned that according to absolutely everyone who knew and worked with him, he was not at all unlike the character he portrayed on TV—a decent and caring person.

Nevertheless, as Susan and I continued our regular advising meetings, I was always waiting for the other shoe to drop, for there to be something dark and conflicted about her motivations, for her to back off of her optimistic ideas and fall closer in line with her fellow grad students' pessimistic criticality. Of course, this never happened. Despite my poking and prodding at the edifice of her optimism, Susan was just like the idealistic character she portrayed through her artwork. This isn't to say that she wasn't struggling with the same doubts that her peers were wrestling with, but her doubts had to do with whether what she was doing was "art" or something else, not whether her desire to make people happy was a less serious pursuit than her peers' desire to make critical art.

In 2004 I started the Independent School of Art (ISA), a nomadic barter-based art school that operated autonomously without grant funding, academic or art world affiliations, accreditation, or a physical site. It was a bit of a one-room schoolhouse of misfits. The student body was made up of currently matriculating students from Bay Area schools as well as people who had recently moved on from art school and were trying to make a go of it. Located temporarily in parks, office buildings, tents, schools, homes, and backyards, the school prioritized social over physical architecture. I asked all involved to imagine how their practice might intersect and respond to a larger set of physical situations and cultural possibilities outside the conventions of academia and the art world.

Even though she was already a student of mine at CCA, Susan decided to join the ISA. I think the fact that we were just making it up on the fly really aligned with Susan's attitude about the role of play in making art. The images on these pages show a range of events and happenings from those early years of ISA: class meetings, dinners, a show-and-tell exhibition . . . you get the idea. In a school predicated on the idea that it only existed if the students showed up and made it exist, Susan was always there in the center of things. She never missed a meeting, signed up for every committee, participated in every event, and believed that the school could be real, even when many of the rest of us—myself included—had our doubts. Many amazing things happened at the ISA in its relatively short two years of existence, and it was the people (and the students especially) that made them happen. Susan was an integral part of that happening.

Top left: ISA class meeting at student Josh Pieper's home. Clockwise from center-top: Helena Del Pesco, Verda Alexander, Thia Jennings, Maggie Foster, Josh Pieper, Rita DiLorenzo, Engelbert Holder, Pablo Guardiola, Corinne Matesich, Lori Gordon.

Center left: ISA class meeting with visiting artist Charles Goldman in the old Hayes Valley Market in San Francisco. Clockwise from center: Susan O'Malley, Amber Cady, Daniel Minnick, Engelbert Holder, Chika Sato, Jennifer Durban, Matt Shain, Charles Goldman, Lissalvy Tiegel, NyQ Bonaventura, Helena Del Pesco.

Bottom left: ISA class meeting in student Helena Del Pesco's home studio. Clockwise from center-right: Susan O'Malley, Jennifer Durban, Helena Del Pesco, NyQ Bonaventura, Engelbert Holder, Matt Shaine.

Top center: Susan O'Malley and artist Keith Boadwee during the ISA's Black Market Auction, held at the old Hayes Valley Market. Artists participating in the auction (which included students from the school as well as over fifty local and national artists) produced high-quality knockoffs of well-known local, national, and international artists' works. The proceeds helped support future ISA events and publications.

Center: The ISA Show and Tell event invited thirty people from throughout the Bay Area to share something unrelated to art that they were passionate about. Each ISA student was responsible for curating people they knew about to participate. Susan O'Malley invited Christina Amini and Elspeth Stowell, shown here displaying Garbage Pail Kids cards. Held at the old Hayes Valley Market, the event was described in its flyer as "*Antiques Roadshow* meets everyday performance art."

Bottom center: The ISA's Black Market Auction

Top and center right: Susan O'Malley and Amber Cady serve food as part of the ISA dinner lecture series held in homes throughout the Bay Area.

Bottom right: Susan O'Malley in the kitchen at the ISA dinner lecture series. Proceeds from the dinners went to pay the lecturers.

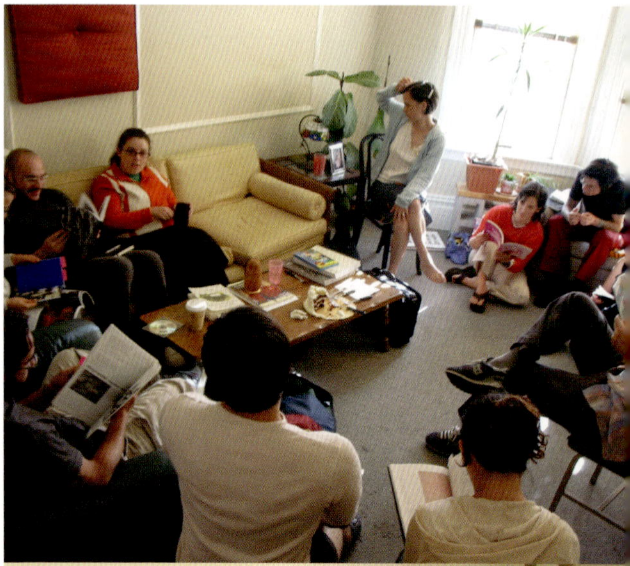

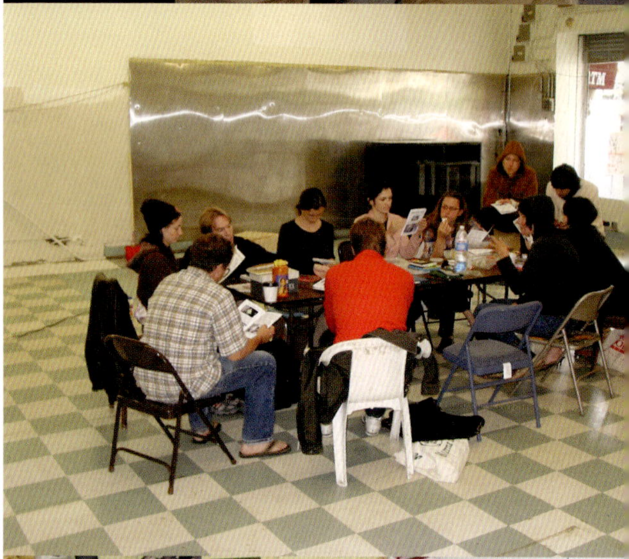

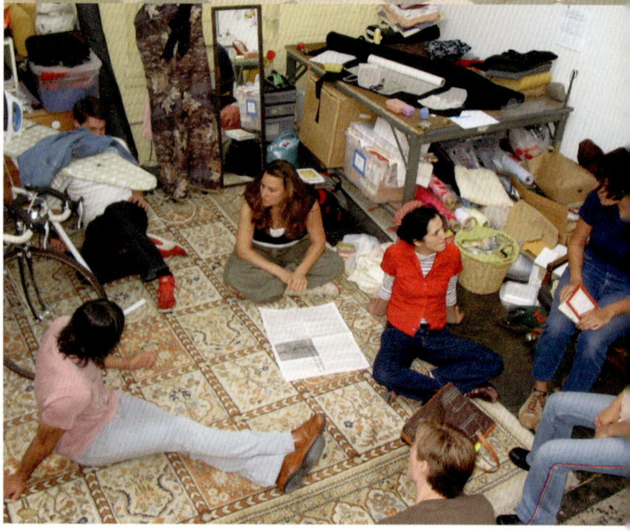

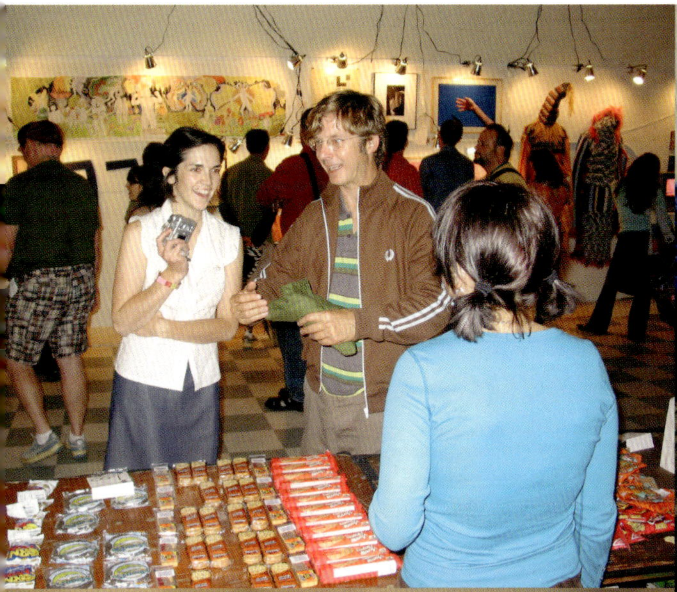
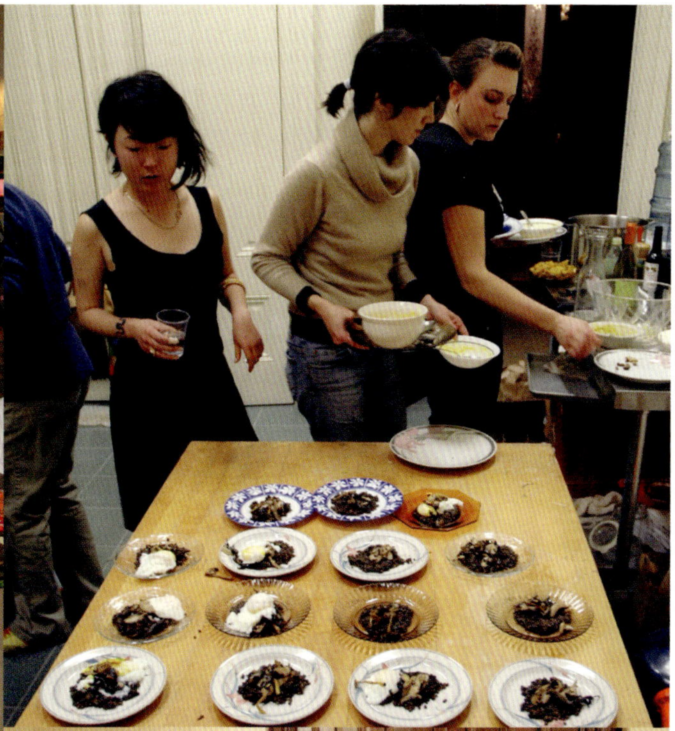
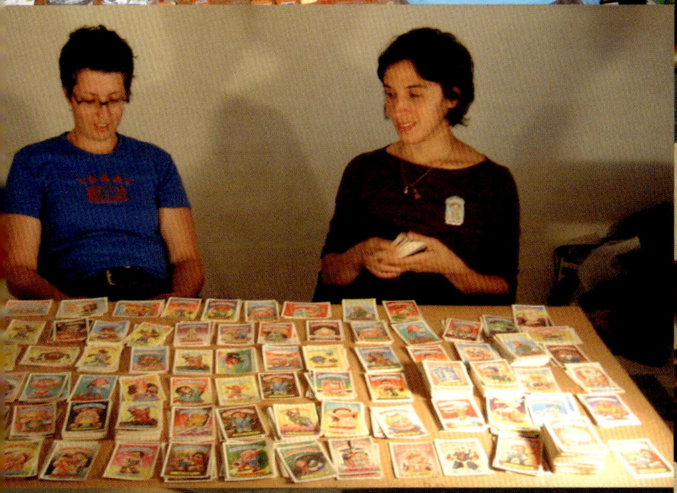
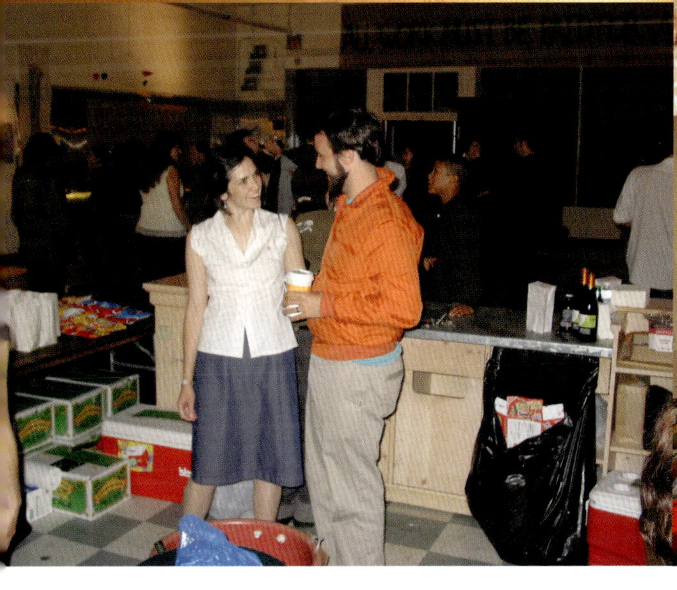
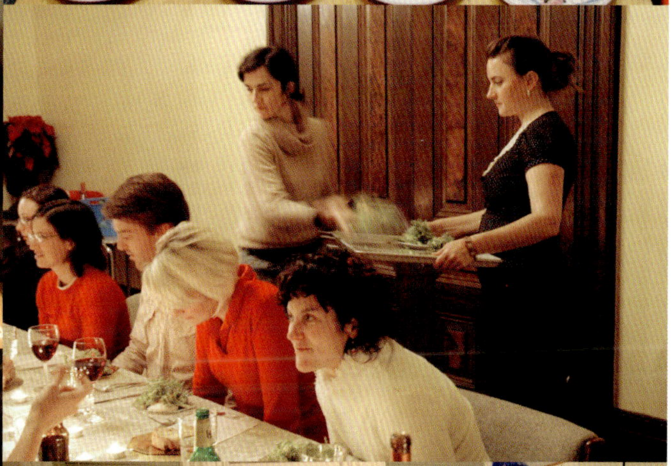
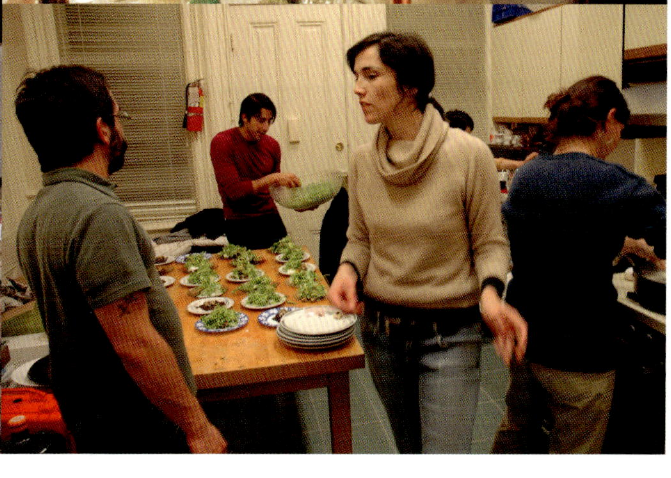

San Jose Artist-in-Residence

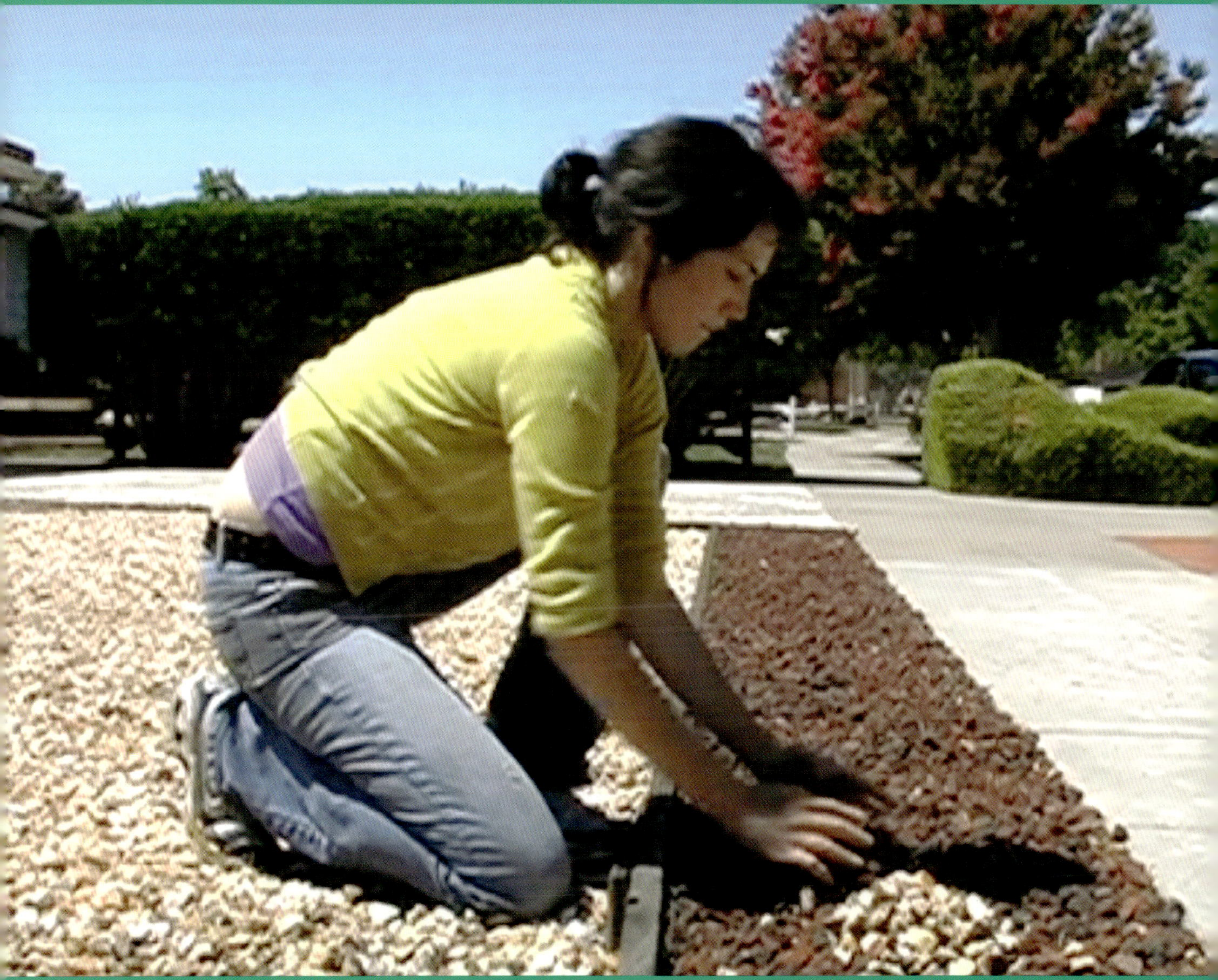

A Simple Change in Your Yard

Ellen Kato

Christina Amini sat down with Ellen Kato—one of Susan O'Malley's sisters—for this conversation. Ellen was Susan's collaborator and assistant on her early project *San Jose Artist-in-Residence*, where Susan appointed herself as an artist-in-residence in a suburb of San Jose called Willow Glen. She left flyers in each of her neighbors' mailboxes, letting them know that she would change items in their front yards. Susan and Ellen captured the results in photos and videos.

Christina Amini: Let's look at a few of the yards in San Jose first, to get us in the mood to talk about *San Jose Artist-in-Residence* by Susan O'Malley.

Ellen Kato: Just as soon as I look at these, my mind goes to: She's such a weirdo, I love her.

CA: Do you remember how *San Jose Artist-in-Residence* started?

EK: First, Susan delivered a bunch of notifications to the neighbors in the area, saying that she wanted to do an artist-in-residency. In the notifications, she told people, "I will modify something in your yard but nothing permanent, nothing that would cause damage."

A bunch of people responded, basically saying, "Yeah, you can do whatever." So we knew which homes we could go to ahead of time, and that they had already consented. She would look at their yards and think, "Well, what can we do here?" And she would come up with these quirky things. The fun thing was imagining what the homeowner would think or what the neighbors would see.

Sometimes we would walk by later and the neighbors would be out looking at the yards—and they didn't know who had been doing it, so we could walk by and see people's responses without them knowing that Susan was the one modifying the yards. People were actually really amused by it, which was fun to watch.

CA: So what was your role in the *San Jose Artist-in-Residence* project?

Page 63: *How to Be an Artist-in-Residence* video still, San Jose, California, circa 2006

EK: I took a lot of photos. I videotaped her. I was kind of like a cheerleader. When she'd come up with something, I'd be like, "Yeah, that's awesome! Let's do it!"

I was working at Planned Parenthood at the time, so oftentimes she'd come by the house early in the morning and we would go do things super early before work—or else after work or on the weekends.

I think Susan had a general sense of things that she was really interested in doing with these videos.

Willow Glen, where we grew up, was really weird because there were these beautiful homes, but they had these overly manicured yards. Like, manicured in a way that was . . . well, it took away all the natural aspects of a yard. They had an element of the bizarre to them.

I think Susan found that really interesting. You know, like having an artificial turf lawn. Nowadays people do have those, but they look real. These ones did not look real. These were the fluorescent green artificial lawns decorated with white statues of life-size lions and weird stuff like that.

I think she just found it so interesting. So she would come up with funny little things to do with the yards. I just was along for the ride.

Like this one with the leaves. We went driving around Willow Glen to some of the houses that she had modified and made a series of pictures with leaves and shadow. For some of them, she had changed the leaves and made these totally pristine clean paths and pushed the leaves aside to play with light and shadow.

Then there was this one dad—he saw what Susan had done to a few of his neighbors' yards, so he created an obstacle course for his kid with the leaves in his own front yard. You could tell it was a play off of her art because he had cleared everything away in just the same way that Susan had, but then he'd used the cleared paths to make a little obstacle course for his daughter who had a little push car.

CA: Will you describe Willow Glen?

EK: Willow Glen is one of the older areas of San Jose. It has single-family homes on pretty good-sized lots. There are a lot of these old ranch homes or bungalow-style homes, 1920s- to 1950s-style architecture. It is definitely quintessential suburbia, where everyone has a manicured lawn and manicured foliage. It's the type of community where every single home has a Christmas tree on their front lawn. You have to decorate it and there's no choice. They purchase it for the block and everyone has to have it. That's kind of the vibe. Some people like the ultimate extreme of lawn maintenance, where it almost has an austerity to it. Everything has its place. It's orderly in those yards. So moving things out of that order, that was what was so hilarious and provocative about what Susan was doing.

CA: Were you surprised by the project?

EK: Well, Susan was such a goof. So, surprised *yes* and surprised *no*. The fact that she wanted to do this, I found that interesting and surprising. But I think the end result was always more clever than I had even thought it would be when she came up with the idea. She'd say, "Let's go do this," and I'd say, "Yeah, that sounds fun. Let's do it." But then, after we took the video, I'd watch it a couple of times, and it would always be way funnier than I had initially perceived it being when we came up with the concept.

CA: Are these single-take videos?

EK: They're pretty much all single takes. I think maybe once or twice we did it twice, but that was just because I forgot to push record. Other than that, single take.

I think it was because they were so quirky and weird. And also I think we didn't want to stick around too long and have people watching us—these weirdos crawling across the lawns in front of people's houses.

CA: Did you see it as art at the time or just goofiness?

EK: Just goofiness at the time, for me. I mean, Susan was super artistic and thoughtful. The way she thought of this had much more depth than I perceived at the time.

CA: Anything else you'd like to share?

EK: The whimsical elements of the project were just so Susan. I loved getting caught up in her energy and her vision. Just following her around, seeing things through her eyes. How clever she was in her thinking about how silly the place we grew up really was.

She found humor in everything and made it whimsical and fun. That captures a lot of who she was. She could turn any situation into something that could bring a smile to your face. Even an interaction with someone angry or annoying, she could turn something like that around. So this is her bringing humor to this neighborhood where we grew up. And making it so much cooler. Seriously.

Honestly, I feel so lucky that I got to spend that time with her doing this. That I got that special time. I could have been doing anything with her. If she was like, "Let's go shave a cat," I'd be like, "Sure, let's go do that." She would have made it fun, right? There were many days where I just felt lucky to spend time with my sister and enjoy the way she saw the world in all its silliness.

I wish I was able to do more of them. Who knows where she would have gone next?

Opposite: Untitled photo from *San Jose Artist-in-Residence*

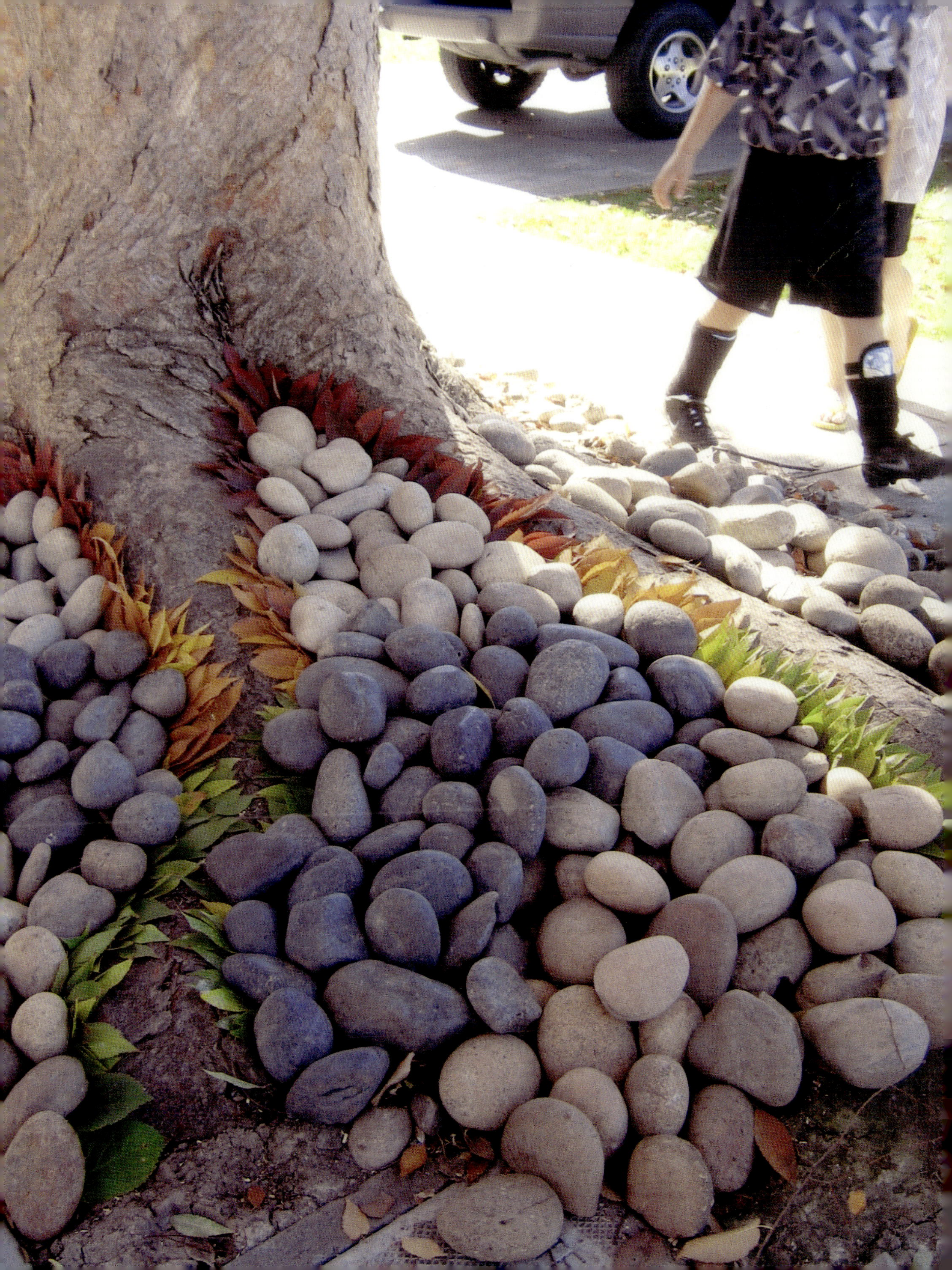

2424

Dear Neighbor,

Hi! My name is Susan O'Malley and I am Landsford Avenue's artist-in-resident. Growing up in this neighborhood, I have always been fond of the front yards and gardens.

From November 29th to December 6th, I will be doing a front yard garden project on your street. I may make a simple change in your yard, such as rolling up a tangled hose in an unusual way or stacking rocks differently. The change will not be destructive but will hopefully bring delight in looking at the front yards on your street.

While I would love for you to participate, you are under no obligation to do so. If you feel like this is not something you want to do, contact me by returning this flyer with your address and by checking the "no thank you" box by November 28th.

I welcome comments and thoughts. Contact me by dropping a note at 2350 Westgate, between Husted and Curtner, by email somalley_99@yahoo.com or by phone 415 810 6436.

Thank you for Reading!

☐ **No Thank You**

Please do not include me in this project.

I live at ________________ Landsford Avenue.

☒ **I would like to learn more**

Contact me at: have fun!

Please return to: 2350 Westgate Ave. by November 28th.

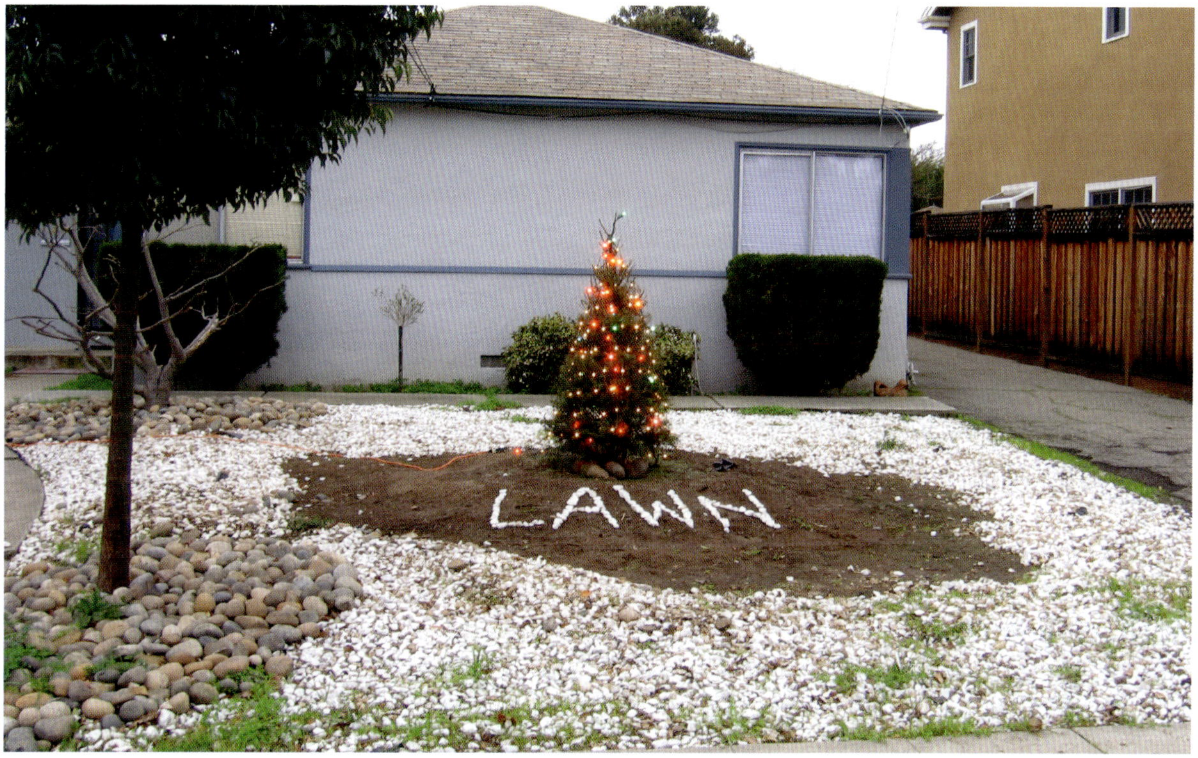

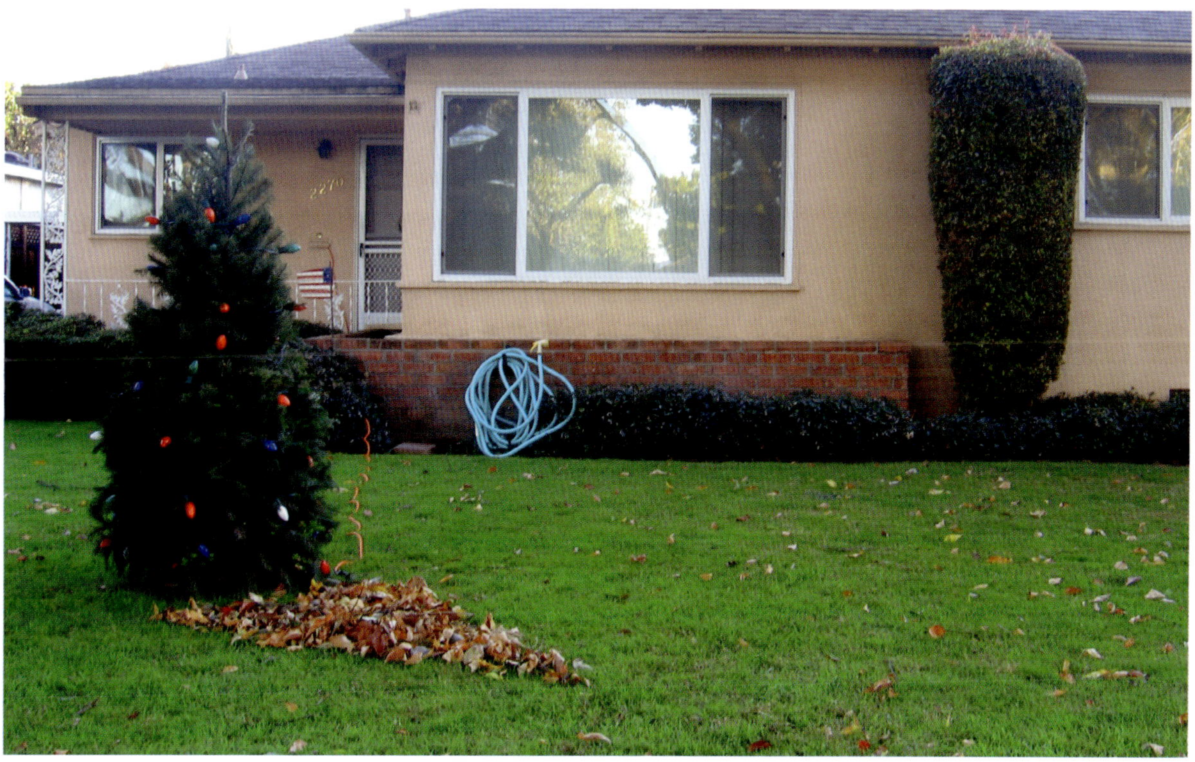

Opposite: *Dear Neighbor* participation agreement, Willow Glen, San Jose, California, circa 2006

Above, top: *Lawn* from *San Jose Artist-in-Residence*

Above, bottom: *2270* from *San Jose Artist-in-Residence*

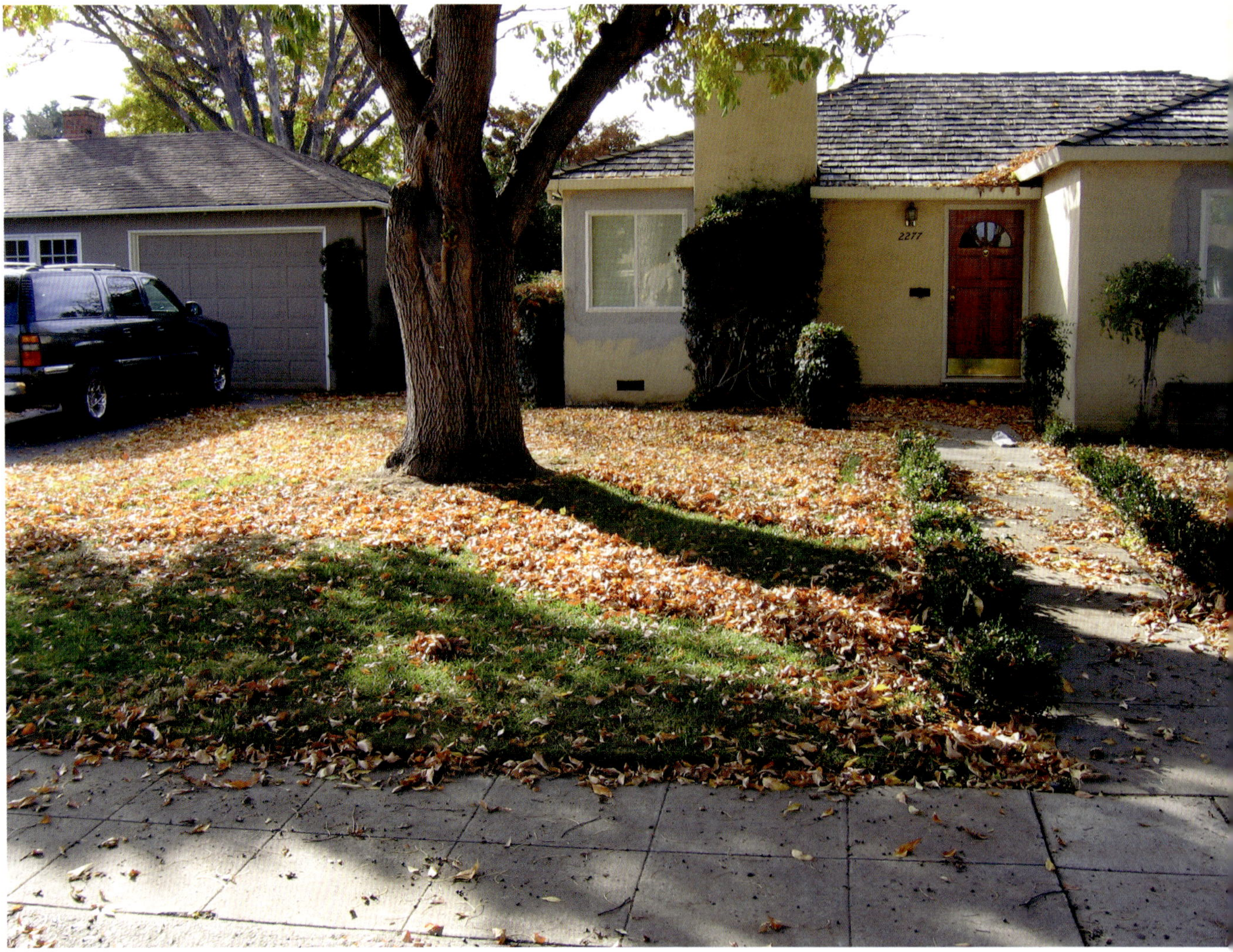

Above: *2277 Lansford* from *San Jose Artist-in-Residence*

Opposite: *2401 Lansford* from *San Jose Artist-in-Residence*

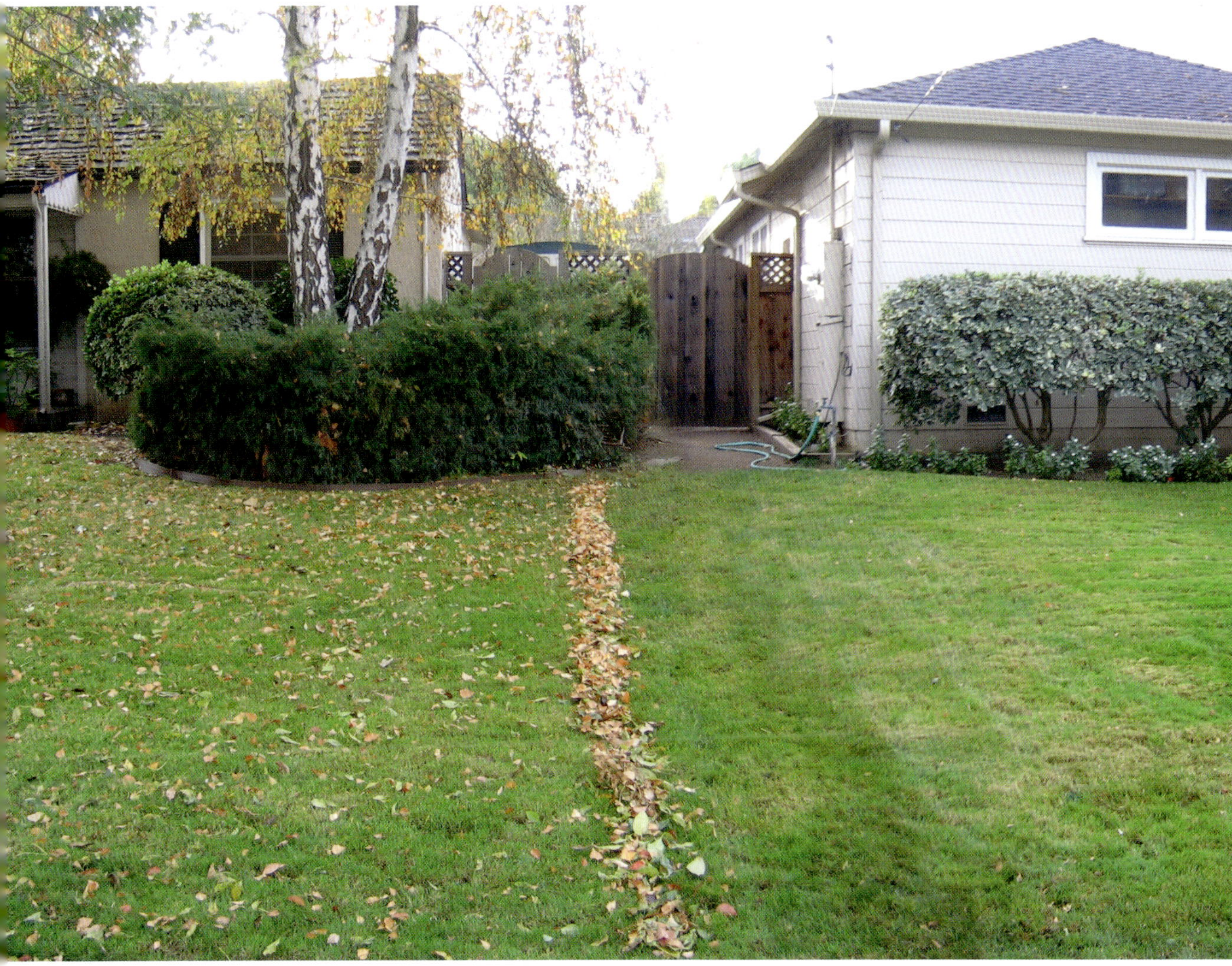

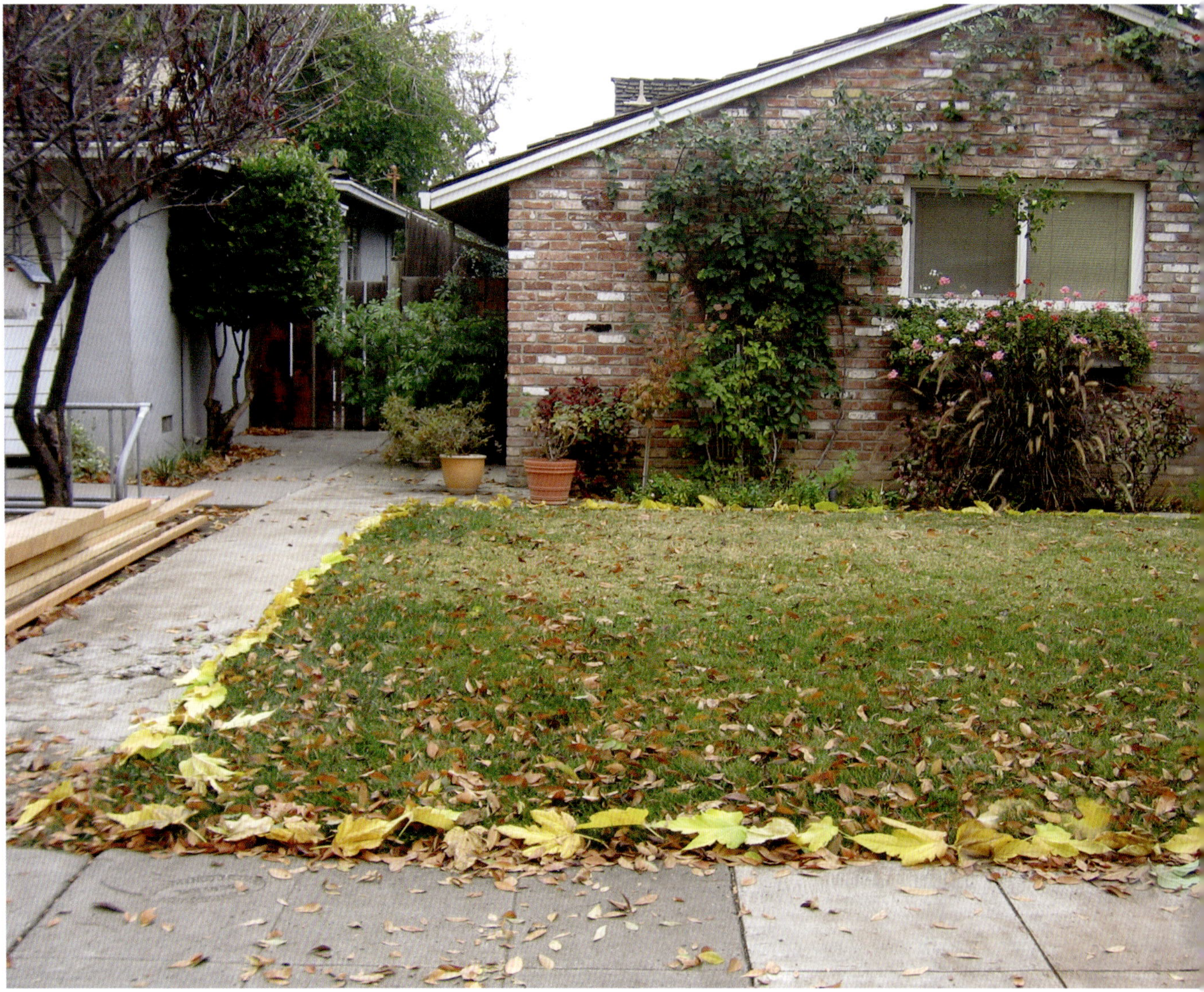

Yellow Lansford from *San Jose Artist-in-Residence*

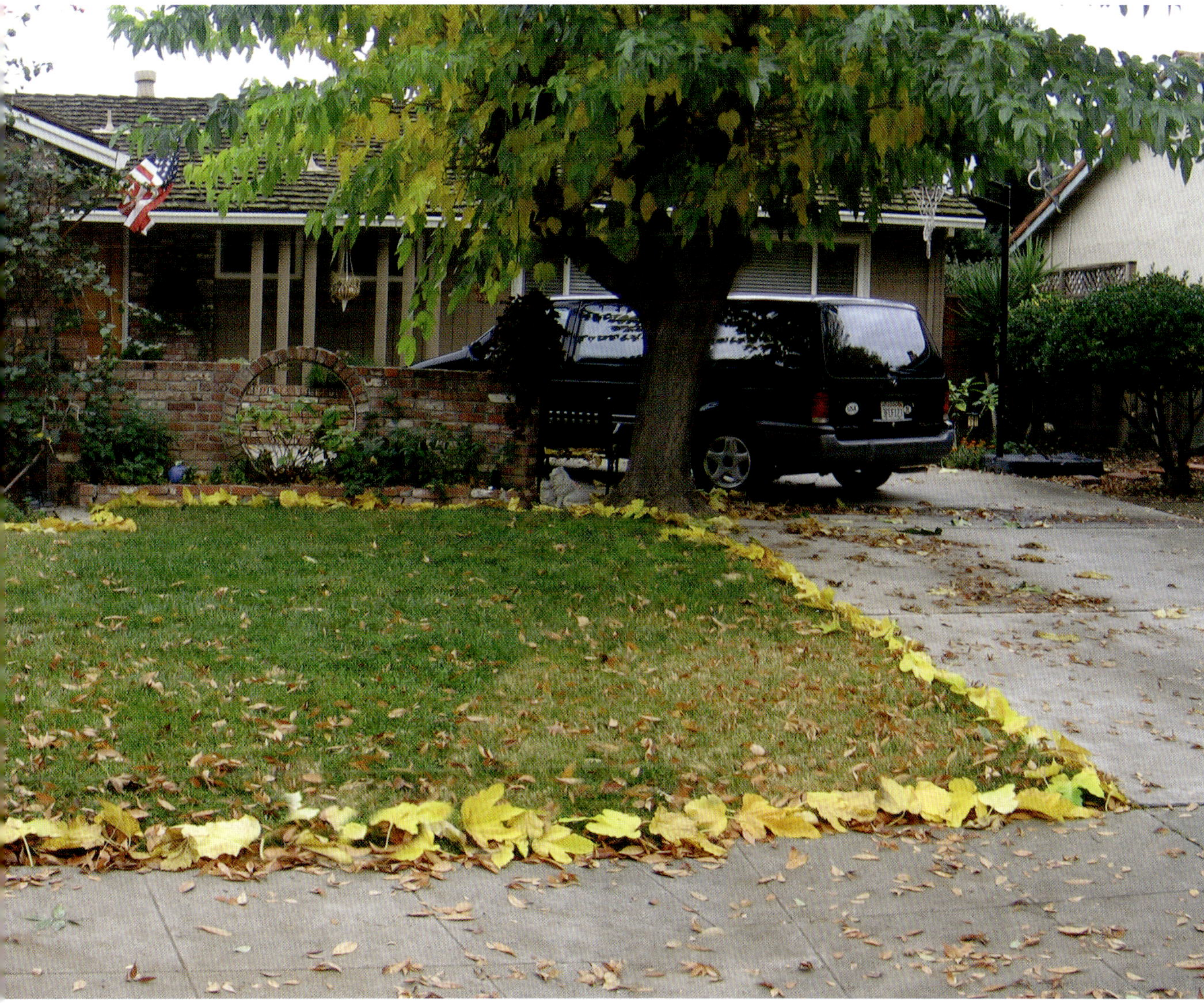

Pages 75–80: Video stills from *A Few Yards in San Jose* and *How to Be an Artist-in-Residence* videos. Videography by Ellen Kato, circa 2006. Video stills from *We've Been Here Before*, joint exhibition with Leah Rosenberg, Romer Young Gallery, San Francisco, 2022.

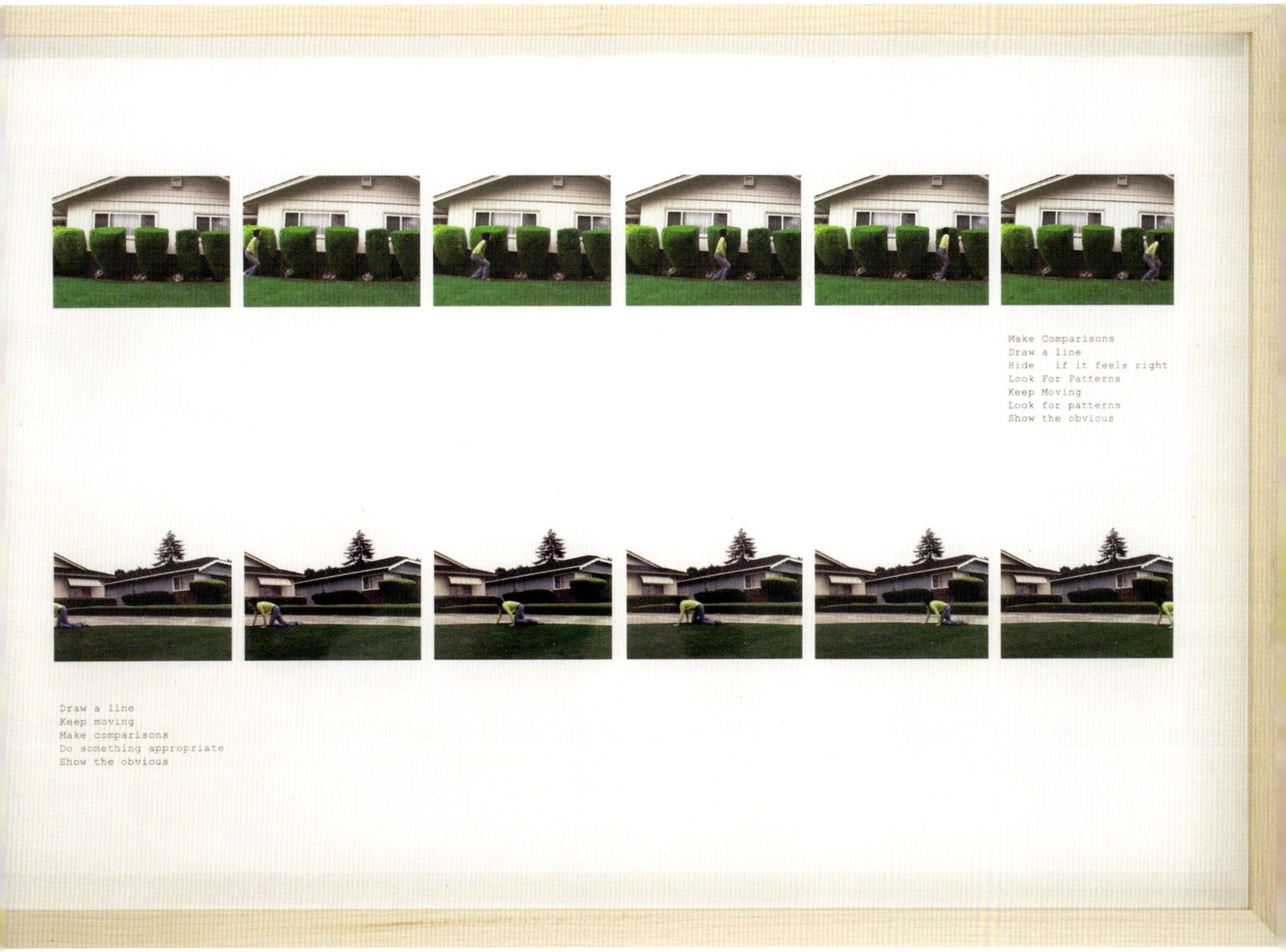
Make Comparisons
Draw a line
Hide if it feels right
Look For Patterns
Keep Moving
Look for patterns
Show the obvious
Draw a line
Keep moving
Make comparisons
Do something appropriate
Show the obvious

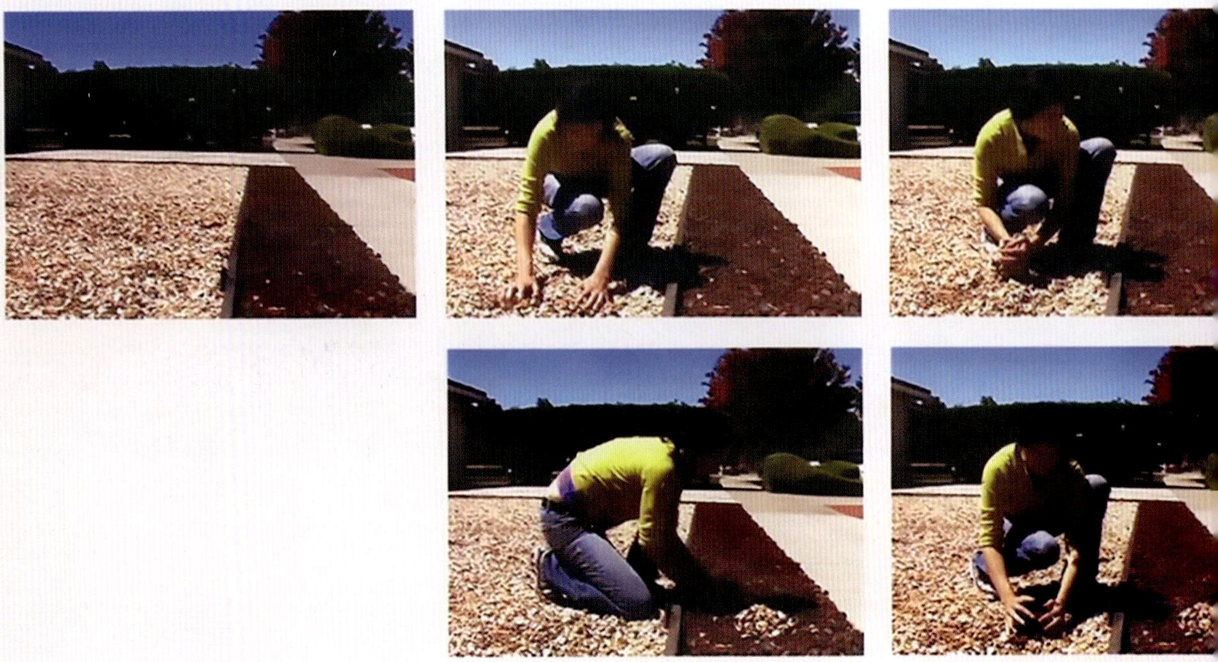

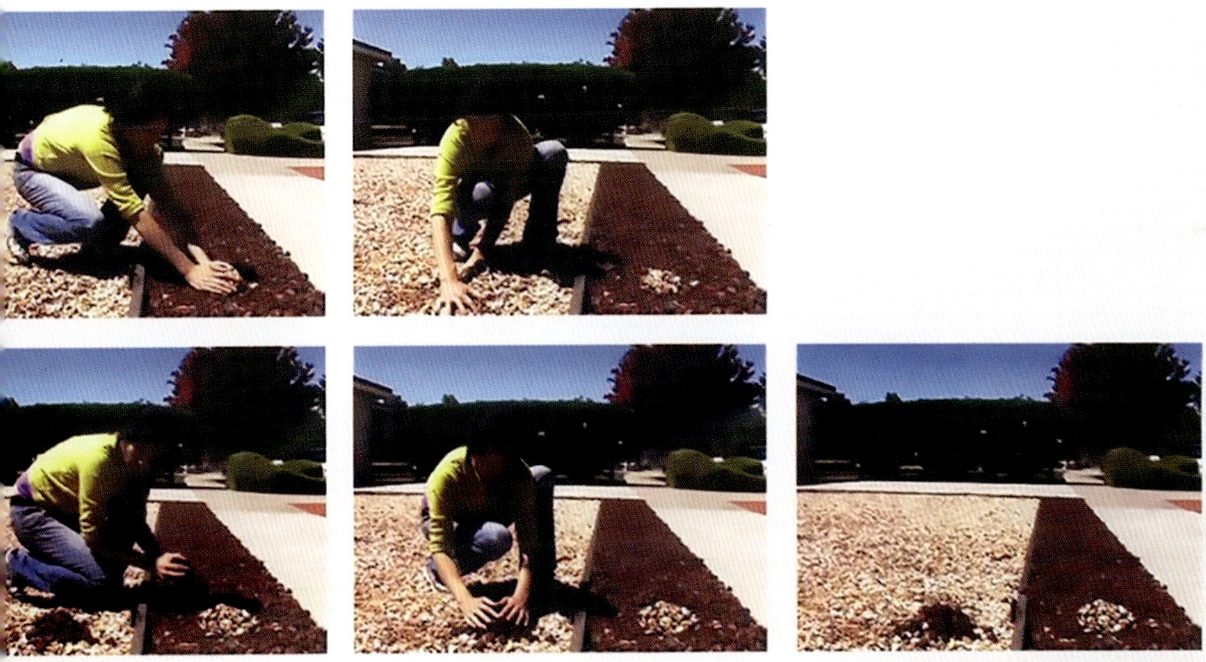

Make a pile
Make a change
Stay awhile
Make comparisons
Misplace an object
Do something wrong

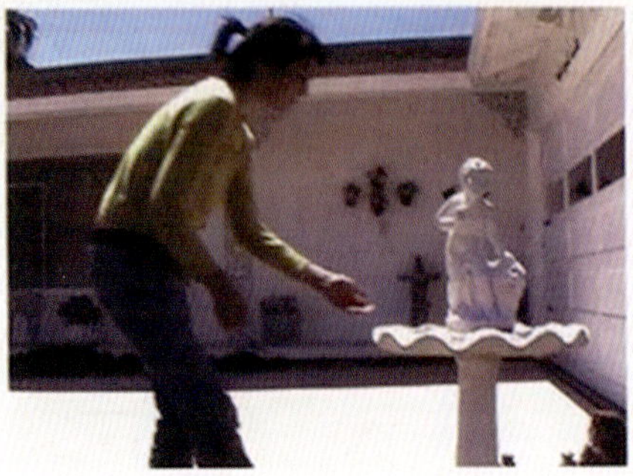

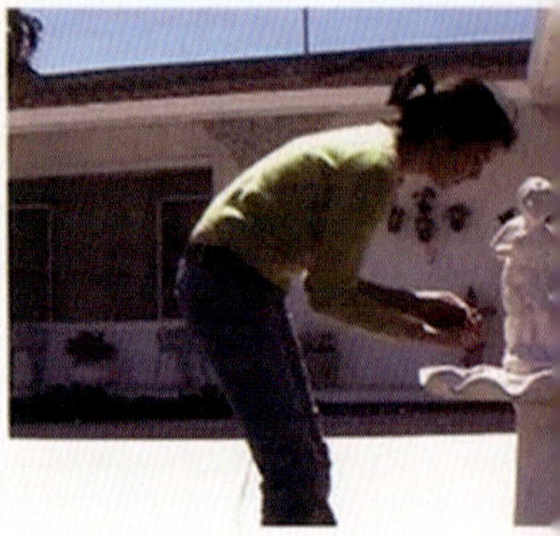

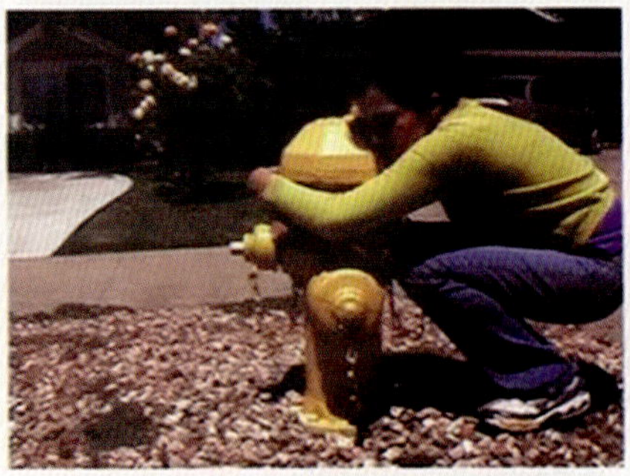

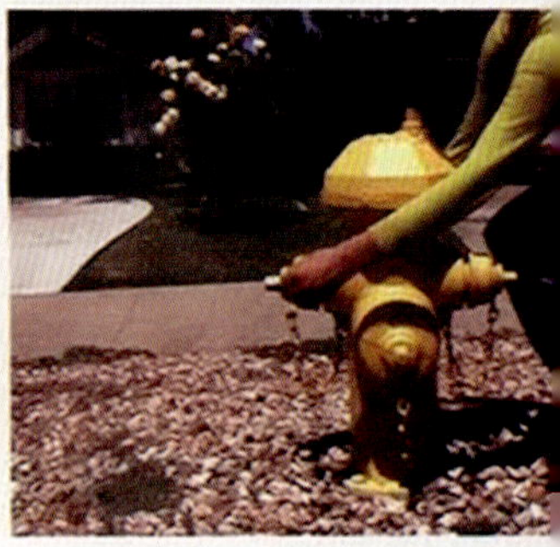

Give something
Do something wrong
Stay awhile
Make comparisons

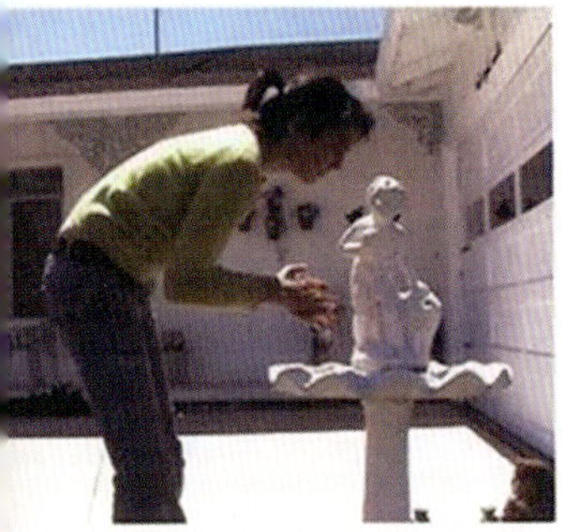

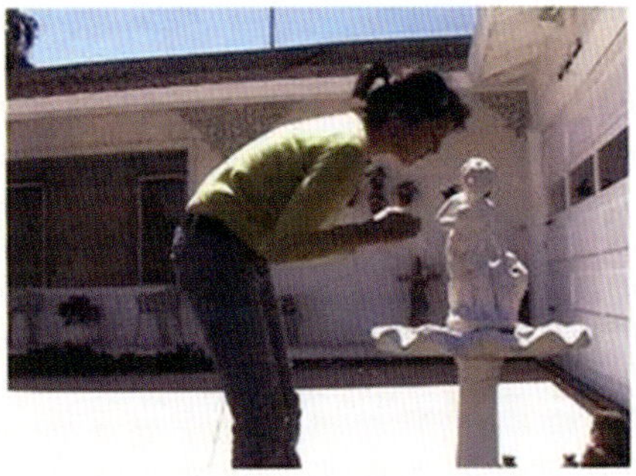

Do something wrong
Keep moving
Show the obvious

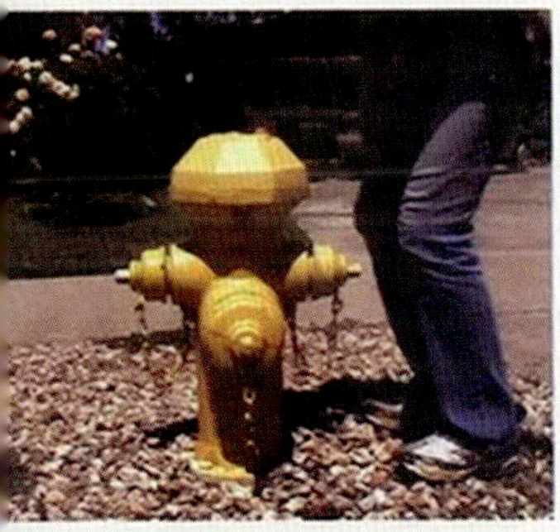

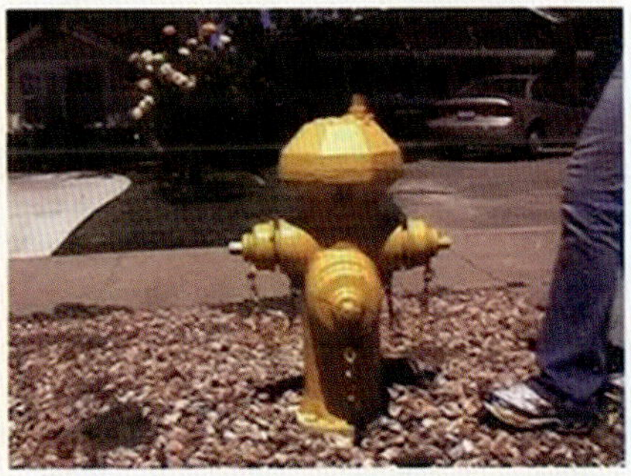

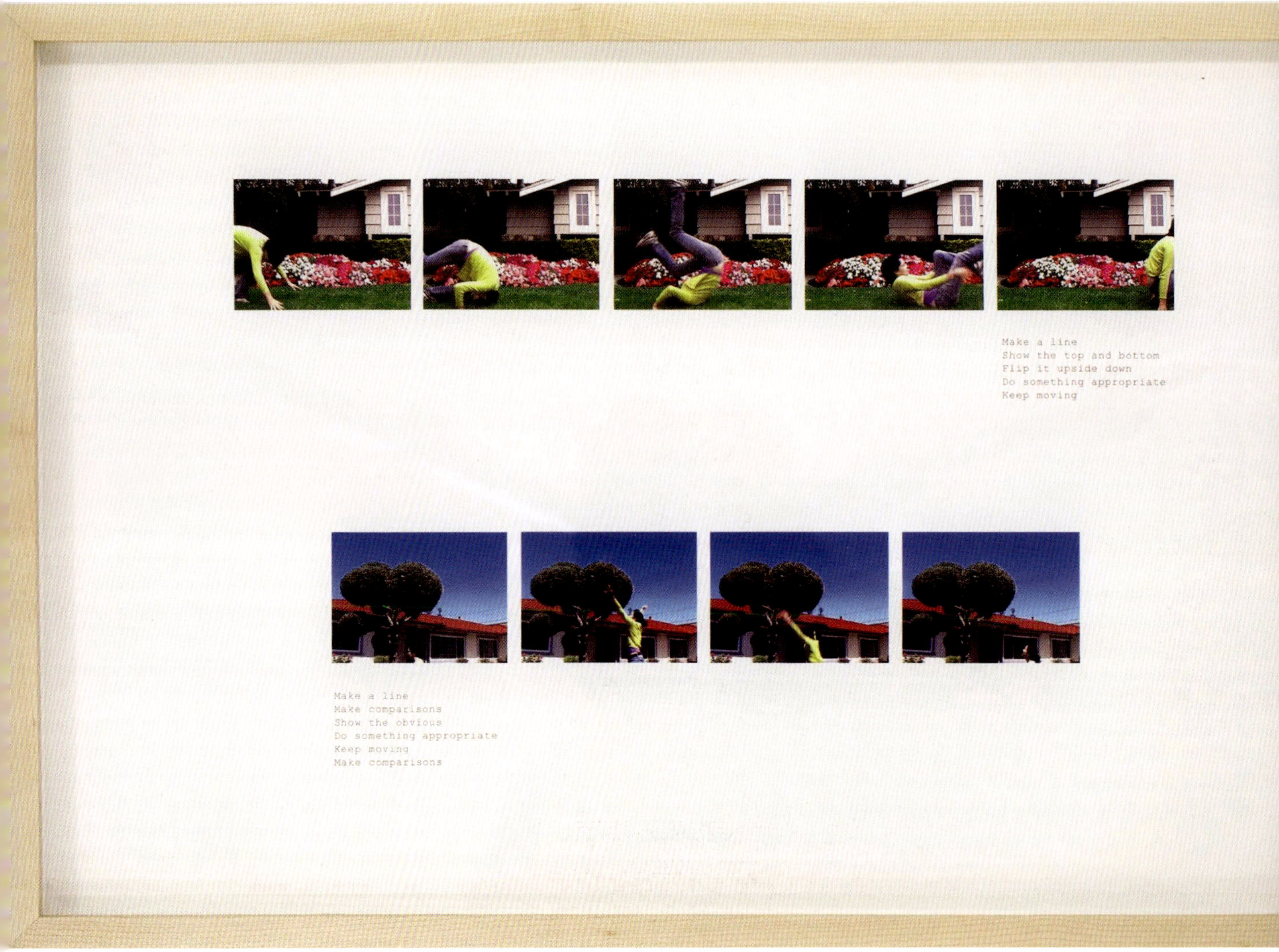
Make a line
Show the top and bottom
Flip it upside down
Do something appropriate
Keep moving
Make a line
Make comparisons
Show the obvious
Do something appropriate
Keep moving
Make comparisons

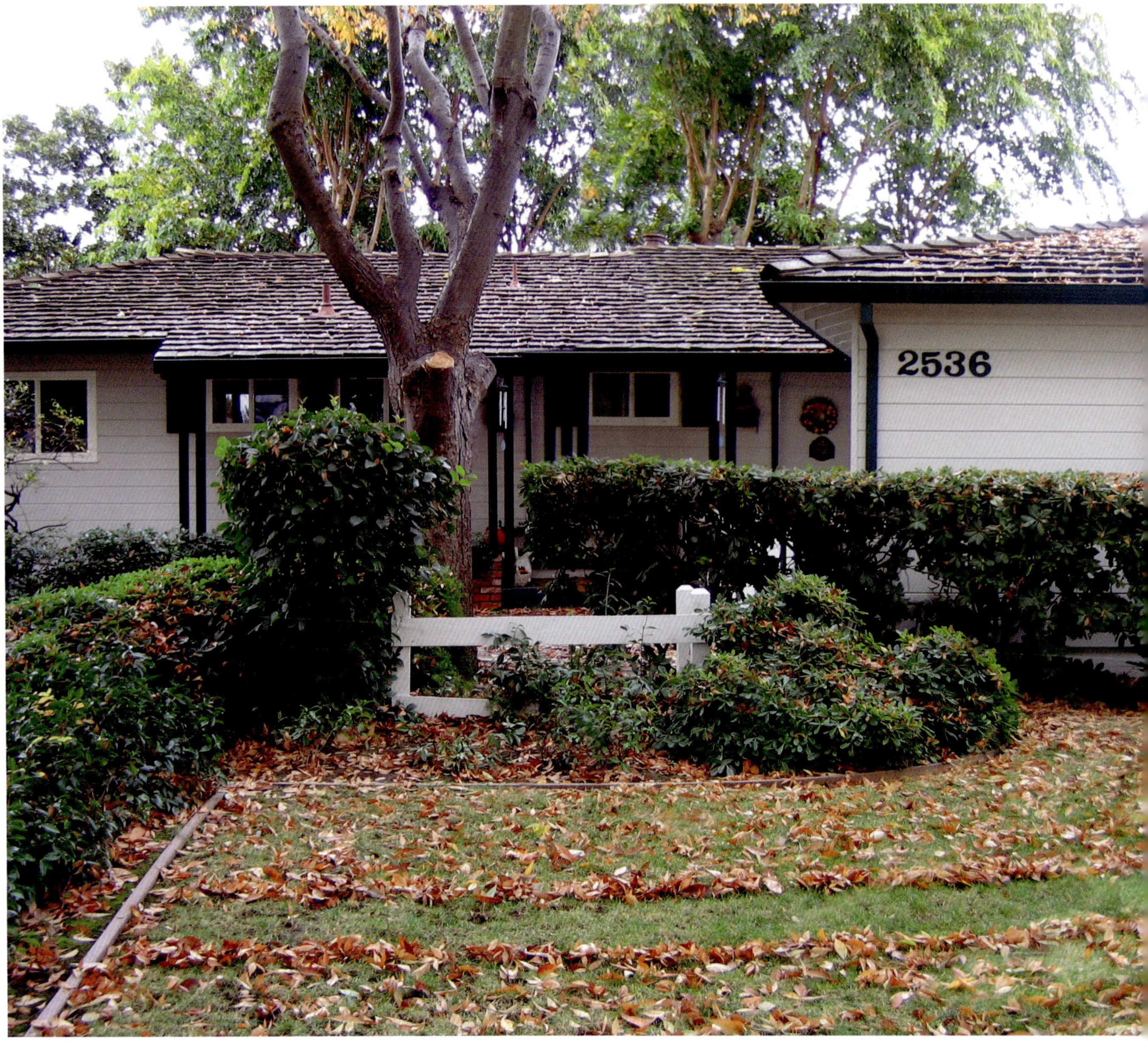

2536 Lansford from *San Jose Artist-in-Residence*

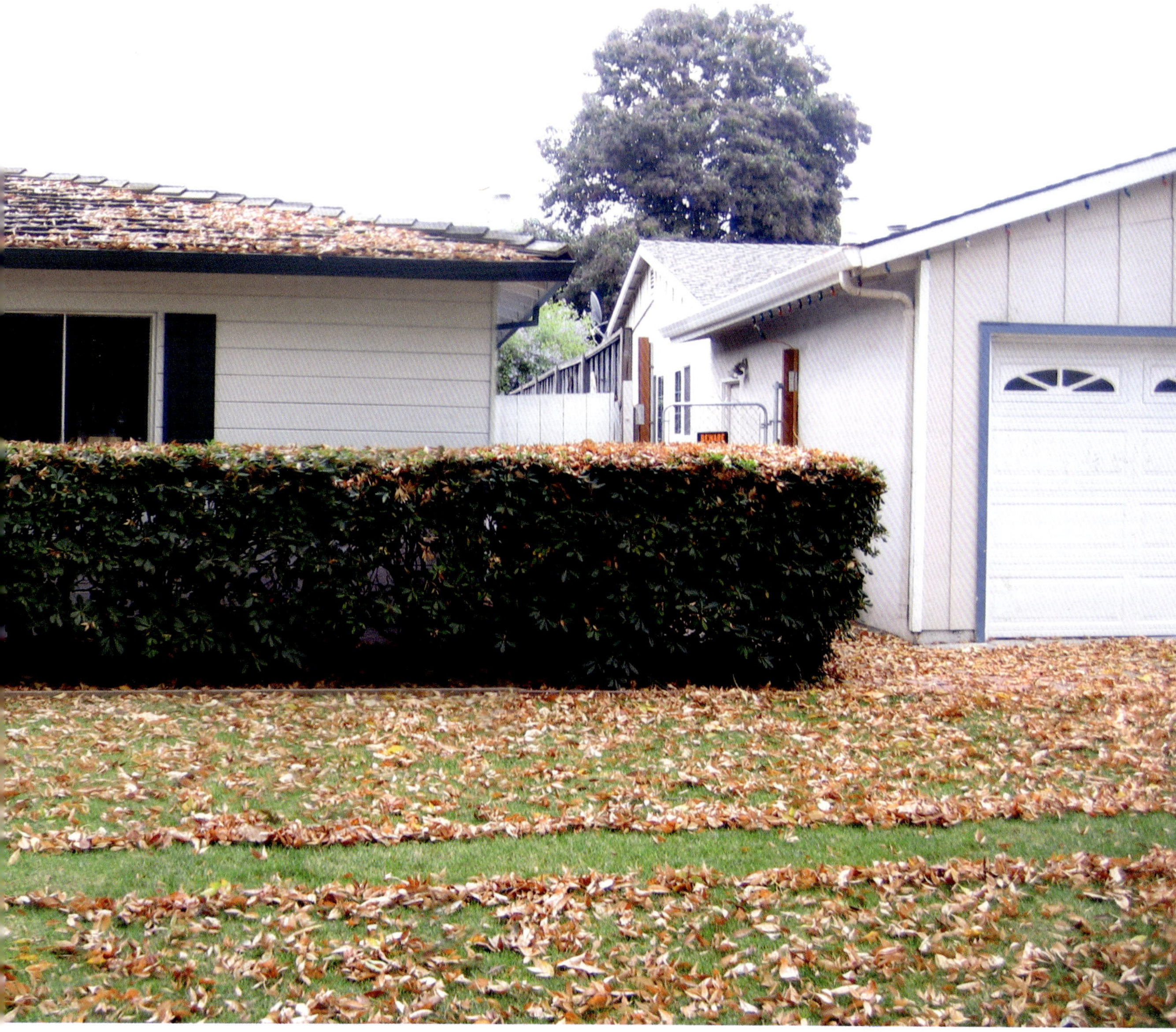

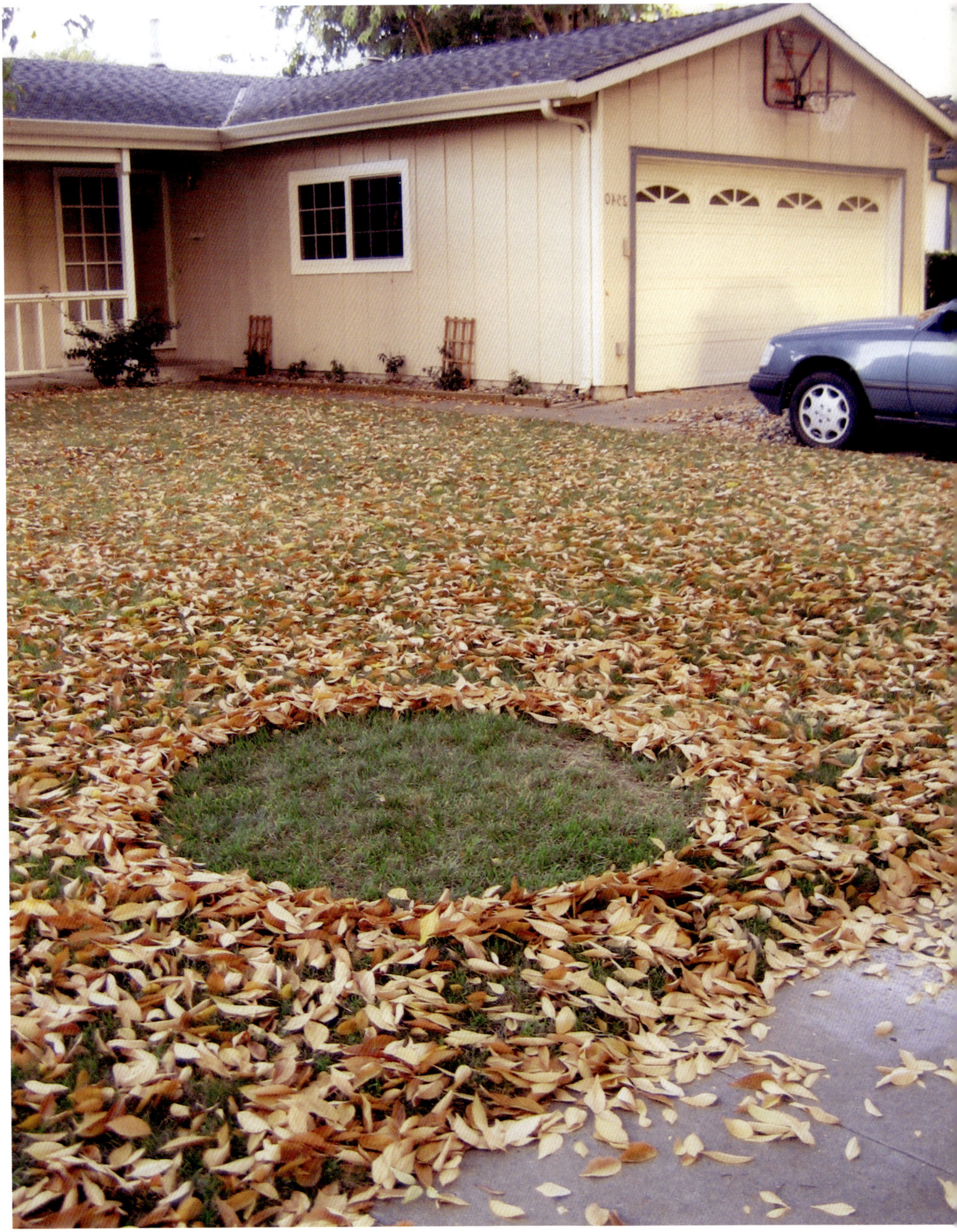

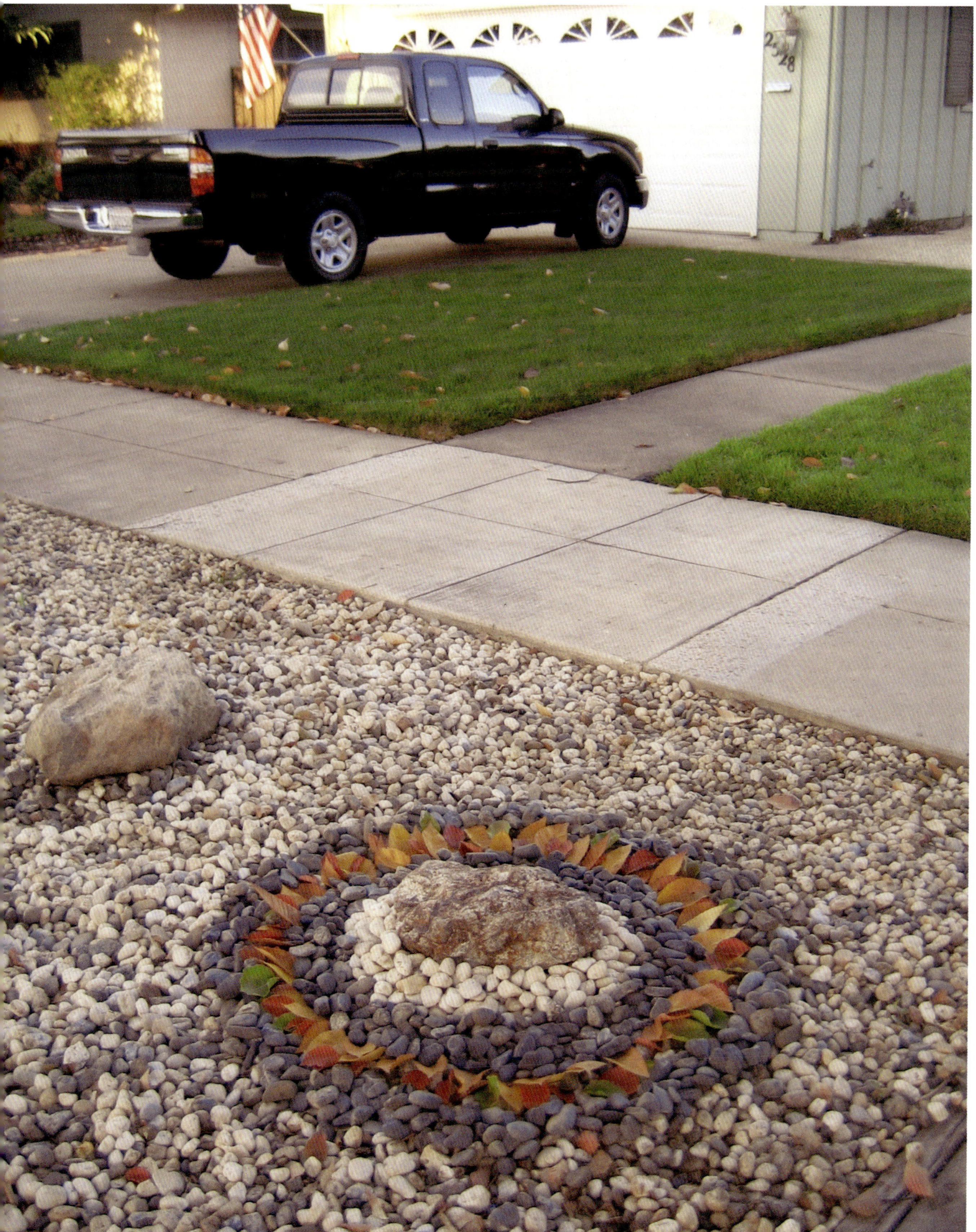

Pages 84–85 and opposite: Untitled photos from *San Jose Artist-in-Residence*

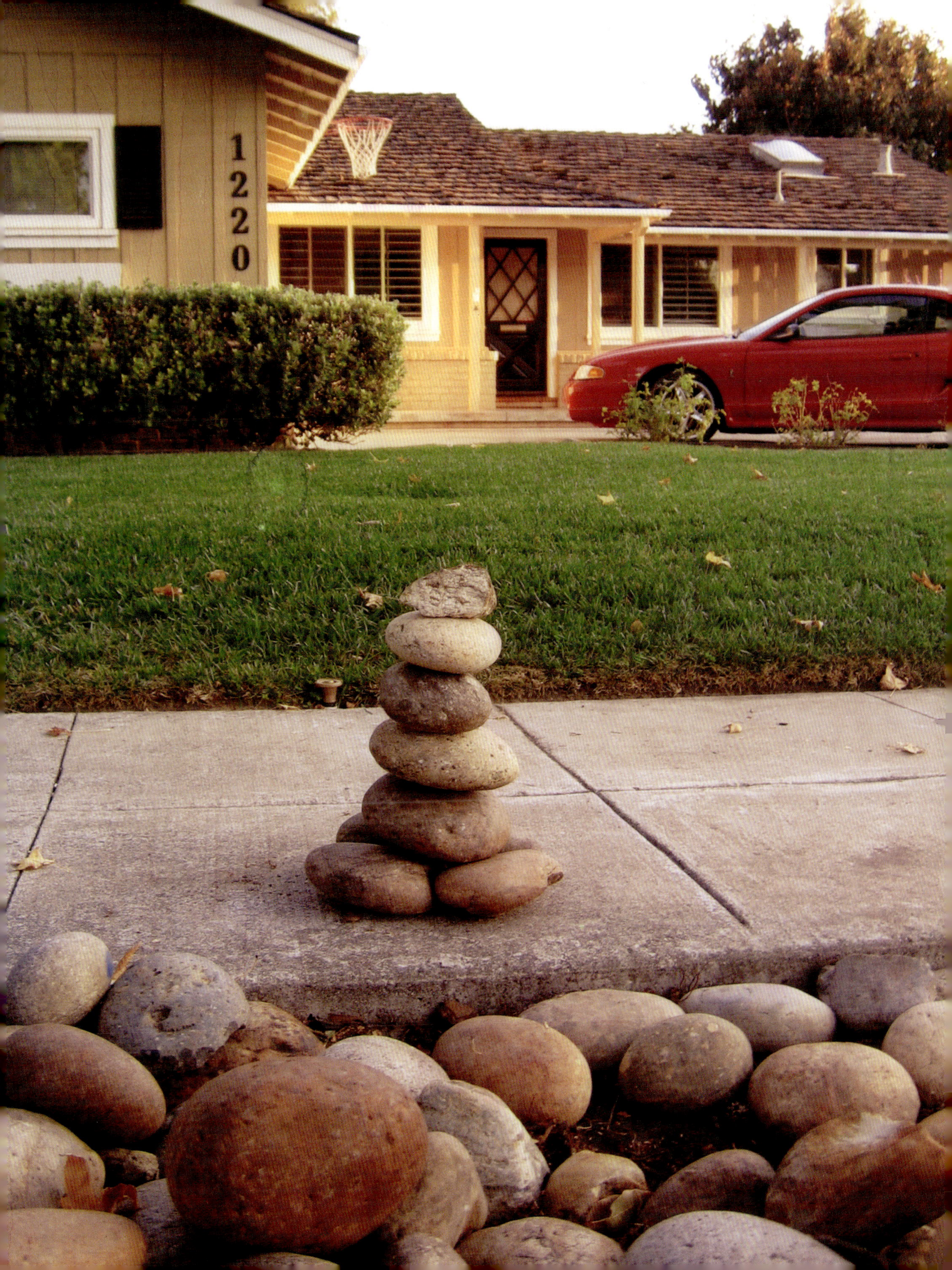
1220

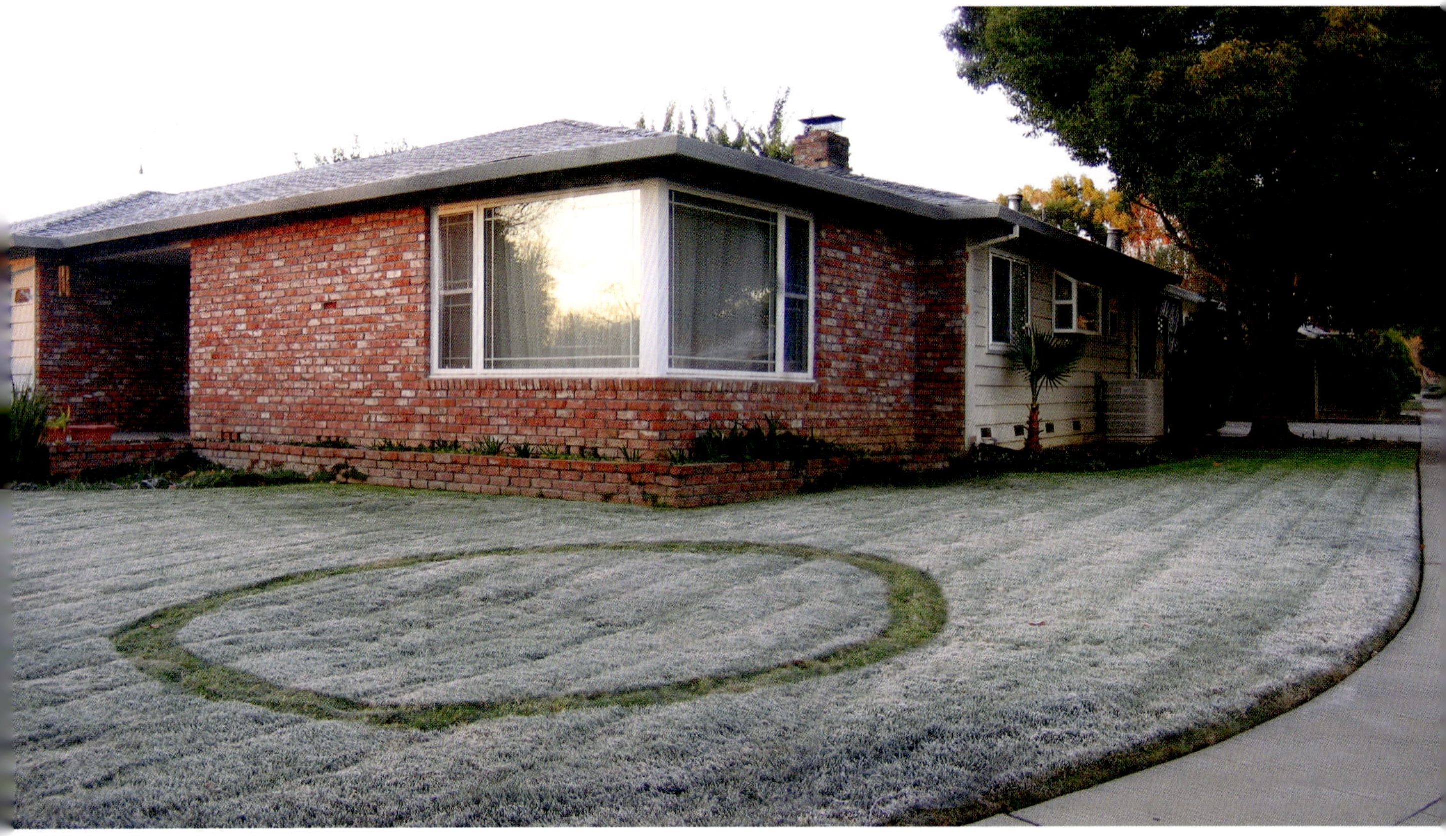

Above: *Corner Circle* from *San Jose Artist-in-Residence*

Opposite: *2235 Lansford* from *San Jose Artist-in-Residence*

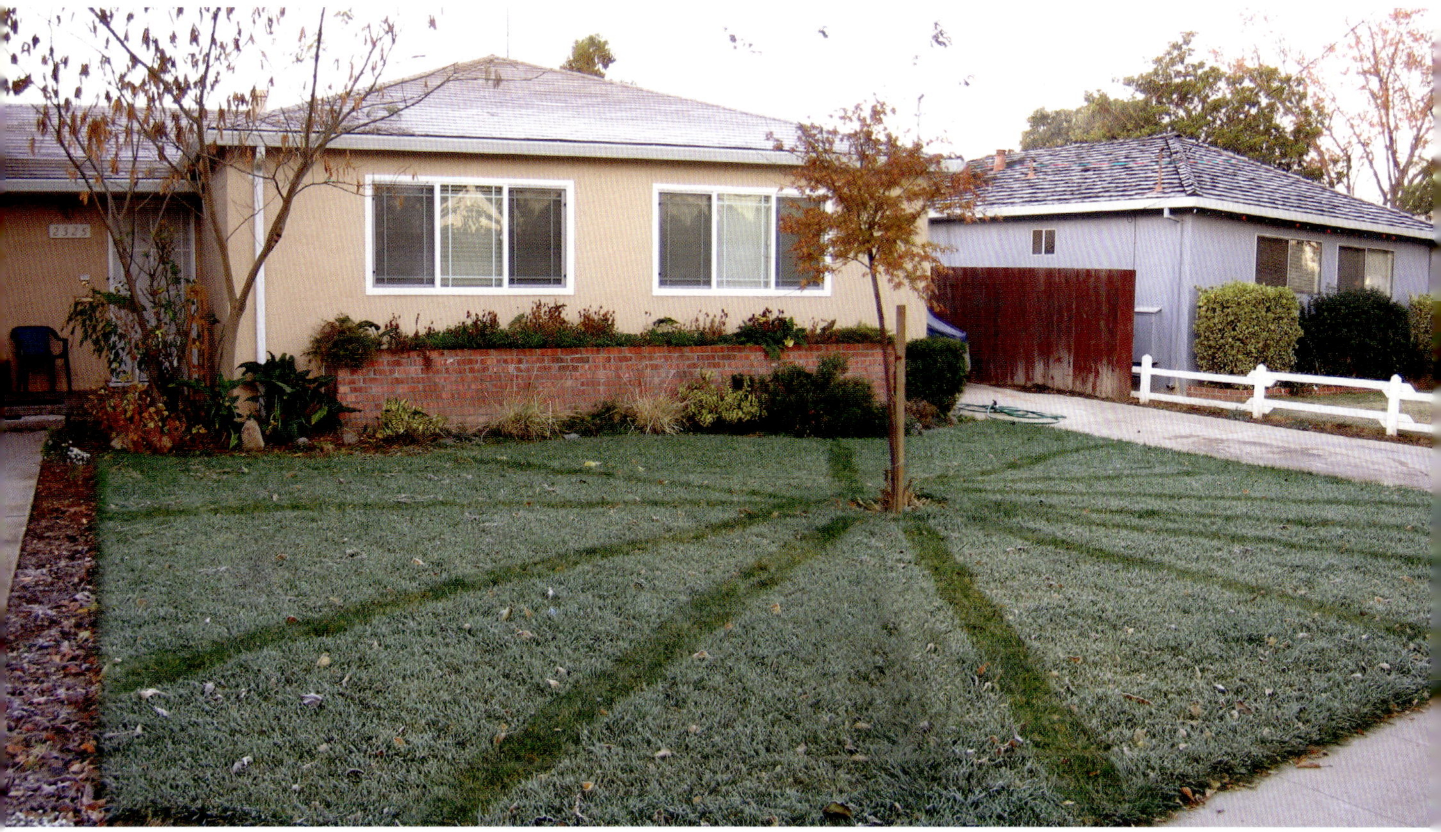

My Healing Garden Is Green

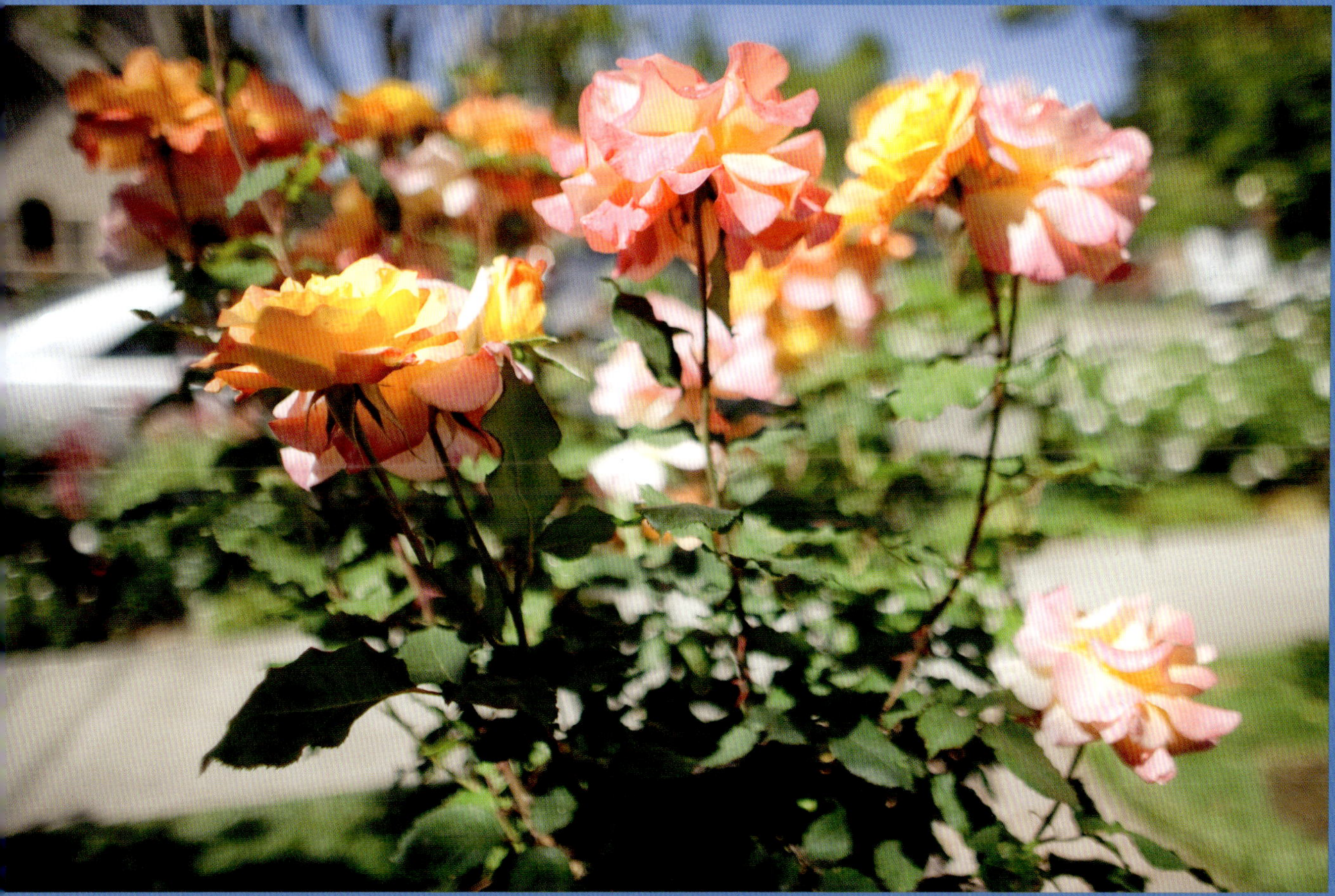

I'M WHOLE HEALING HEALED + HOLY I'M HOME

Joey Piziali and Vanessa Blaikie

Susan O'Malley was an "electric light." Like the whimsical mynah birds in Aldous Huxley's novel *Island*, who cry out "Attention!" and "Here and now!," she was always patiently bringing us back to the present moment and reminding us to be here, awake and alive.

For many of us, Susan's work was a life force, like breathing.

IN (be here now) . . . OUT (everything will be OK) . . . IN (this is all part of the process) . . . OUT (we are all in this together).

Over the years Susan planted seeds of love, compassion, joy, humor, and positive intent with her fierce generosity and collective acts of engagement. Things bloomed in the path she walked. Homes, galleries, city streets, suburban lawns, and forest trails all flowered with her work: colorful mantras, optimistic affirmations, gentle reminders, and emboldening calls to action. Susan was planting symbolic gardens, a legacy of meaningful exchanges and happiness directives that have come to be the tender, healing spaces we continue to seek out.

In 2012, during the months leading up to her second solo exhibition at our gallery, Romer Young, Susan's mother was diagnosed with a rare and rapidly degenerating neurological disease. So often the healer, Susan struggled to find the emotional space and time to make work for the show, and she was considering canceling it so she could be fully present for her mother, Guadalupe Reyna O'Malley.

We took many walks up and down San Francisco's 22nd Street during that time. Many days, Susan's laughter turned to tears as she grappled with the speed at which things were progressing. She was lost, and the positivity and optimism of her mantras—the ones she so often relied on for guidance—no longer grounded her. Gently, but somewhat insistently, we encouraged Susan to think about doing the show as an opportunity to find where the light could enter. It could be whatever she needed it to be. A space filled with a thousand tear-soaked tissues. A space to sit in meditation and recenter herself. A space to host a collective support group. A space to gather friends around the Tamale Lady's nourishing food. Anything. After much uncertainty, Susan found the answer closer to home, with her mother.

Page 91: Guadalupe O'Malley's roses, San Jose, California, 2013

My Healing Garden is Green included some of Susan's most personal and heartfelt work. In some search for permanence, Susan asked Guadalupe to write down messages. "I think she wrote me things both of us needed to remember," Susan reflected. With a strained hand, her mother wrote, "I love you baby" and "It is the little things in life that count." Her handwriting was just one part of the loss. She could no longer do many of the activities she loved, like tending to her garden or walking independently. Yet Susan and her mother invited strangers into the intimacy of their life at that tenuous, but ultimately deeply loving, time. Their collaboration shared an essential truth about unshakable love and created a healing garden within the gallery. The show featured a series of handwritten phrases, a photograph, and an inspirational poster. Susan had taken her mother's handwritten phrases, enlarged them, and made prints. The photograph was of her mother's actual garden. And the back wall of the gallery was painted green and featured Susan's inspirational print that read, "I'M WHOLE HEALING HEALED + HOLY I'M HOME." Together they offered up peace, light, and connection as possible pathways through the impermanent and sometimes unforgiving human condition.

As we have grown older, and lived through experiences that we believed (at the time) would break us, we have come to understand that happiness and joy don't come from living a life without gravity. They come from living this impermanent life with love, grace, courage, and a sense of humor. Susan's life—one we tend to look back on because of the joy that filled her artwork, in simple hues—was not frictionless, and certainly not without pain, heartache, and struggle. She lived and loved fiercely, and she believed in the power of art to connect us to each other.

Susan left us with a garden of love. The poet Rumi called love "the life-giving garden of this world." We must always remember to tend to this beautiful, expansive garden.

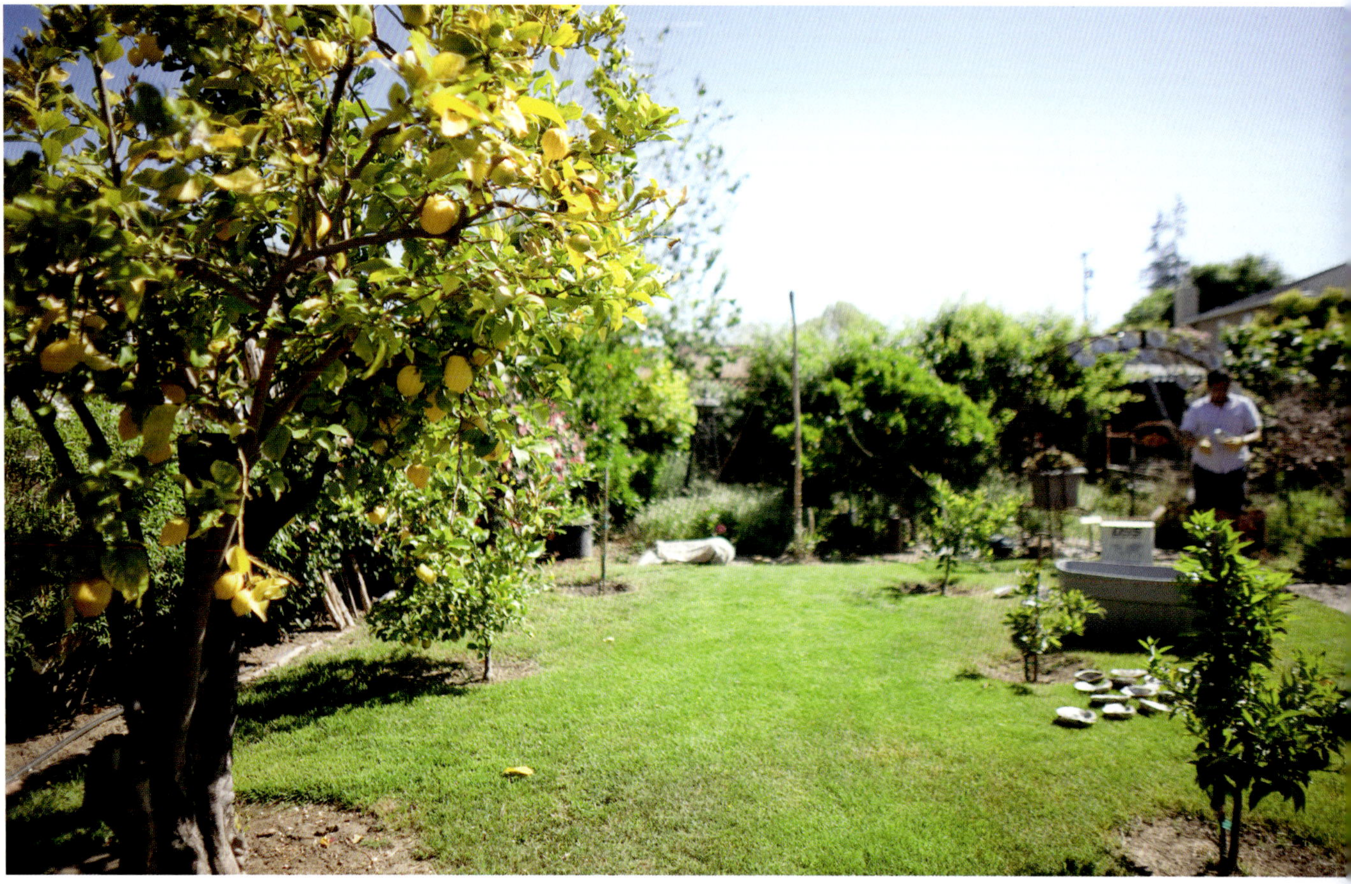

Above: Guadalupe O'Malley's garden, San Jose, California, 2013

Pages 95–100 and 102–3: Process work in preparation for *My Healing Garden is Green* show at Romer Young Gallery, San Francisco, 2012. Susan O'Malley's questions to her mother, Guadalupe O'Malley, and her mother's answers.

Mom,

Can you write about
your healing garden?
What it looks like,
what it means to you...
write as little or as much
as you like.
↪

you can describe a specific
plant or write about it
overall.

A cut-paper collage (ca. 1943) by Ray Eames. Photo: Eames Office

Write a list of your
favorite flowers. ✓

Write a list of your
favorite plants. ✓ (2)

You can use several
cards for this.

EAMES OFFICE P.O. Box 26 Venice, CA 90294 www.eamesoffice.com

Flavors

I LIKE THEM ALL!

FLAVOR

Good Lord
Astonishing
Amazing   Linkers   Gawk

CB-roses
Kerr love roses

COOL & refreshing

CALM

Happy

elated

Hopeful

Empowered

CHEERFUL

CHEERFUL

HEALING

BECOMING - EXISTING BECOMING

BECOMING WAITING

NEW LIFE / BIRTH
BIRTH NEW LIFE & death

Lecture 1 was an early media presentation by Charles and Ray Eames. First given by Charles in 1945, the show included this flower slide which was NOT an image, but an actual flower pressed into a slide casing and then projected. Photo: Eames Demetrios

What words describe your garden?
you can make a list or use several cards for this.

4

EAMES OFFICE P.O. Box 268 Venice, CA 90294 www.eamesoffice.com

EAMES OFFICE

My HEALing garden is

ALIVE

feeling LOVE

new life

My healing garden is

is

GREEN

Opposite: *The Backyard*, a map of Guadalupe O'Malley's garden, San Jose, California, 2012

THE BACKYARD

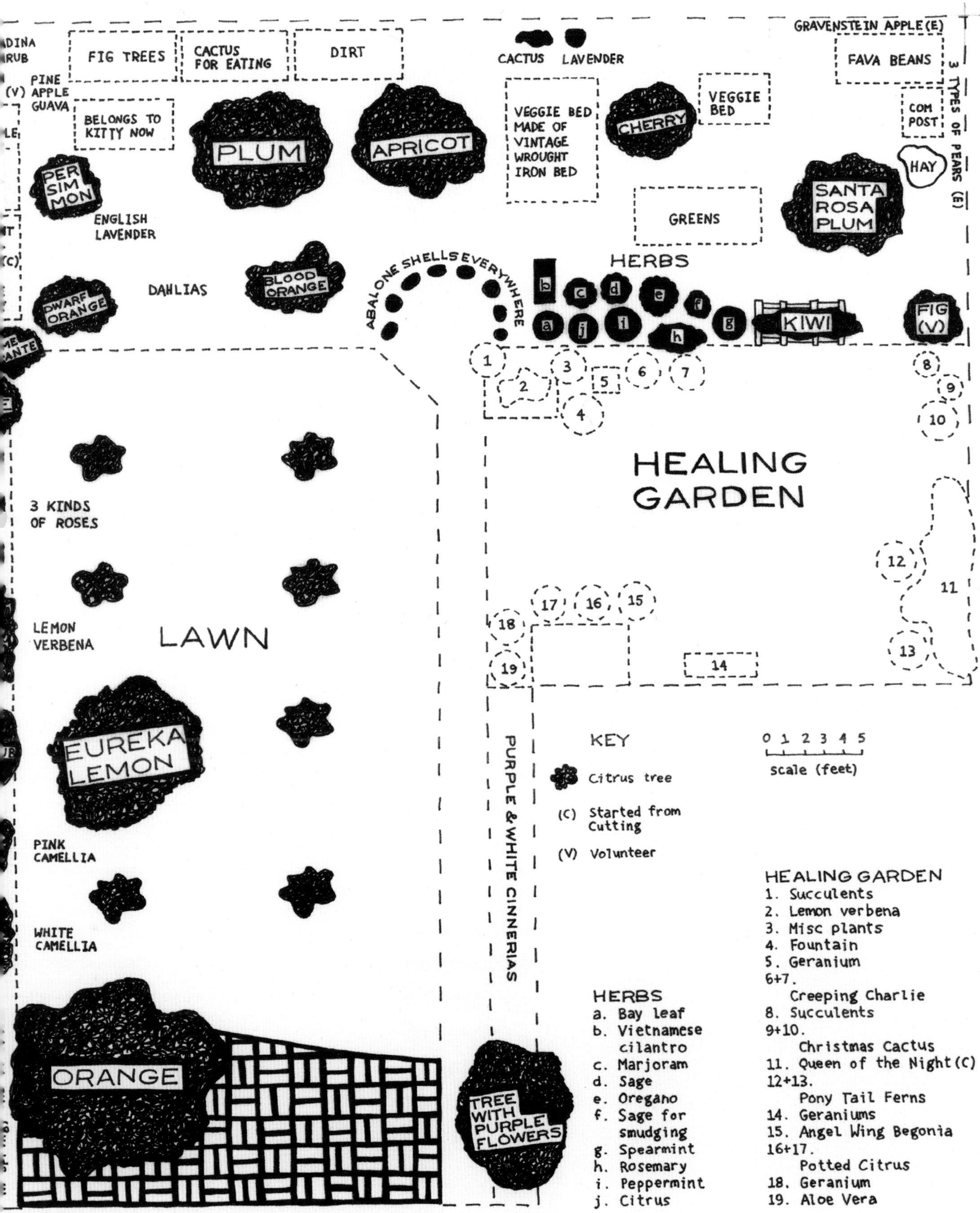

ENVISION Healing like a wild seed.

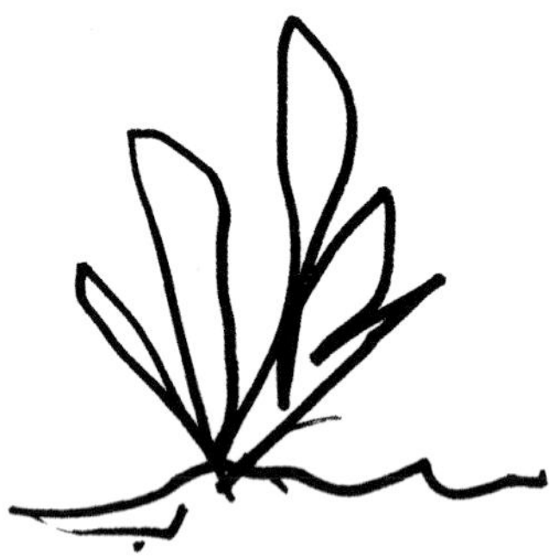

Growing into the garden like a wild seed

ITA's garden

I'm

Whole

healing HEALED

\+

HOLY

I'm

HOME

Opposite: *I'm Whole Healing Healed + Holy I'm Home* from *My Healing Garden is Green*, Romer Young Gallery, San Francisco, 2012

Pages 106–7: *She still takes me through her garden*, from *My Healing Garden is Green*, Romer Young Gallery, San Francisco, 2012

I'M WHOLE
HEALING
HEALED +
HOLY
I'M HOME

she still
through

takes me
her garden

I Love You Baby

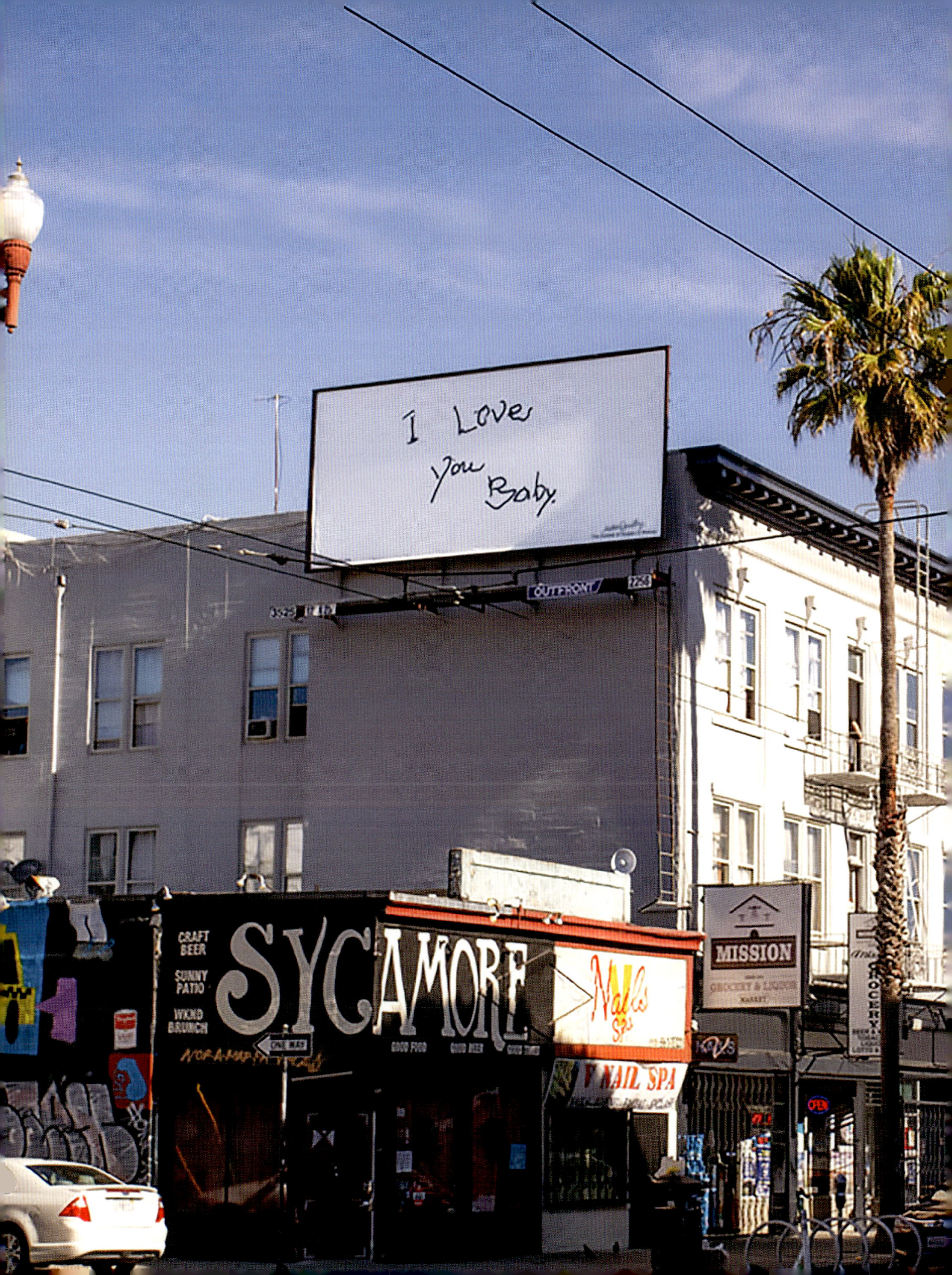

I Love
you Baby.
OUTFRONT
CRAFT BEER
SUNNY PATIO
WKND BRUNCH
SYCAMORE
ONE WAY
GOOD FOOD
GOOD BEER
V NAIL SPA
MISSION
GROCERY & LIQUOR
MARKET
OPEN

Memory, Aliveness, Words: The Beauty in Sadness

Carissa Potter

Sometime between 2010 and 2023, my grandmother lost her mind. That could mean anything, really, but the gene that put her at risk, I also carry. A mutation on our CFTR gene. There was never an exact moment it happened; the progression was slow. It showed up as stories of eating meatloaf for dinner when we had just had pasta and progressed to forgetting our names. We begged her to write her life down. She didn't. She said she would get around to it and then never did. Her stories had shaped our family; every member thought they were her special someone. And we all were.

Why is it that we want to remember? What is important about memory? We see the end coming—it's natural. We know it is coming for us all. And yet we fight to keep whatever makes us human, relational beings alive. Memory is an ever-changing and energy-intense process wherein we work to remember things so that we can learn and grow and do better. Each time we access a memory, it changes. It is never static. We long for it to be fixed, but existence is porous.

The first time I saw Susan O'Malley's work *I Love You Baby*, I had just had my first and only living child. It was after the baby was diagnosed with cystic fibrosis and after we had gone into COVID lockdown and come out again, some of us still living in the traditional sense. I cried.

In the literal sense, O'Malley's piece *I Love You Baby* consists of four words written on a sheet of white paper. Four words. *I. Love. You. Baby.* However, those four words explore the complexities of time, memory, existence, and records. Those four words are grappling with the idea of life and death: that we all were young once and that those of us who are lucky age—experience time, have relationships, and make meaning as a means to survive.

Words are translations of feelings. Historically we thought that humans react in real time, feeling things based on external stimuli directly perceived by the senses. It is now understood, however, that such a process would not be energy efficient. More accurately, our feelings are in essence predictions of how we *might feel*,

---

Page 109: *I Love You Baby* billboard, San Francisco, 2020. Created as part of the "lone some" project with Montalvo Arts Center, Saratoga, California, which featured works in twenty-five independent public sites around the Bay Area.

gleaned from past experience. We predict so that we can act in what we hope is our best interest in order to stay alive.

O'Malley's four words were written by her mother, who had been diagnosed with a rare and terminal neurological disease called multiple system atrophy. Guadalupe Reyna O'Malley, Susan's mom, rapidly lost her ability to do most things she enjoyed, such as walk, write, and tend to her garden.

The saying "I Love You Baby" is initially read as something so sweet. It instantly alludes to a loving relationship between a mother and a child. In theory, the origins of love as we know it come from this connection, this binding energy between two beings that once were one but somehow, through the reproduction process, became two. But after a moment, the sugary taste becomes complex as the context of the words expands. The four-word message, the cherished moment between loved ones, is also, in all its greatness, punctuated with the knowledge of the shaky hand, the awareness that all of this is about to end.

O'Malley's work is relatable. For all of us. There is no human reading this who was not once a baby, who has not loved and been loved, who has not had a relationship end whether through illness or death or departure. The work reminds us of the persistence of a parent's love for their child, but then it also forces us to confront the thing we spend so much of our lives avoiding—the inevitability of dissolution—in one simple, poetic, bittersweet moment.

In Susan Cain's book *Bittersweet* she asks the question, "Why do humans like sad music?" Why would someone choose to invite something sad into their lives? In my personal experience, sadness is comforting. The idea that there is comfort in pain might seem weird, and yet we've all enjoyed a sad song. Knowing that you are not alone, that others are there with you, or have been where you are now, feels connective. Your brain releases soothing hormones, such as prolactin, to help you deal with and prepare for what is coming.

It is impossible not to feel something when you see Susan O'Malley's heartbreaking yet beautiful work. If we hold that feeling—that prediction of what our future selves might want and need—it is comfort. It reminds us that we are humans who love, who are connected. It reminds us to celebrate the moments we are together, in awe of the mind-boggling and weird nature of being alive in the same form, in the same time, out of all the times that have ever existed.

If we love, we will want to love again. Even if it hurt, we want to remember it because we want those feelings for the future: connection, comfort, and the warmth of coexistence. Memory, in all its forms, is a form of aliveness.

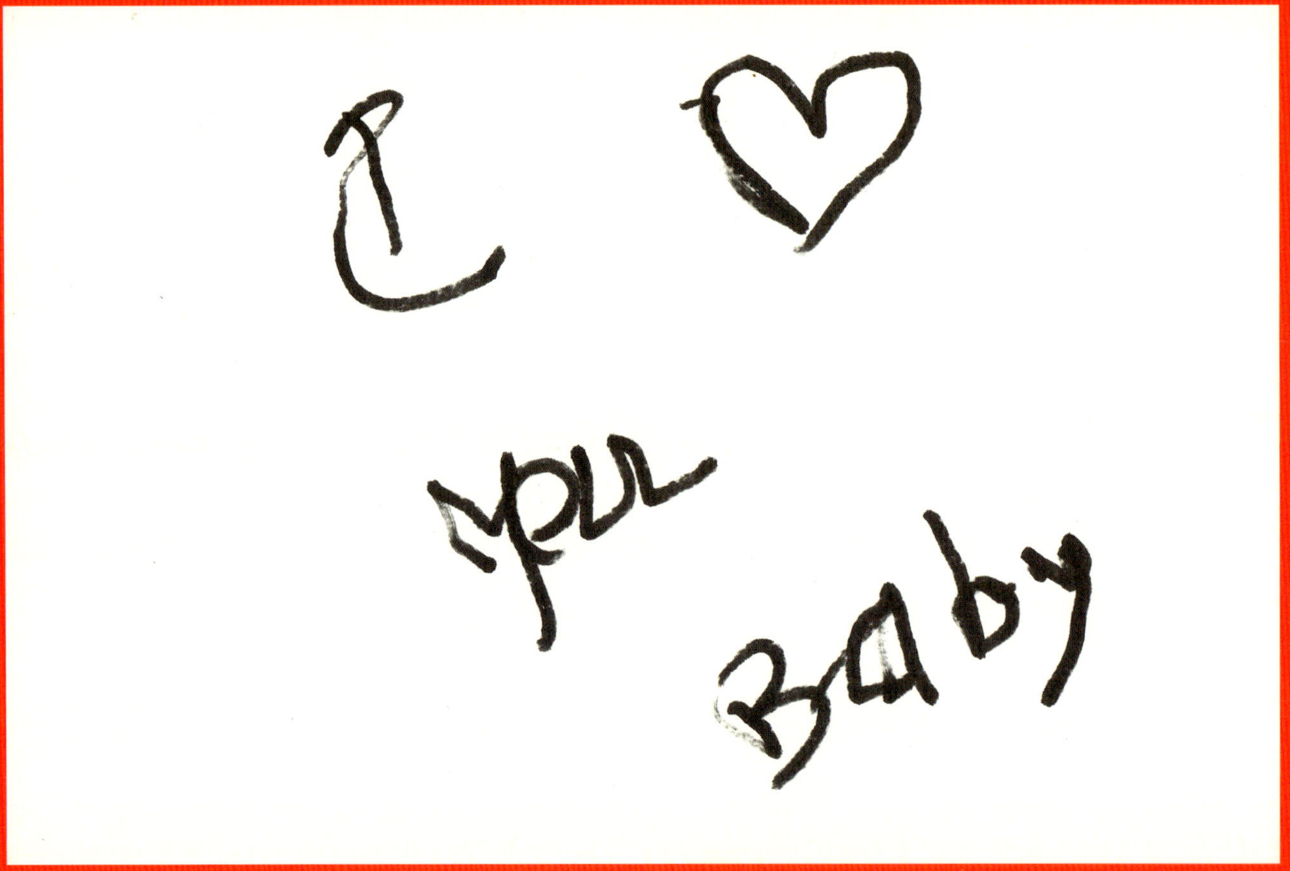

Above: *I Love You Baby (2)* from *My Healing Garden is Green*, Romer Young Gallery, San Francisco, 2012, digital print, 24 x 36 inches

Opposite: *I Love You Baby (1)* from *My Healing Garden is Green*, Romer Young Gallery, digital print, 24 x 36 inches

Pages 114–15: *I Love You Baby (3)* from *My Healing Garden is Green*, Romer Young Gallery, digital print, 24 x 36 inches

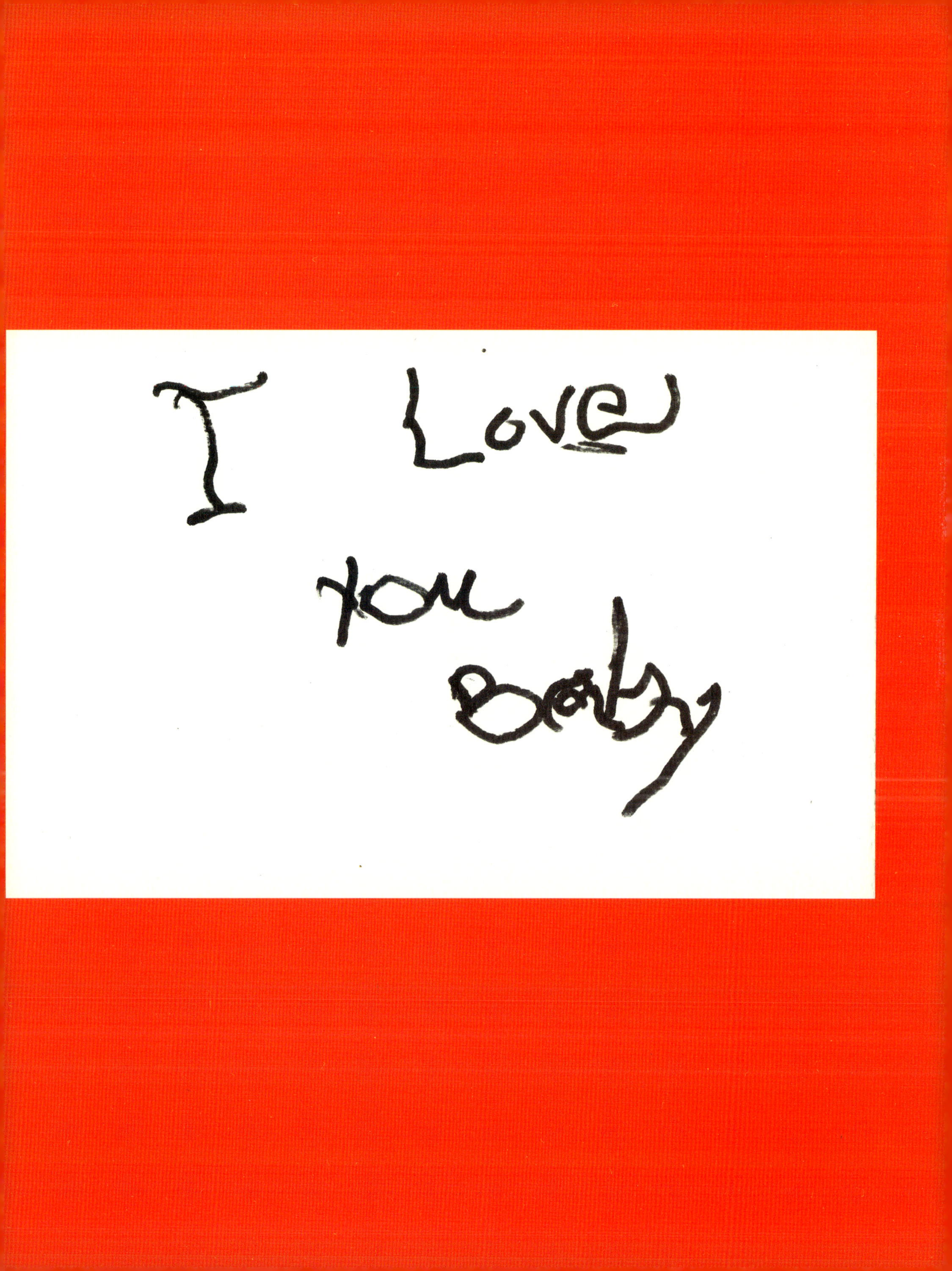
I Love
you
Baby

I L

yo

ve

Baby.

Trick Your Brain and Smile

Bonnie Tsui

We live in a time when skepticism and pessimism are the norm in all things. Humanity is confronted with climate catastrophe and ongoing war; public discourse has skewed so far from civility that we despair of any progress being made to alleviate the suffering of so many. In this hierarchy of needs, in the midst of such grief, what can art do?

In the face of divisiveness, art that makes the effort to connect—that *insists* that a conversation with a stranger is still a route to discovery and delight—is disruptive, radical, and more essential than ever.

Susan O'Malley knew this. She made art that was preoccupied with the social connections in our lives. It often took the form of big, colorful, hand-printed posters and public murals that distilled simple life lessons and transmitted nuggets of wisdom. Her work could comfort and subtly provoke, no matter the specific preoccupations of the day.

"Take More Chances, Make More Friends" in red, white, and blue type; "Love Is Everywhere, Look for It" in bubblegum pink; "Enjoy Your Hair While You Have It" in shades of orange. She thought of these messages as community-authored public service announcements. They conveyed a zest for life, a love of serendipity, and a generosity of spirit. The art was a beacon, beaming out fellow feeling for anyone who needed it.

What does it mean to be an artist of optimism? Because, of course, life is never all joy and rainbows. O'Malley was well acquainted with grief. In the years before she died unexpectedly, she had reflected on the illness and physical decline of her mother, Lupe, by making art with her.

In two years Lupe went from being an independent, energetic teacher of children with special needs to someone who was largely paralyzed and used a wheelchair. But her wit and sense of humor remained intact. "Our mom really raised us to be tender with each other. . . . Susan had my mom write out messages, things she wanted us to remember, and she made these prints," Susan's sister Sharon, the youngest of the six O'Malley children, told me. "'I love you baby' or 'Trick your brain and smile'—things she used to always say when we were growing up."

Finding light in the darkness, being able to locate optimism even in life's hardest moments—this was a place where O'Malley was beginning to find resonance as an artist.

It was when her mother was dying that O'Malley created her installation at Montalvo Arts Center, *A Healing Walk*. She installed brown National Park Service–style wooden signs along a steep nature trail there. In a grove of redwoods, one sign reads, "You Look Up." Mid-trail, there are other signs: "Your Mind Quiets." And finally, before the summit lookout, "You Are Here Awake and Alive."

After O'Malley's death, Montalvo made the walk a permanent installation. Being able to walk with others in a time of grief is profound. It does not erase the grief, but the act alchemizes it into something different.

The filmmaker and writer Ava DuVernay has said that the job of art is to meet us where we are, and to invite us to imagine. She edited a special February 2019 issue of *TIME* magazine that was devoted to the art of optimism, in all its forms, from visual art and film to music and literature. Her argument for "art as a weapon for dynamic optimism" is that it revives us in times of despair. It creates the space to breathe, to think, to feel. It shows us how the pain of a traumatic event can instigate a radical connectedness, the kind of long-term mutual engagement that makes real change.

"Art is worthy of our interrogation," DuVernay writes, "and is in fact the antidote for our times."

What this means is that optimism shouldn't be equated with false hope. It isn't papering over ugliness and pretending all is well. In its best incarnation, optimism is daring to dream and working collectively for a vision of the future that is worth fighting for.

In this way, Susan O'Malley was an optimist, because she wanted to live in a world in which people stopped to listen to each other. One of her goals was to come up with creative, guerrilla ways to engineer the simple act of making a stranger a friend. In this, as in so much else, she was essentially, intentionally optimistic about humanity and our ability to connect. There is something both poignant and important about her art continuing to carry out that original intent.

There is a long tradition of young artists' works being reevaluated after they pass away. Think of Eva Hesse, Jean-Michel Basquiat, Keith Haring, Francesca Woodman. Forever arrested in youth, the artist becomes as much martyr as maker, and their work is subsequently invested with more profundity and pathos than it may have ever possessed in life. Now, ten years after O'Malley's passing, it's clear that her work keeps reaching out to the world. It is not mythologized, not romanticized, but doing the hard work of pushing us to be our best selves. What can O'Malley's loved ones and admirers do in her absence? Try to follow her instructions as best they can:

Take More Chances, Make More Friends
Love Is Everywhere, Look for It
Trick Your Brain and Smile
You Are Here Awake and Alive

"There is something magical about breaking the silent space between a stranger and myself," she wrote in January 2015, about *Advice from My 80-Year-Old Self*. "I have a theory that people are waiting to be asked and to be heard."

Opposite: *Trick Your Brain and Smile* from *Advice from My 80-Year-Old Self* series, 2015

TRICK YOUR BRAIN AND SMILE

One Minute Smile

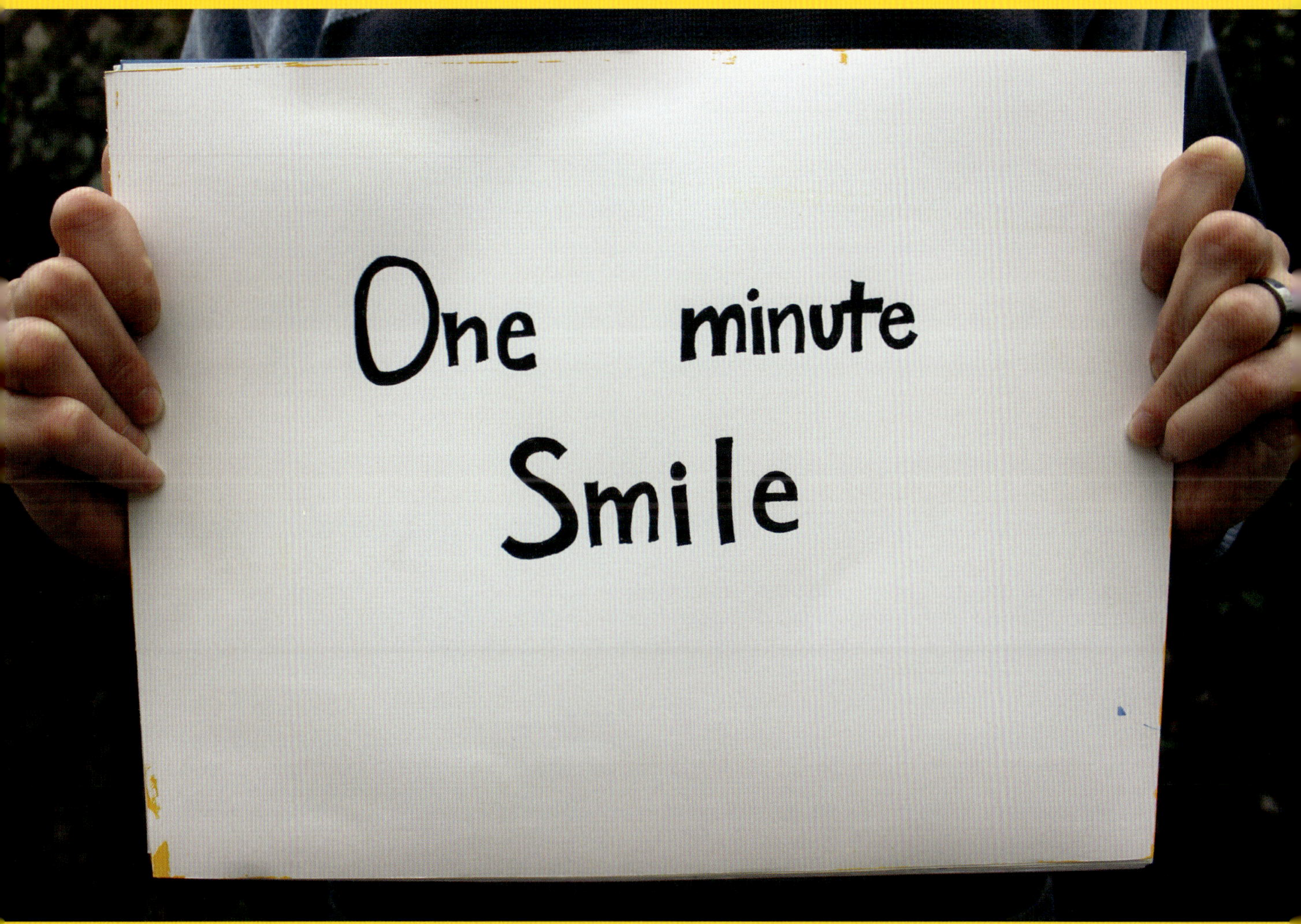
One minute
Smile

Nod If You Are Ready

Kelly Sicat

In January 2013, Susan O'Malley, Leah Rosenberg, and Christine Wong Yap participated in the exhibition *Happiness Is . . .*, the inaugural exhibition for Montalvo Arts Center's twenty-month initiative *Flourish: Artists Explore Wellbeing*. The three artists sought to address this question: How do we foster happiness and build a contented life? Building upon their shared interests, each drew from a variety of influences, including scientific research, visual experimentation, and grand gestures, to create their individual and collaborative responses. They examined the role of aesthetic pleasure in inspiring positive emotion, and they created events and engagements for the public that emphasized the importance of community ritual and active participation in cultivating happiness.

The first of those activations was held on the Saturday following the exhibition's opening. The three artists were in conversation with Carole Pertofsky, director of wellness and health promotion services at Stanford University, in the villa's historic library. To begin the session, O'Malley led the audience through a participatory and performative piece, *One Minute Smile*.

O'Malley silently stood at the front of the room and presented handwritten placards that instructed the participants about what to do. She began with the title card, which read, "One minute Smile." She dropped it to the ground and went on to the next card, and the next, and the next, each containing brief words for her audience. You can read the complete text of the first seventeen cards (including two, the fifth and the seventh, written in another person's almost illegible writing) in the photos of the performance on pages 121–41. When she reached the penultimate card, "Let's start now," one minute was provided for all participants to smile with one another. To share a big, colorful, peaceful smile. And they did, with a nervous delight, as they giggled and found joy together in that moment. O'Malley then lifted the last card, which read, "Thank You." She returned to her seat and joined the others as they engaged in the conversation with Pertofsky and the audience about the science, circumstances, and aesthetics behind finding happiness.

O'Malley was a socially engaged artist, long known for her offerings of affirmation, inspiration, hope, and care. She provided just that as she invited participation in *One Minute Smile*. The performance was inspired by a work developed in collaboration with the artist's mother, Guadalupe (Lupe) Reyna O'Malley. After Lupe was

---

Pages 121 and 124–41: *One Minute Smile*, performance at Montalvo Arts Center, Saratoga, California, 2013

diagnosed with multiple system atrophy (MSA), a rare and terminal neurological disease, O'Malley asked her mother to write down the words of advice she had always provided her daughters. Lupe agreed. In her shaky handwriting, she provided phrases to be remembered and words to live by. "Trick your brain and smile" was one of these handwritten phrases that comprised O'Malley's 2012 exhibition, *My Healing Garden is Green*. Her mother's words encouraged O'Malley to continue to deepen her commitment to her own artistic practice, transforming her grief into inspiration.

For O'Malley, the point of the work was to touch as many people as possible and to provide moments of reflection—pep talks, words of encouragement—as an aesthetic form of community care. It has often been said that O'Malley's work delivered optimism. And that day in the historic library of Montalvo Arts Center, O'Malley shared herself fully. That was something she had done on many occasions; this time, however, she silently offered to all present the opportunity to experience Lupe's words. And out of that experience, they then each offered one another those big, bright, colorful, peaceful smiles. *One Minute Smile* is a profound work. It is a gift that expands in silence beyond its creator, beyond Lupe O'Malley's words, and into the hearts of all who experience it. A gift that can be employed in the darkest of times and shared with another, offering a gentle reminder of our connectedness and providing a sense of possibility or a moment of true joy.

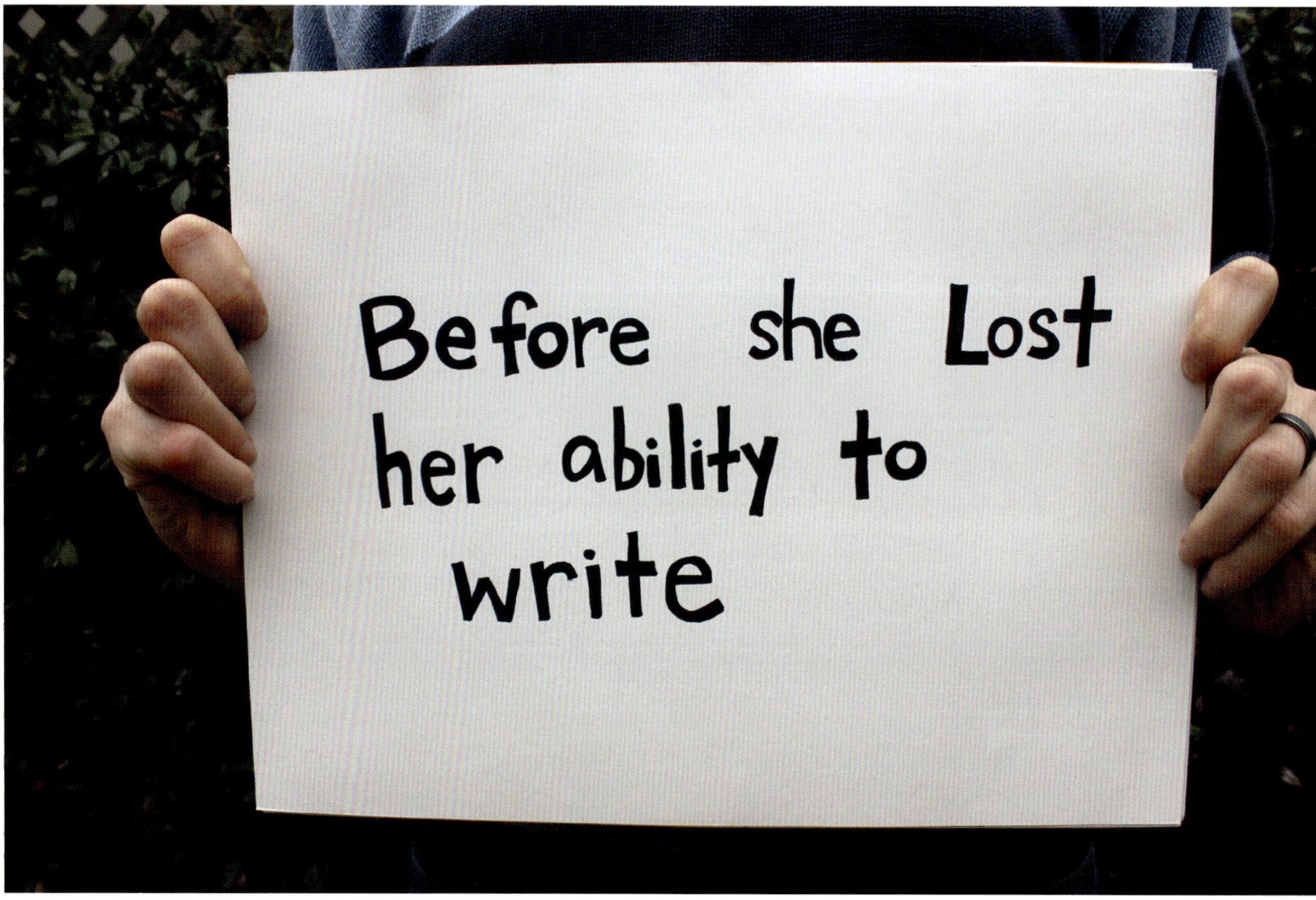
Before she Lost
her ability to
write

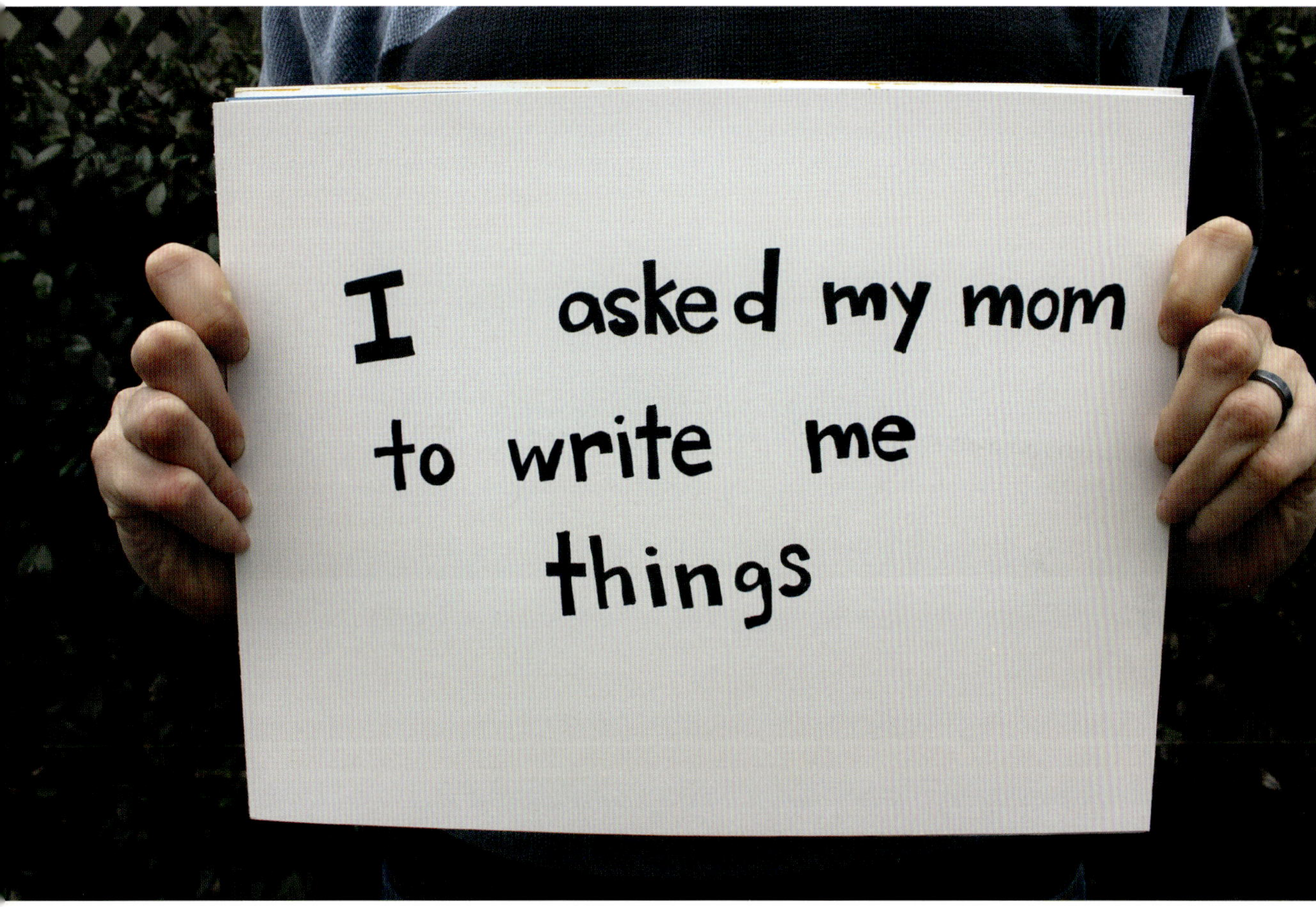
I asked my mom
to write me
things

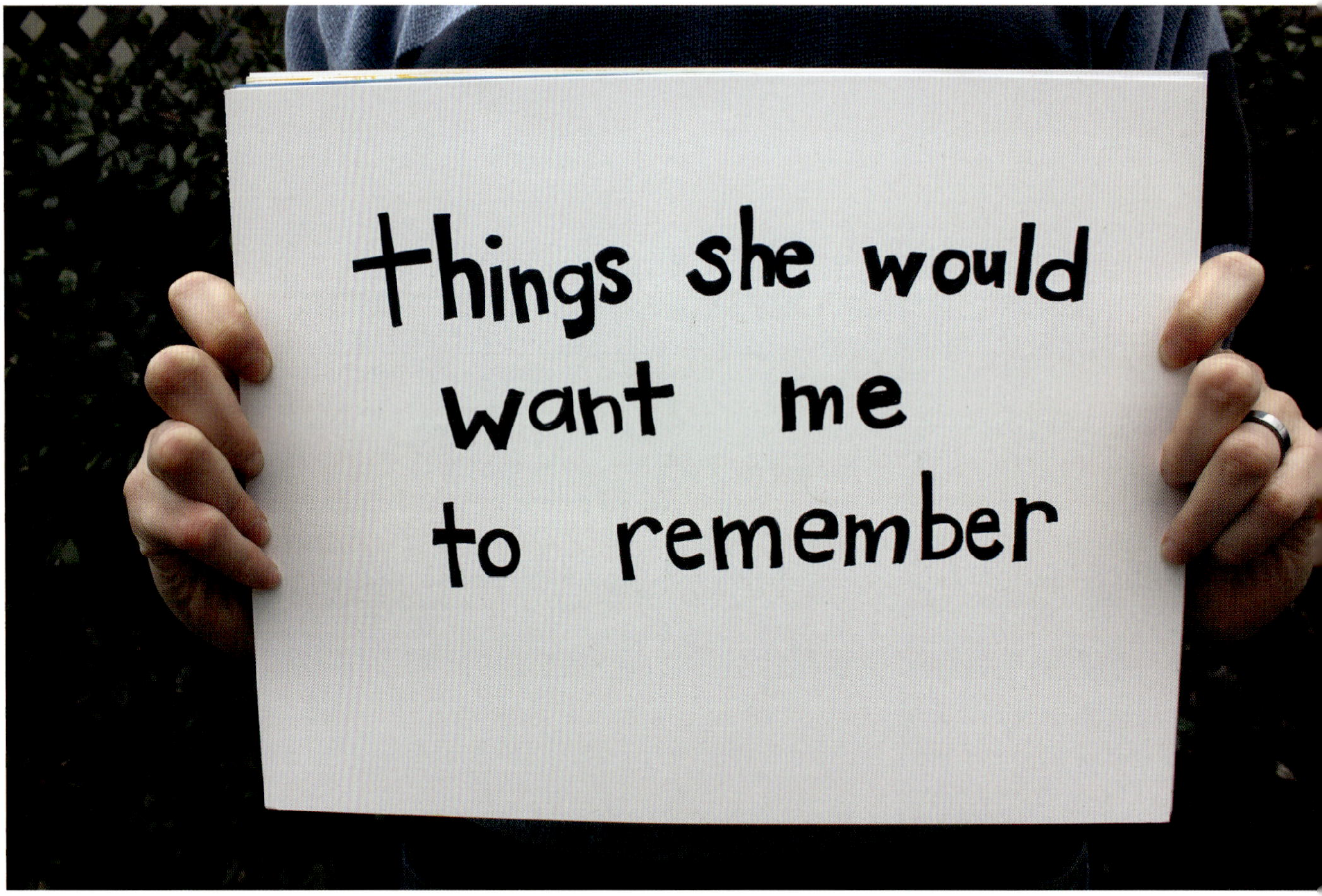
things she would
want me
to remember

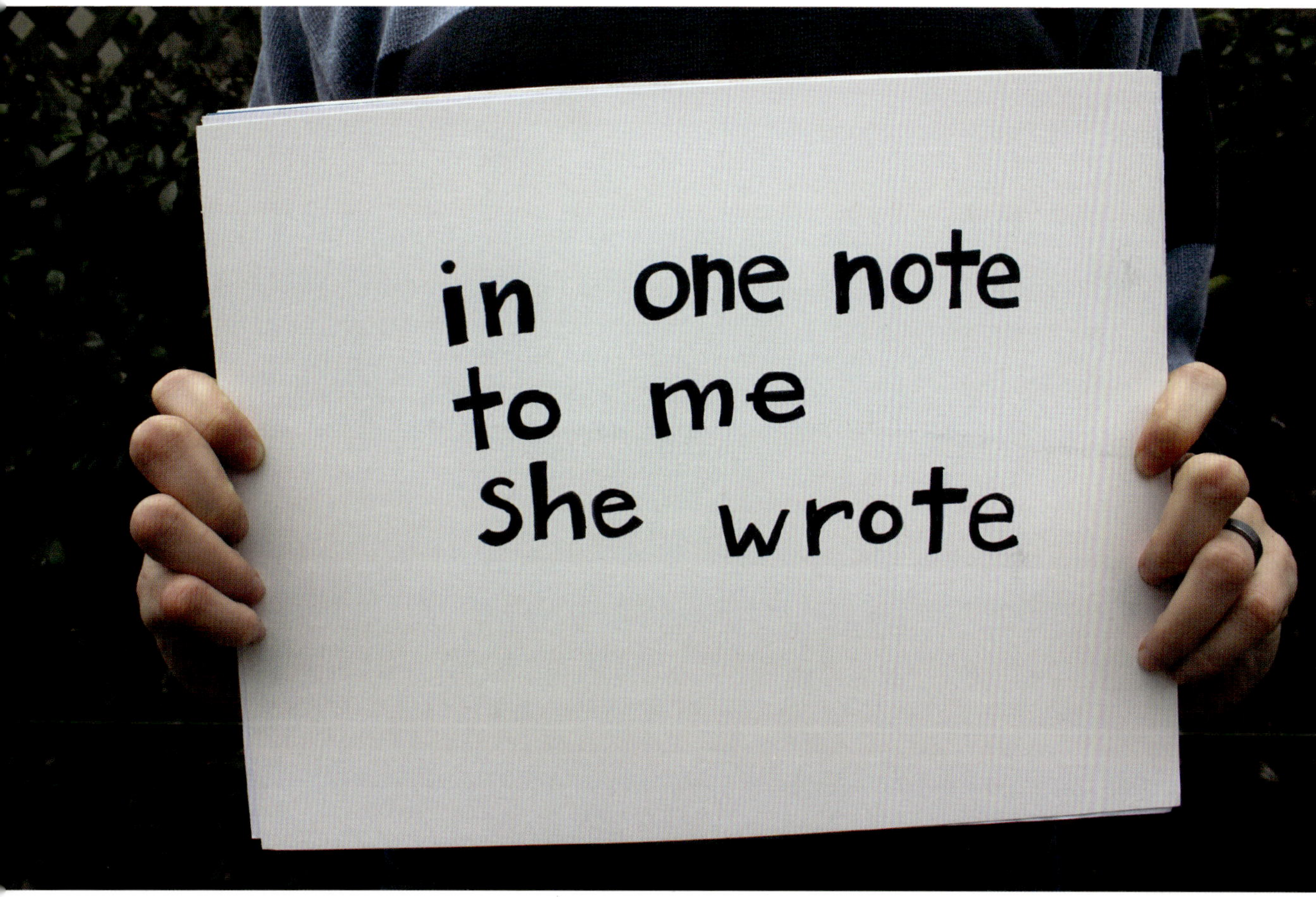
in one note
to me
she wrote

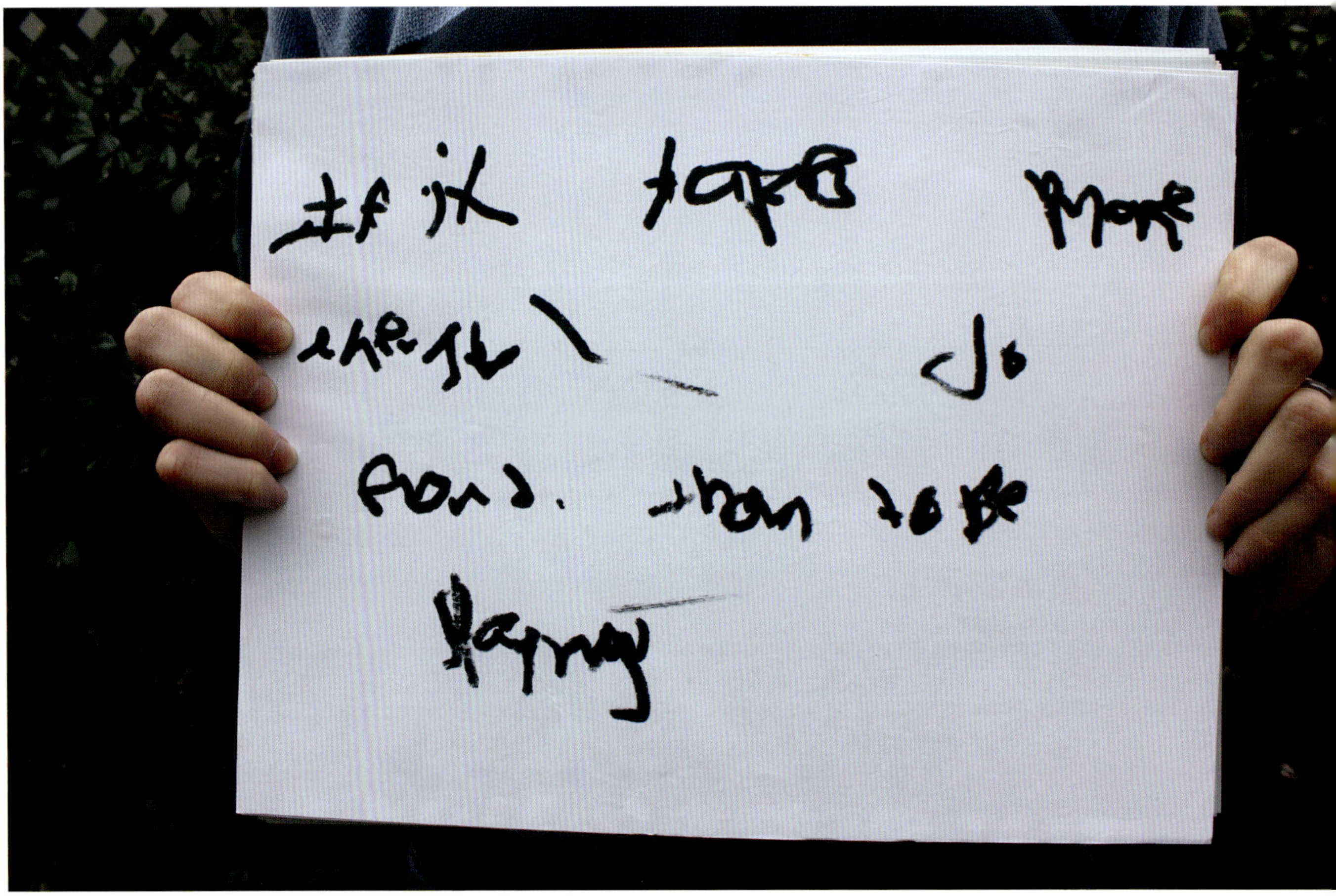

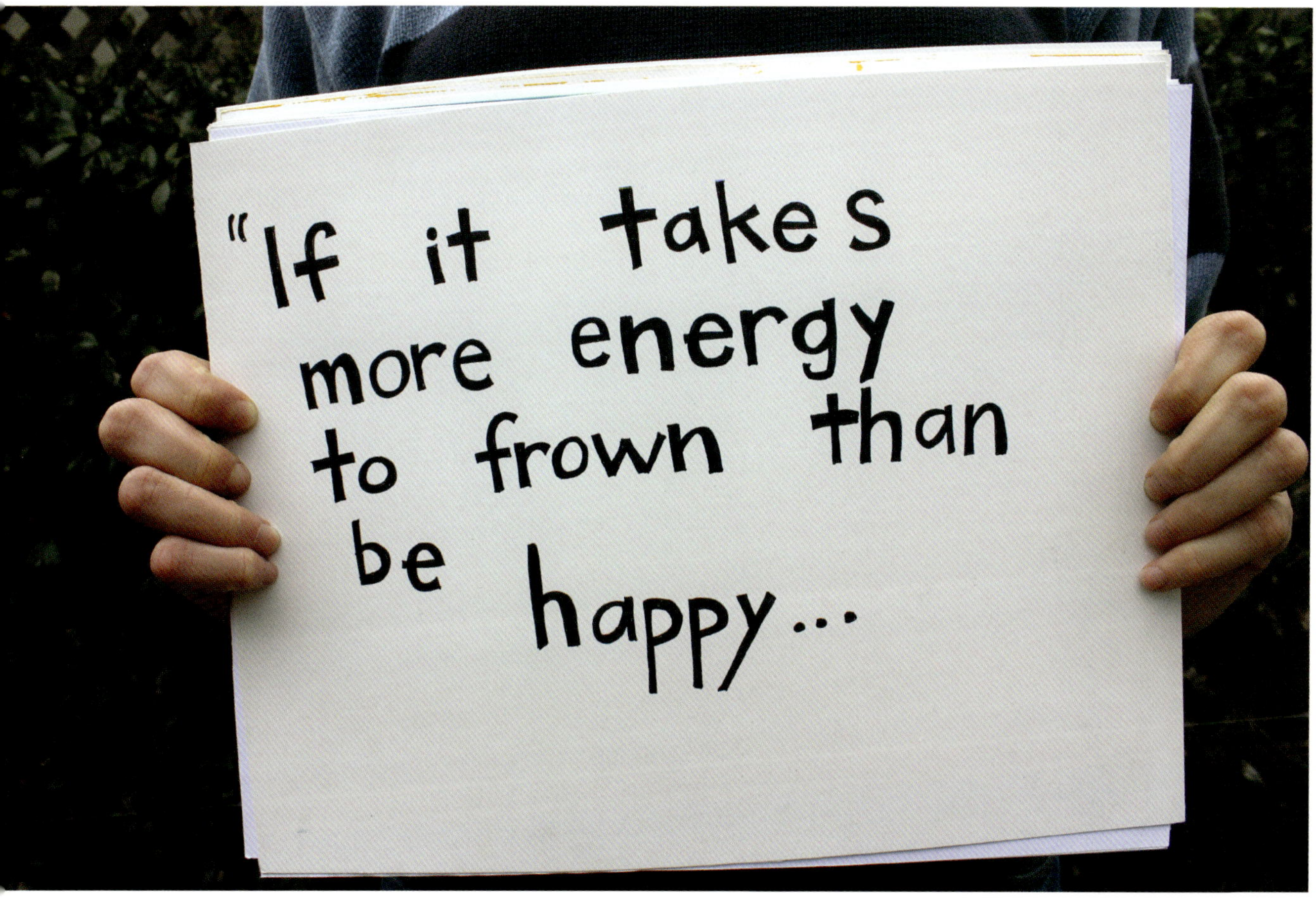
"If it takes
more energy
to frown than
be
happy...

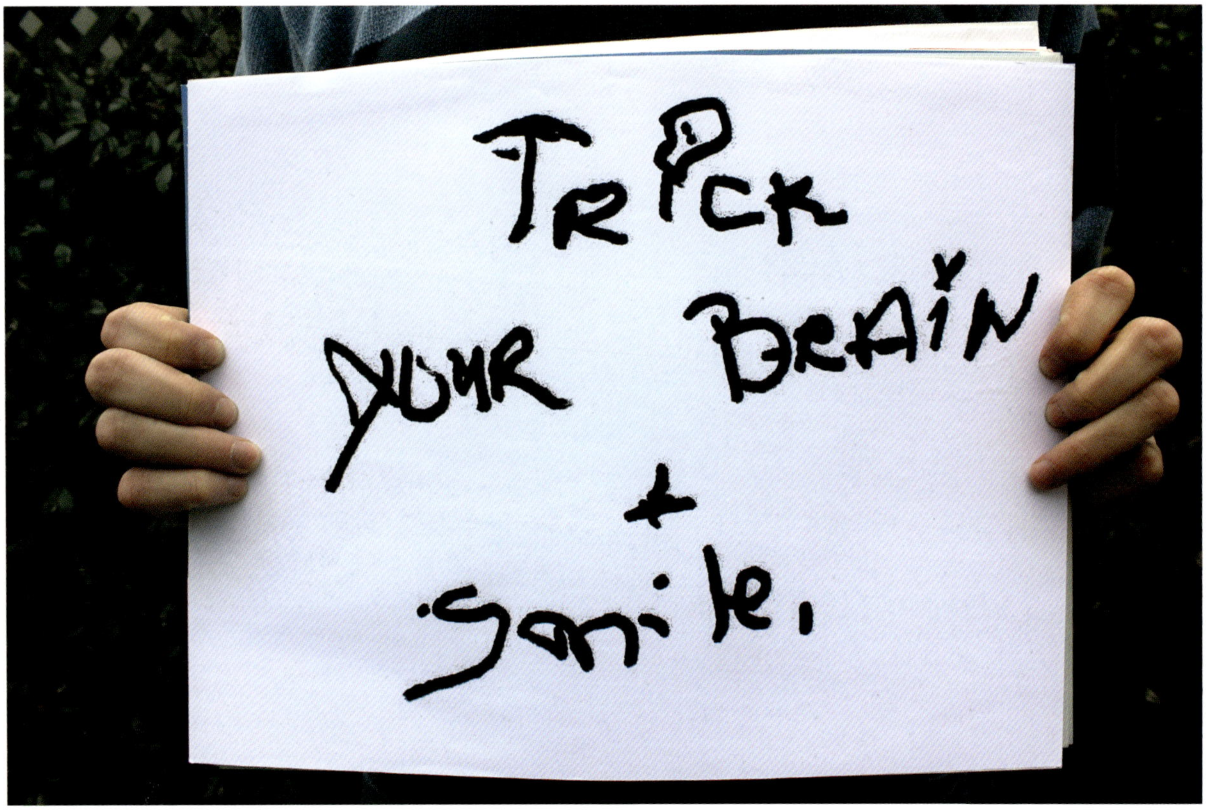
TRICK
YOUR BRAIN
+
Smile.

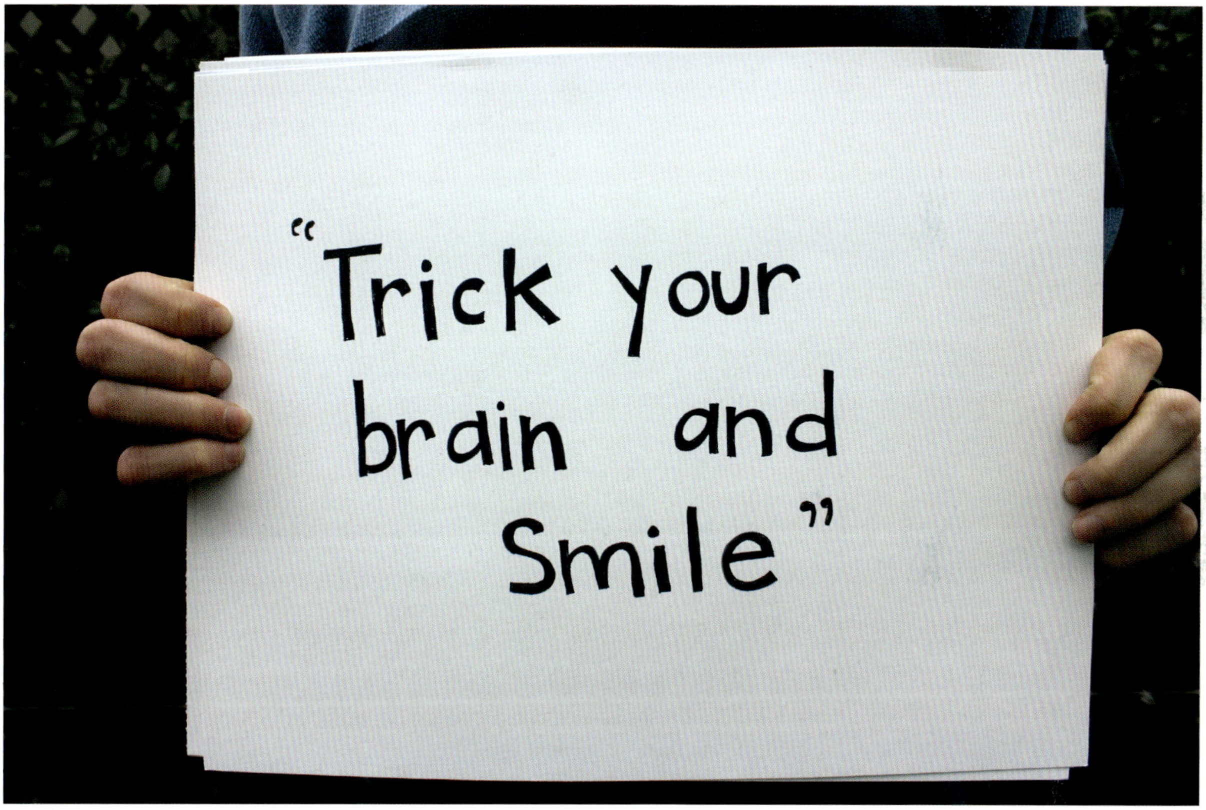
"Trick your
brain and
Smile"

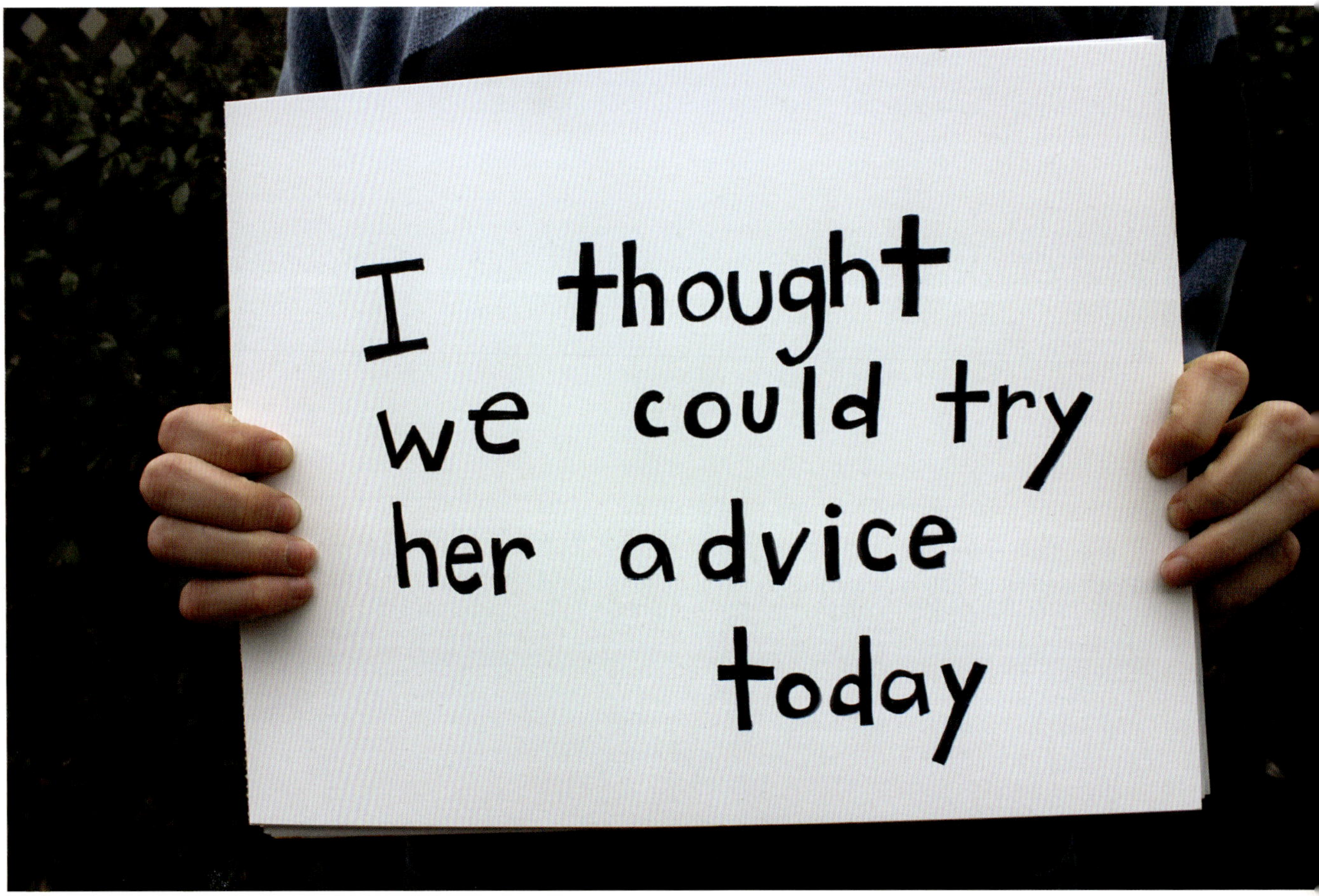
I thought
we could try
her advice
today

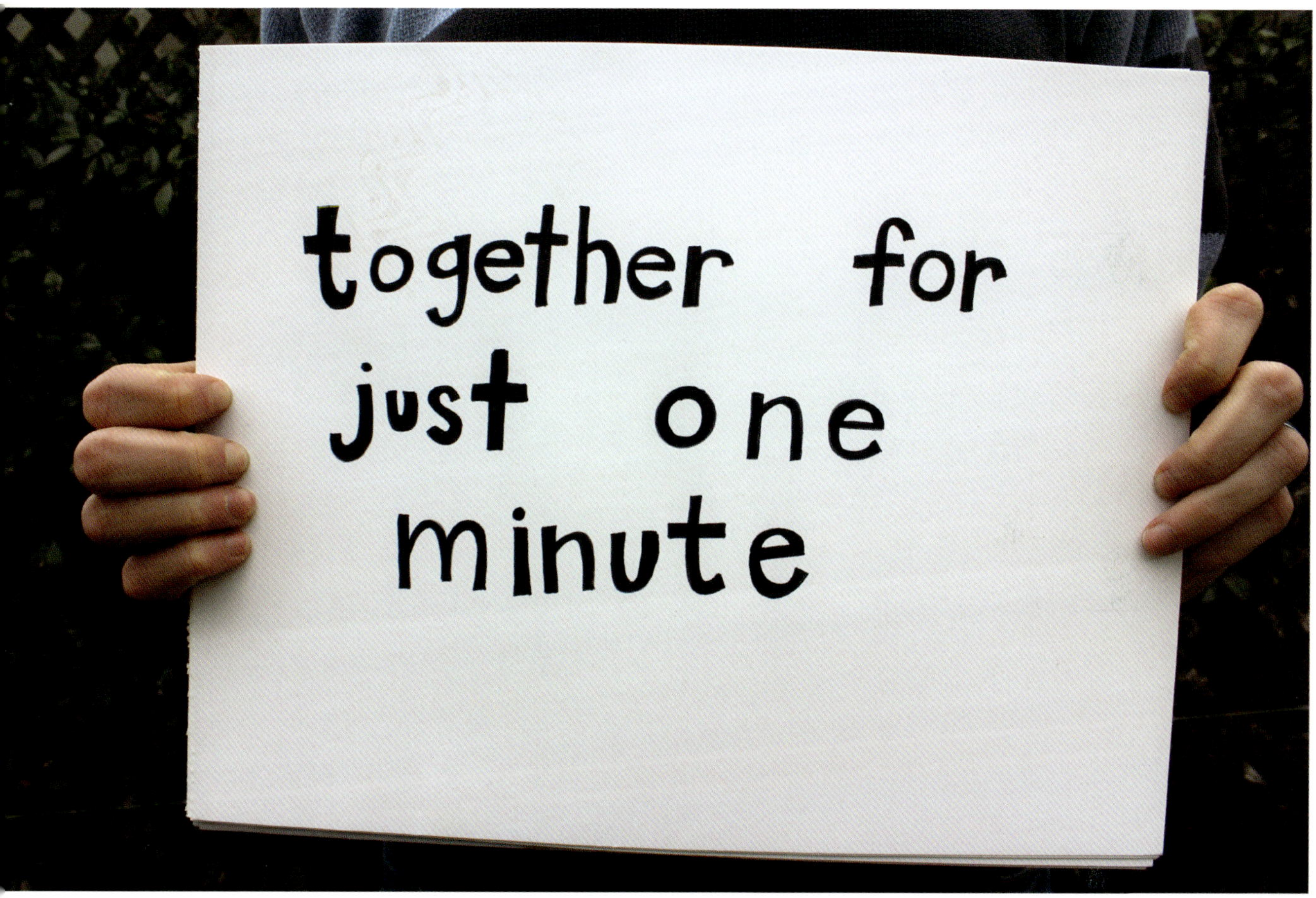
together for
just one
minute

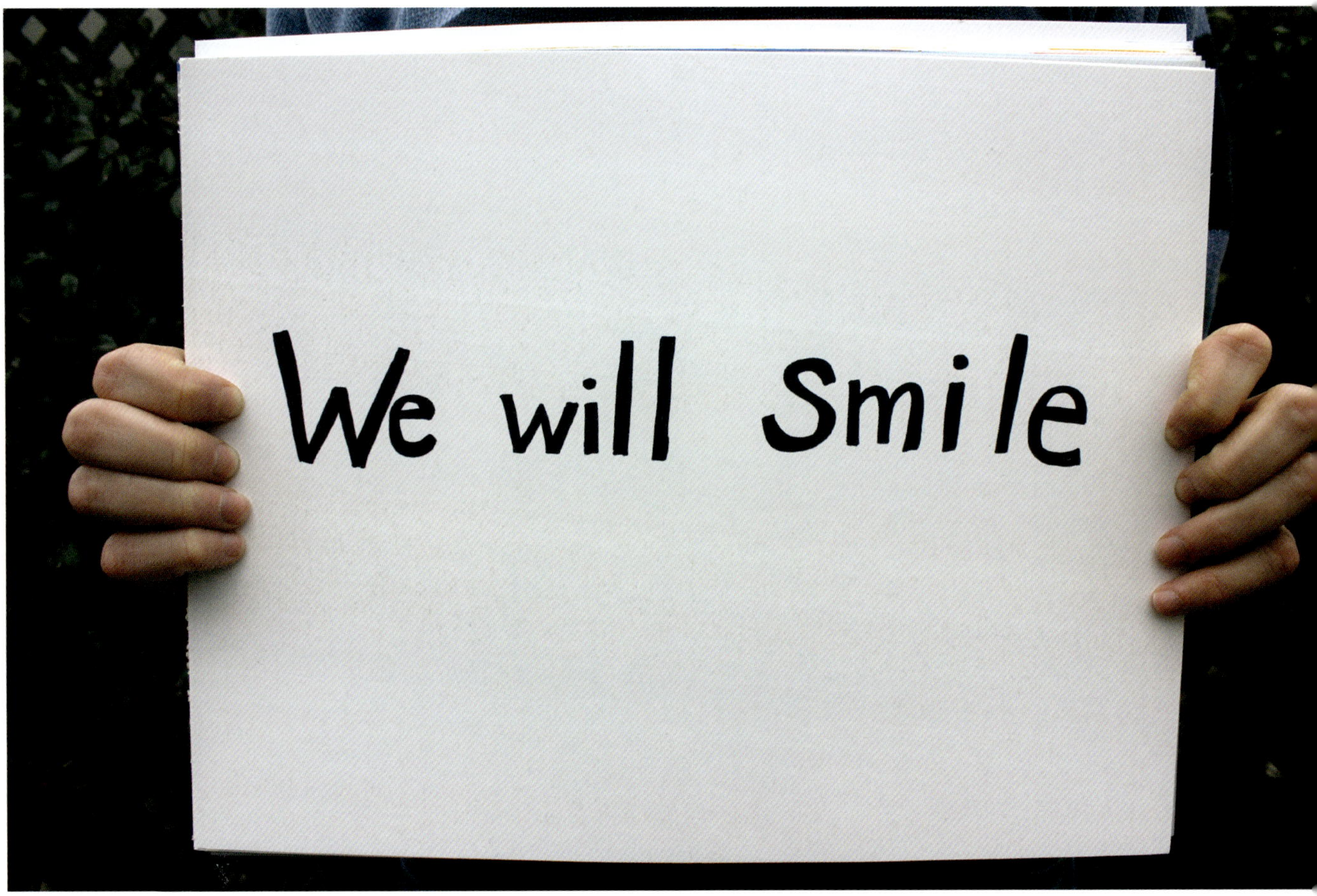
We will Smile

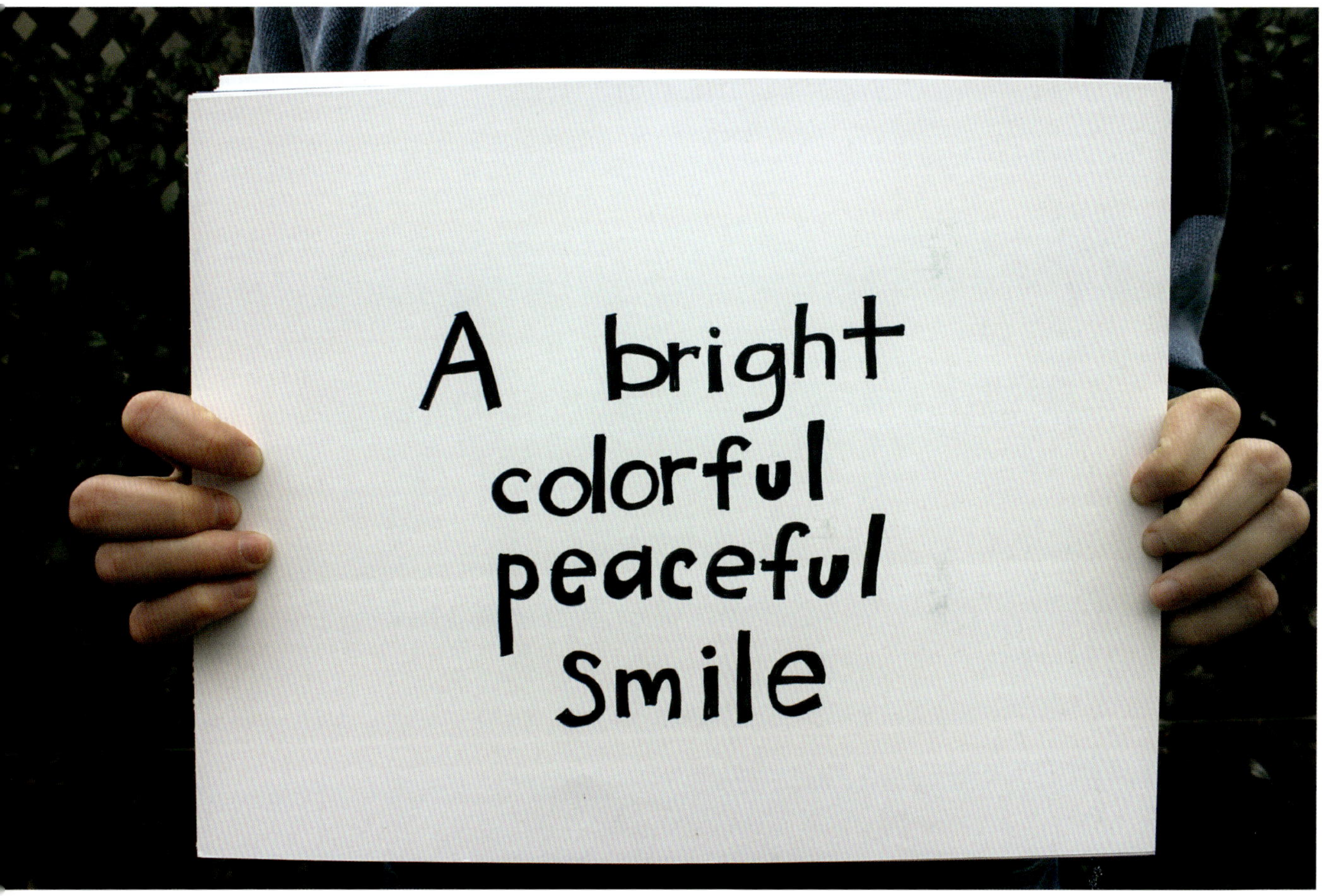
A bright
colorful
peaceful
Smile

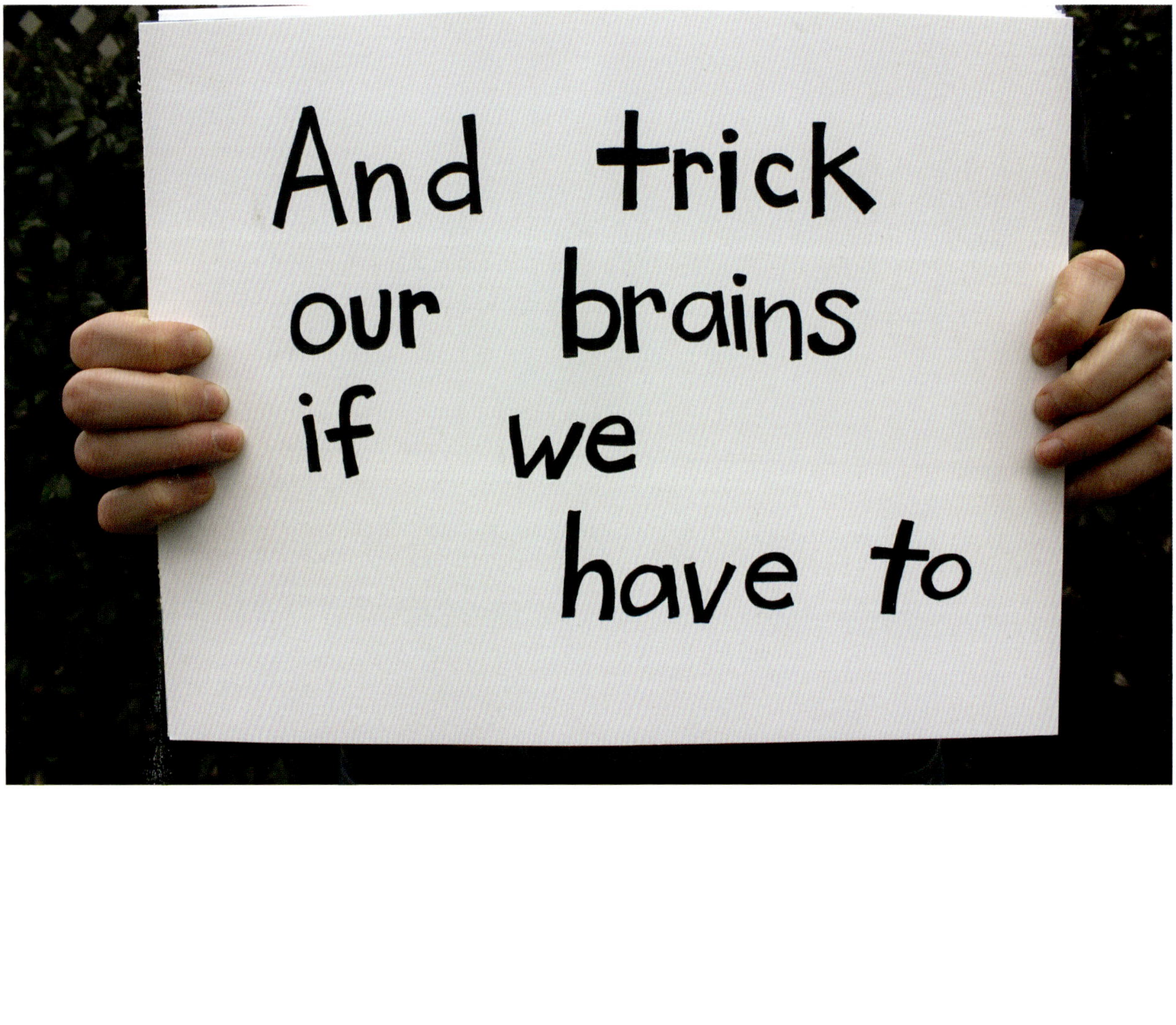
And trick
our brains
if we
have to

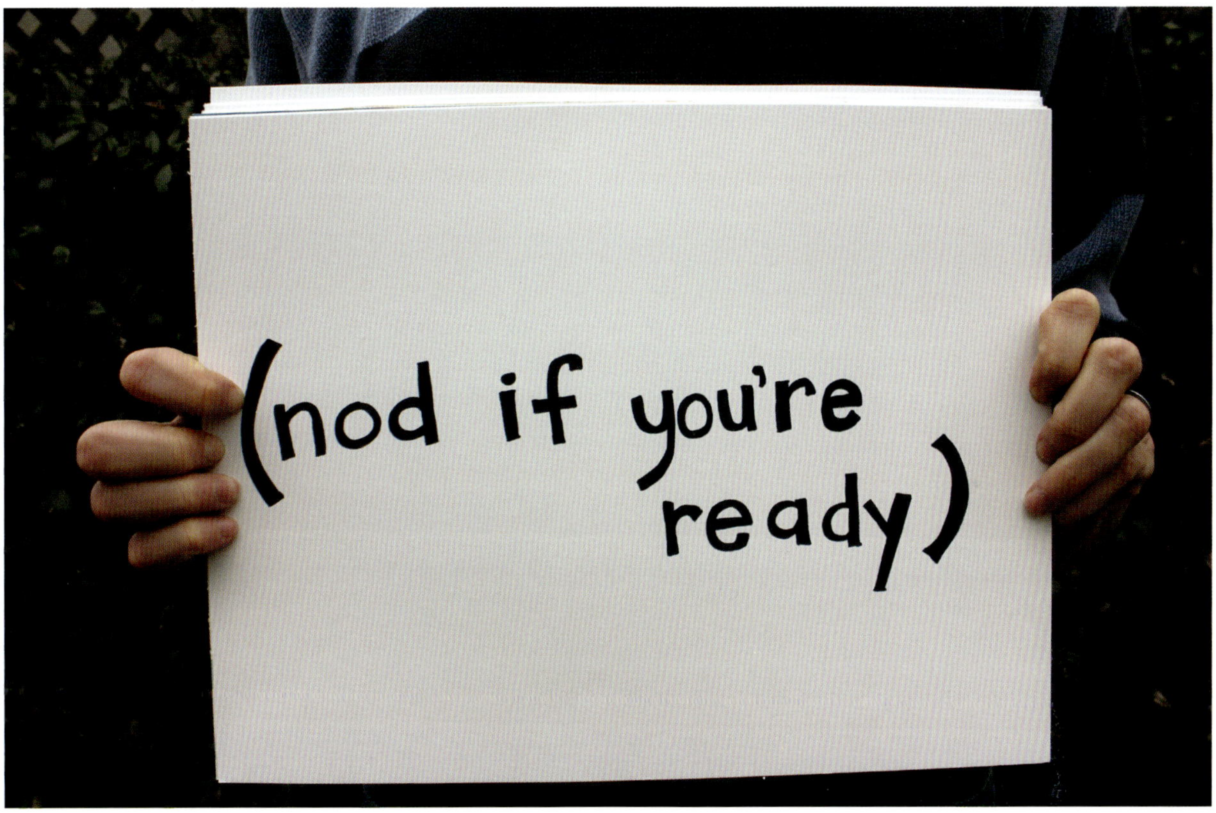
(nod if you're
ready)

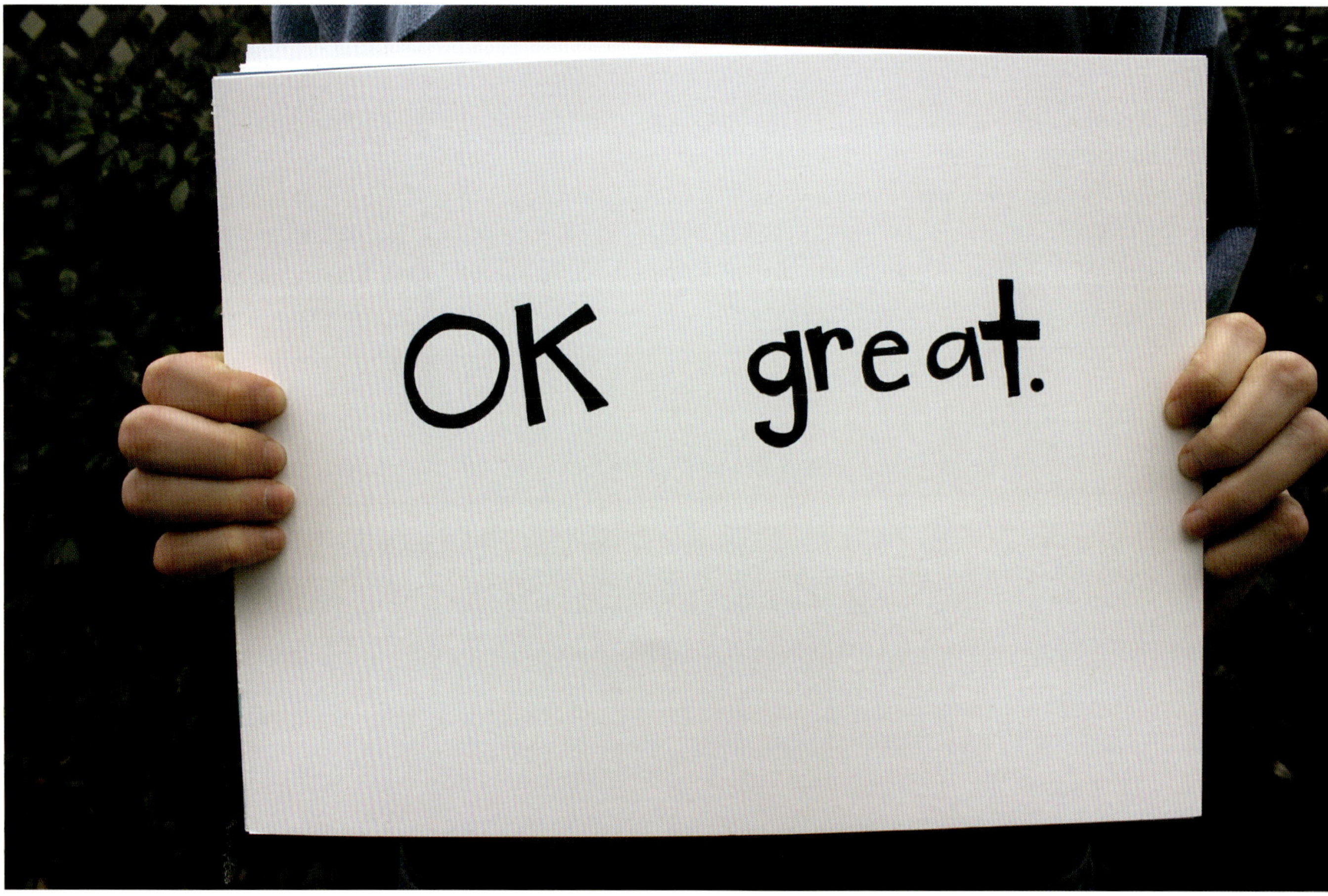
OK great.

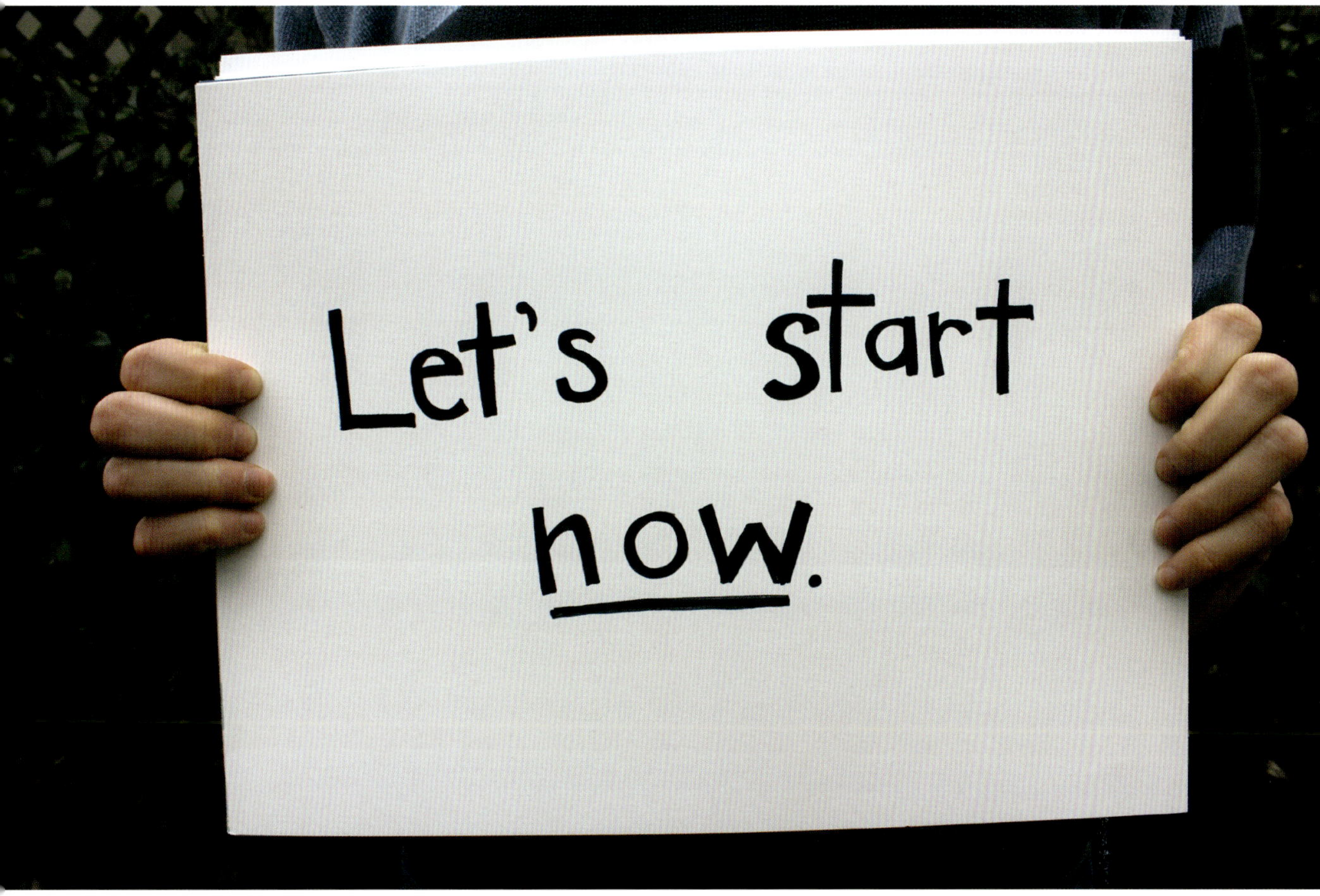
Let's start
now.

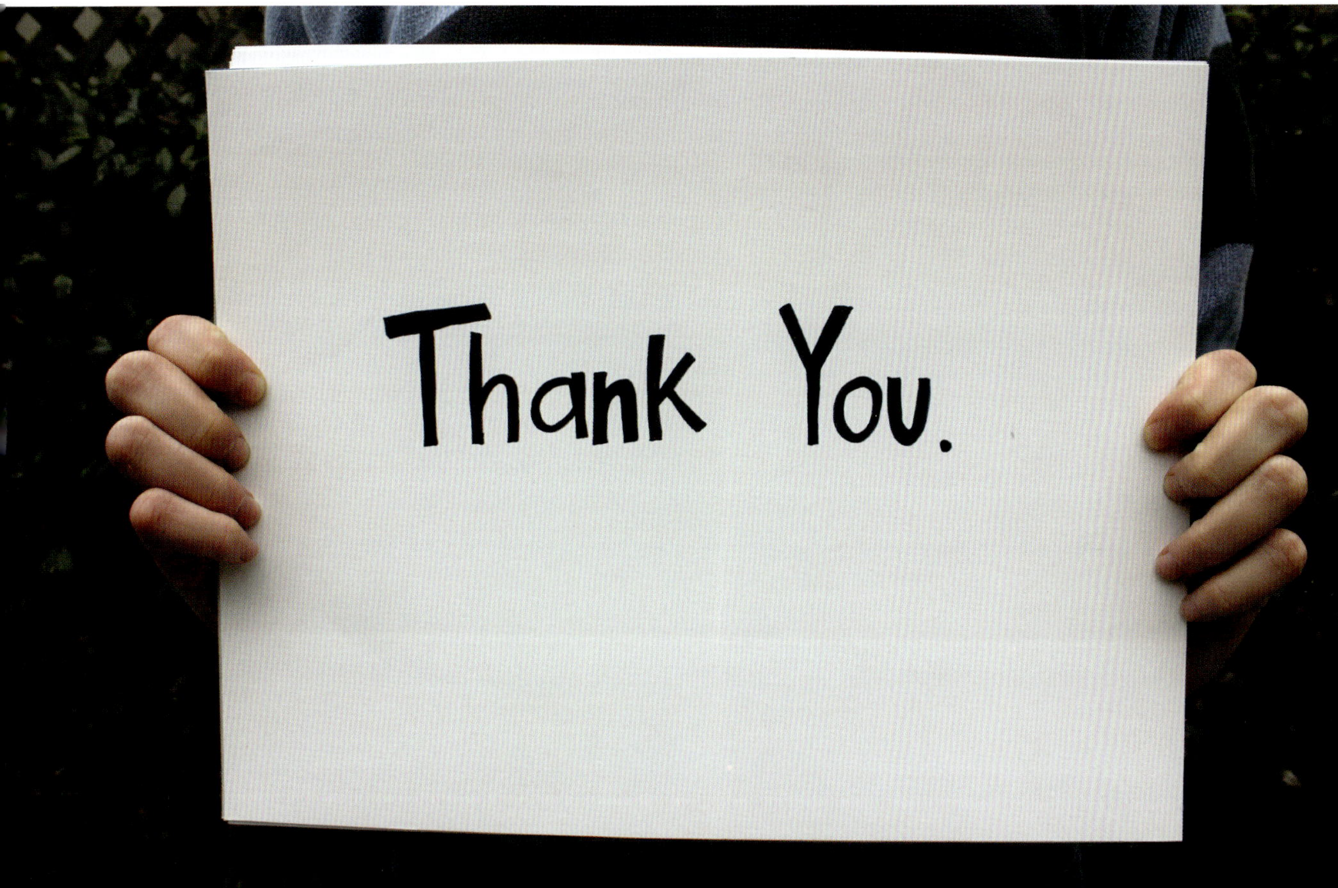
Thank You.

A Healing Walk

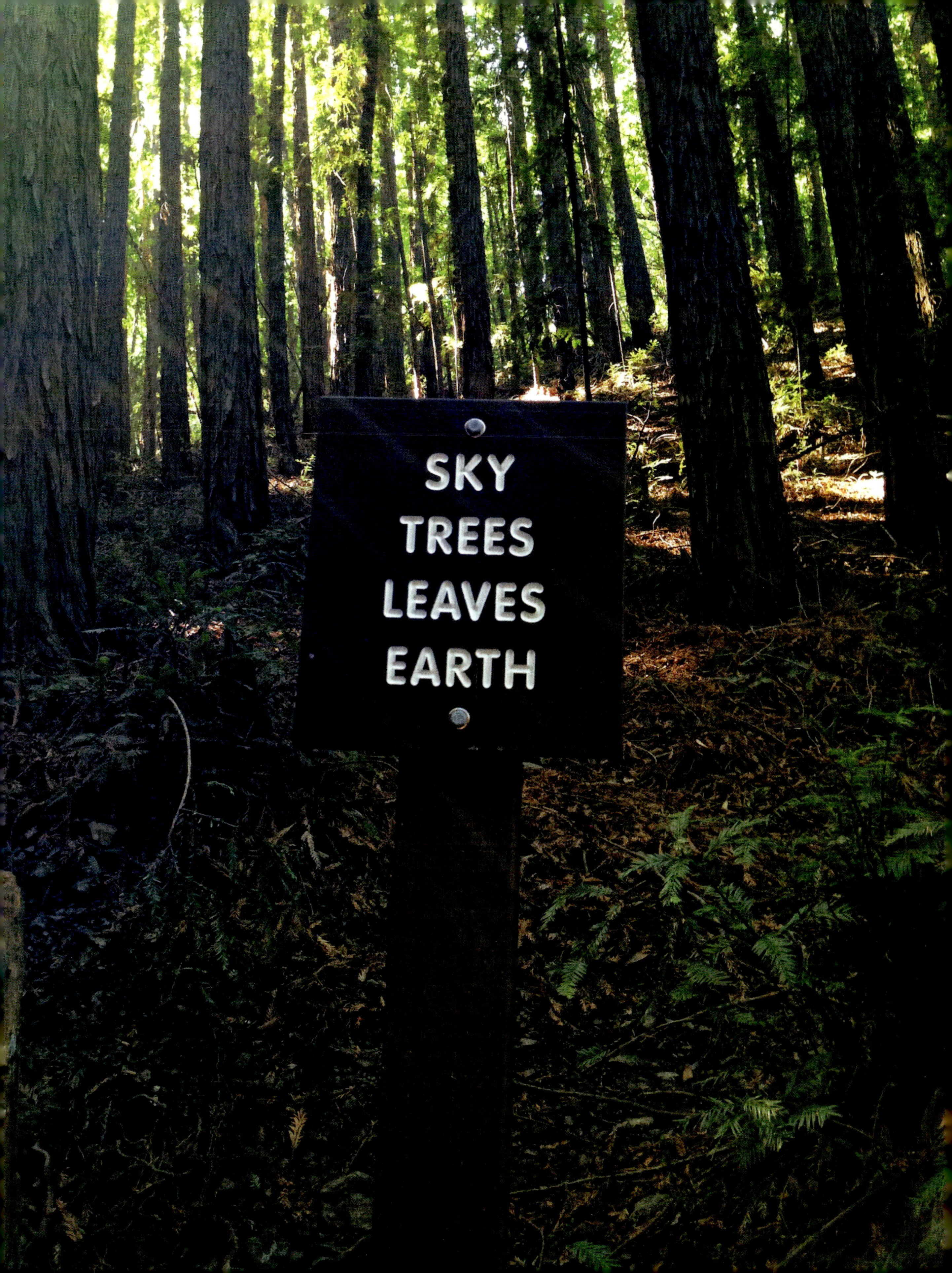
SKY
TREES
LEAVES
EARTH

It Begins with Feeling

Donna Conwell

Montalvo is a 175-acre estate turned public park and art center in the Saratoga foothills. Its manicured gardens, historic villa, and 3½ miles of hiking trails attract visitors from all over the Bay Area and beyond. At a trailhead behind the villa is a sign that says, "A Healing Walk." As you follow the steep trail through a dense and shady second-growth redwood forest up to a lookout point with a panoramic view of the Santa Clara Valley below, eight more signs accompany you. The words are etched into wooden posts, and at first glance they look like park signage. But instead of providing informational or interpretive content, the texts encourage you to center yourself in the experience of being in this beautiful forest, to be fully present with all your senses.

SKY TREES LEAVES EARTH
IT BEGINS WITH FEELING
THEN THERE IS COLOR
YOU LOOK UP
YOUR MIND QUIETS
HERE YOU LEAVE YOUR WORRIES
THIS BEAUTIFUL MOMENT
YOU ARE HERE AWAKE AND ALIVE

In 2012, the curatorial team at the Sally and Don Lucas Artists Residency Program at Montalvo Arts Center began to develop a multidisciplinary, twenty-month thematic program on the subject of well-being. On January 25, 2013, we launched the program, titled *Flourish: Artists Explore Wellbeing*, with an exhibition exploring the topic of happiness. The exhibition featured new and extant work by three artists: Susan O'Malley, Leah Rosenberg, and Christine Wong Yap, all of whom had studied at California College of the Arts. The show, called *Happiness Is . . .*, was intended to be an open-ended inquiry into the elusive question of how we can cultivate contentment in our daily lives. The artists collaboratively designed and installed the exhibition and presented sculptures, installations, light works, drawings, participatory site-specific works, and innovative public programs. Susan created *A Healing Walk* and *A Space for You* for the exhibition. *A Space for You* was an area in the gallery designed for visitors to rest and recline among comfy cushions that included positive affirmations such as "So Glad You Are Here." *A Healing Walk* also included uplifting texts but

---

Page 143 : *A Healing Walk*, Montalvo Arts Center, Saratoga, California, 2012

conversely focused on the actions of moving and walking, and the way that being outside in nature contributes to a sense of well-being.

One of my first in-person conversations with Susan was when she arrived at the residency program in November 2012. After some chitchat, Susan casually mentioned that she was undergoing IVF treatment. I was completely taken aback by her candor. The truth was that while I was working on a program about happiness, I was struggling with deep sadness after several pregnancy losses and my own failed IVF journey. At that time in my life, I was withdrawn and rarely talked with anyone about how I was truly feeling. Later, Susan and I took a walk through the woods along the trail where she would install *A Healing Walk*. We talked about the social expectations and assumptions that often conflate femininity with motherhood and the stigma of infertility. We breathed the earthy and sweet smell of the redwood trees. We talked about forest bathing and how being in nature can be so healing, and we shared stories about the role of movement in our sense of well-being. Susan told me that she was having trouble thinking about the idea of happiness and instead had been considering the whole spectrum of human experience and how happiness and sadness can coexist in a single moment. She was interested in the journey of getting to a more contented space, and she told me about the importance of her mindfulness practice to that journey, how she sought to focus on being in the moment instead of becoming caught up in thoughts about the future or ruminating on the past.

My walk in the forest with Susan was deeply healing. Humans are relational beings; we all long to be heard and understood, yet so often we respond to pain by retreating inward. Susan's openness recalls the words of the faith leader Rabbi Sharon Brous: "When so many of us feel that we are breaking, do not take your broken heart and go home, don't isolate, step toward those you know will hold you tenderly. . . . Trust there is someone on the other side who will hold your heart with kindness."[1] I would come to learn that this was how Susan approached not just her in-person interactions with others but also the art she made.

Susan said, "I make art that connects us to each other." Her text-based work exemplifies this approach. There is no ironic coolness that might leave a viewer alienated and confused. Rather, Susan used text to create a sense of trust between herself and anyone willing to read and receive her words. She held her viewers with empathy and care, and she leaned into our shared experiences. Writing about her 2013 text-infused solo show *You Arrive My Life Begins* at the Galleri Urbane in Dallas, Texas, she said,

> Without you, without an audience, without the belief that there is something here—a connection between yourself and the work—between you and me—things stand still. We're going nowhere. What I'm interested in is what will happen if you accept the gratitude and

> affection of this work. . . . My hope is that by sharing my own feelings through the work, others will feel it too.

For *A Healing Walk*, Susan chose to share texts that drew on her practice of mindfulness meditation and the mantras she used in her daily practice. She believed that they might resonate with park visitors. As with her other text-based work, she sought to create a disruption in visitors' everyday lives by presenting the text in a way that feels familiar (park signage) but with "different language than you expect to see. . . . It creates a pause or a shift so that the reader . . . might be able to internalize the texts in their own ways of thinking."[2]

During my long and difficult journey to becoming a mother, I ventured up the trail along Susan's *A Healing Walk* many times. Sometimes I had to stop to rest as the trail inclined steeply upward—the path to healing is not easy. I was always struck by the rhythm Susan created on the trail upward, punctuating the journey with encouraging words and gentle suggestions to pay attention—like the sign "You Look Up," which reveals a delightful green canopy of encircling trees and calming blue sky. Today, as I play with my two-year-old daughter, Susan's advice along *A Healing Walk* still resonates: to be present, to be in the moment, and to keep going. As you emerge out of the shady forest into the sunlight, the last sign of the walk reads, "You Are Here Awake and Alive."

---

[1] https://www.kqed.org/forum/2010101904623/rabbi-sharon-brous-on-saying-amen-to-each-others-joy-and-pain

[2] Archived podcast interview between The Aphorists and Susan O'Malley, Leah Rosenberg, and Christine Wong Yap. Held in private archive.

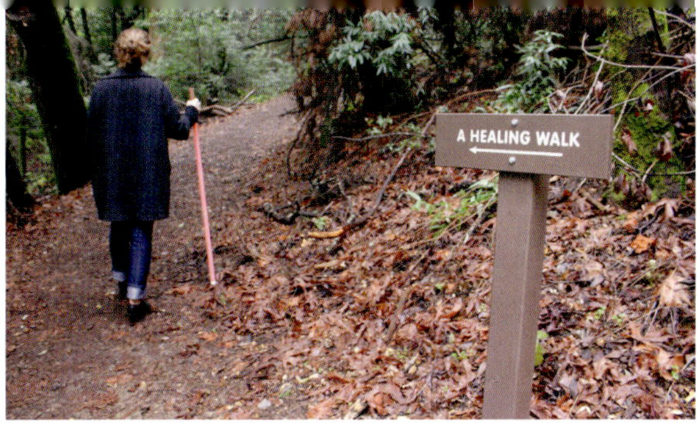
A HEALING WALK

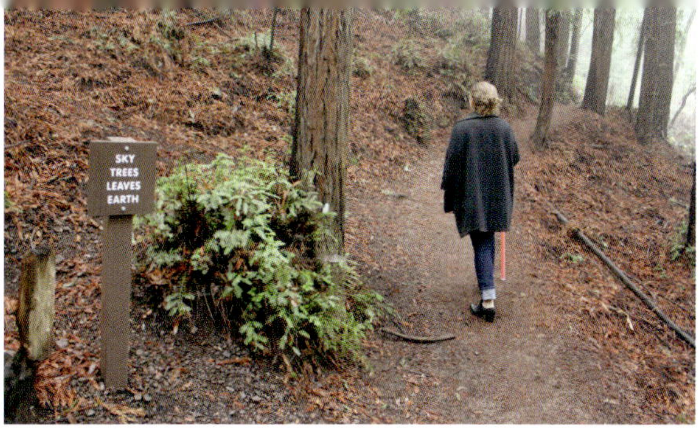
SKY
TREES
LEAVES
EARTH

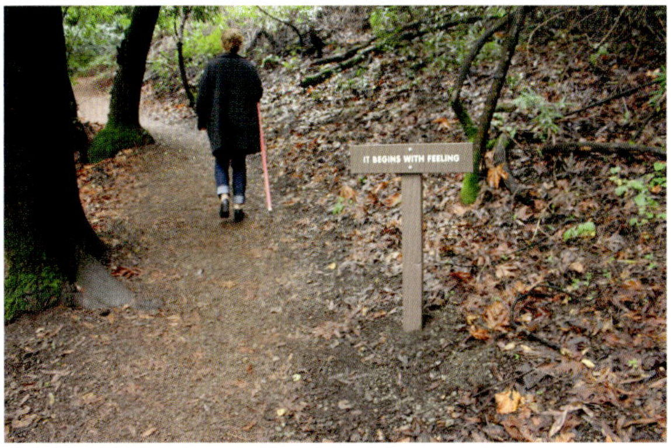
IT BEGINS WITH FEELING

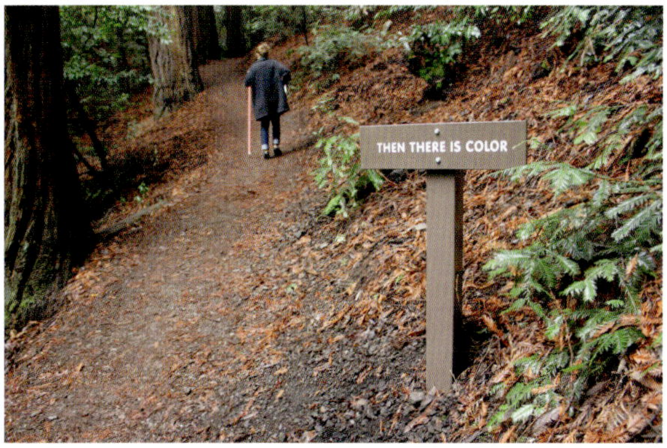
THEN THERE IS COLOR

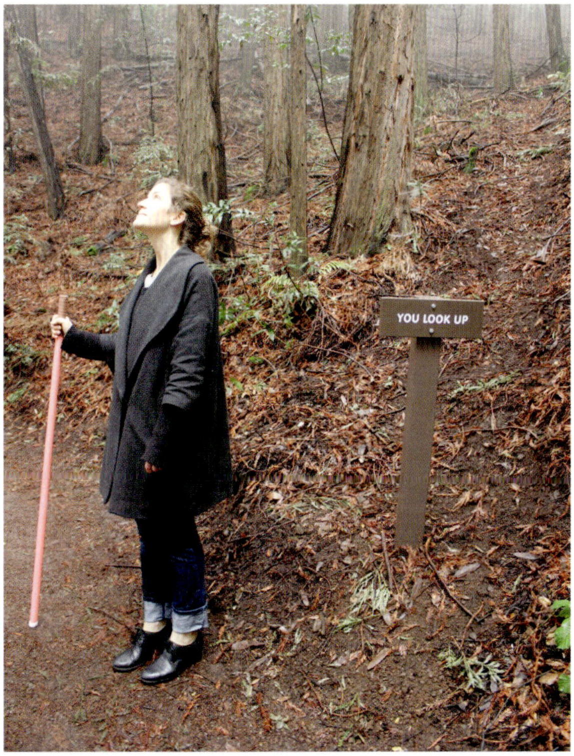
YOU LOOK UP

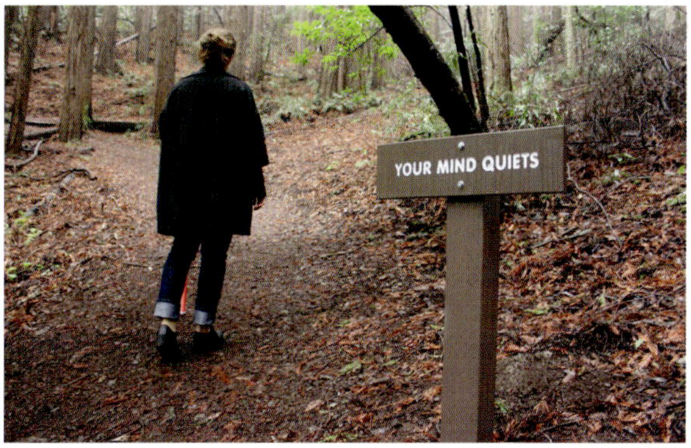
YOUR MIND QUIETS

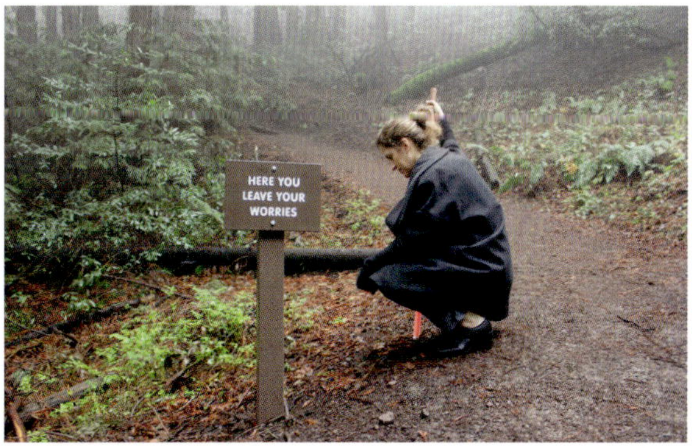
HERE YOU
LEAVE YOUR
WORRIES

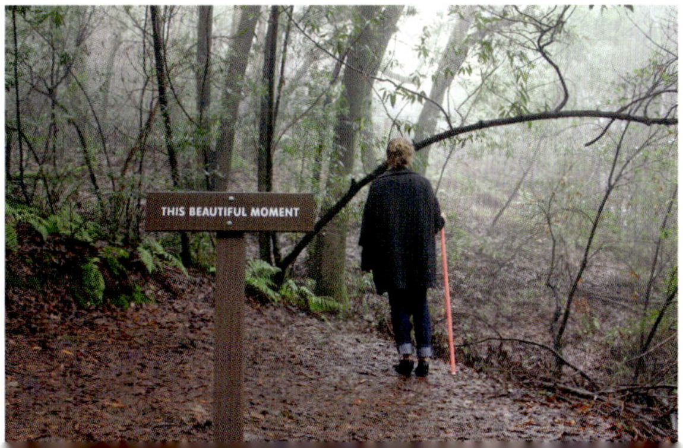
THIS BEAUTIFUL MOMENT

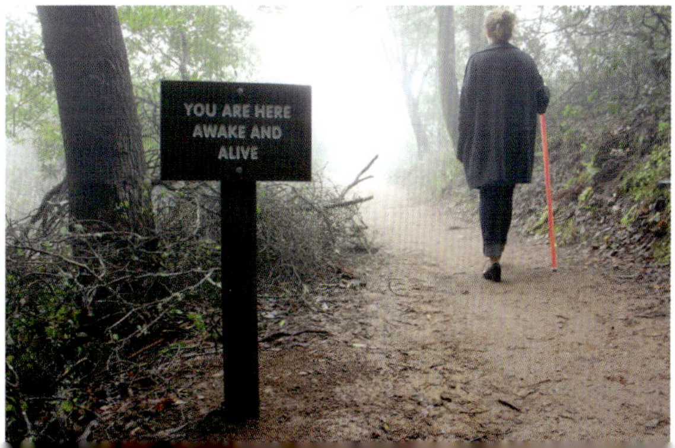
YOU ARE HERE
AWAKE AND
ALIVE

Page 147: Leah Rosenberg photographed walking through *A Healing Walk*, Montalvo Arts Center, Saratoga, California, 2012

Pages 149–61: *A Healing Walk*, Montalvo Arts Center, Saratoga, California, 2012

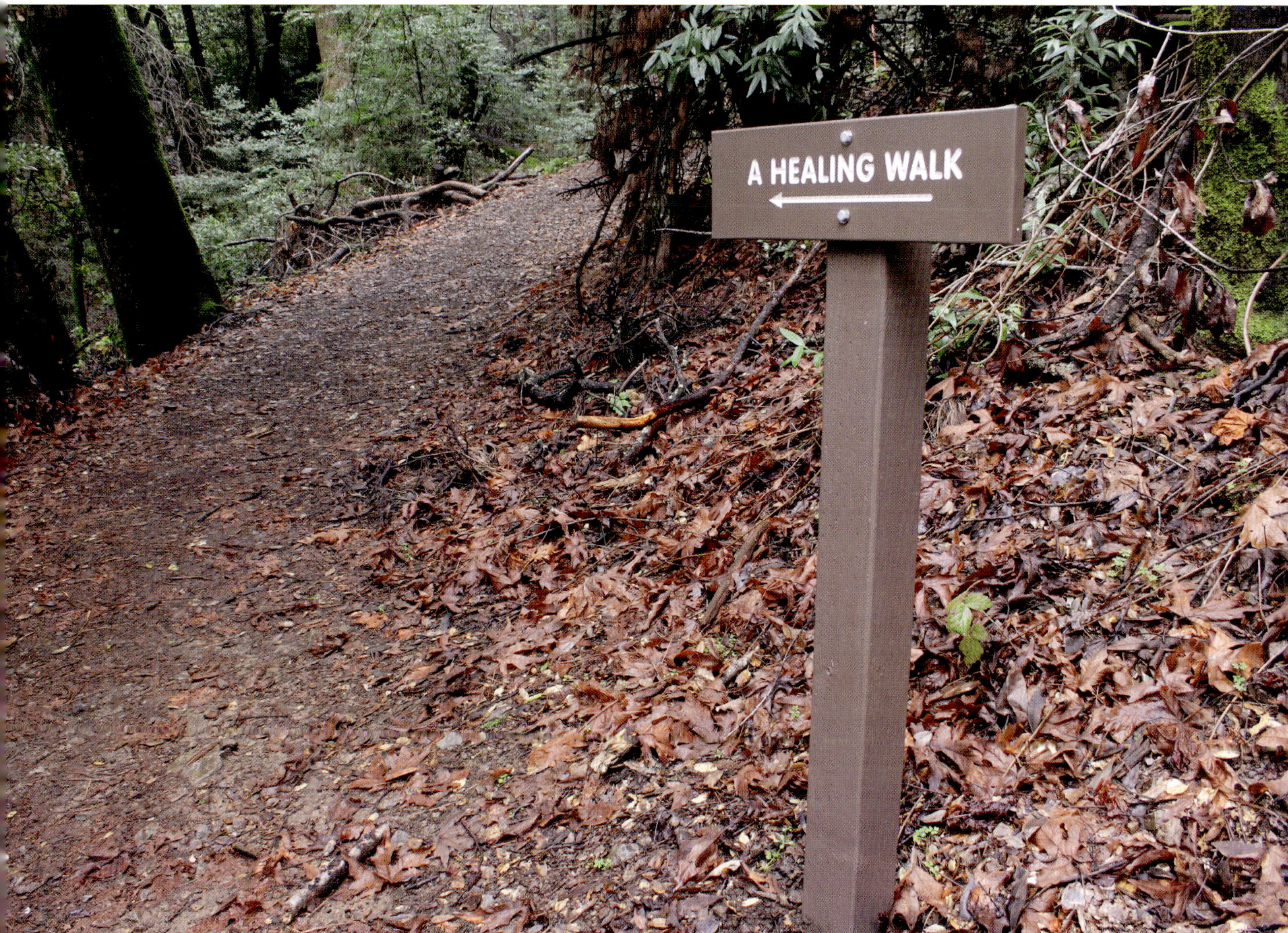
A HEALING WALK

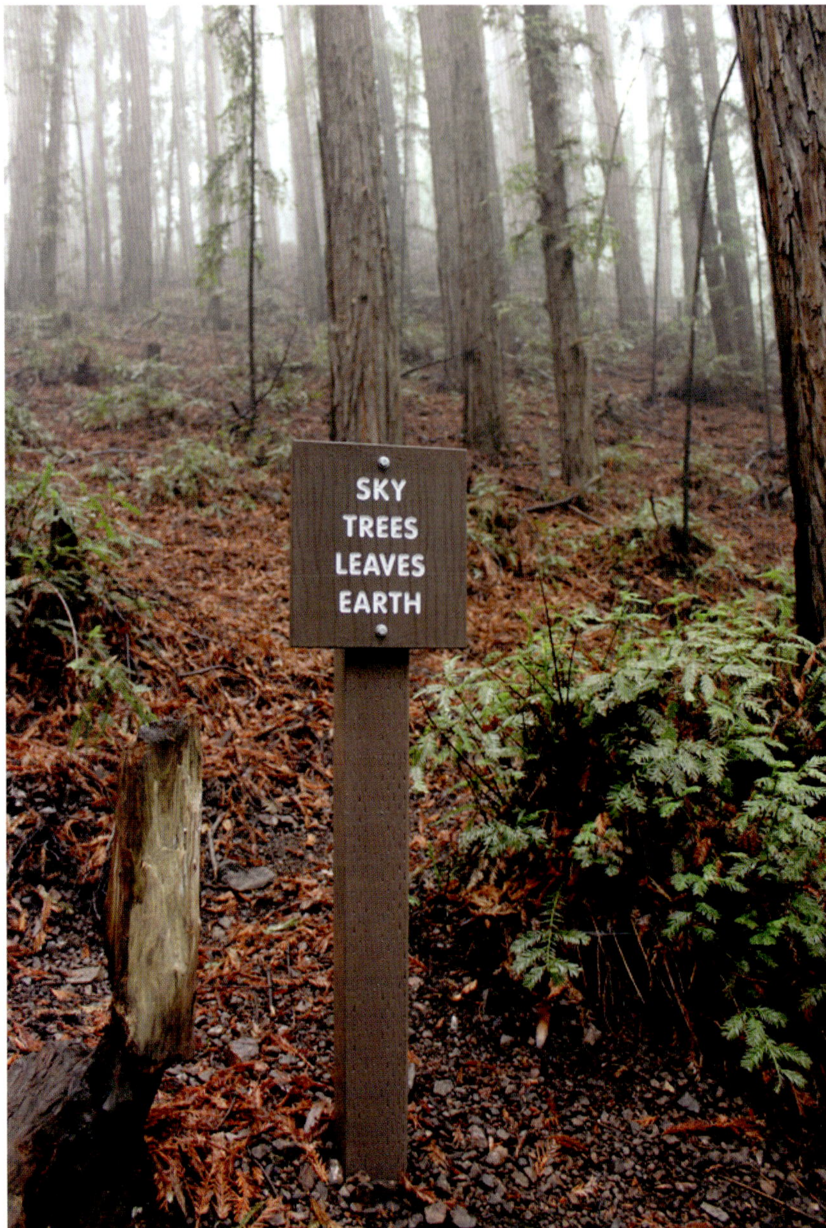
SKY
TREES
LEAVES
EARTH

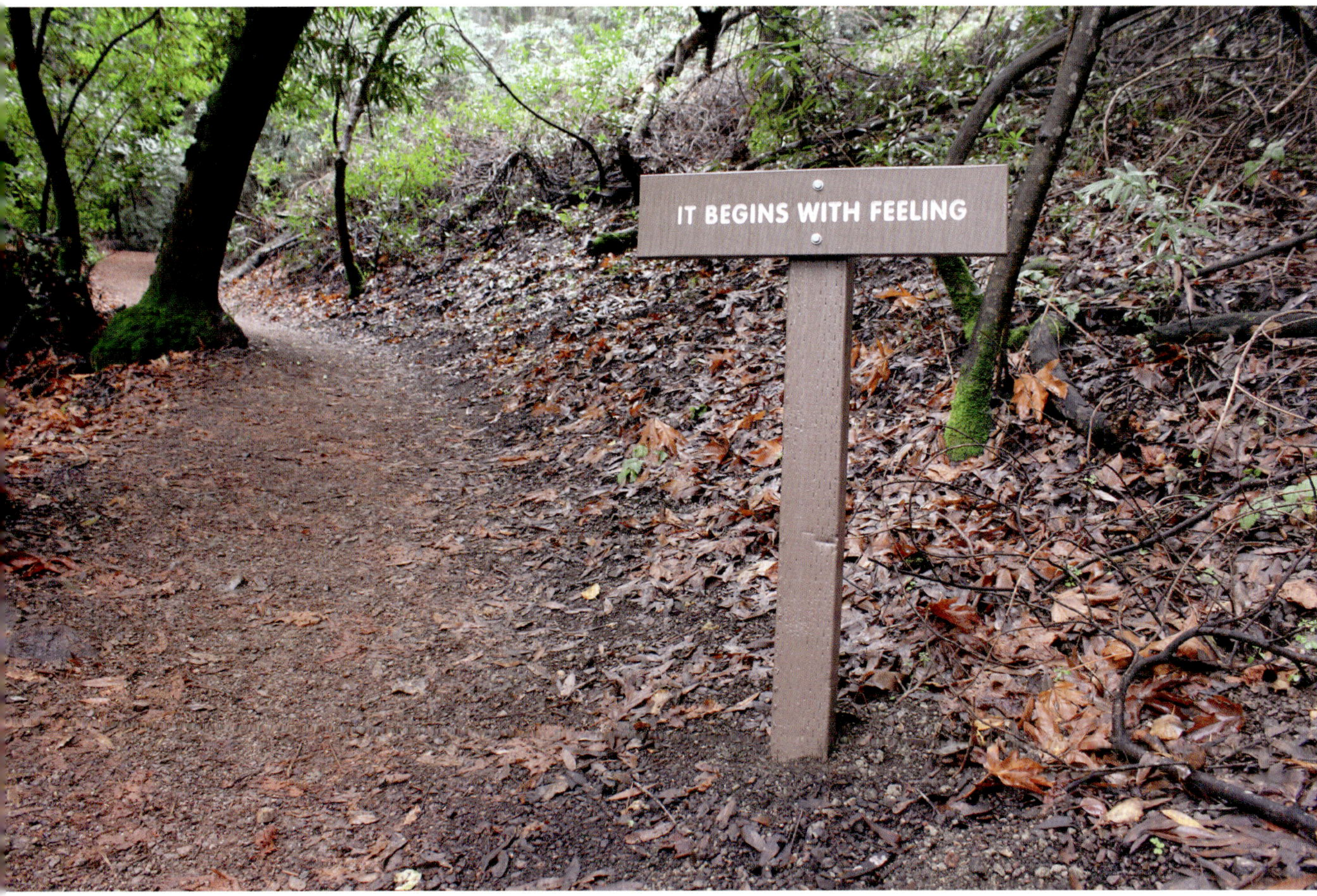
IT BEGINS WITH FEELING

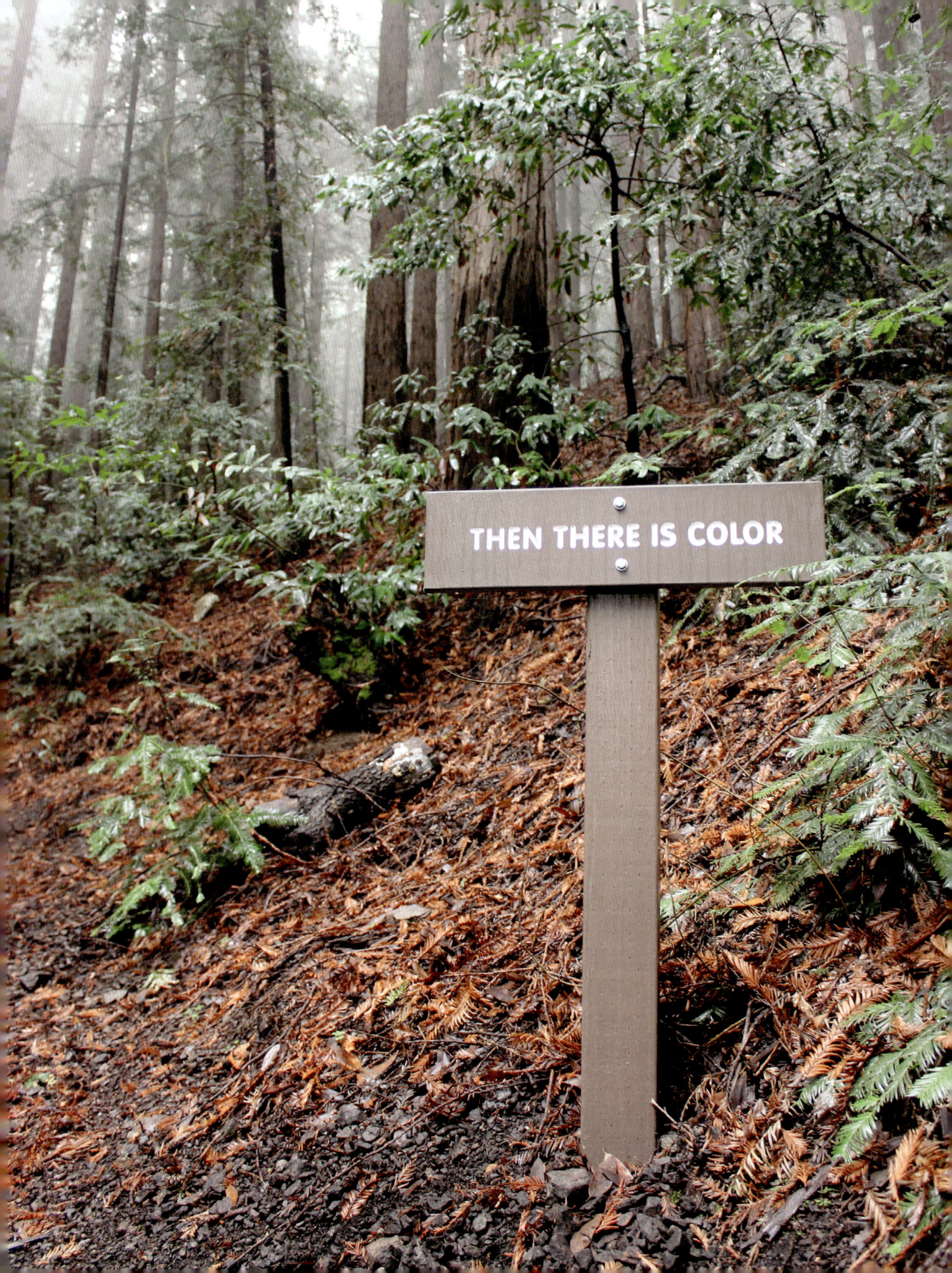
THEN THERE IS COLOR

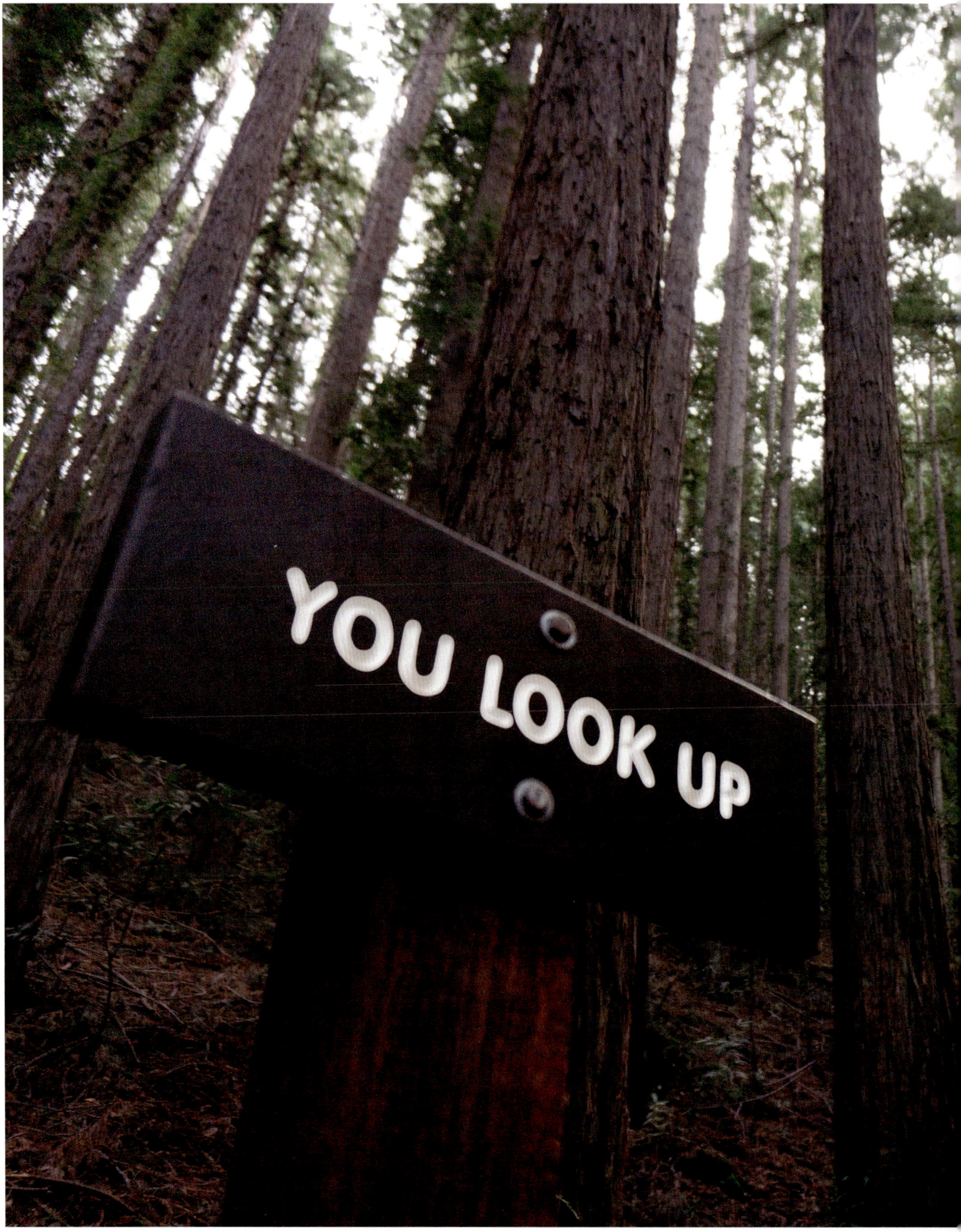
YOU LOOK UP

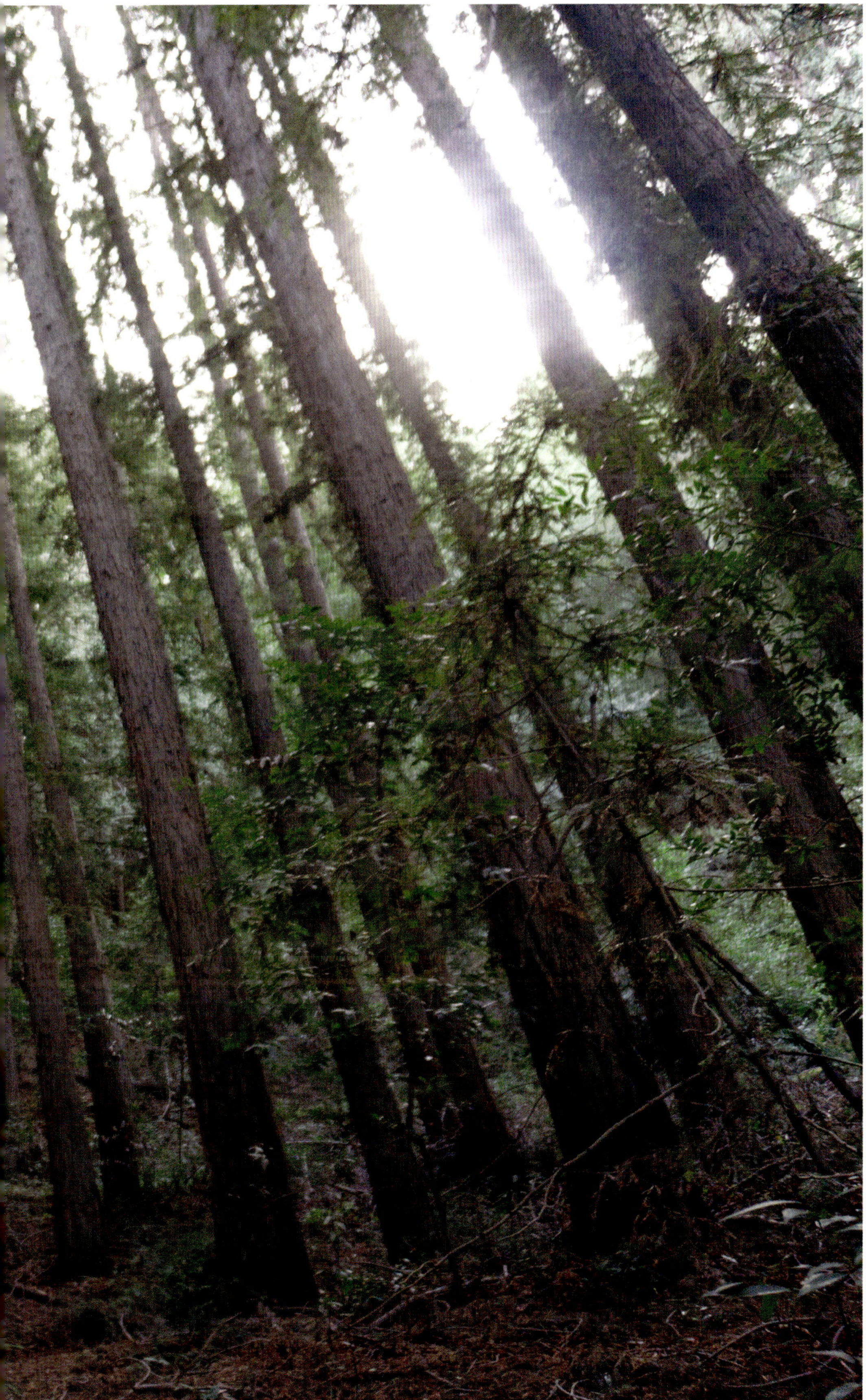

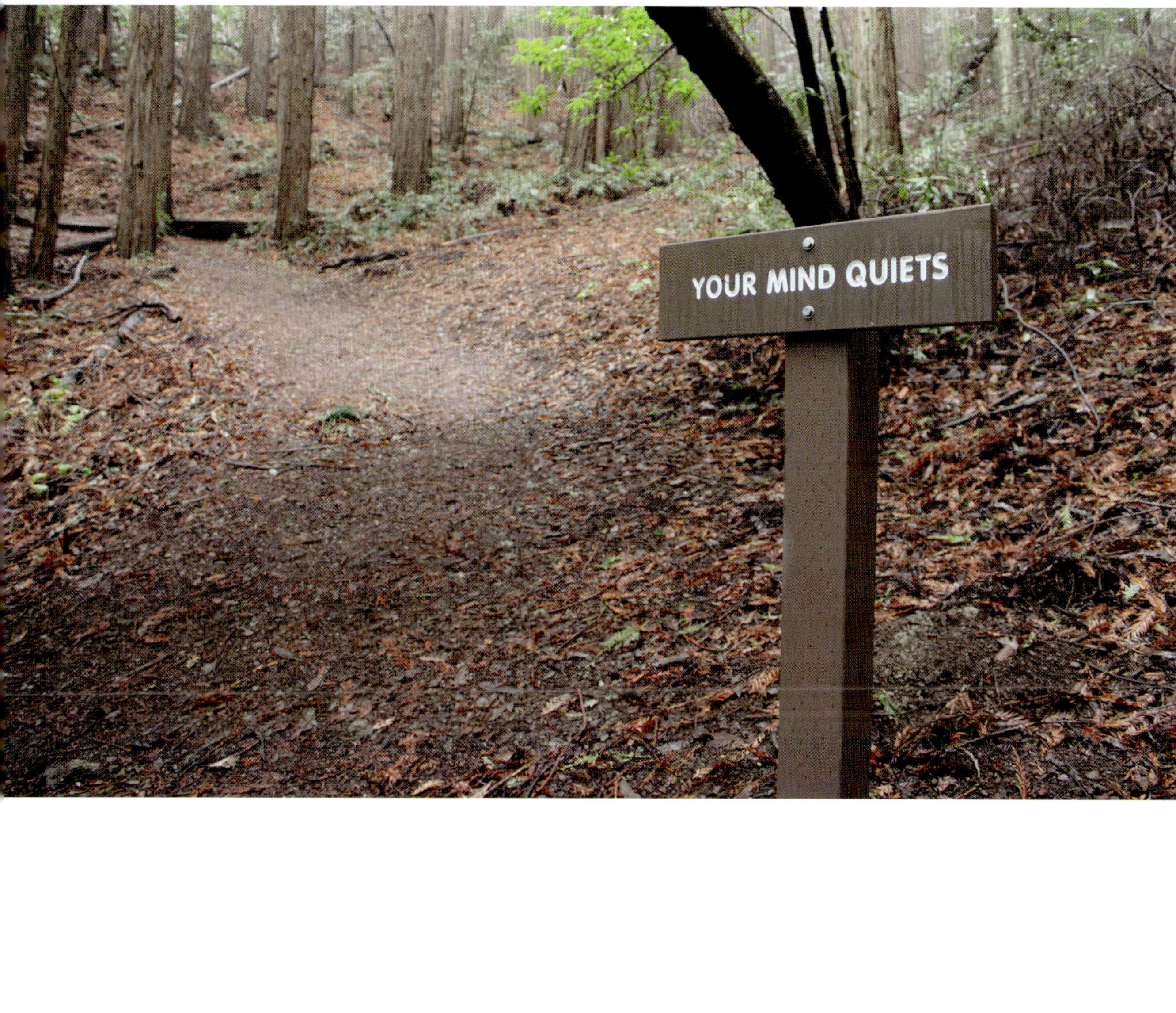
YOUR MIND QUIETS

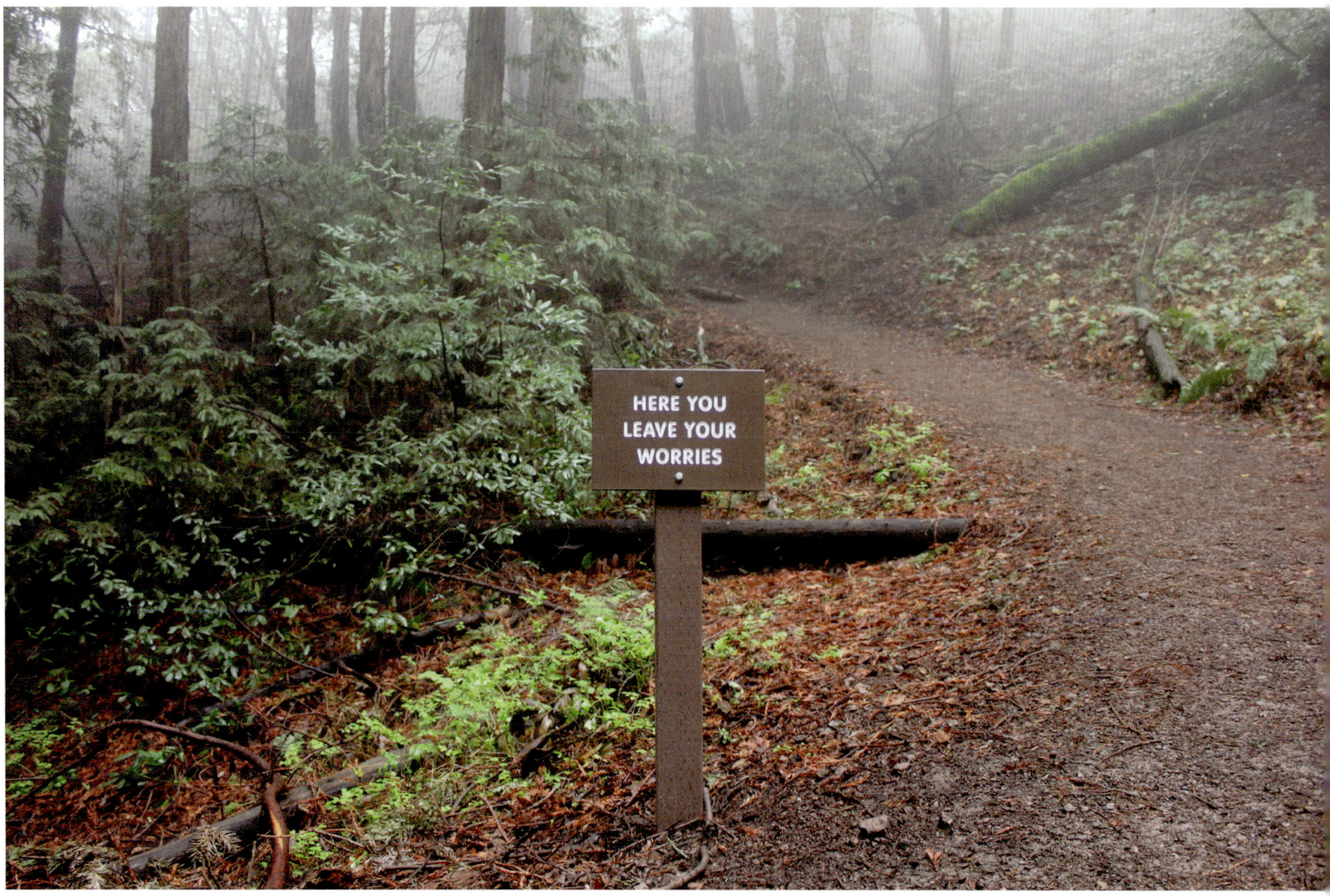
HERE YOU
LEAVE YOUR
WORRIES

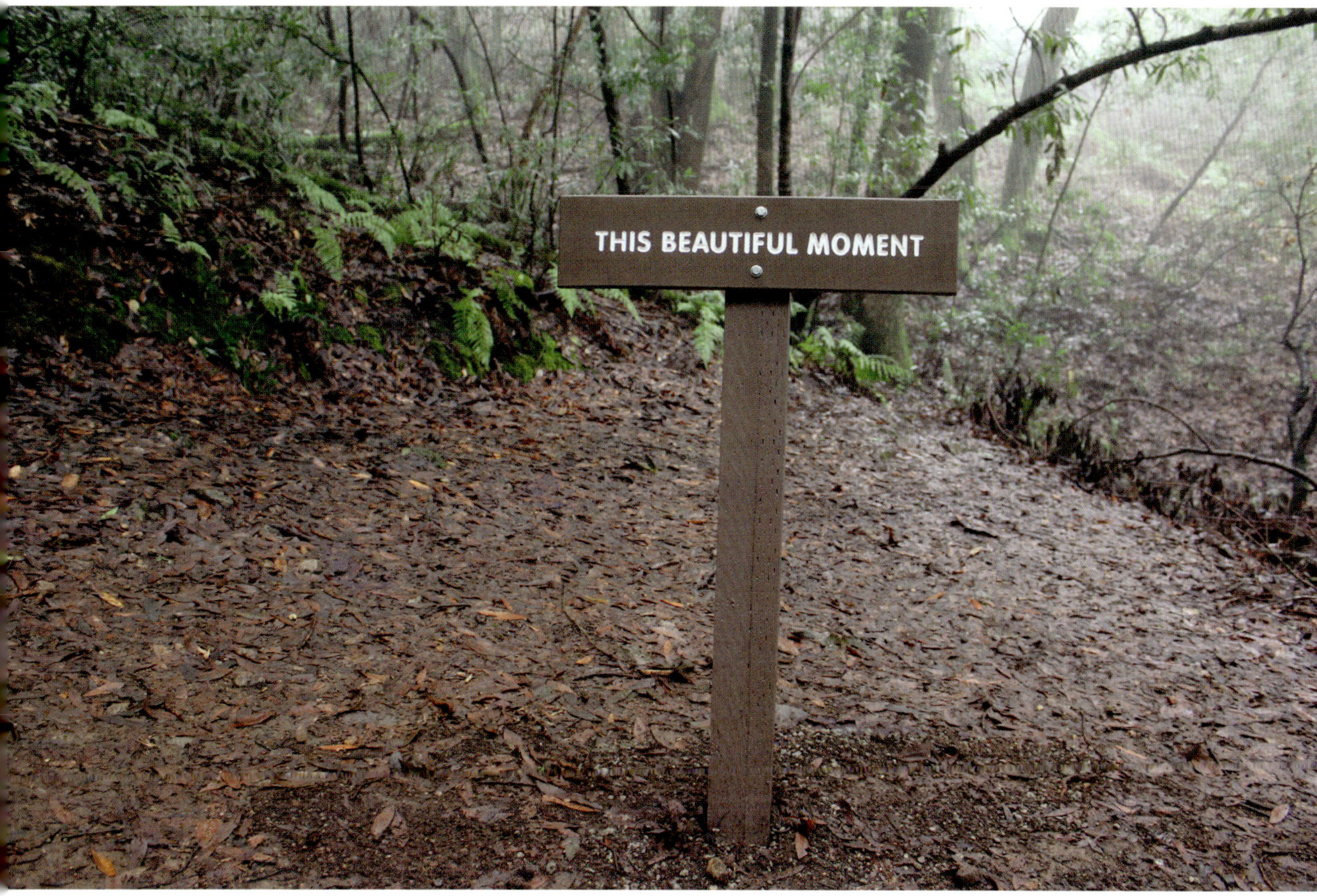
THIS BEAUTIFUL MOMENT

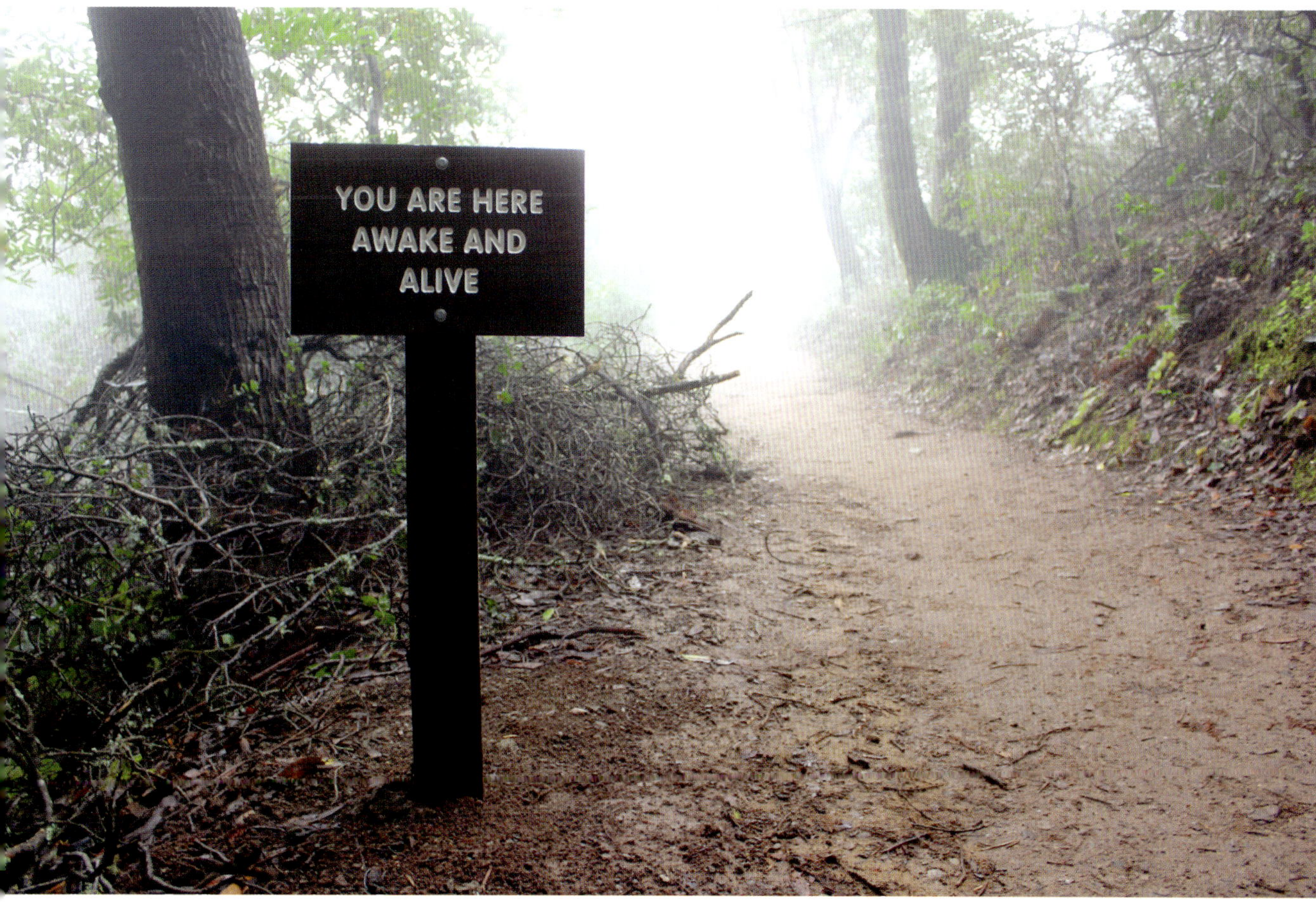
YOU ARE HERE
AWAKE AND
ALIVE

Good Vibes

Lawrence Rinder

In 2004, I returned to San Francisco after four years in New York City, having become disillusioned with the competitive, money-driven mainstream art world. Soon after I took up my new position as dean of graduate studies at California College of the Arts (CCA), it became obvious to me that something new and fresh was happening in the Bay Area art scene. Drawing on numerous local precedents from the Diggers and Ant Farm to the interactive conceptual work of Bonnie Sherk and Tom Marioni, artists were evolving new forms of practice that combined social activism, political organizing, radical pedagogy, and anti-capitalism.

Ted Purves and Susanne Cockrell's Oakland-based *Temescal Amity Works* (2004–7) was one example. As part of this project, they drew on Lewis Hyde's theory of the gift economy of art to create *Big Backyard*, an initiative that aimed to generate community through acts of gleaning and mutual care. This project grew out of their knowledge of their neighborhood's agricultural history and their observation that while many of the old orchard trees still existed and were producing bountiful fruit, these nutritious items were often left to rot on the ground. Purves and Cockrell built a cart to gather fallen fruit, which they then made into marmalade and distributed to the community.

Another project from the same era, Jon Rubin's Independent School of Art (2004–6) was both a work of art and a radical effort to redefine art education. For the two years of its existence, the ISA fostered a sense of a possibility based on diversity, multidisciplinarity, and the power of shared labor and a barter economy.

Inspired by these projects, as well as other similarly interactive art experiments, I worked with my colleagues at CCA to help found the nation's first MFA in Social Practice. Although we recognized the irony—and possible detriment—of institutionalizing practices that were often by their very nature anti-institutional, it was impossible to ignore the groundswell of interest in this art form. So we attempted to place it responsibly in the art historical continuum.

Susan O'Malley, who received a BA from Stanford University in urban studies in 1999, was a student at the Independent School of Art and joined the inaugural 2005 class of CCA's Social Practice MFA. At CCA, O'Malley would have been exposed not only to the work of her instructors—including Purves (first chair of the department) and Rubin—but also the rich history of performance art presented in seminars, readings, and visits to the renowned library and archive of Steven Leiber, who was on the faculty of the college.

Leiber collected and dealt in materials from major figures such as Joseph Beuys, as well as important but lesser-known artists such as the Dutch-Surinamese conceptualist Stanley Brouwn (whose key work, *This Way Brouwn*, 1960–64, consisted of asking passersby to draw maps of directions to various locations on scraps of paper). Leiber was particularly interested in the ways that artists fashioned coherent, powerful identities—what might now be called "brands"—by taking control not only of the works of art but also their modes of presentation, publication, and promotion. Leiber's groundbreaking 2001 exhibition at CCA, *Extra Art: A Survey of Artists' Ephemera, 1960–1999*, validated the aesthetic value of artist-designed announcements, exhibition posters, flyers, buttons, and other seemingly ancillary materials.

O'Malley's own work combined an interest in creating socially engaged, uplifting experiences with a close attention to the look and feel of the accompanying ephemera. One piece, included in her 2006 CCA MFA exhibition, was *A Button of Every Person I Met and Remember*. It consisted of an ordinary button printed with the first and last name of every person she personally knew and remembered. While recalling the social network web of Amanda Eicher's 2004 mural, *Genealogy*, at Adobe Books, O'Malley's project leaned toward the affect of a marketing or political campaign.

O'Malley's collaboration with Christina Amini, *Pep Talk Squad* (2005–7), similarly embraced a business-y look and feel. This project offered a problem-solving, morale-boosting service complete with wordmark, uniforms, and other accoutrements of a commercial consulting agency. Their service, however, was completely free and consisted simply of close listening, empathy, and constructive feedback. A local precedent for pseudocorporate branding was T.R. Uthco (Doug Hall, Diane Andrews Hall, and Jody Procter), a performance group active in the 1970s. However, unlike T.R. Uthco and other Dada-based performance projects, O'Malley's work was never sardonic or satirical; rather, her art was imbued with earnest sincerity and a genuine desire to positively impact people's lives and make the world a better place.

In this regard, O'Malley's work—and that of many of her Bay Area peers during the 2000s and 2010s—was part of a transformational, therapeutic artistic thread of performance art that can be traced to the work of artists such as Lygia Clark,

Barbara T. Smith, and Linda Montano. These artists created experiences intended to psychologically heal and spiritually uplift their audiences/participants. Their projects were intimate, interactive, and highly experimental, positioned at the outer fringe of both the therapeutic profession and the art world. In the Bay Area, this tendency was expressed—in wildly divergent ways—in the work of Theresa Hak Kyung Cha and Frank Moore. Cha created shamanistic performances that induced deeply meditative states and spiritual insight, while Moore's events veered toward the bacchanalian, empowering his audiences with a message of universal love and empowerment.

O'Malley's drive to cut through the elitism of the art world to create a universally accessible, positive message inspired her to utilize a style of vernacular street poster popularized by Los Angeles's Colby Poster Printing Company (1948–2016). These distinctive posters, which featured block lettering set against bright bands of color, had been used for decades to publicize music shows, wrestling matches, and other everyday entertainments. As early as 1962, the Pasadena Art Museum borrowed the Colby style for a poster promoting their exhibition of paintings by Ed Ruscha, Jim Dine, Joe Goode, and others. O'Malley adopted the Colby style for her important project *Inspirational Signs* (2009–12), as well as *Advice from My 80-Year-Old Self* (2015). She used color for its overt appeal as well as for its capacity to signal a cheerful mood, and in so doing aligned with her CCA classmate Leah Rosenberg, a painter and cake baker. Rosenberg's bright, colorful paintings, installations, and baked goods were like a Good Vibes Formalism to O'Malley's Good Vibes Conceptualism.

Good vibes were in the air. Susan O'Malley's career coincided, in part, with the presidency of Barack Obama; with a period of tremendous economic growth; with optimism about digital tech; and with an era of expanding civil rights, including the Supreme Court's legalization of same-sex marriage. Despite myriad serious problems—national, global, and personal—it can sometimes be tempting now to think of that time, just a few scant years ago, as the "good old days." O'Malley passed away in 2015. She did not experience the presidency of Donald Trump; the COVID pandemic; the murder of George Floyd; the Capitol insurrection; Russia's invasion of Ukraine; or the descent of the Middle East into unfathomable horror. With the untimely loss of Susan O'Malley the person, we also lost the work of Susan O'Malley the artist. How might O'Malley's Good Vibes Conceptualism have responded to the dark days we have experienced in the decade since her death? This is something we cannot know. Her art can seem to us now like a bittersweet artifact of a more peaceful and hopeful time—but it is universal and timeless in its message.

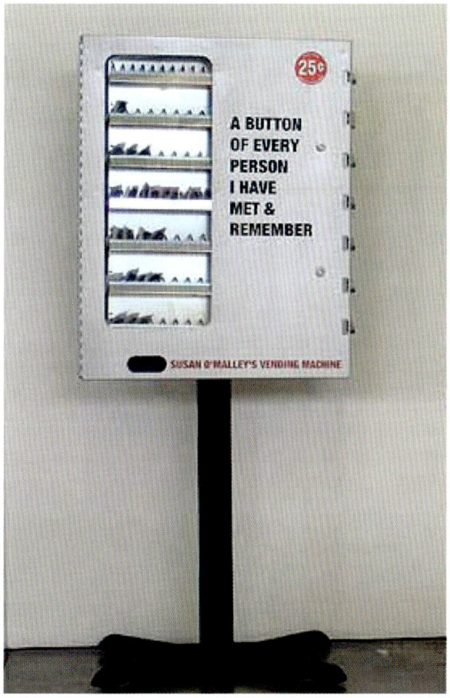

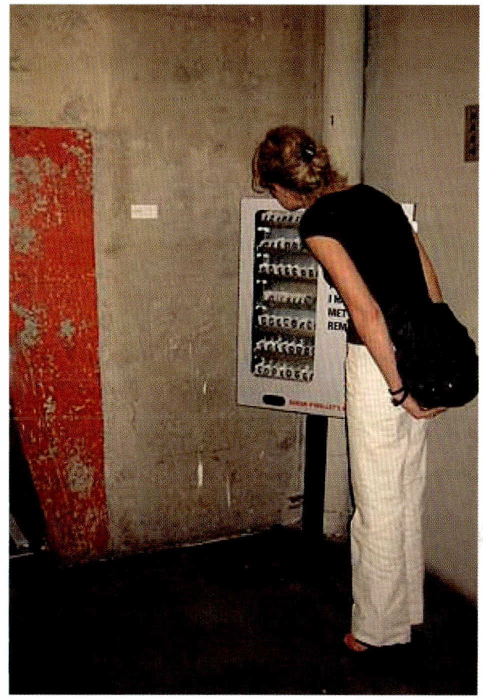

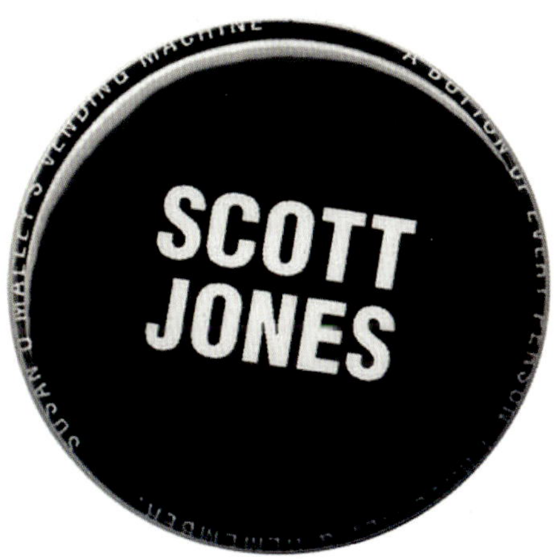

Above: *A Button of Every Person I Have Met & Remember* button vending machine and *Scott Jones* button, California College of the Arts, San Francisco, circa 2006

Pages 166-67: *Plaques*, a series of twenty-four plastic engraved plaques located throughout the gallery and the building, as part of *In Other Words*, curated by Kevin Chen, Intersection for the Arts, San Francisco, 2012

THIS PLACE BEGINS WITH YOU.
HI.

BEHIND THESE WALLS HUMANS MAKE THINGS.

THIS PLAQUE IS DEDICATED TO UNDERUTILIZED SPACES EVERYWHERE.

ANOTHER SPOT FULL OF GOOD GROWTH POTENTIAL.

THE FINEST HALLWAY IN THE WHOLE ENTIRE WORLD.

YOU ARE SAFE HERE.

THE PLACE WHERE YOU CAN PEACEFULLY STARE INTO SPACE.

A CROWD OF FRIENDS AND STRANGERS CHEERING YOU ON BECAUSE YOU HAVE DONE SOMETHING SO GREAT. AND IT'S TRUE.

SPACE AVAILABLE FOR DANCING AND WALKING AND STANDING.

IMAGINE EVERYONE YOU LOVE TOGETHER IN ONE PLACE. GIVING YOU THE GROUP HUG OF YOUR LIFE.

WHERE PLACE MAKING HAPPENS. WELCOME. WE'RE SO HAPPY YOU ARE HERE.

MAXIMIZATION OF THIS LIMITED SPACE.

THE TIME YOU LAUGHED SO HARD YOU CRIED AND PEED AND FARTED ALL AT ONCE.

IMAGINE THE COLOR GREEN SO LUSH AND FRESH AND VIVID YOU CAN SMELL IT.

IMAGINE THIS PLAQUE IS NOTHING LIKE A PLAQUE BUT IS THE MOST PERFECT RAINBOW.

YOUR BEST FRIEND SMILING AT YOU.

WAITING
WAITING
WAITING
FOR YOU TO ARRIVE.

HERE YOU CAN JUST BE.

THE BIG BLUE OPEN SKY.

IMAGINE THIS PLAQUE IS NOT A PLAQUE BUT THE MOST STUNNING SUNSET YOU'VE EVER SEEN.

Finding Your Center

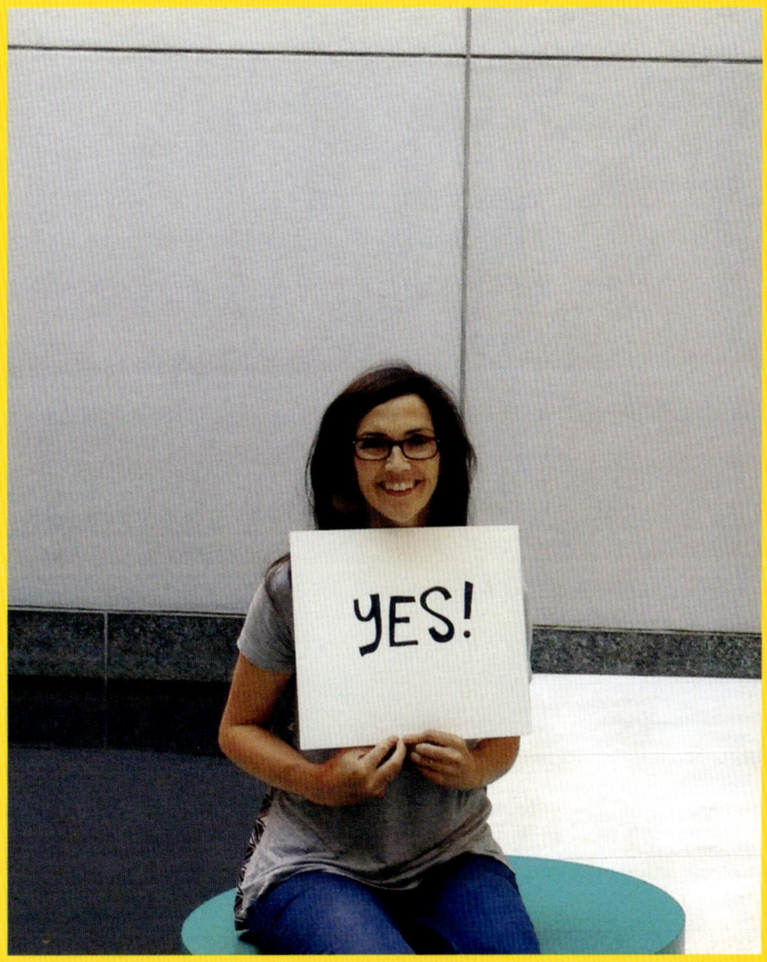
YES!

(Re)Finding Your Center

Benjamin Laramie

When Susan O'Malley and Leah Rosenberg approached me with their idea for *Finding Your Center*, I was honored. Honored and also confused.

This collaboration they were planning for the *Bay Area Now 7* show at Yerba Buena Center for the Arts (YBCA) was to be "a self-help audio tour and distributed sculptural installation that playfully responds to our quest for calm, balance, and equilibrium in the face of the demands of modern life." [1]

Given that unique and ambitious brief, I was honored to be considered, while at the same time surprised that they thought I, of all people, could help them realize their vision.

I remember them describing the specific pieces they hoped I could make: five large, brightly colored cylindrical elements—four to sit on and one suspended as a light fixture. The idea was that these forms would appear as if sliced from a structural column in the gallery, which Leah would paint with colorful bands to match the objects I would build. I recall confidently saying I could do it—while having no idea how I actually would.

At that point in my career I had only a few pieces in my portfolio as a designer and fabricator—and nothing resembling what these two artists had in mind. I typically gravitate toward straight lines, rectilinear forms, and natural materials, tones, and textures. This project pushed me well beyond my comfort zone.

Finding Your Center was a project of many firsts: the first time I had ever built large cylindrical forms, worked with suspended lighting, or used such bold, saturated color. It was also the first time anything I had a hand in was featured in a prominent public setting.

These creative and professional milestones were made possible through collaboration with Leah and Susan, along with their other collaborators, the writer Christina Amini and composer Tiffany Lin. Their support wasn't just verbal—it came primarily through *trust*. They gave me the freedom and responsibility to experiment with materials and construction methods. I ended up sourcing a 28-inch industrial-grade

Page 169: Susan O'Malley holding *Yes!* from *Finding Your Center*, a self-help audio tour and distributed sculptural installation and collaboration between Susan O'Malley and Leah Rosenberg, at Yerba Buena Center for the Arts's *Bay Area Now 7* (*BAN7*), San Francisco, 2014

cardboard tube, cutting it into five equal sections, capping them with plywood disks, and wrapping them in smooth polystyrene. They didn't ask for a detailed plan or second-guess the process. They trusted me to make key decisions—like insetting the bases of the seating elements to give them the illusion of floating, and sanding the acrylic disk on the hanging fixture to diffuse its light. That level of autonomy pushed me to take risks and trust my own judgment.

In retrospect, I see that time and that project as the beginning of a major shift in my professional trajectory. To be invited into meaningful collaboration with such thoughtful and visionary artists as Susan and Leah, and to see objects I had made featured in a public exhibition for the first time, helped me begin to imagine a future shaped less by what I already knew how to do, and more by what I was willing to try.

---

[1] https://www.leahrosenberg.com/findingyourcenterybca/

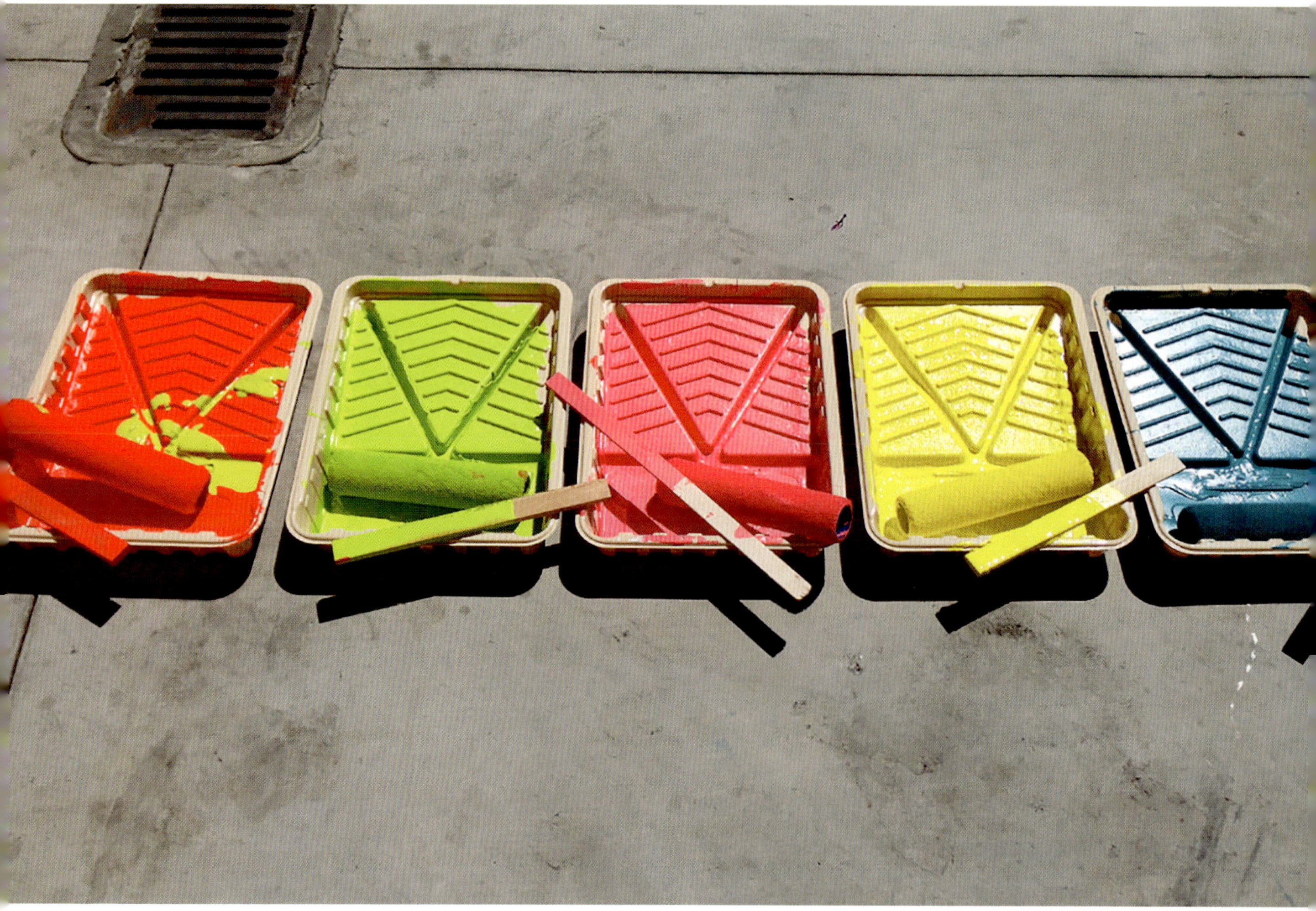

Above and opposite: Process photos for creating cylindrical seating for *Finding Your Center*, Yerba Buena Center for the Arts, San Francisco, 2014

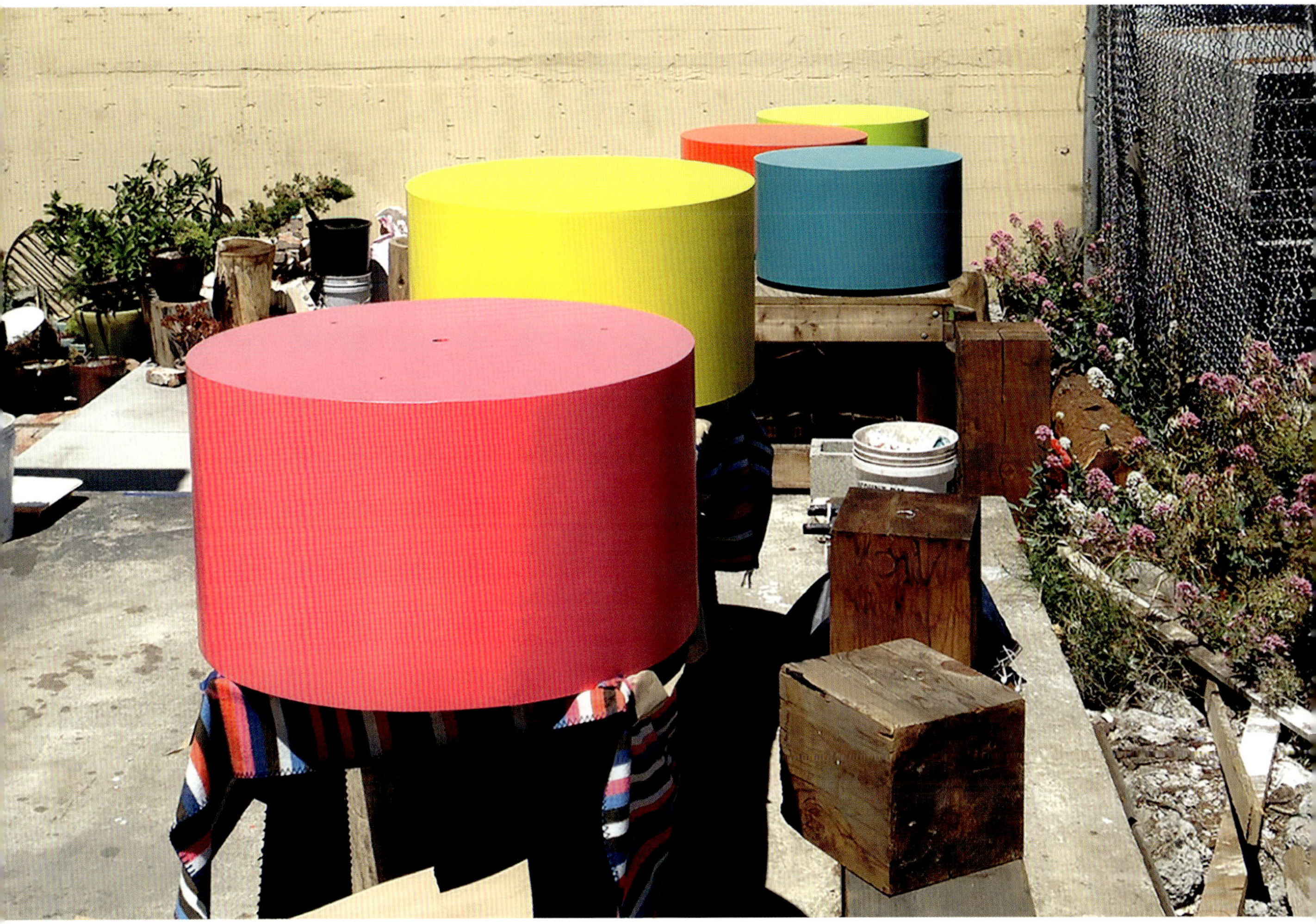

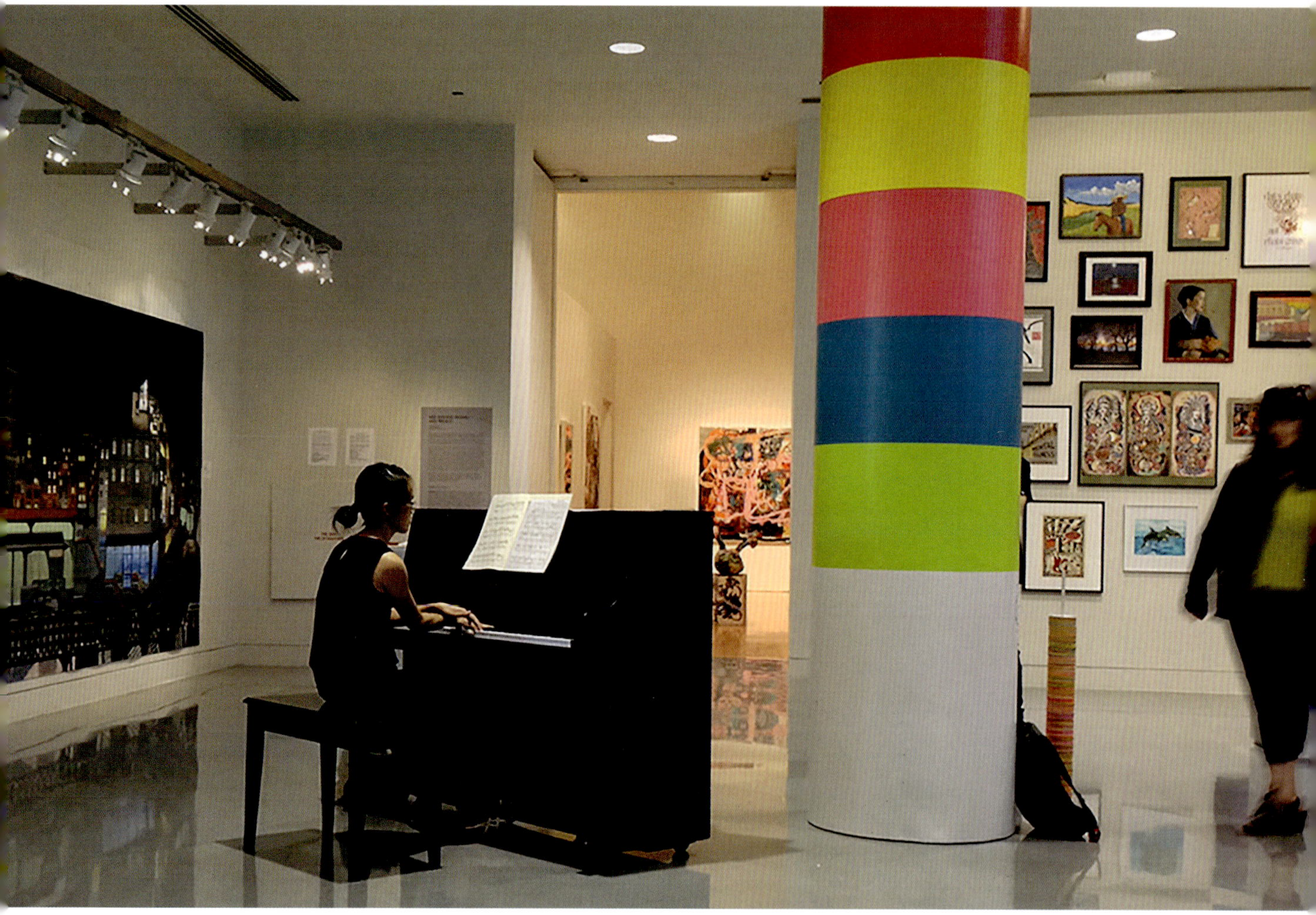

Above: Tiffany Lin playing piano composition in *Finding Your Center*, Yerba Buena Center for the Arts, 2014
Opposite: Participant listening to the audio tour for *Finding Your Center*, Yerba Buena Center for the Arts, 2014

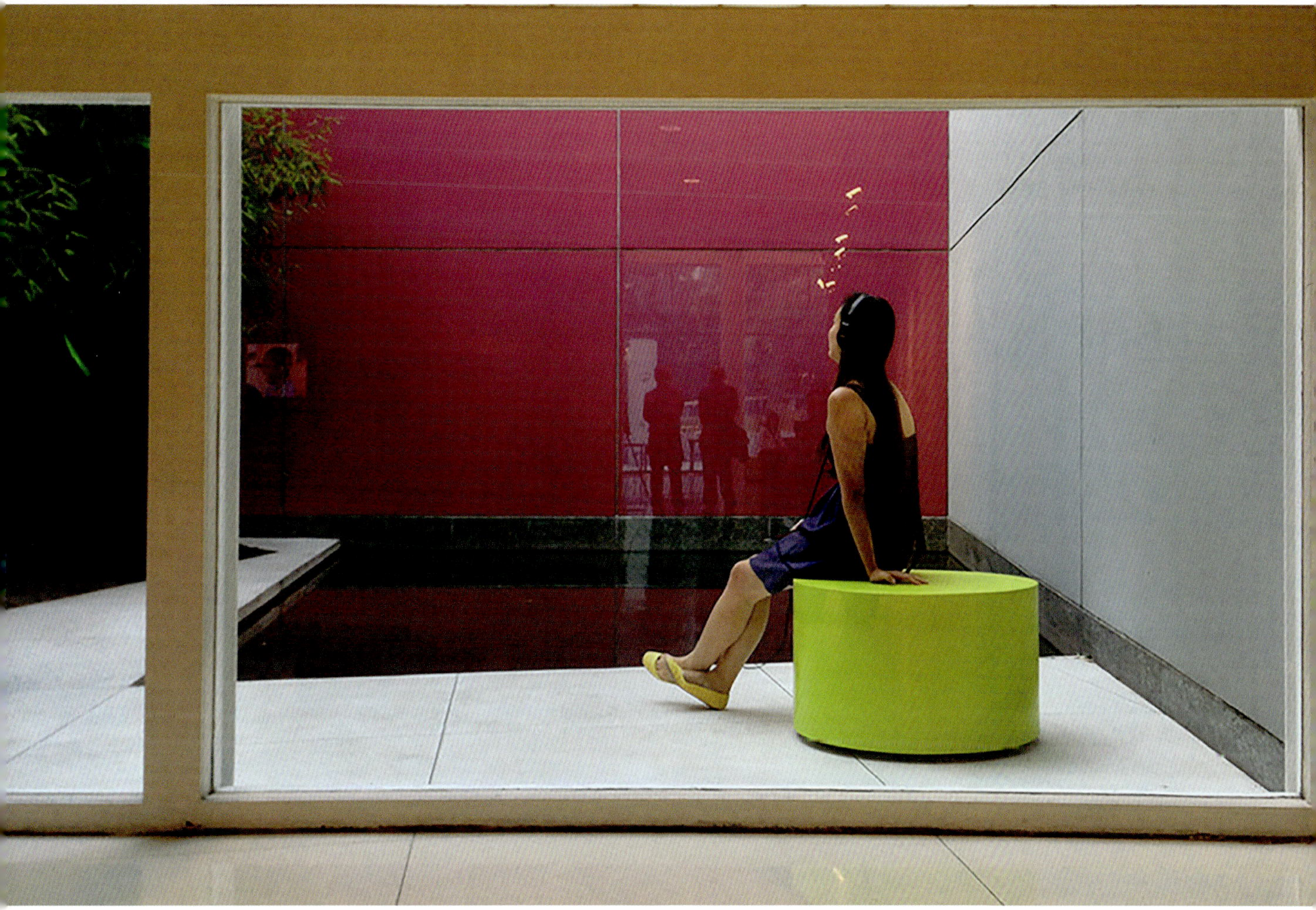

On Collaboration

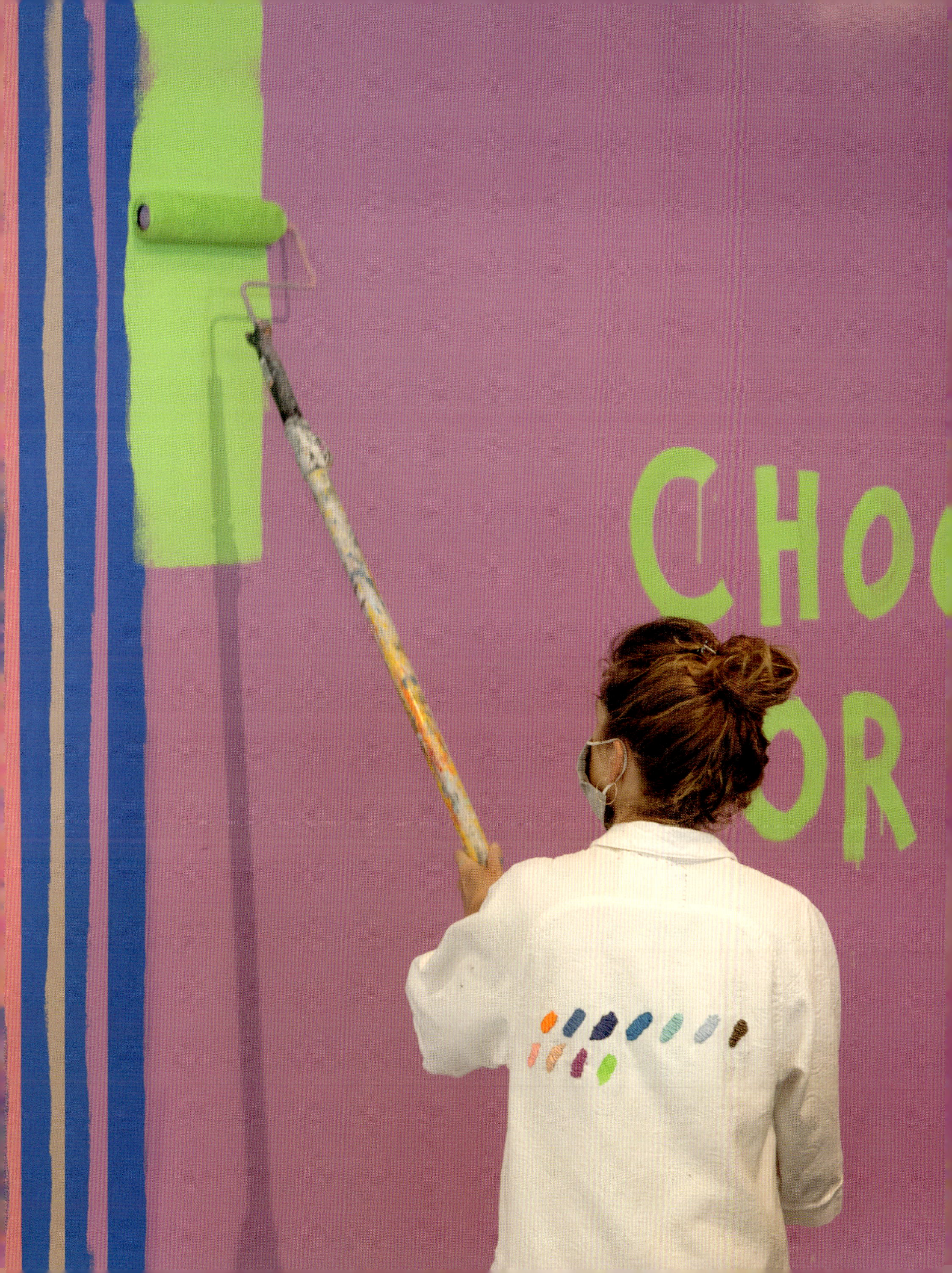

Hot Pink for Susan

Leah Rosenberg

Happiness Is . . . (2013)

Susan O'Malley and I talked about happiness a lot. What it means. How to get it. How to give it. We struggled with it and realized that the clumsy and surprising space of pursuing happiness was what interested us the most. Susan wrote, "It turns out that Yes! Happiness can be a burst of elation, but it is also a journey, which includes everything from falling in love to falling in something you love."

Our happiness conversations began in earnest when the Montalvo Arts Center invited Susan, Christine Wong Yap, and me to explore the question "How do we cultivate happiness?" We called it *Happiness Is . . .*, an exhibition and public program that invited artists and audiences to explore happiness not as an endpoint but as an ongoing practice.

The exhibition extended out onto the Montalvo grounds with *A Healing Walk*, which featured happiness-affirming signage and colorful walking sticks. For many of her projects, Susan talked to people about ideas: happiness, healing, advice. She always reached out to include people; her heart just invited people in. At one point she turned to Craigslist to find people to interview. "What does healing mean to you?" she asked. One man described healing as the color purple.

Page 177: Leah Rosenberg painting *Day 11: Choose a Bright Color for Your Front Door* from *Getting Better Everyday a Color*, San Francisco Museum of Modern Art, 2021

Opposite: *A Space for You* by Susan O'Malley, from *Happiness Is . . .*, Montalvo Arts Center, Saratoga, California, 2013

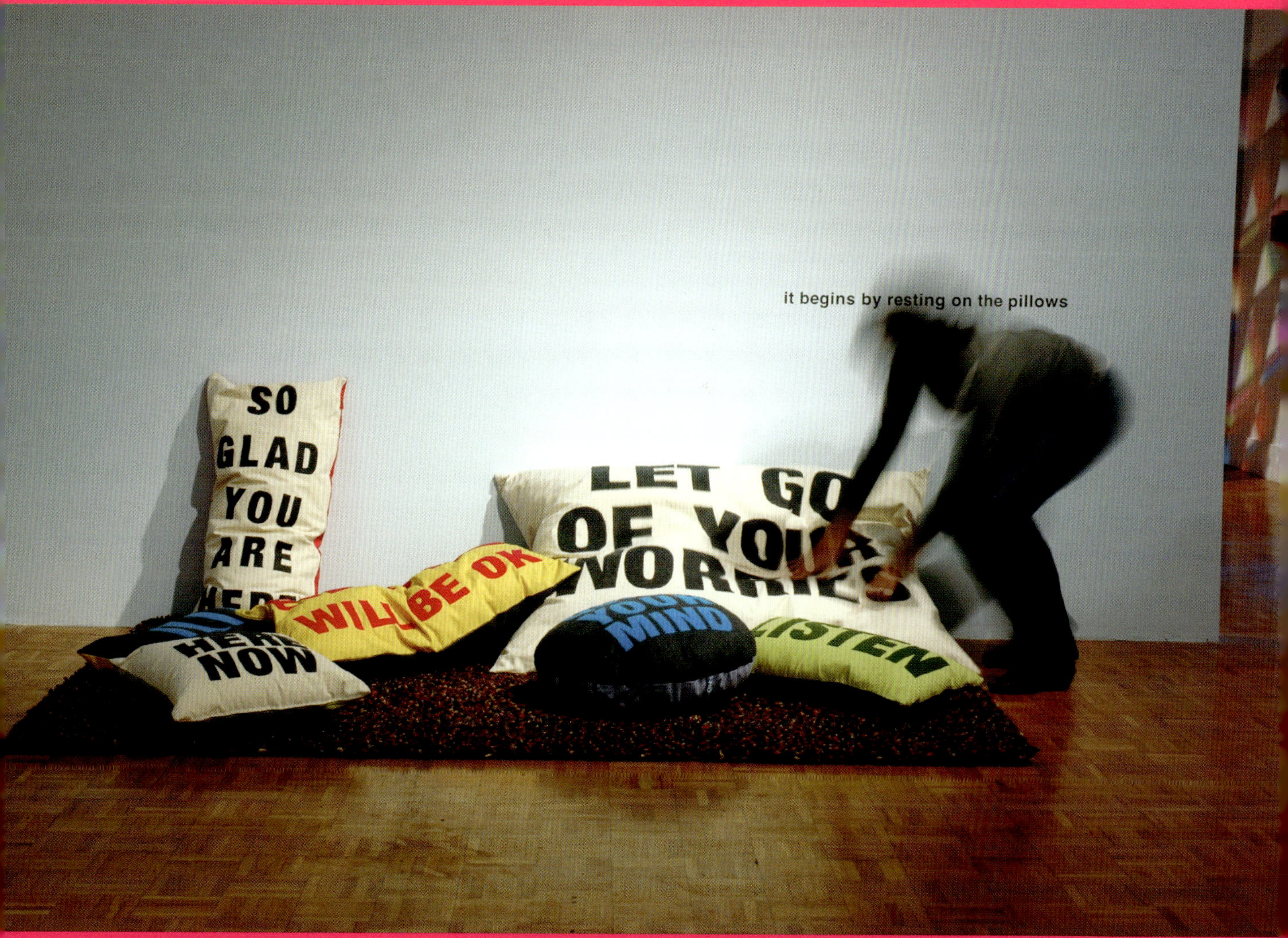

it begins by resting on the pillows

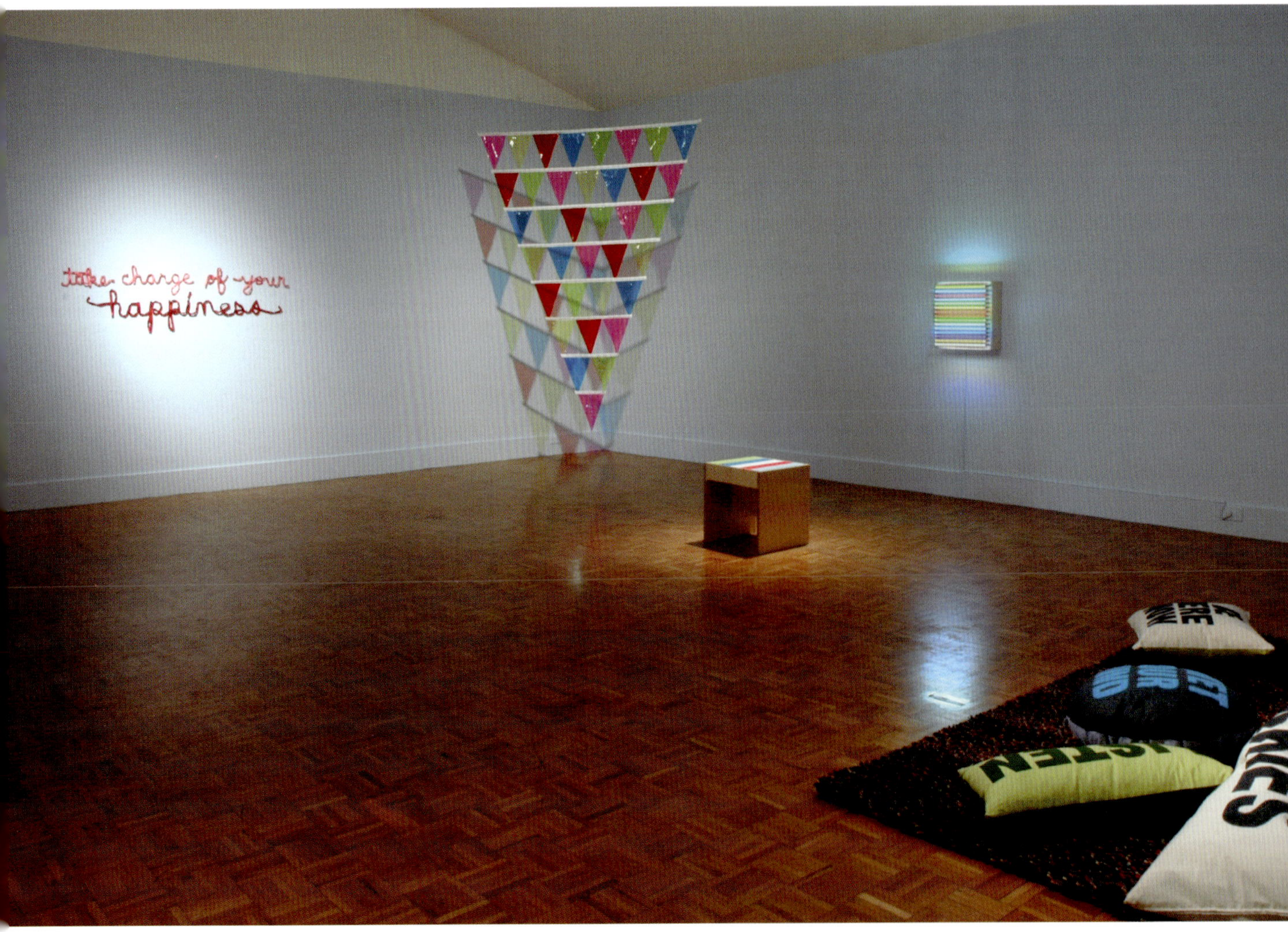

Above: *Take Charge of Your Happiness* and *MegaPennant* by Christine Wong Yap; *Striped Stool* and *Illuminated Stripes 1* by Leah Rosenberg; and *A Space for You* by Susan O'Malley from *Happiness Is . . .*, Montalvo Arts Center

Opposite: *Walking Sticks* by Leah Rosenberg, from *Happiness Is . . .*, Montalvo Arts Center

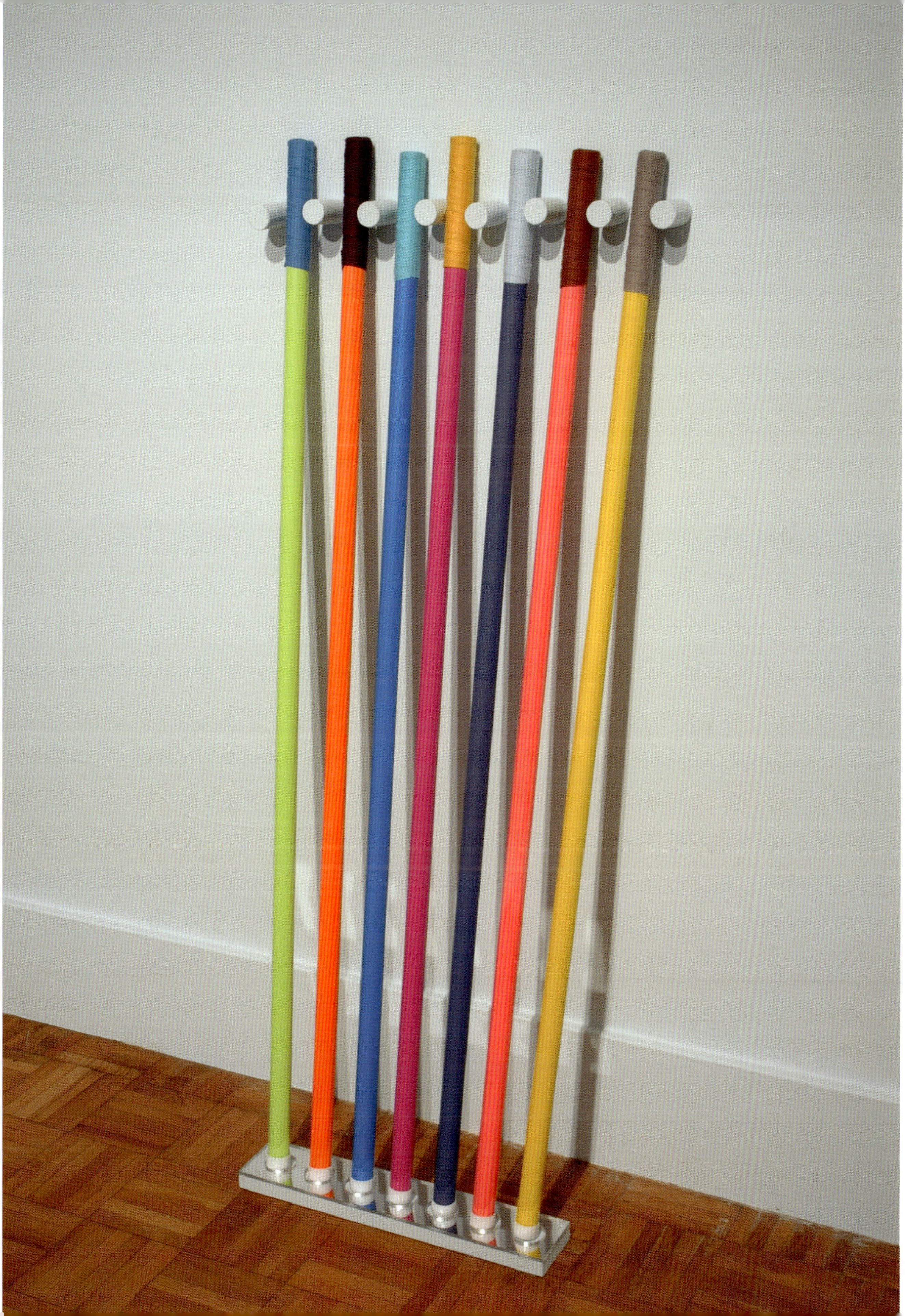

Getting Better Everyday (2013)

Susan made a list while thinking about various healing- and happiness-inducing actions in preparation for the *Happiness Is* . . . exhibition. Some are ideas she incorporated in her own life; others are exercises she borrowed from other artists, gurus, and friends. I keep this list from Susan's blog pinned to my studio wall.

Pages 183–85: *Getting Better Everyday* from susanomalley.org, 2013

GETTING BETTER EVERYDAY

- Breathe. Remember you can always return to your breath.
- Focus on your breath for one minute, then two minutes, then five minutes all the way up to 20 minutes. Do this everyday.
- Find a comfortable space and trust it for awhile.
- Take a walk.
- Surprise someone with a handmade gift.
- Throw a surprise party for someone you love.
- If you are stuck, turn on the music and dance.
- Write down three things you are grateful for at the end of the day. Do this for one week, a month, a year. Notice what happens.
- Lean up against a very tall building and let it support you.
- Lean up against a very tall tree and let it support you.
- Lean up against someone you love and let her support you.
- Think of all the people you love in the world, imagine each of their faces smiling at you one by one.
- Do not look at facebook for one day, then two days, then an entire week
- Make lunch for a friend and include a note written on a napkin.
- Call a dear friend you haven't heard from in a long time.
- Call your best friend on a regular basis.
- Talk to a stranger.
- Join a club or start one of your own.
- Take a class on something you know nothing about.

- Teach a class on a subject you are passionate about or want to learn more about.
- Check out books at the library on subjects you've always wanted to learn about.
- Give yourself permission to write bad poetry and make bad art.
- Start a one-sentence daily journal.
- Make a cup of tea for someone else. Bring it to them without them even asking for it.
- Give your money away.
- When someone compliments you on something that you have (your sweater, your earrings etc), give it to her.
- Invite friends over and make a big pot of soup to share with them.
- Have a dinner party with friends and eat in a circle on the floor (with plenty of pillows etc).
- Eat your meal outside.
- When you eat fruits and vegetables, thank yourself for being kind to your body.
- Raise your arms up as high as you can. Pretend you are a redwood tree.
- Give your belly a gentle massage at the end of the day.
- Close your eyes and smile for at least one minute. Try doing this the first thing in the morning.
- Pretend you are 20 years older than you are today. Dress like that person pretend you are her for an entire day.
- Drink a glass of water for 15 minutes and do nothing else.
- Write a hand written letter to someone who lives far away from you but you think of often.
- Notice the things that you enjoy doing. Then make sure you do those things every day.
- Smile at three people during the day.
- Every morning commit yourself to being kind to yourself and to others.
- When in line at the market, focus on your breathing instead of looking at trashy magazines.

- Make a poster with an inspiring story or phrase on it. Hang it somewhere in public for others to feel inspired too.
- Take a walk during your lunch hour.
- Find a place – maybe it's a tree, a building, a lobby, a patch of grass – to leave your worries. Go there every day and let go of your worries.
- Give away things you have that you don't use to someone who will appreciate it.
- Use your nice things every day, don't just save them only for "special" occasions.
- Find time everyday to sit on the floor.
- Lie down on the floor and try to imagine your body sinking down. Do this for at least 10 minutes.
- Describe a beautiful place or event to someone who is no longer here.
- Revisit your favorite thing to do when you were 8 years old.
- Swim in an open body of water.
- Cultivate a simple daily practice that reflects something you love to do.
- Hold a baby until she falls asleep.
- Watch something grow.
- Keep track of all the movies that really make you laugh. Revisit when necessary.
- Take a nap.

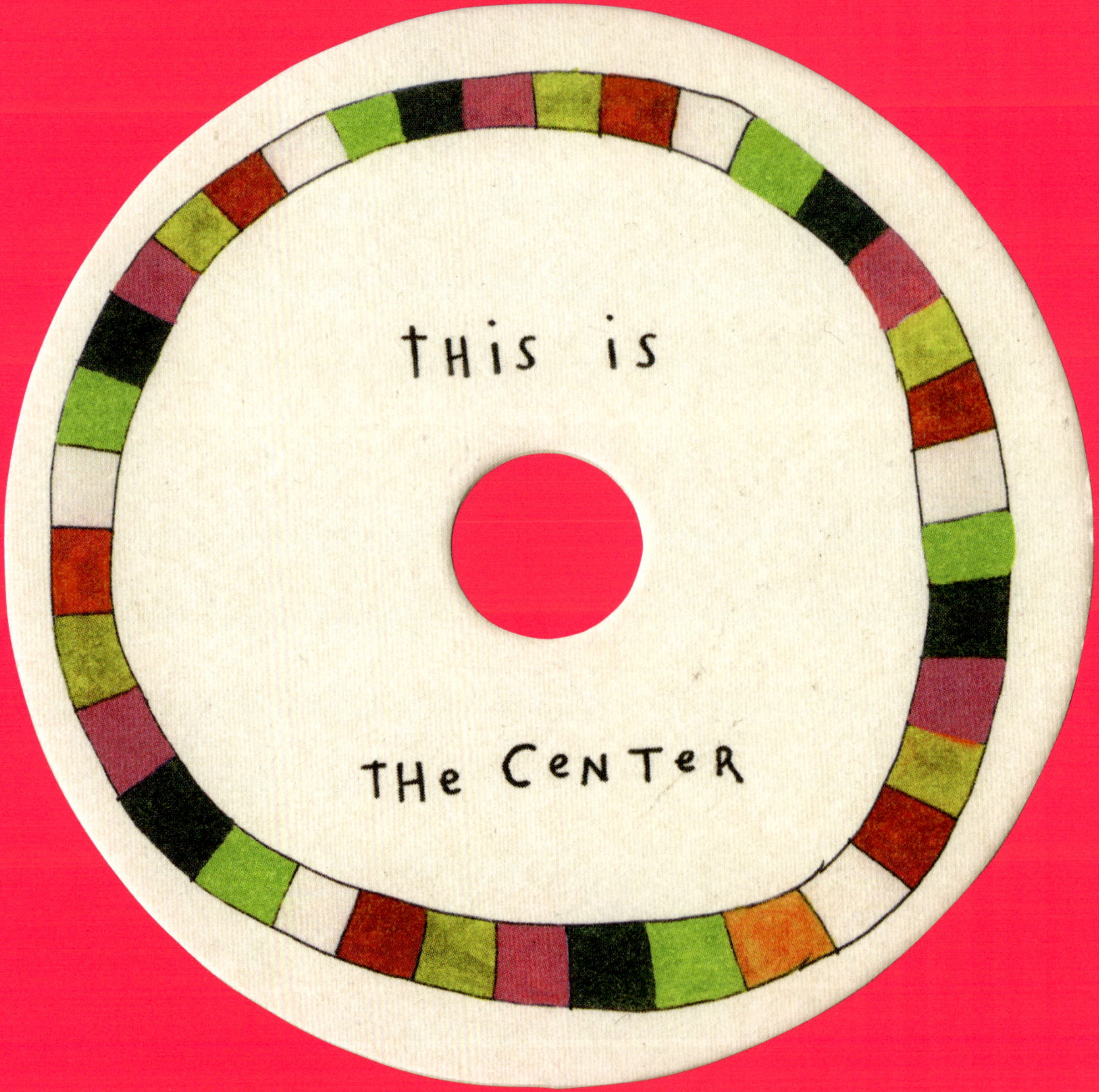
THIS IS
THE CENTER

Finding Your Center (2014)

Susan was one of my favorite collaborators. She knew how to keep things simple and silly while also making them deeply meaningful and connective. In 2014 we worked with the Montalvo Arts Center to create a project called *Finding Your Center* for the *Bay Area Now 7* show at the Yerba Buena Center for the Arts (YBCA). It was a weird, wonderful project: a self-help audio tour and sculptural installation that featured seven bright colors and Susan's guiding voice (she was channeling Scarlett Johansson) to lead visitors through the various exhibition spaces and architectural features within the institution. I loved the way she said the word *turquoise*.

But it was the color hot pink, in particular, that became a *thing* for us in the course of preparing for that show. It was what we would say when we thought an idea was good, when we needed to find "the sparkle" in our own center, or when we'd spot something inspiring. HOT. PINK. Those two words had a magic that could bring joy to any situation or get us back on track when we lost focus.

Opposite: *This Is the Center* takeaway by Leah Rosenberg from *Finding Your Center*, Yerba Buena Center for the Arts, San Francisco, 2014

Everyday, a Color (2015)

In February of 2015, Kelly Inouye contacted me about doing a three-month residency at her Irving Street storefront space in the Outer Sunset, a San Francisco neighborhood by Ocean Beach. I accepted with enthusiasm. I was looking for a place to work outside of my house, where I could create a new routine.

I visited the space and had a conversation with Kelly about the community that exists in the Outer Sunset and how the neighborhood is known for often being gray and foggy. It's a perfect environment for color to pop. I loved the idea of creating something that would change every day, so that people passing by—walking their dogs or on their way home—would be surprised to find that yesterday's "yellow like oxalis by the dunes" was now "lime green like the fence down the street." I imagined that the execution of this project would be a solitary one, even though the entire process would be visible through the large front windows. It would be about process, time, color, and the neighborhood.

Then, four days before I was set to begin, I lost my dear friend Susan, suddenly. Faced with an immense loss and a small white space, I painted the space hot pink, for Susan. Another good friend of Susan's, Christina, and her family came and helped. The space glowed. I left it that way throughout the following week. Painting the space felt like something good in a time when nothing else did. So I repeated the process forty-nine more times. Hot pink for Susan was the first color, and the forty-nine colors after that were a practice in living a life in color without her here.

I painted the space—the walls and furniture—a different color every day, a monochromatic tableau. I mined the environment for various shades: saffron from a sunset, lavender from a morning fog, powder blue from a serendipitous spill of Silly String on the sidewalk, and coral from a lone Converse sneaker sunbleached on the beach. *Everyday, a Color* was a durational performance, much like the observance of a Jewish mourning ritual, which provides somewhere to go, something to do, and ways of sanctifying time. The space became both a gathering place for friends and family of Susan's and a portrait of the neighborhood *for* the neighborhood. Over time I realized the project was all about presence: walking the avenues, collecting the colors, mixing the paint, painting the walls, and folding in personal encounters along the way.

It turns out that colors really do glow in the gray and the fog. But what makes hot pink glow is all the colors in its company. So, hot pink for Susan. And in the truest spirit of Susan, I pulled all the colors in, all the neighborhood in, all the care in. This collaboration with Susan became hot pink in collaboration with all the colors.

After applying fifty layers of paint over the course of the residency—leaving a stripe of the previous day's hue visible with each new layer—the plan was to paint the walls back to white at the residency's conclusion.

Opposite: *Day 1: Hot Pink (for Susan)* from *Everyday, a Color* by Leah Rosenberg, Irving Street Projects, San Francisco, 2015

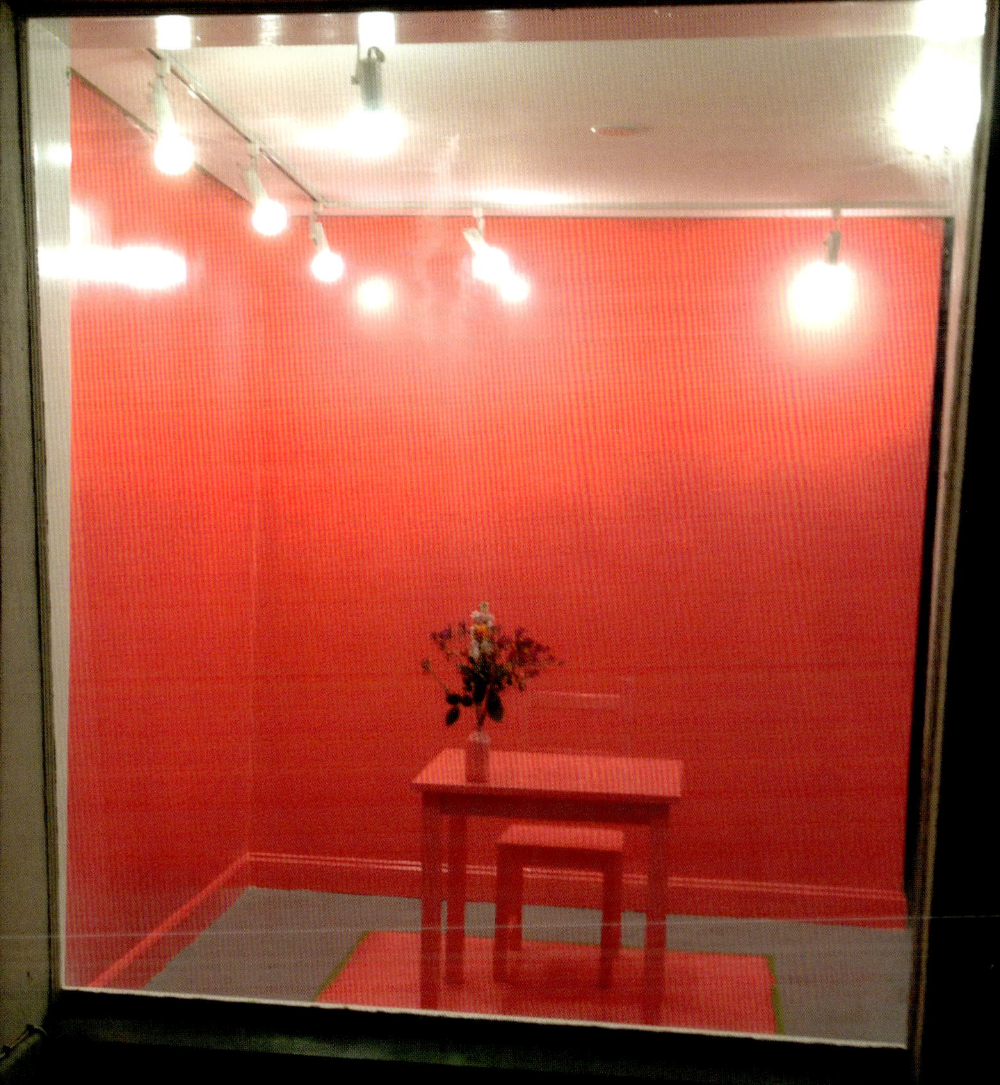

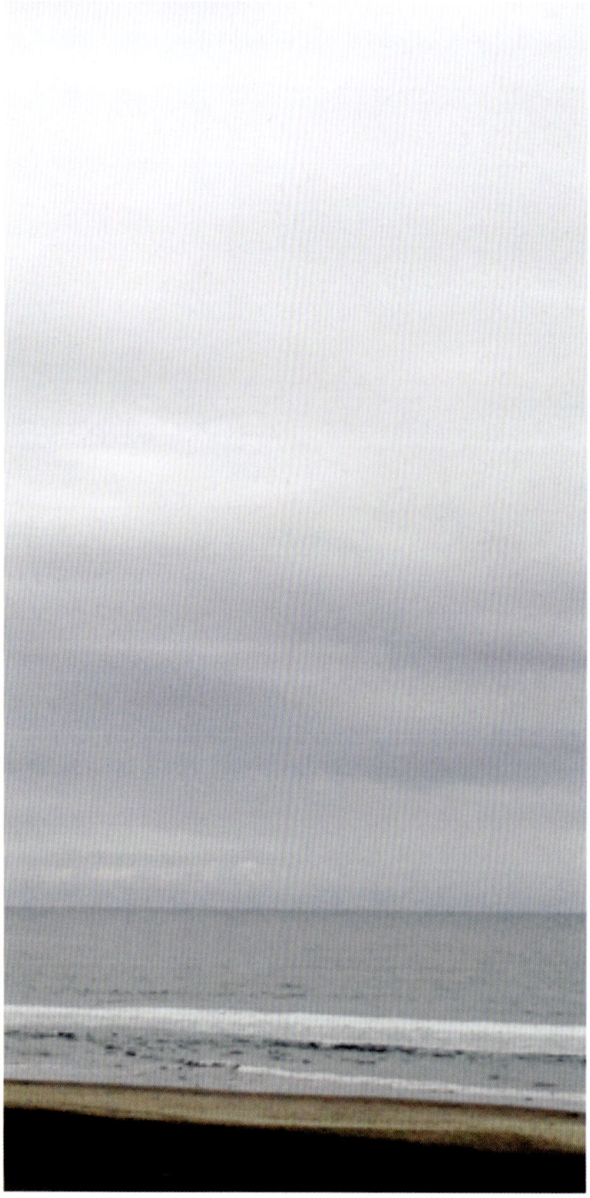

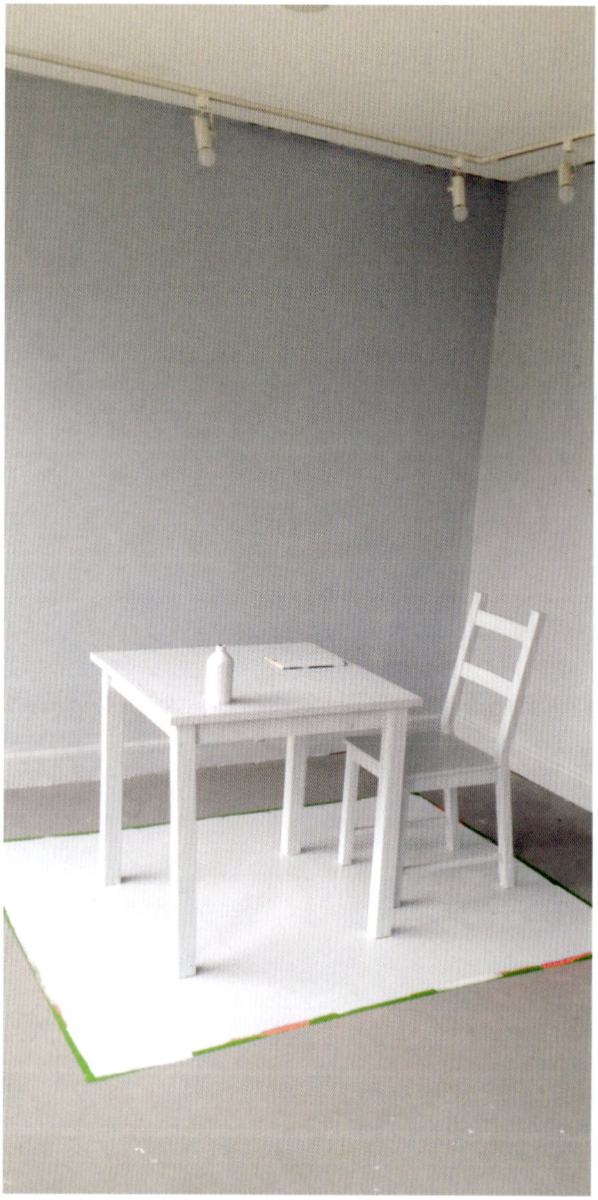

Above: *Day 2: Ocean Mist* from *Everyday, a Color* by Leah Rosenberg, Irving Street Projects

Opposite: Clockwise from top left: *Day 3: Yellow Oxalis, Day 4: Window Frame, Day 5: Lime Green Fence, Day 23: Echium* from *Everyday, a Color* by Leah Rosenberg, Irving Street Projects

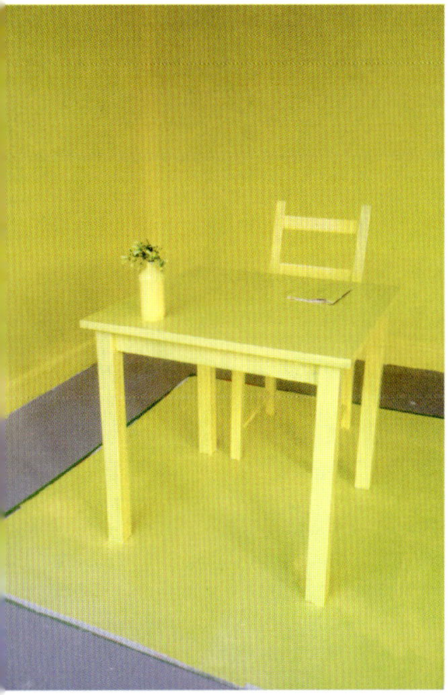
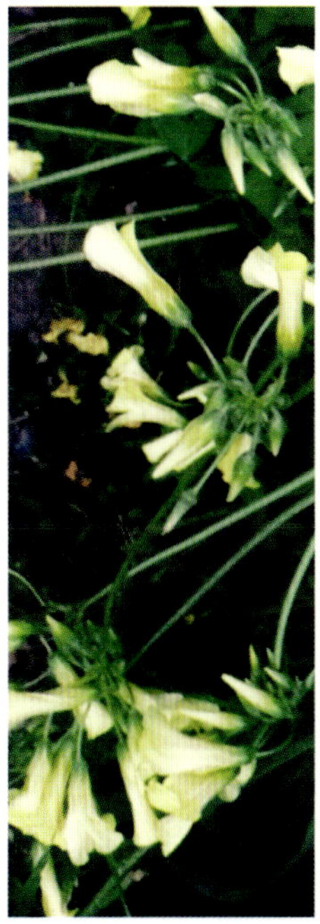
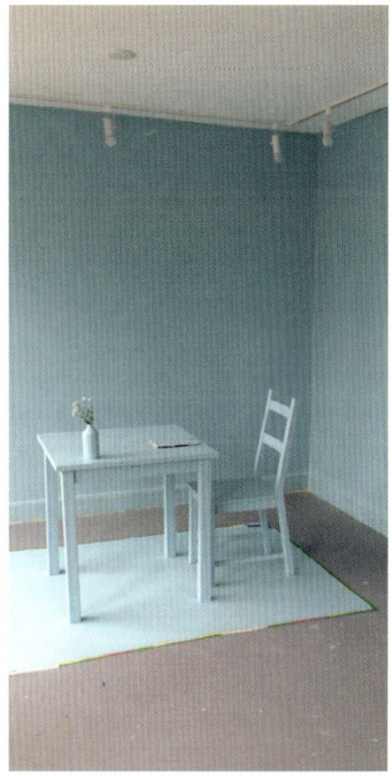
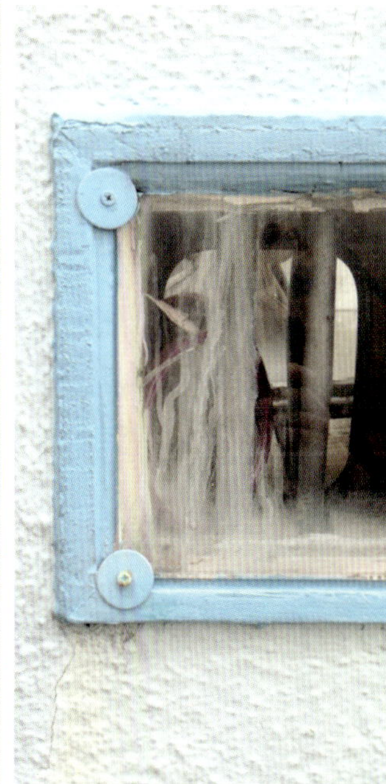
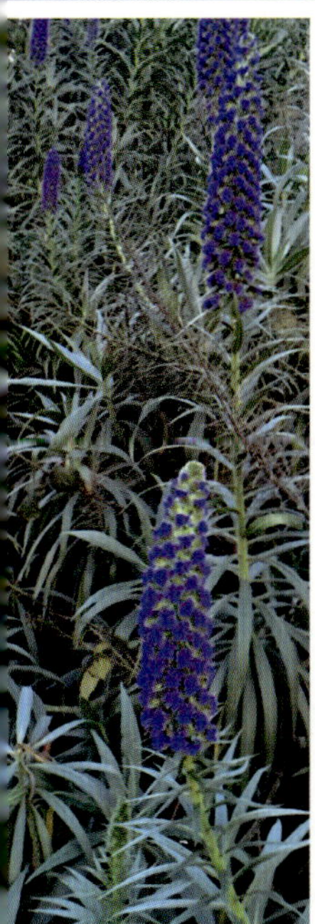
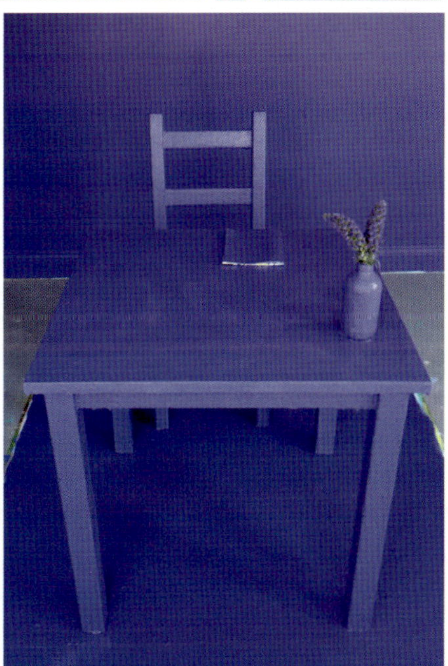
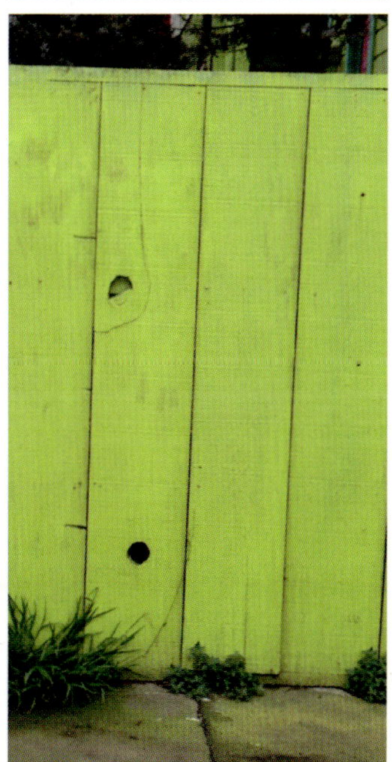
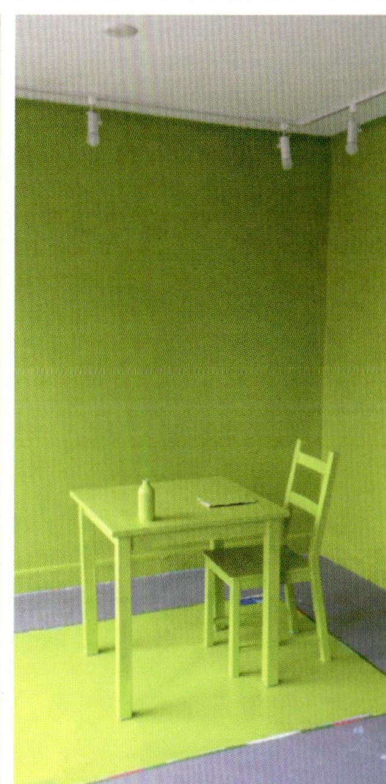

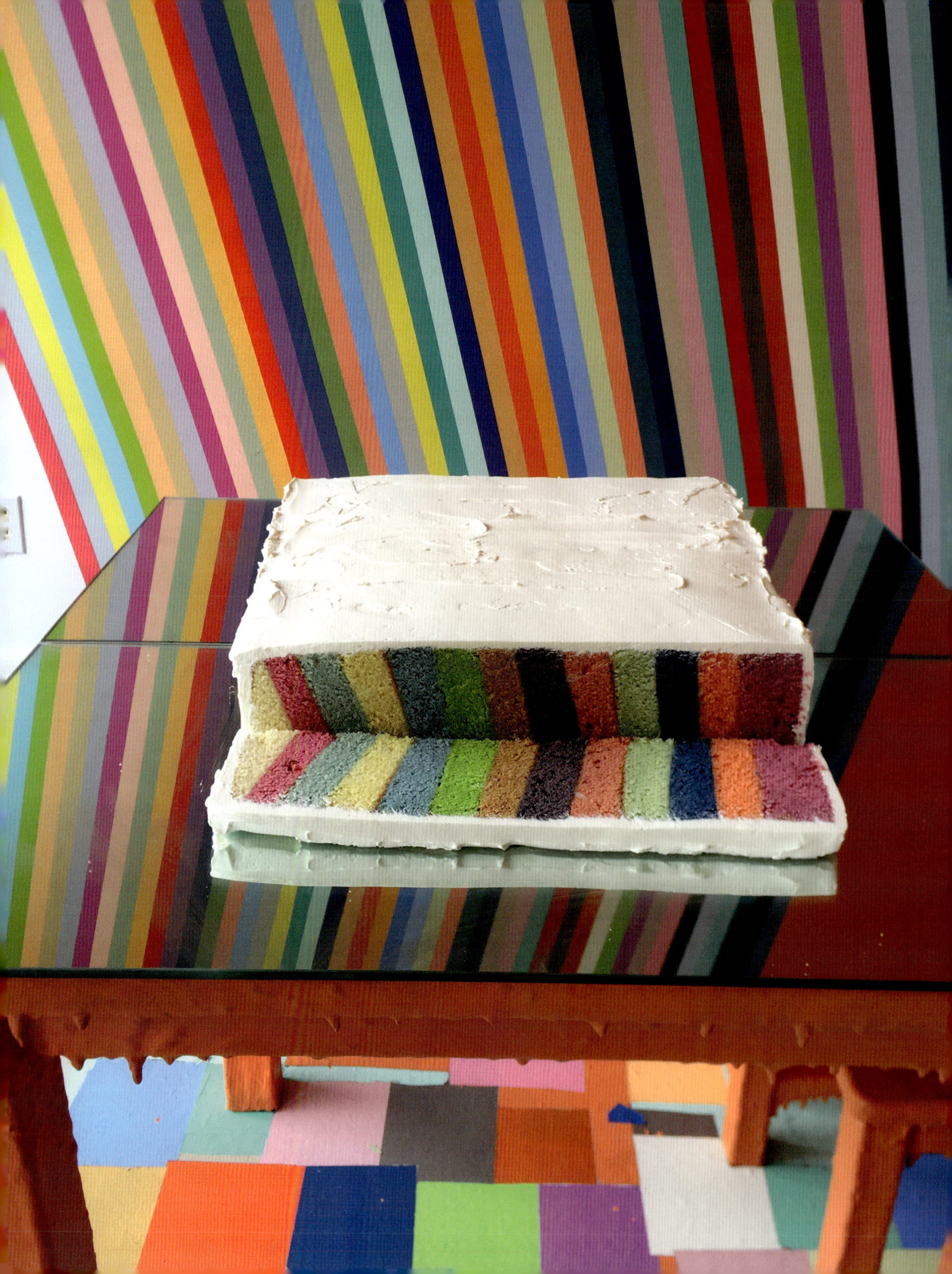

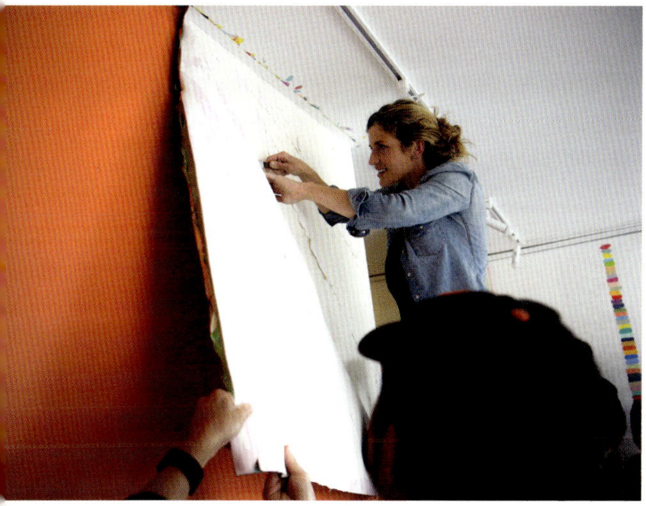

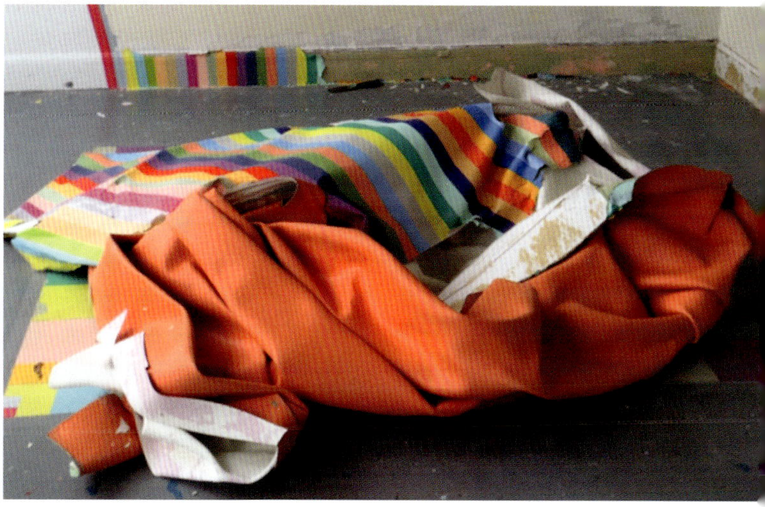

For a public program at the end of the residency, I invited visitors to help paint over all fifty layers. I made a cake for the occasion. The cake was frosted white but, when cut, revealed the same colored stripes as the ones on the wall. In the end, both the cake stripes and the wall stripes would be gone. But what made the eating of the cake and the painting of the wall memorable was a complete surprise. I was up on the ladder, guests down below ready with their paintbrushes. As I peeled off the painter's tape from the ceiling, the layers of paint started to come off with it. By some twist of fate, and with a little coaxing with a cake spatula, the layers of paint peeled off the wall in a massive sheet of color. The giant rolls of paint formed a relief of the space that I had gone to every day after Susan died. Only a single stripe of hot pink remained.

Opposite: *Everyday, a Color* cake for the end of the residency by Leah Rosenberg, Irving Street Projects

Above: Paint sheets from *Everyday, a Color,* which became *One Day at a Time* by Leah Rosenberg, San Francisco Museum of Modern Art, 2015

Getting Better Everyday a Color (2021)

Everyday, a Color evolved into another posthumous collaboration with Susan called *Getting Better Everyday a Color*. I returned to the palette and process from my residency at Irving Street Projects, this time in reverse and at SFMOMA. What was the first color there, hot pink for Susan, was the final color here.

It turned out that when the paint layers peeled off the wall at Irving Street Projects, the only color that remained was hot pink for Susan. Years later, I wanted to give the expansive color to her.

For the new project, it did not make sense to me to have the colors reference the Outer Sunset when I was painting a wall inside the museum. So much had happened since 2015, and I wanted to acknowledge the additional loss and grief associated with the pandemic, shifting politics, the climate crisis, and the art world in general. What would Susan be making at this time in the face of it all? Once again I returned to Susan's list "Getting Better Everyday" in pursuit of happiness and healing. I amended the list to include some recent research and ideas expressed by artists on view at SFMOMA at the time in an attempt to acknowledge our continuous and collective need for healing.

Each day for fifty days, I put on my uniform and painted a phrase inspired by Susan's list in that day's color on top of the color from the previous day. Then I'd paint the whole thing over in that day's color. The phrase was then hand painted on a board, like a "now serving" deli sign, to the left of the mural, paired with a swatch of its corresponding color. The list grew longer as the paint layers accumulated. As I had turned to the everyday for my color palettes, I now turned to Susan's list, giving the colors new names that incorporated her spirit. Since viewers couldn't see the phrases, painted and covered every day, the sign board offered what began as a suggested practice for happiness and was now a color legend, or an ever-evolving healing poem for the times.

Opposite: Process photos for *Getting Better Everyday a Color* by Leah Rosenberg, San Francisco Museum of Modern Art, 2015

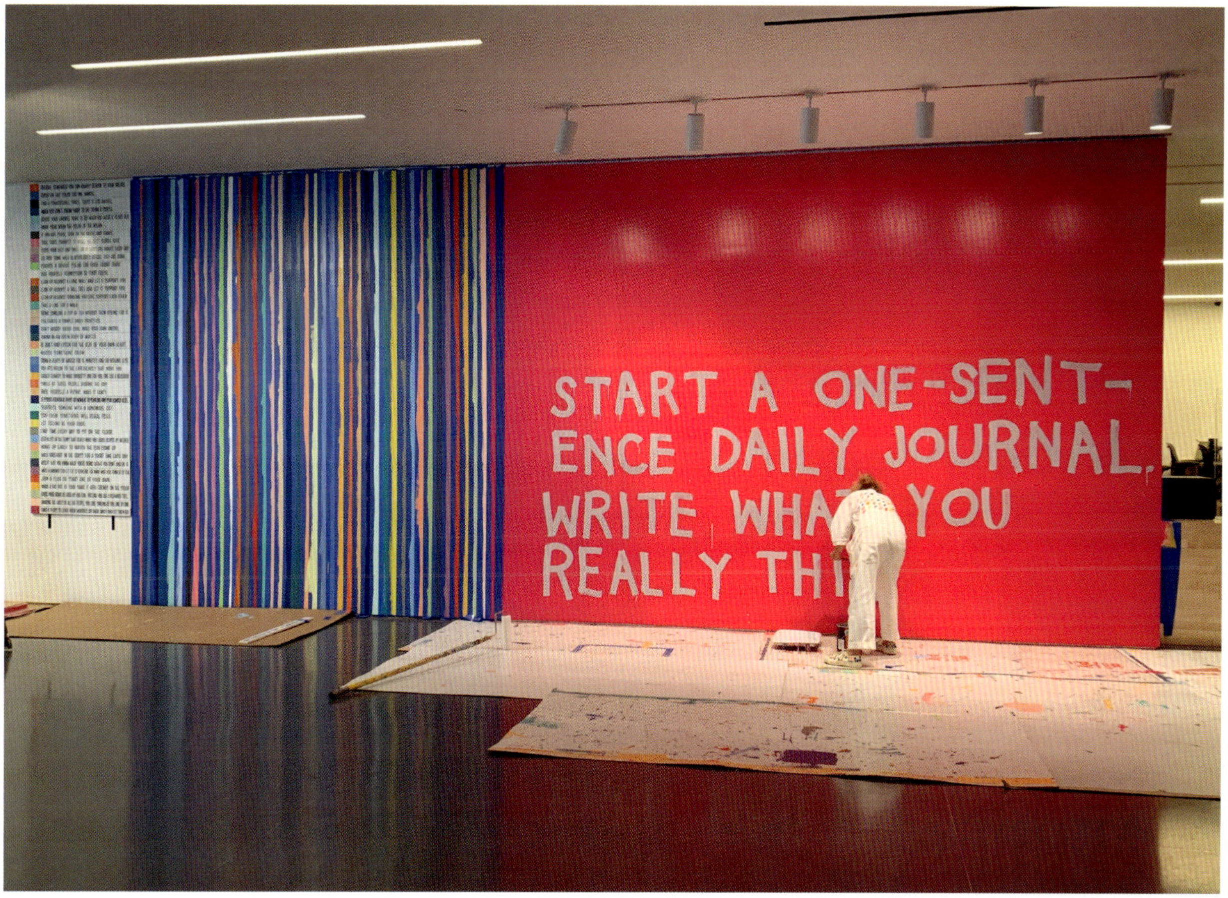
START A ONE-SENT-
ENCE DAILY JOURNAL.
WRITE WHA YOU
REALLY THI

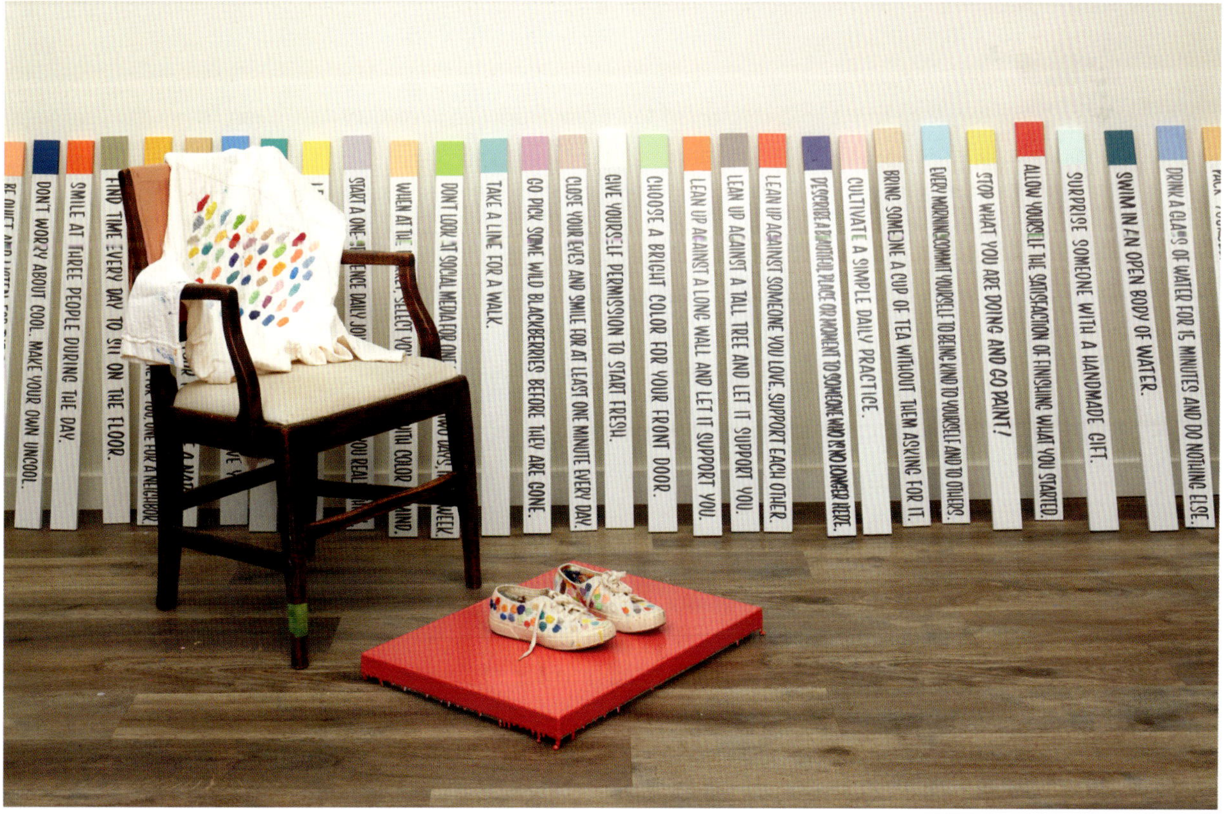
DON'T WORRY ABOUT COOL. MAKE YOUR OWN UNCOOL.
SMILE AT THREE PEOPLE DURING THE DAY.
TAKE A LINE FOR A WALK.
GO PICK SOME WILD BLACKBERRIES BEFORE THEY ARE GONE.
CLOSE YOUR EYES AND SMILE FOR AT LEAST ONE MINUTE EVERY DAY.
GIVE YOURSELF PERMISSION TO START FRESH.
CHOOSE A BRIGHT COLOR FOR YOUR FRONT DOOR.
LEAN UP AGAINST A LONG WALL AND LET IT SUPPORT YOU.
LEAN UP AGAINST A TALL TREE AND LET IT SUPPORT YOU.
LEAN UP AGAINST SOMEONE YOU LOVE. SUPPORT EACH OTHER.
CULTIVATE A SIMPLE DAILY PRACTICE.
BRING SOMEONE A CUP OF TEA WITHOUT THEM ASKING FOR IT.
STOP WHAT YOU ARE DOING AND GO PAINT!
ALLOW YOURSELF THE SATISFACTION OF FINISHING WHAT YOU STARTED.
SURPRISE SOMEONE WITH A HANDMADE GIFT.
SWIM IN AN OPEN BODY OF WATER.
DRINK A GLASS OF WATER FOR 15 MINUTES AND DO NOTHING ELSE.

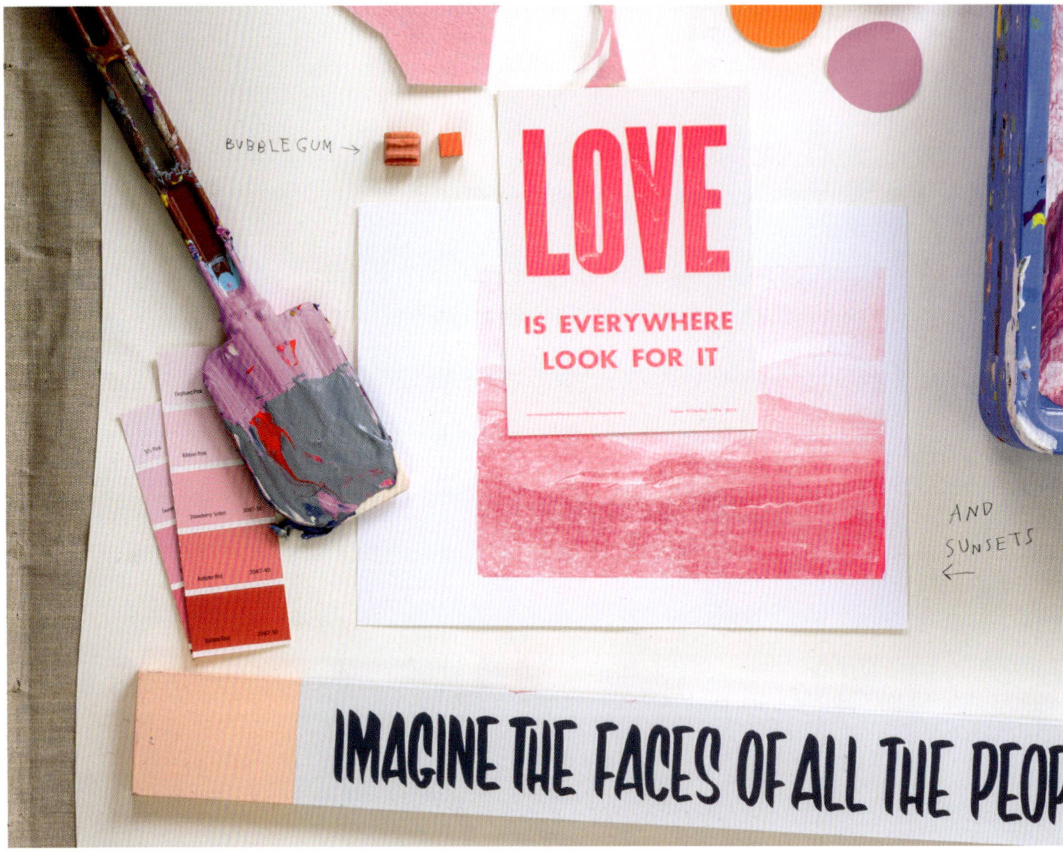
BUBBLEGUM →
LOVE
IS EVERYWHERE
LOOK FOR IT
AND SUNSETS ←
IMAGINE THE FACES OF ALL THE PEOP

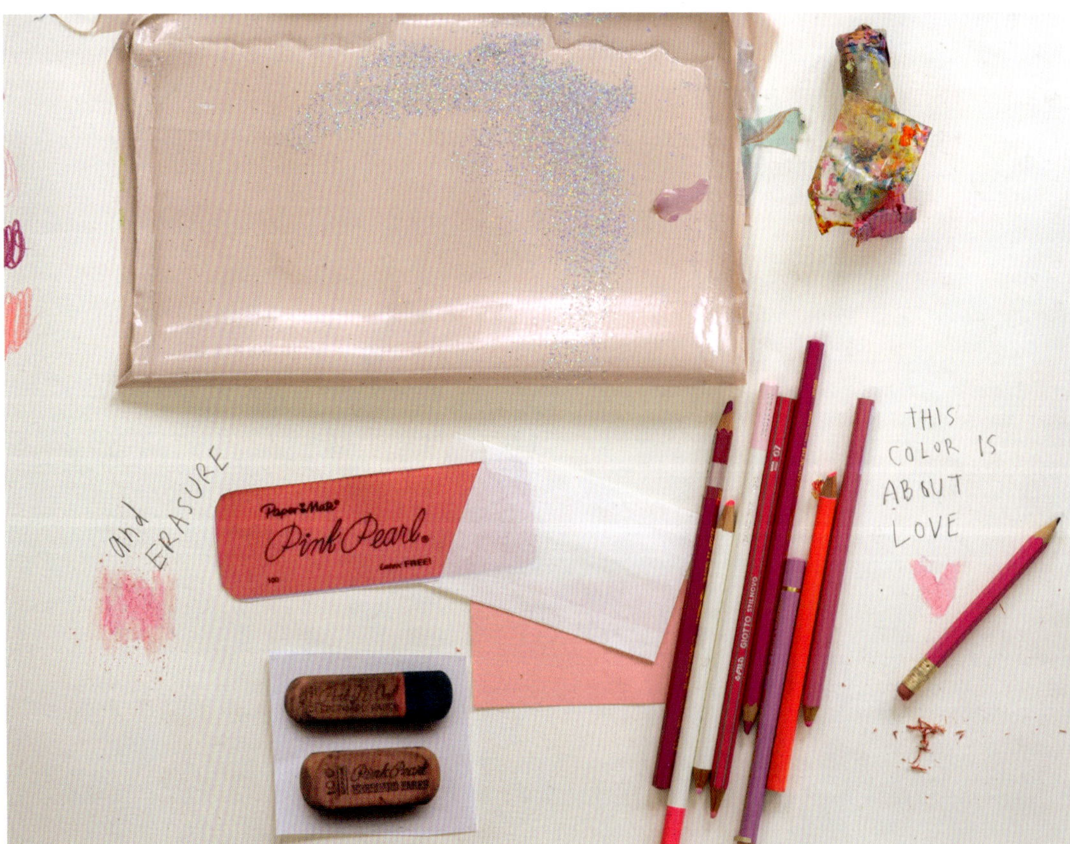
and ERASURE
Paper Mate
Pink Pearl
THIS COLOR IS ABOUT LOVE

Susan left us with wise words, good humor, great art, and an understanding of the serious benefits of stopping to ask questions and really listening to one other.

Susan is gone. But in a lot of ways, she's still here. Her mark is on the world, on us, on walls, in windows, in the pages of books. She continues to bring us endless joy and healing through her art. Her work charges us with the task of taking it all in, of noticing the beautiful things we encounter despite the horrible things, and then enjoying them to the fullest and sharing them with others.

Color is everywhere and always. I love it for its ability to hold different meanings, for different people, at different times. But to me, no matter what, hot pink will always be for Susan.

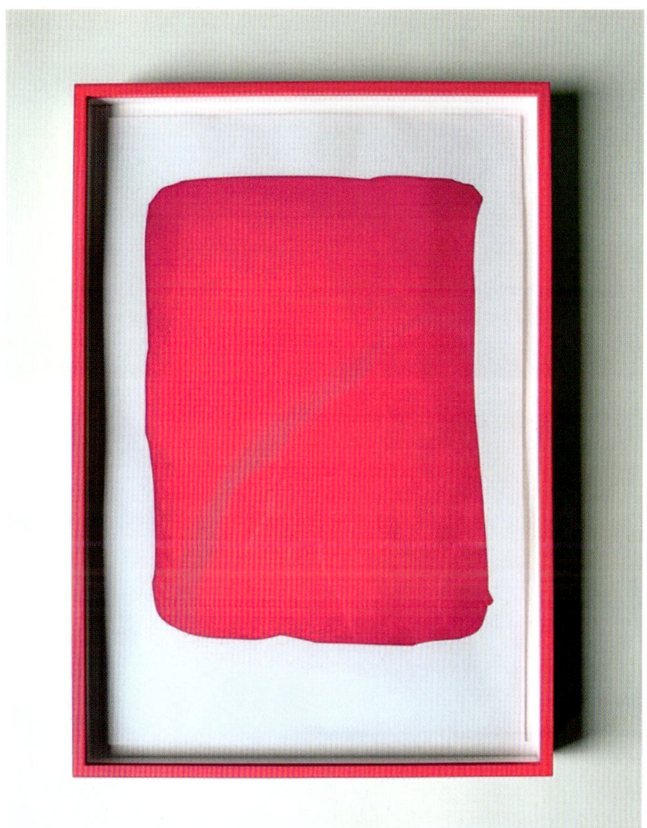

Opposite: Process photos for *Getting Better Everyday a Color* by Leah Rosenberg, San Francisco Museum of Modern Art, 2015

Above: *Hot Pink* silkscreen on paper from *Color Separation* series by Leah Rosenberg, Kala Art Institute, Berkeley, California, with custom frame by Small Works, San Francisco, 2016

The Hot Subway Air and Other Collaborations

Jonn Herschend

In the summer of 2014, I was working with Susan O'Malley on an installation inside Bedford Avenue station, a subway stop on the L line in Brooklyn. Her proposal was a simple series of texts that would be placed on each of the metal I beams that ran the length of the station. It was a lengthy process to get approvals from the MTA, but they liked the project and it was greenlit. When the installation was unveiled, however, we discovered that the MTA had decided to alter one of the lines from "the hot subway air" to "the hot summer air." Apparently they felt a reference to subway air might have negative connotations for riders who were experiencing that air. But instead of checking with Susan, someone at the MTA took it upon themselves to change the text on their own. It wasn't a major change, but this was a fairly large-scale installation with an artist who was precise about her words. When I realized what had happened, I reached out to Susan to explain the issue. I had worked with her quite a bit at that point, but I wasn't sure how she would react to this last-second institutional edit. I was braced for some disappointment from her. But instead she laughed and said that the project was now truly a collaborative conversation with the writers at the MTA.

The story and her reaction have stayed with me over the years. I've worked with a lot of artists, and Susan's response was rare. Most artists (myself included) are hyperprotective of their work, and with good reason. Every element of an artwork is considered and important. Editing art is just not something that happens. The artist usually presents their work as full and complete. Suggestions to change elements of a painting are usually met with hostility. Yet Susan's reaction was beautifully aligned with her approach to art, which was always about conversation and positivity. Her work is an invitation to participate in something larger than yourself, to catch people outside of the typical art constraints (such as museums and galleries) and engage people in ways that are infectious, funny, goofy, and beautiful. Ultimately, Susan asked viewers to become participants, which the MTA clearly took to heart.

When I first came across Susan and her work in the early 2000s, during San Francisco pre-tech boom, she was one of a handful of us who felt that art had become trapped in the tropes of institutions. We were excited about ways that art could engage audiences who didn't expect to find it. We wanted art to be ridiculous, funny, and beautiful, and far outside of the confines of galleries and museums. Artists like Jon Rubin, Lindsey White, and Heidi Hove were pushing art experiences into places like elder care facilities, comedy clubs, and commuter train stations. Susan wanted to democratize the art experience. She put art in vending machines; she and writer Christina Amini created the *Pep Talk Squad*; and she became the self-appointed artist-in-residence in a suburb of San Jose, modifying elements of front yards and rearranging lawn furniture.

In 2009 I was invited to organize a show in Houston with an artist space called Skydive, which was headquartered in an office building. I titled the show *Sisyphus Office* and decided to embed the artists in businesses around the city. I asked Susan to participate and assigned her to a Copy.com in a strip mall. At first, she wasn't sure exactly what she wanted to do, and her project evolved in conversations with the Copy.com staff. She decided that she would send the staff text files of slogans each day. They would then print these out as posters and arrange them in the shop's front window in order to offer "pep" to the customers of the Houston strip mall as they walked past.

The staff were so excited and became eager participants in Susan's work, arranging the posters in the window each morning. Her piece in the show was a massive hit. And when the exhibition came down, the Contemporary Arts Museum Houston asked if they could bring the exhibition inside their walls. But, in an even more interesting twist, in keeping with the idea that the work needed to be seen outside of normal institutions, Susan determined that the museum's administrative offices made the most sense as the place to display her posters. Museum visitors had a map of the show, which invited them to walk into the offices to view Susan's piece, as though this workplace were part of the gallery. The staff loved the show so much (in spite—or perhaps because—of the art viewers regularly walking through their office space) that they asked to keep some of the posters up in their office afterward. It was simple and radical at the same time. But people connected with her work immediately—just like they always have.

Inspired by the intensity of text-based artists like Jenny Holzer and the humor of artists like Lawrence Weiner and John Baldessari, Susan began to find other opportunities for producing text on billboards and posters. In 2012 she participated in the Art Moves Festival in Toruń, Poland, and worked with billboards for the first time. It was the turning point for her creatively. She suddenly realized the power that simple, bright colors and large-scale text have on the viewer/reader. It's a warm, open invitation to participate. Billboards and posters are the perfect vehicle for communication. They exist out in the world and are meant to be viewed. Artists have utilized posters for art, so this in itself was nothing new, but her work was also completely new and fresh: It was unabashedly positive and supportive . . . a celebration.

Art in general is considered a serious endeavor. An artist is seen as someone serious about their work. Humor and goofiness are a tough sell to larger institutions. Although I think a lot of that is changing, it's still safe to say that you won't find a lot of humor when you visit museums and galleries. There are exceptions for sure (William Wegman's dogs, Miranda July's sculptures, and anything by John Baldessari, for example). But Susan's text was the ultimate form of rebellion. It was positive, celebratory, and full of heart. A sentence on a billboard that asks you to consider something that will be more beautiful than you can ever imagine cannot simply be dismissed. Something solemn can be passed by, but something this full of life makes you look.

The amazing thing about text is that the viewer is involved in making the piece. Text is universal (as long as you can read the language). The reader becomes the collaborator, completing the meaningfulness of the words by interpreting them in their mind, which worked perfectly for Susan and her work. She wanted to catch us in places where we live our lives: the copy store, the subway, the office, the suburban street. And she wanted us to participate with her in the moment: to celebrate the liminal, to acknowledge the hot summer (or subway) air, to try to imagine things more beautiful than we can ever imagine. But the real beauty in all of this is that we (as the viewer) are bringing our own experiences and ideas to her words. So the MTA's collaboration really wasn't far off from what Susan wanted. She was setting in motion a collaboration that we would complete with her, starting a sentence and asking us to finish it.

Opposite: *Mantras for the Urban Dweller* from *The Thing Quarterly's* "Moment to Moment" installation, New York City Subway, 2013

Pages 202–3: *Mantras for the Urban Dweller (You've Been Here Before)* from *The Thing Quarterly's* "Moment to Moment" installation, Oxford Circus Underground Station, London, 2013

Pages 204–5: *Mantras for the Urban Dweller* from *The Thing Quarterly's* "Moment to Moment" installation, Los Angeles, 2013

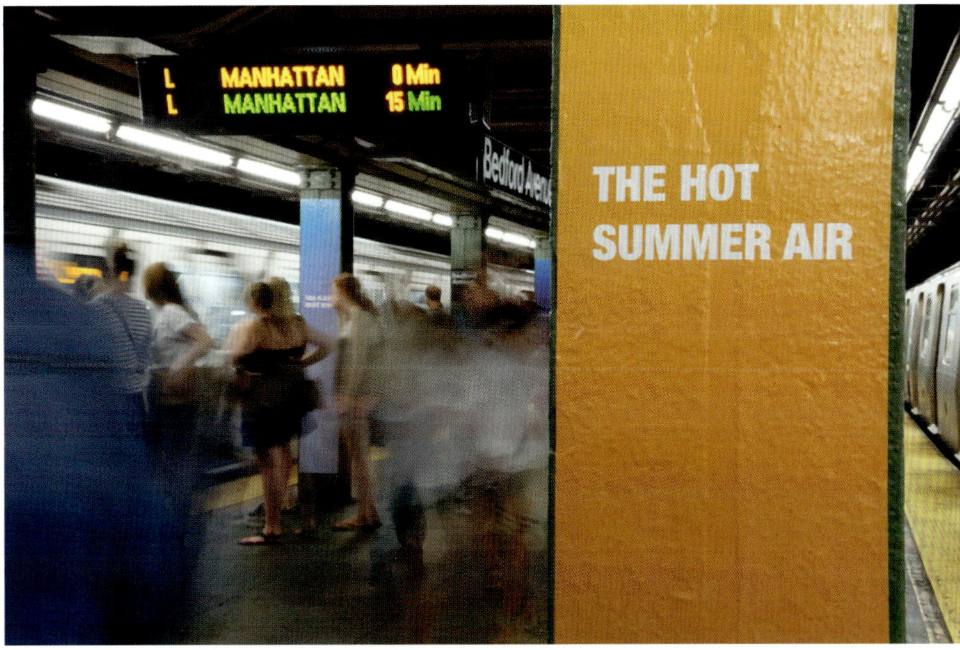
L MANHATTAN 0 Min
L MANHATTAN 15 Min
THE HOT
SUMMER AIR

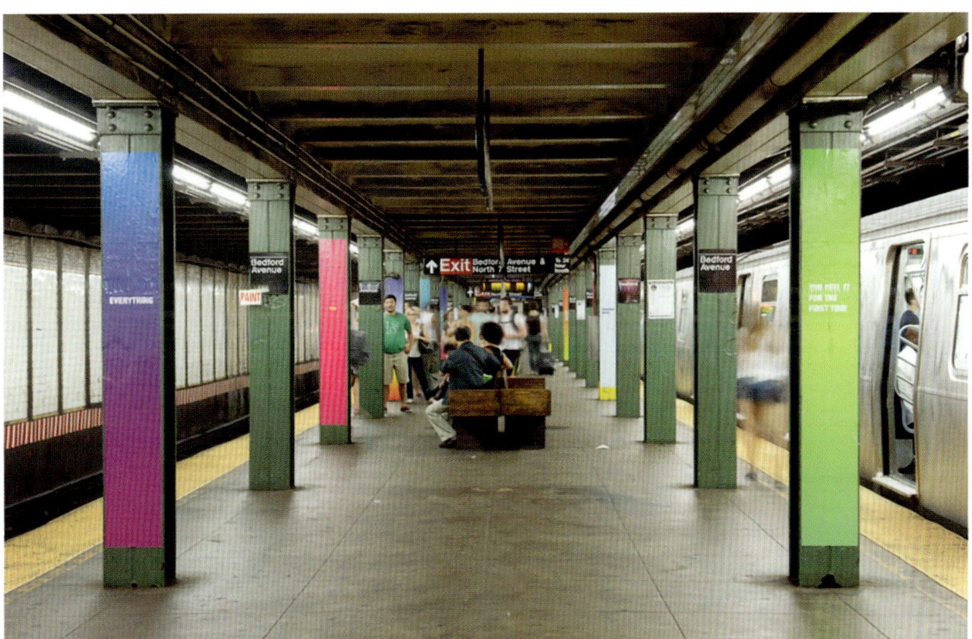
Bedford Avenue
EVERYTHING
PAINT
Exit Bedford Avenue & North 7 Street

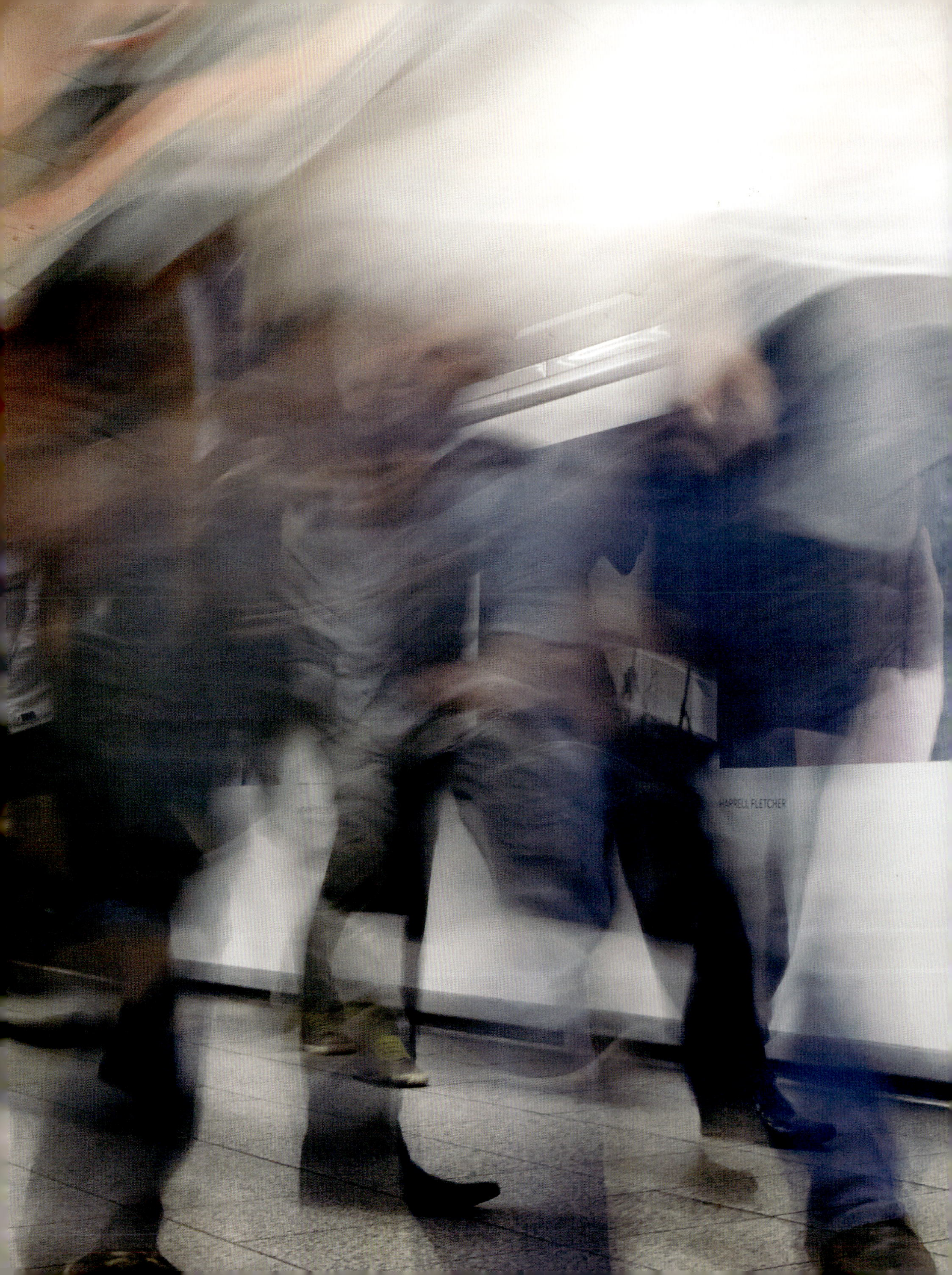
HARRELL FLETCHER

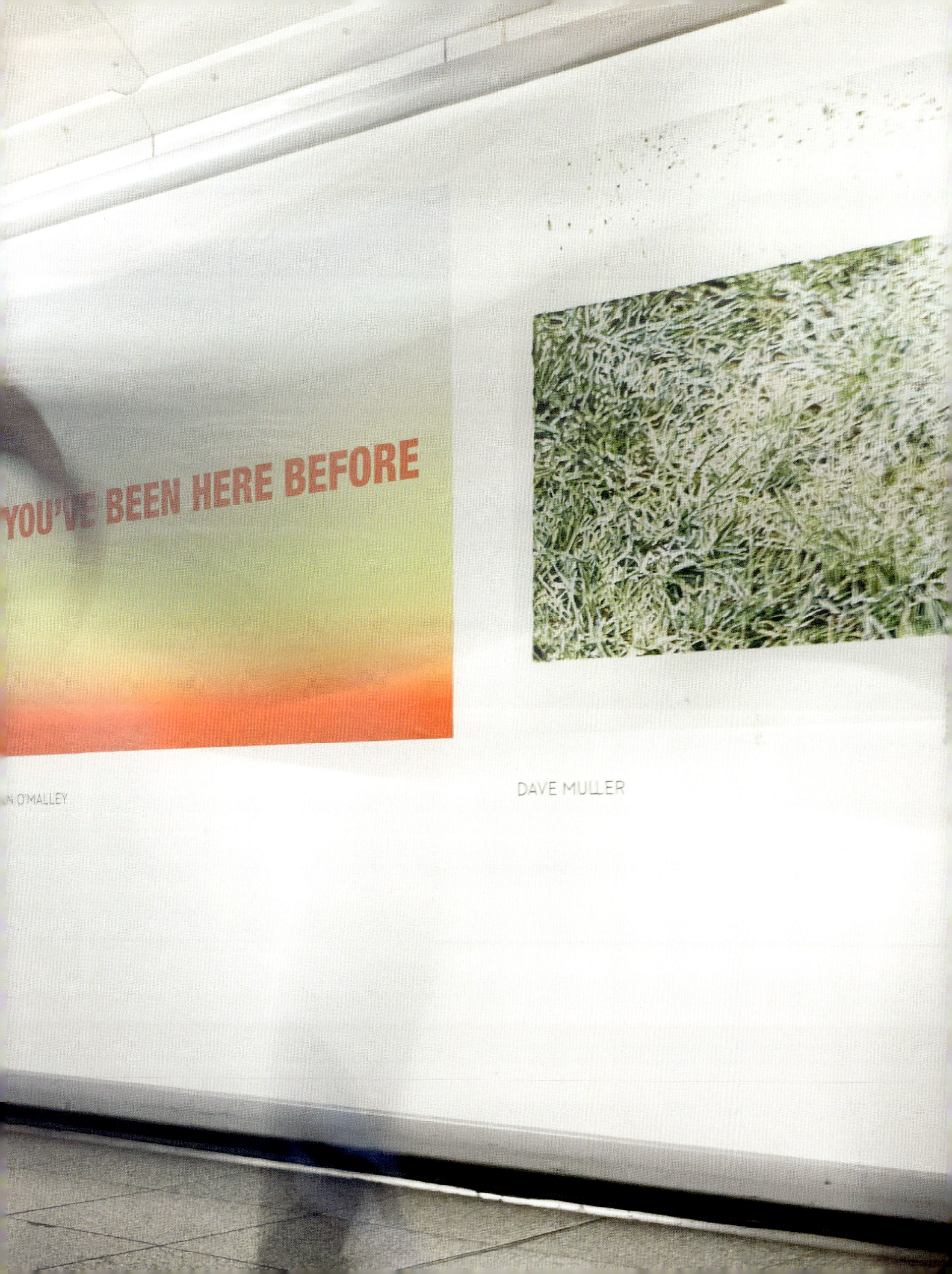
YOU'VE BEEN HERE BEFORE
N O'MALLEY
DAVE MULLER

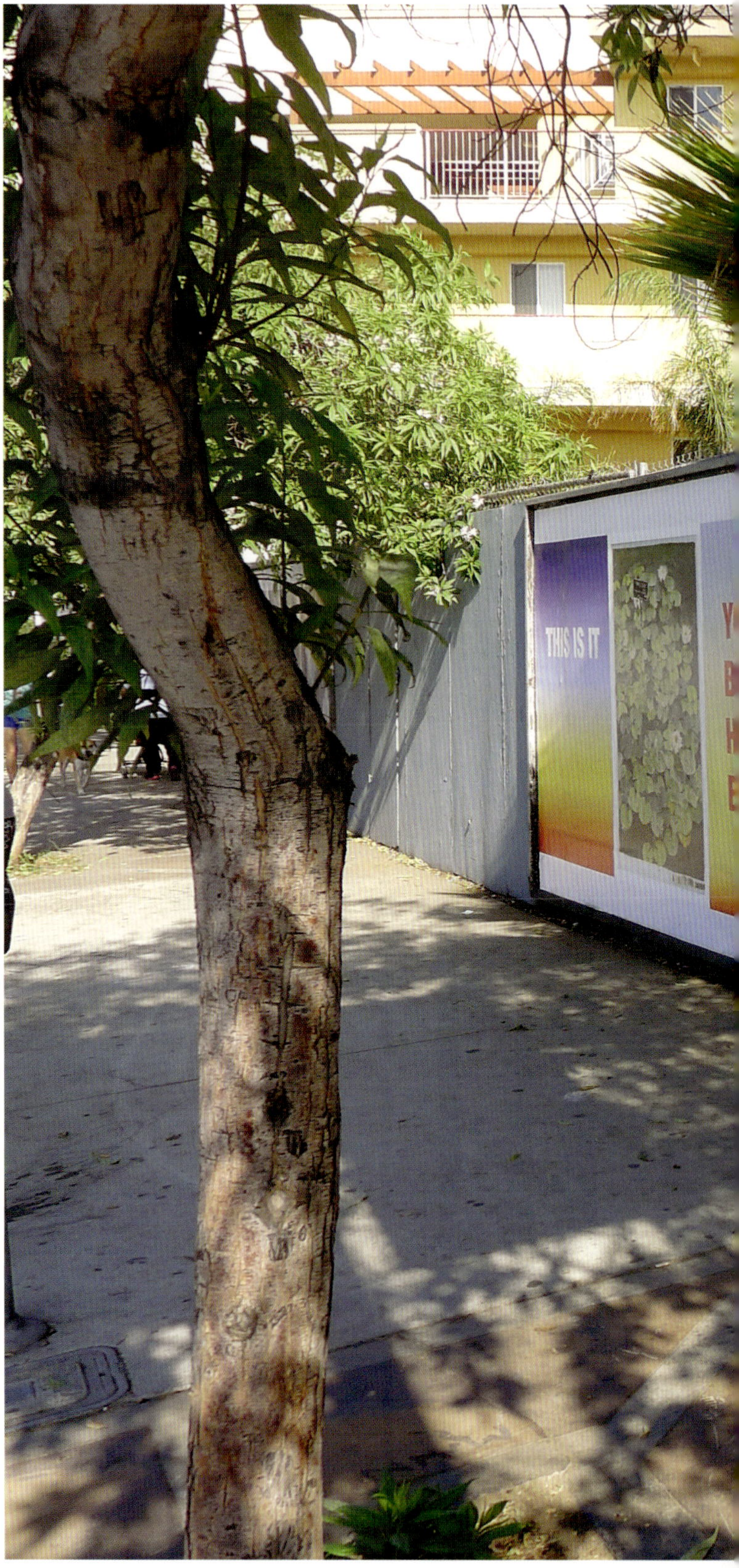
THIS IS IT

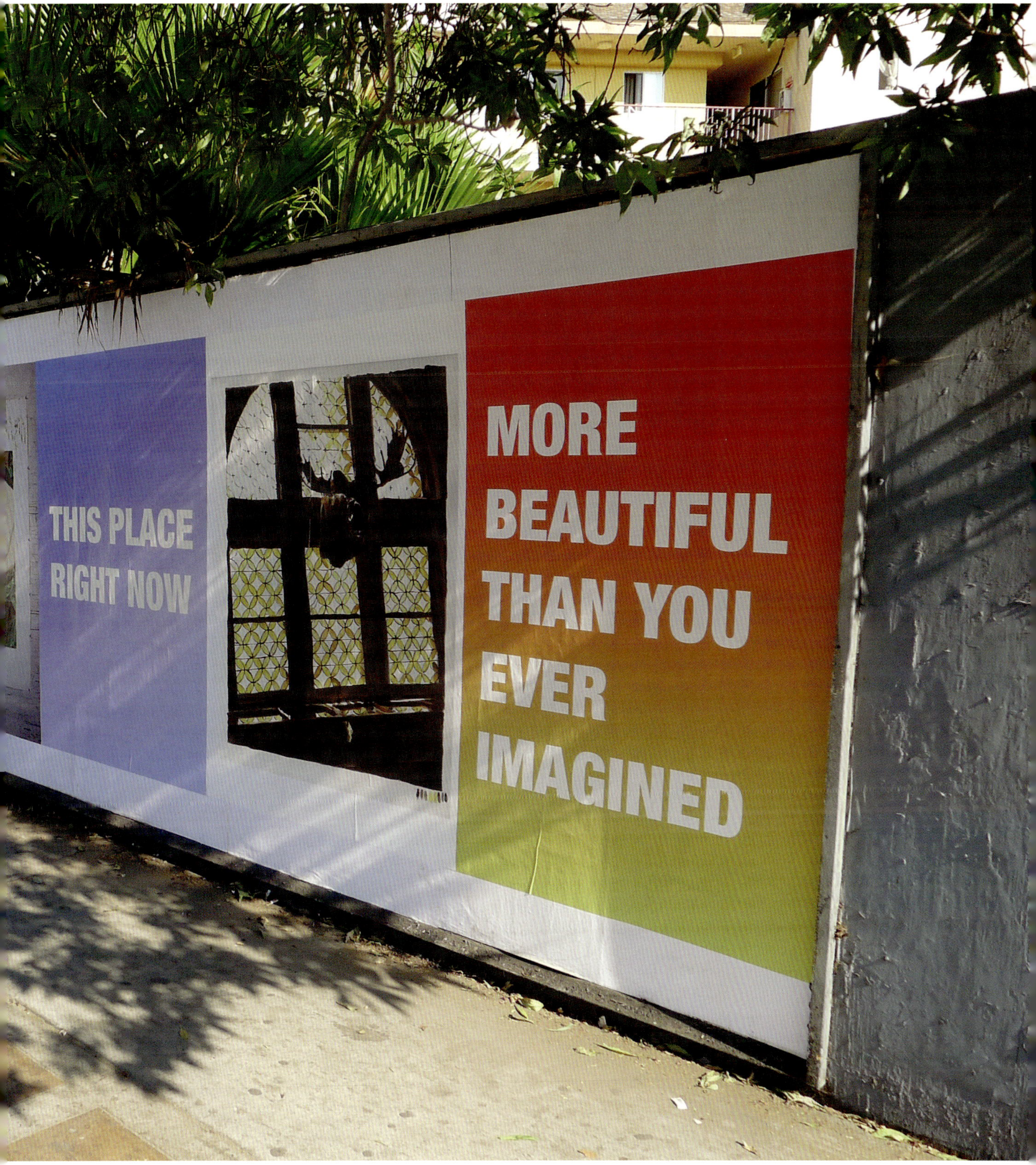
THIS PLACE
RIGHT NOW
MORE
BEAUTIFUL
THAN YOU
EVER
IMAGINED

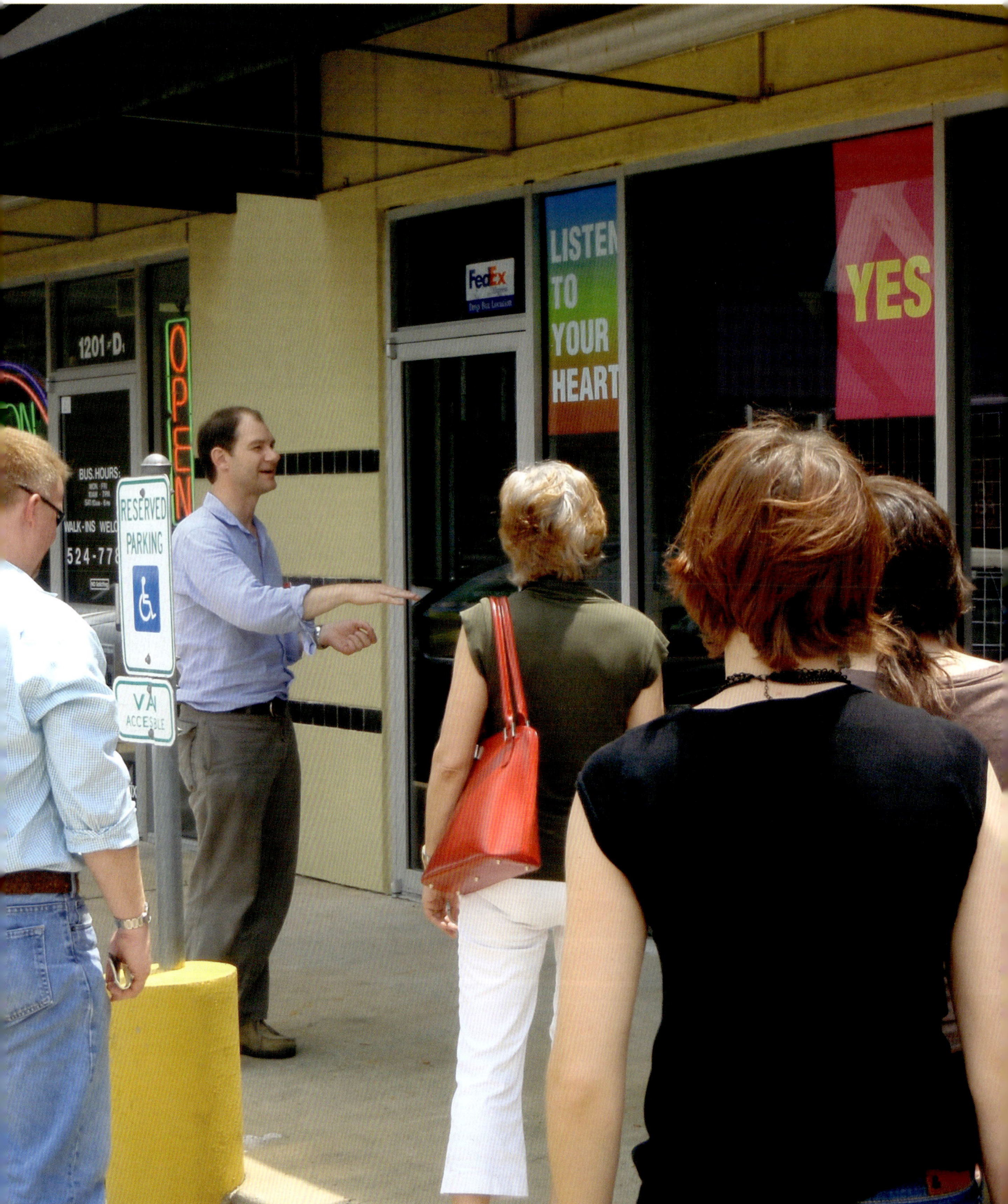

1201-D
OPEN
BUS. HOURS:
RESERVED PARKING
FedEx
LISTEN TO YOUR HEART
YES

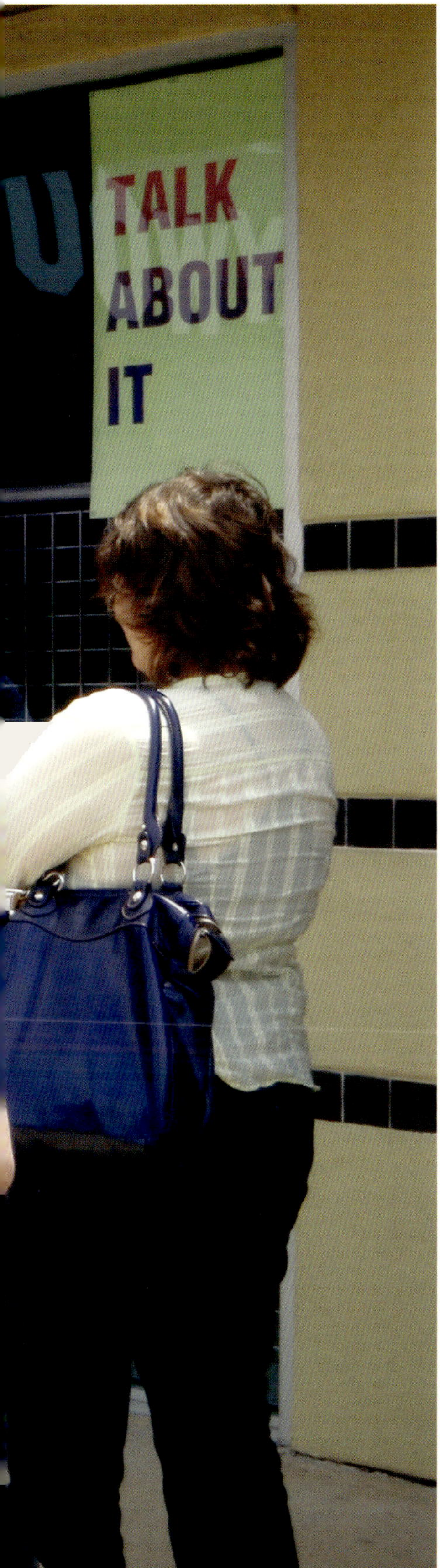

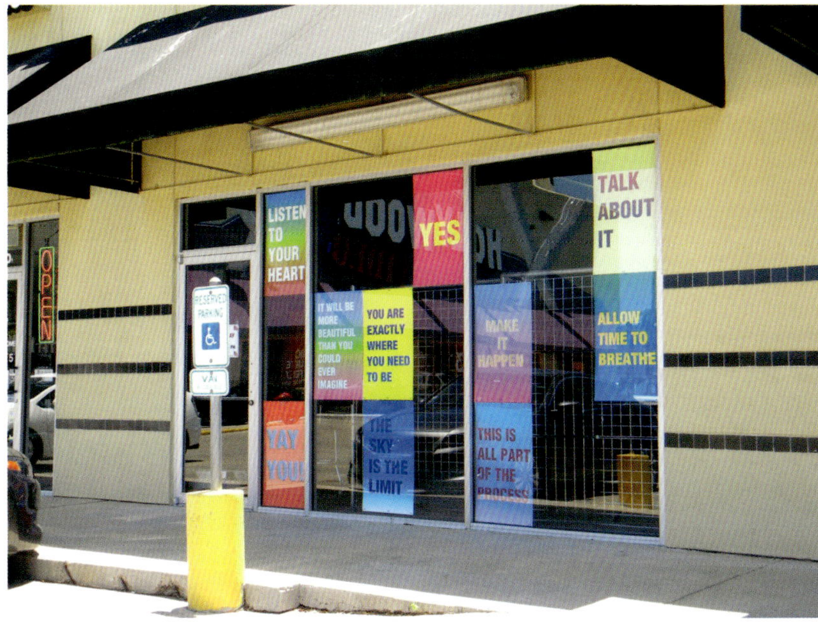

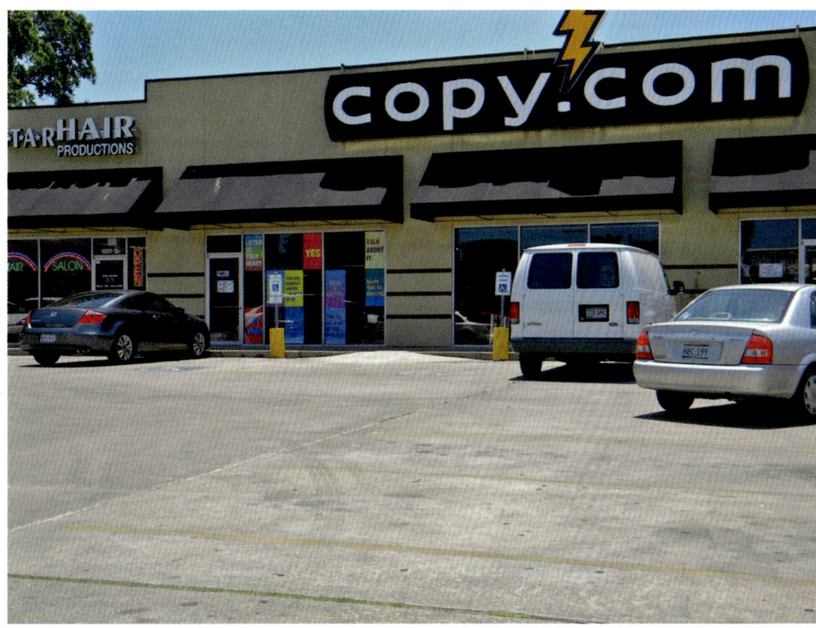

Opposite and above: Inspirational posters at Copy.com in *Sisyphus Office*, Houston, Texas, 2009

Pages 208–11: *Mantras for the Urban Dweller (This Is It)* and *Mantras for the Urban Dweller (More Beautiful Than You Ever Imagined)* from *The Thing Quarterly*'s "Moment to Moment" installation, San Francisco, 2013

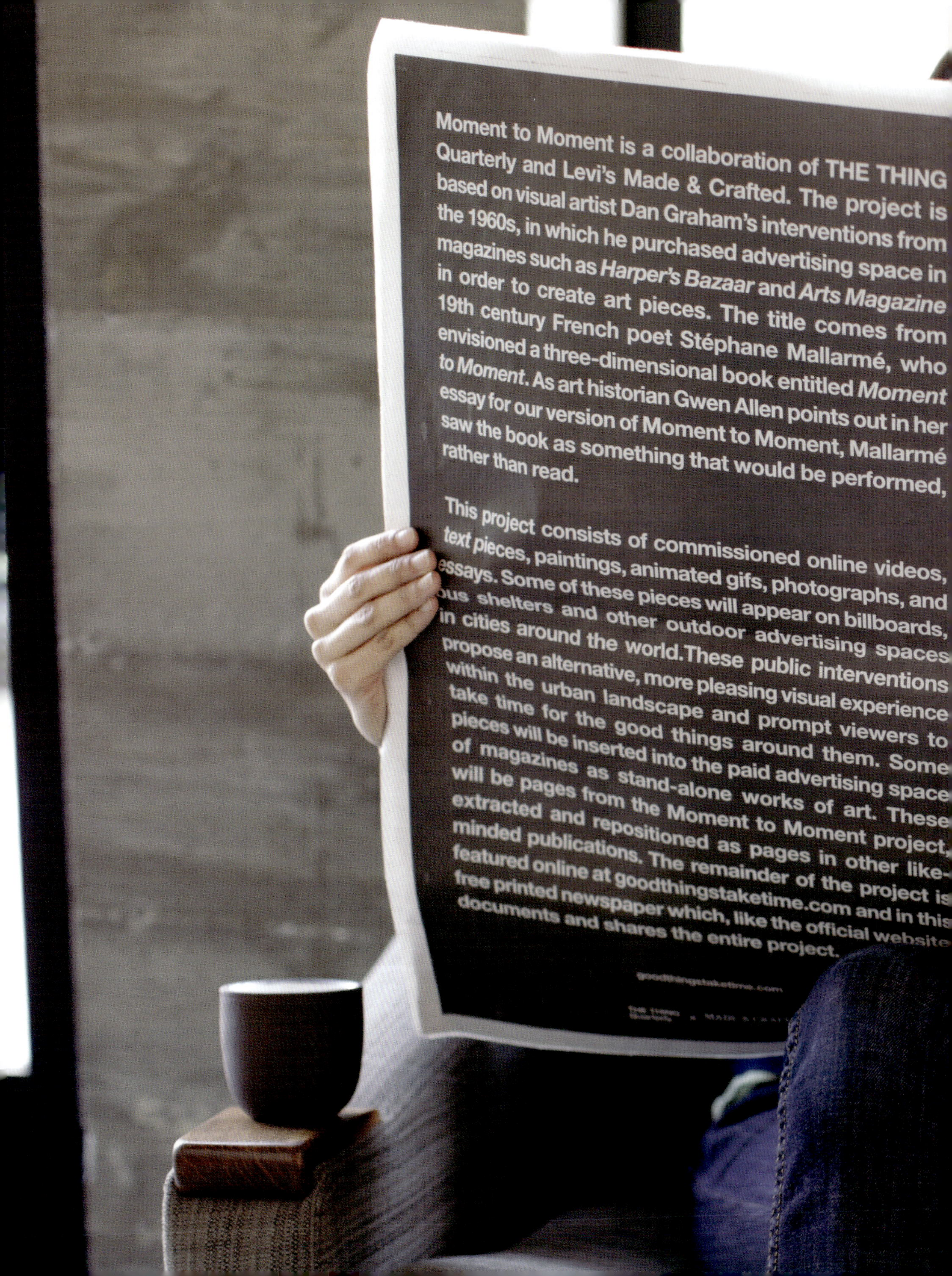
Moment to Moment is a collaboration of THE THING
Quarterly and Levi's Made & Crafted. The project is
based on visual artist Dan Graham's interventions from
the 1960s, in which he purchased advertising space in
magazines such as Harper's Bazaar and Arts Magazine
in order to create art pieces. The title comes from
19th century French poet Stéphane Mallarmé, who
envisioned a three-dimensional book entitled Moment
to Moment. As art historian Gwen Allen points out in her
essay for our version of Moment to Moment, Mallarmé
saw the book as something that would be performed,
rather than read.
This project consists of commissioned online videos,
text pieces, paintings, animated gifs, photographs, and
essays. Some of these pieces will appear on billboards,
ous shelters and other outdoor advertising spaces
in cities around the world.These public interventions
propose an alternative, more pleasing visual experience
within the urban landscape and prompt viewers to
take time for the good things around them. Some
pieces will be inserted into the paid advertising space
of magazines as stand-alone works of art. These
will be pages from the Moment to Moment project,
extracted and repositioned as pages in other like-
minded publications. The remainder of the project is
featured online at goodthingstaketime.com and in this
free printed newspaper which, like the official website
documents and shares the entire project.
goodthingstaketime.com

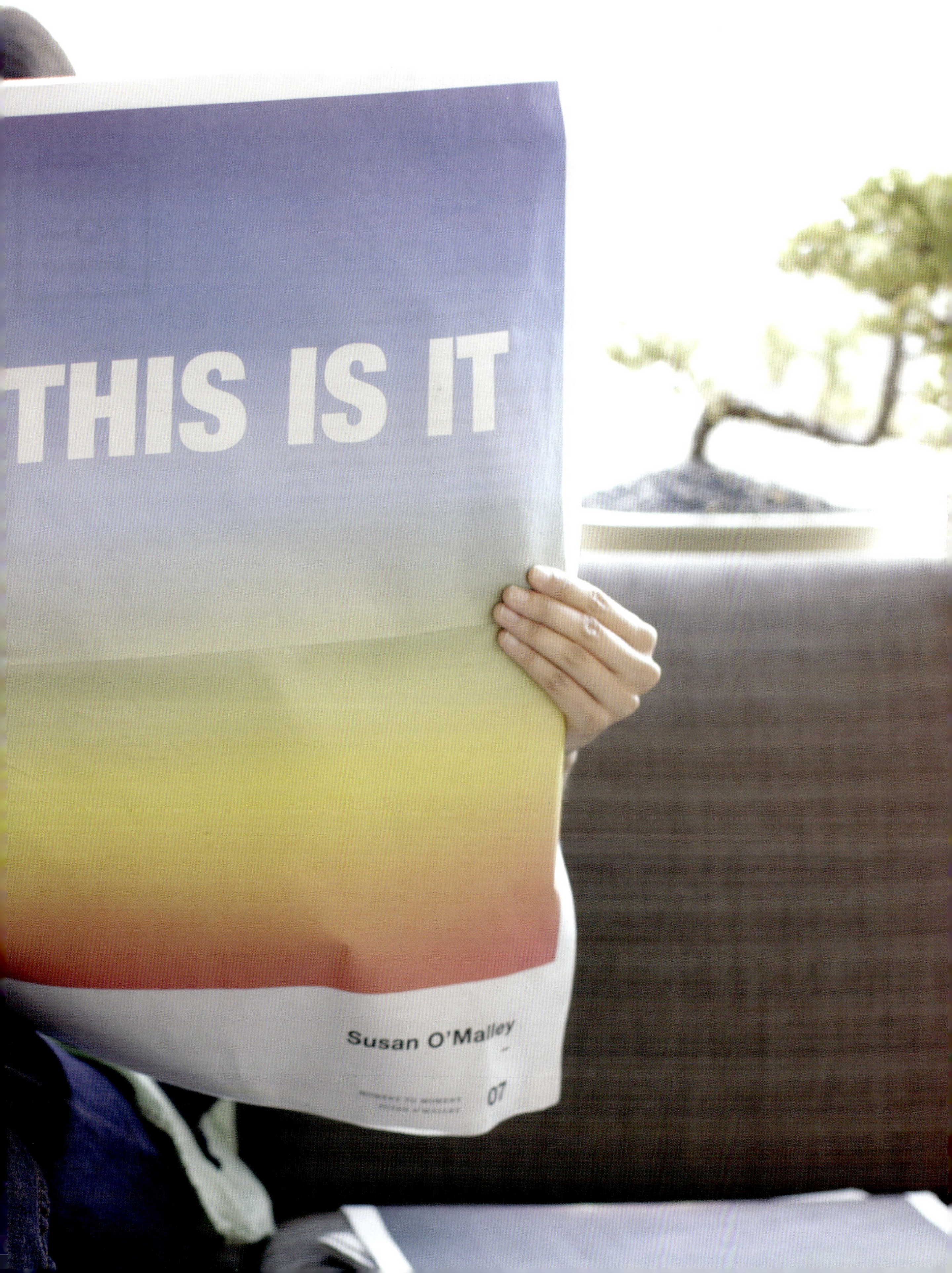
THIS IS IT
Susan O'Malley
07

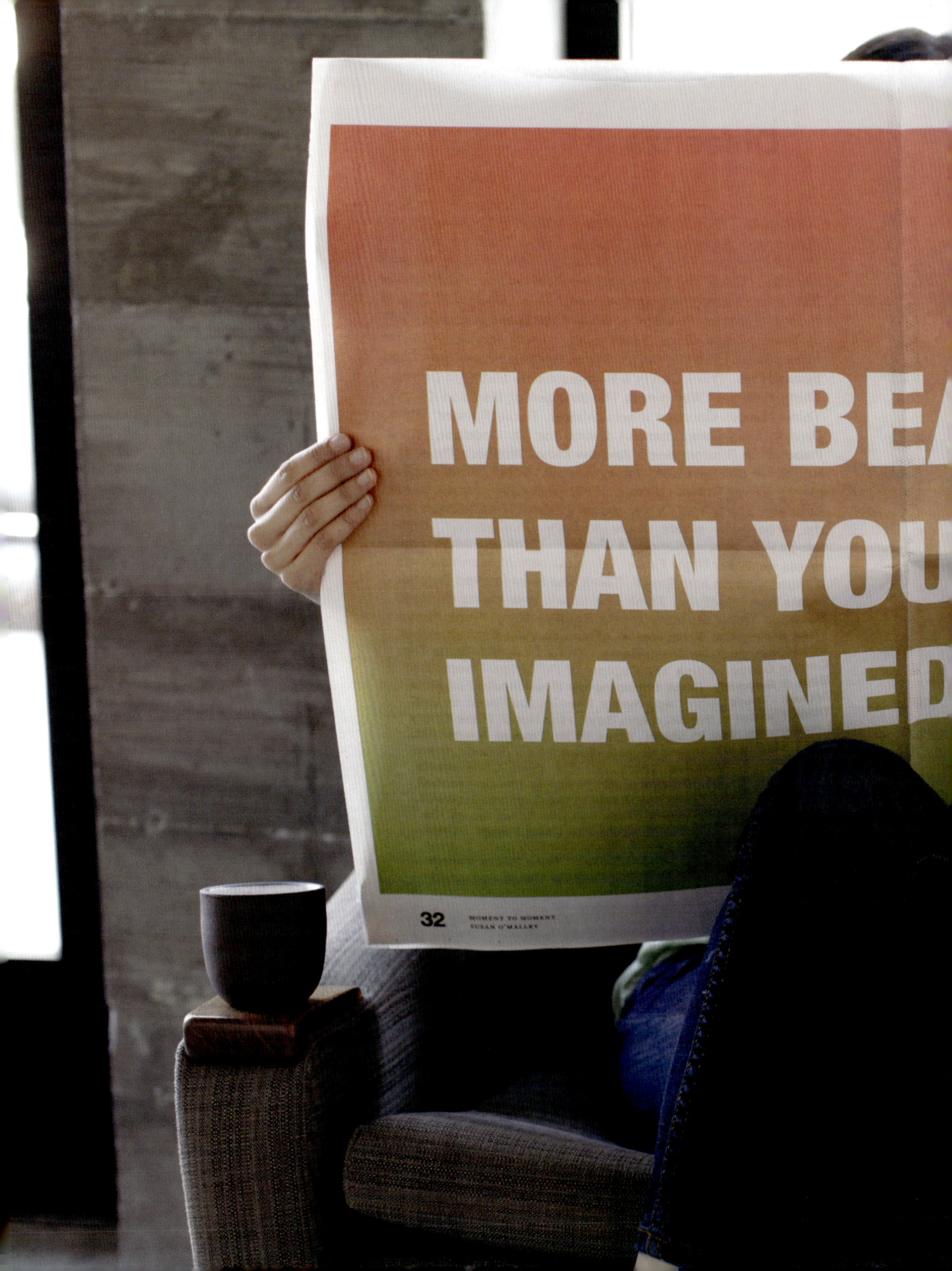
MORE BE
THAN YO
IMAGINE
32
MOMENT TO MOMENT
SUSAN O'MALLEY

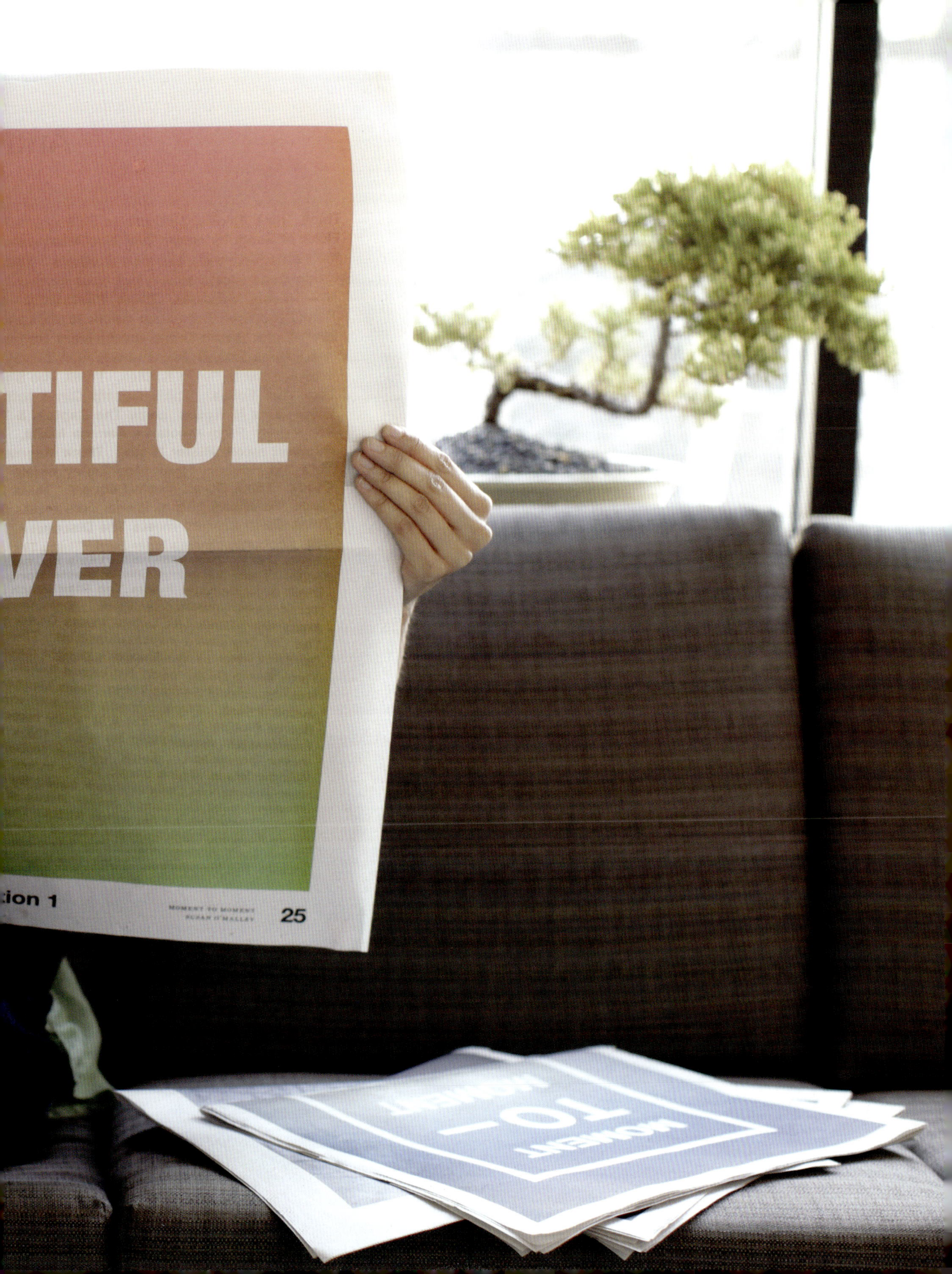

TIFUL
VER
tion 1
MOMENT TO MOMENT
25

Community Advice

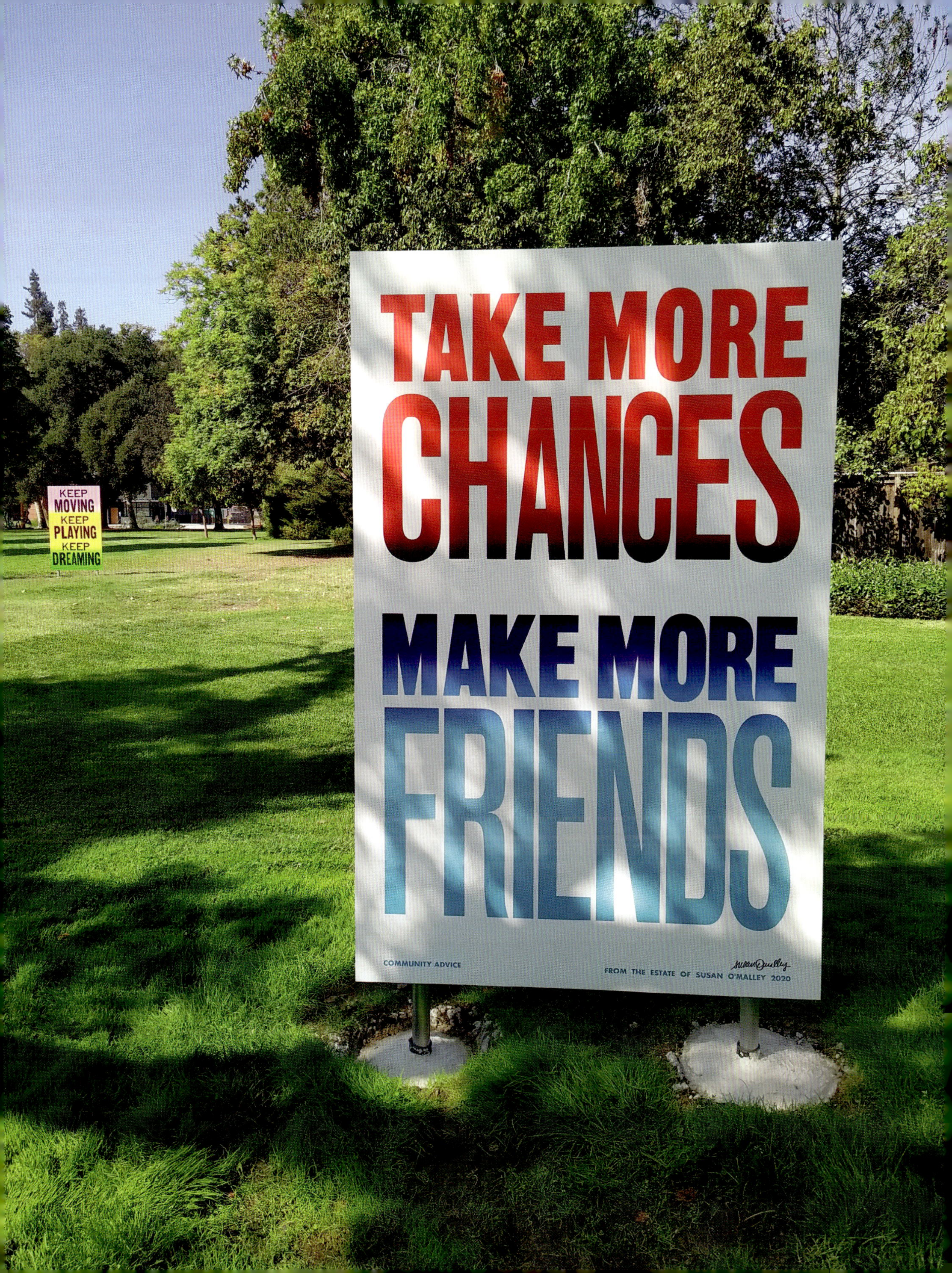
KEEP
MOVING
KEEP
PLAYING
KEEP
DREAMING
TAKE MORE
CHANCES
MAKE MORE
FRIENDS
COMMUNITY ADVICE
FROM THE ESTATE OF SUSAN O'MALLEY 2020

Keep Moving Keep Playing Keep Dreaming

Karen Kienzle

Back in 2011, in the midst of a large-scale renovation, we at the Palo Alto Art Center started thinking about a reopening exhibition to showcase the center's role in building connection through art. Susan O'Malley was one of the very first artists we reached out to for the show that would become *Community Creates*. Her vision perfectly matched our interest in meaningfully partnering with the community.

Susan proposed *Community Advice*, a project in which she reached out to people to ask them two simple questions: What advice would they give to their eight-year-old selves? And what advice would they give to their eighty-year-old selves? To produce the project, Susan met people where they gathered—at farmers' markets, in libraries. Their responses to her questions inspired an edition of prints that were exhibited both at the art center gallery and throughout the city of Palo Alto.

Community Advice represented everything that was amazing about Susan, both as a person and as an artist—a consistent belief in the best of everyone, boundless optimism, and an inspiring ability to see beauty in everything. Today, more than a decade later, community members still talk about the value of the project and their delight and surprise in seeing her prints on telephone poles along Embarcadero Road in Palo Alto. These powerful images and messages live on.

At various times since Susan's original installation, the art center, our staff, and our community have needed this inspiration. We have drawn upon *Community Advice* for hope and healing. When we lost Susan in 2015, staff and friends gathered to remember her by reenacting a portion of *Community Advice*, stapling her memorial poster to telephone poles along Embarcadero Road. During the worst of the COVID lockdown in 2020, we worked with her estate to blow up the posters on billboards along Embarcadero Road and collaborated with the original letterpress printer (Horwinski Printing Company in Oakland) to produce a run of limited-edition posters that were distributed to first responders in the community.

Page 213: *Take More Chances, Make More Friends* installation view of *Community Advice Revisited*, on view at the Palo Alto Art Center, California, October 2020–January 2021

Opposite: In conjunction with *Community Advice Revisited*, the art center worked with the estate and Horwinski Printing Company to reprint a selection of *Community Advice* posters, distributing them to senior centers, outreach centers for the unhoused, and first responders in the community. Here, emergency room staff at Stanford Hospital.

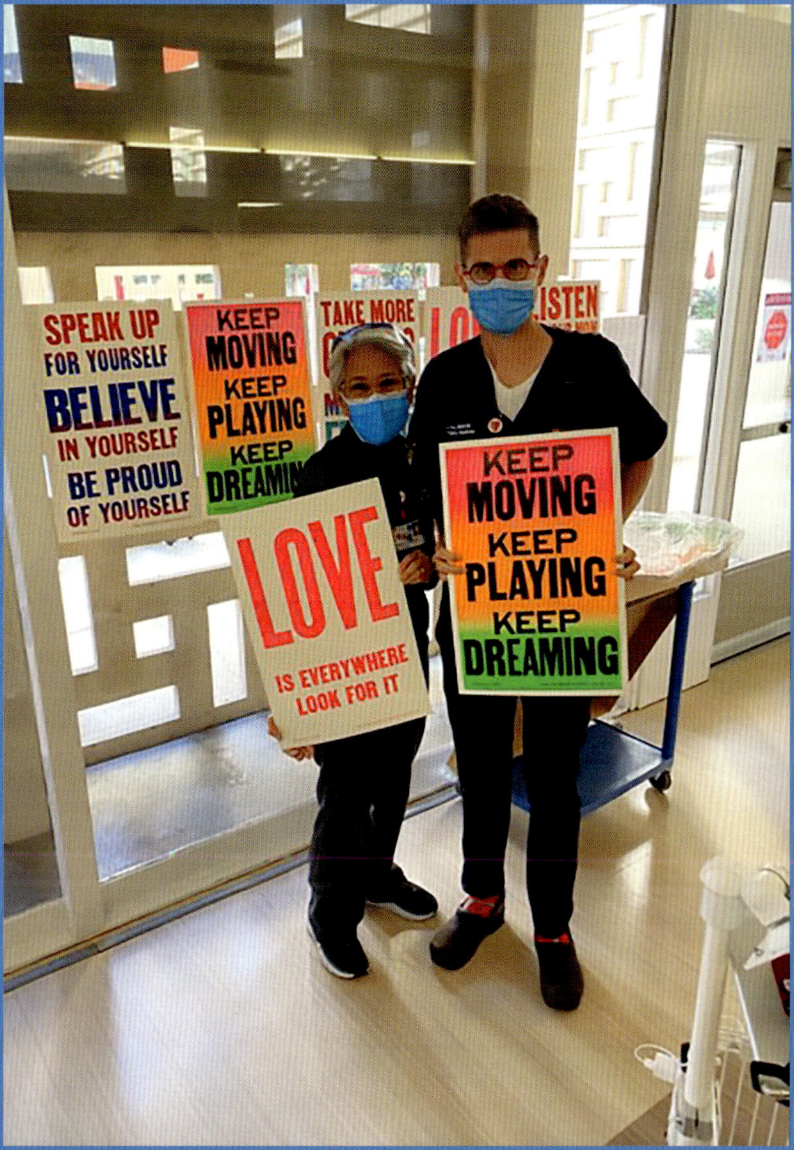
SPEAK UP
FOR YOURSELF
BELIEVE
IN YOURSELF
BE PROUD
OF YOURSELF
TAKE MORE
LISTEN
LOVE
IS EVERYWHERE
LOOK FOR IT
KEEP
MOVING
KEEP
PLAYING
KEEP
DREAMING

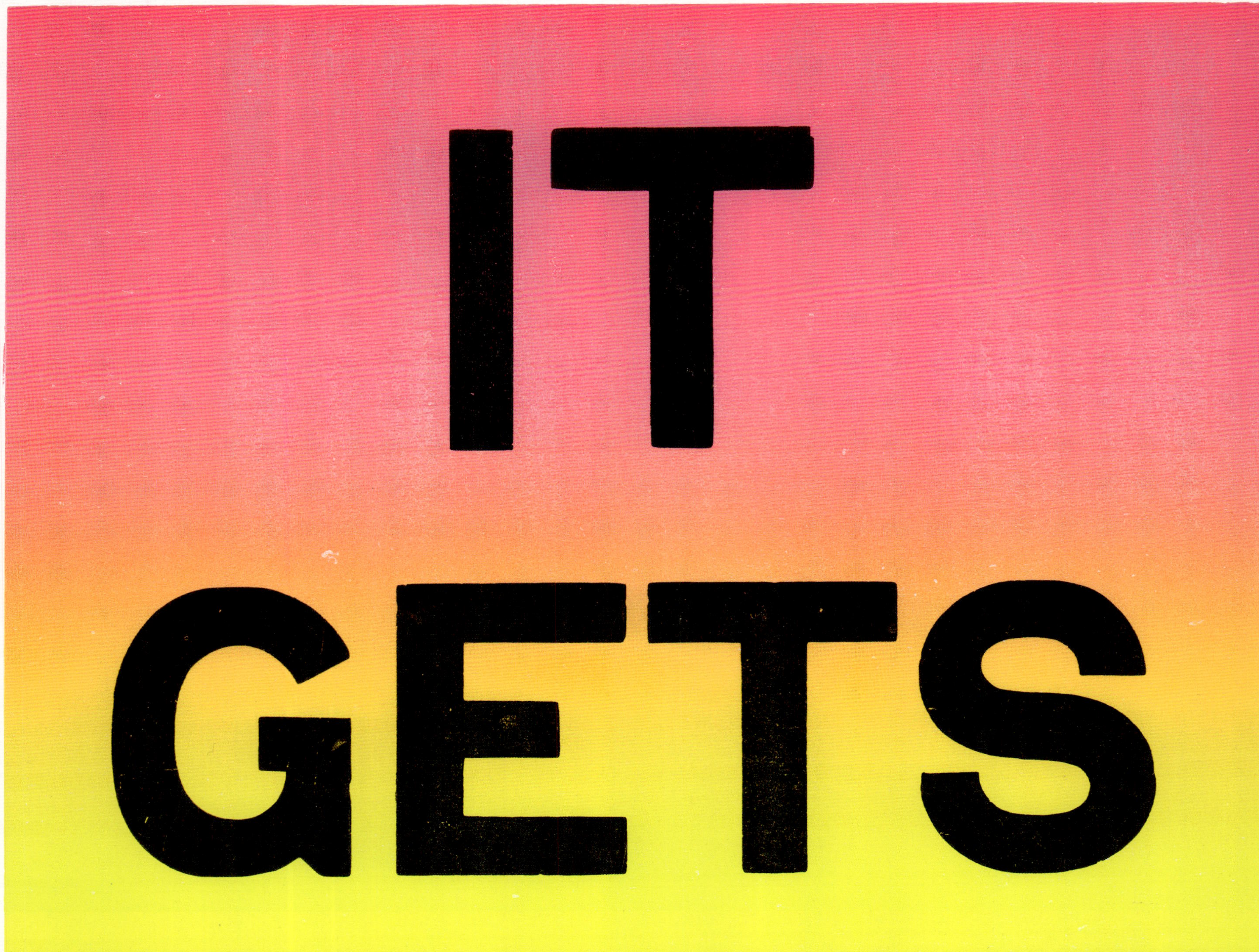
IT
GETS

MORE FUN

COMMUNITYADVICE.ORG

A PROJECT BY SUSAN O'MALLEY 2012

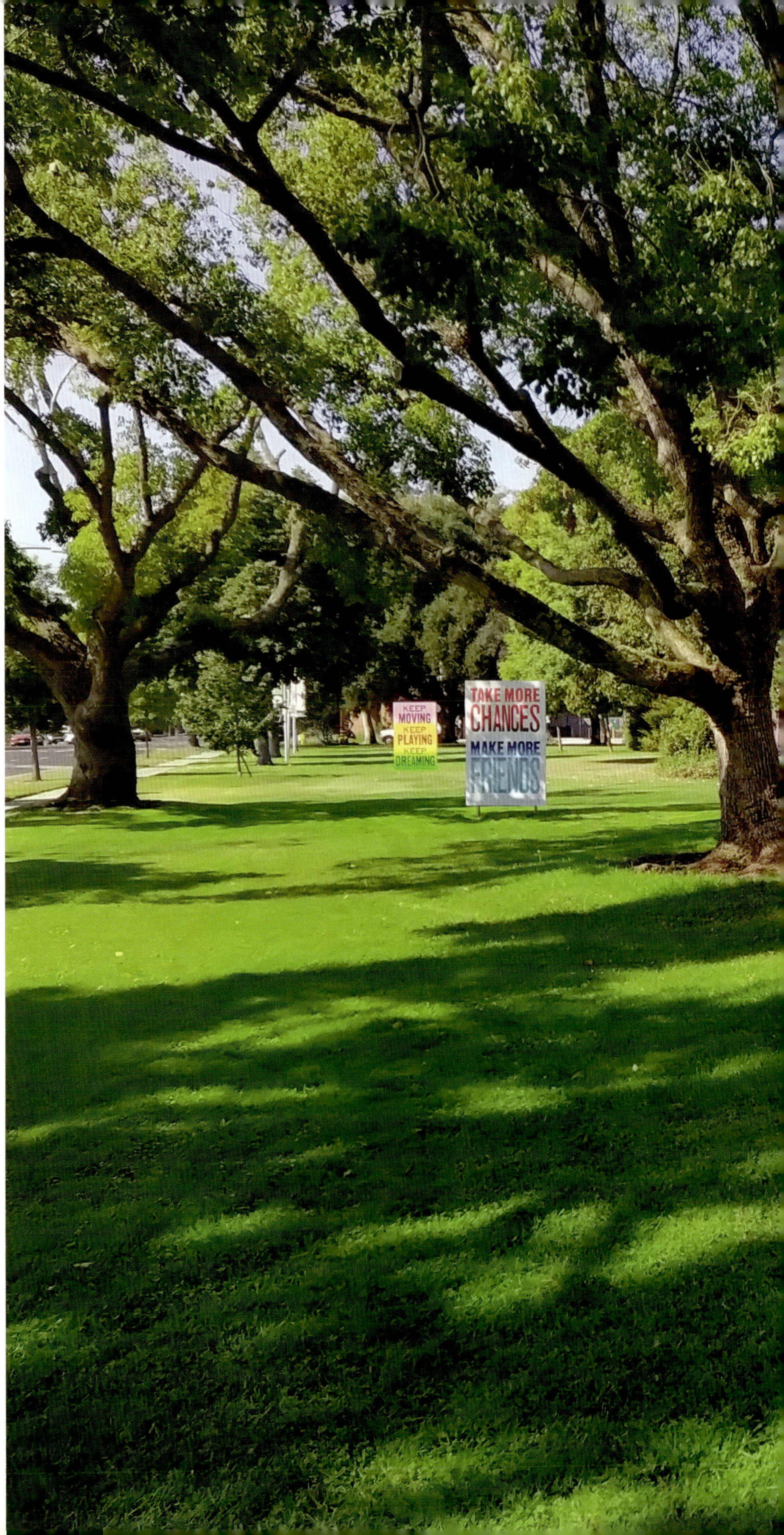
KEEP MOVING
KEEP PLAYING
KEEP DREAMING
TAKE MORE CHANCES
MAKE MORE FRIENDS

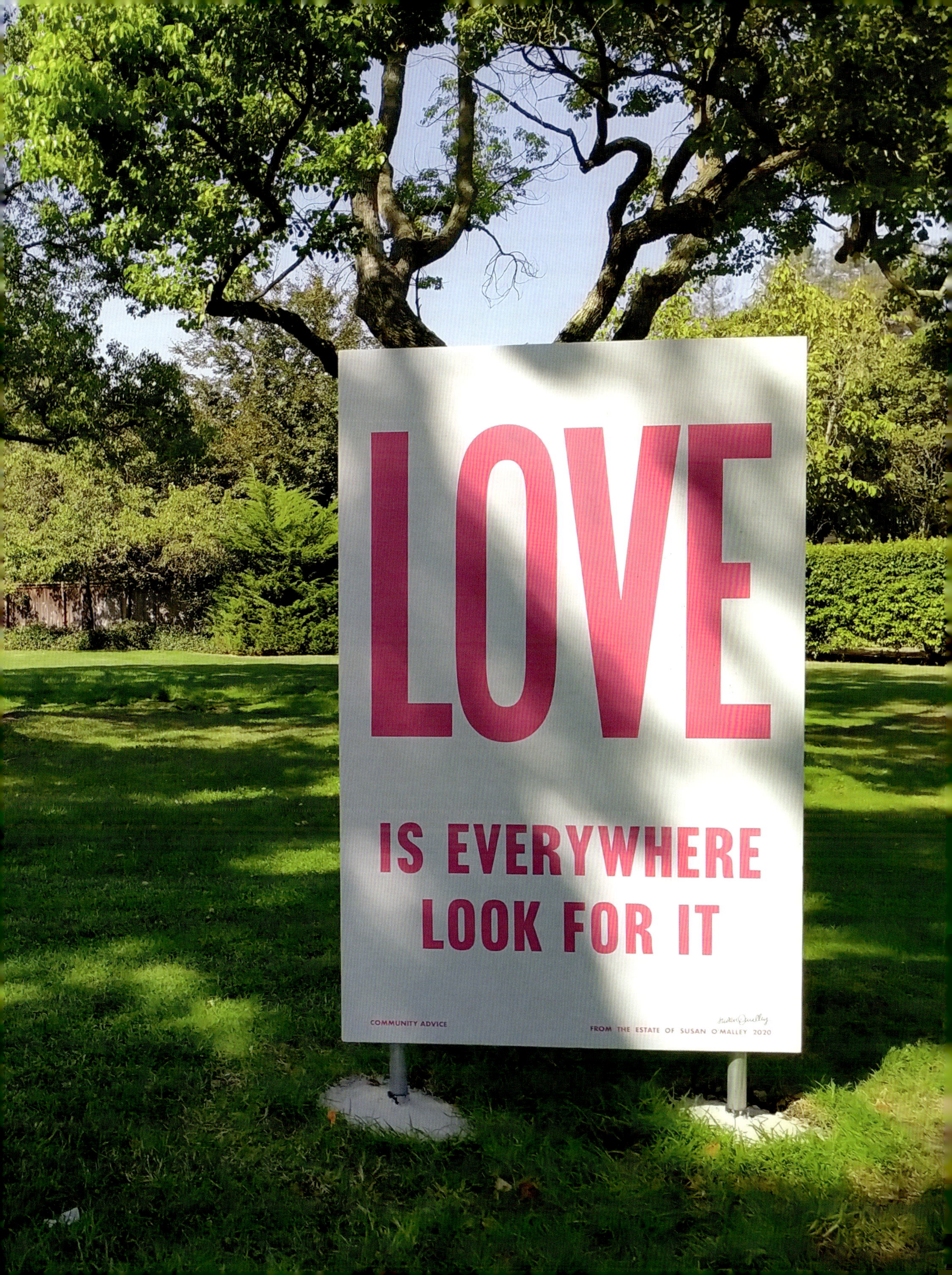
LOVE
IS EVERYWHERE
LOOK FOR IT
COMMUNITY ADVICE
FROM THE ESTATE OF SUSAN O'MALLEY 2020

Community Advice continues to have resonance and impact. Its lessons are universal: Trust yourself, remember what is really important, listen to your mom, be kind, find happiness, and remember that it gets more fun. The latter poster has been hanging in my office for more than a decade, consistently inspiring laughs, stories, and contemplations about our shared and hopeful humanity.

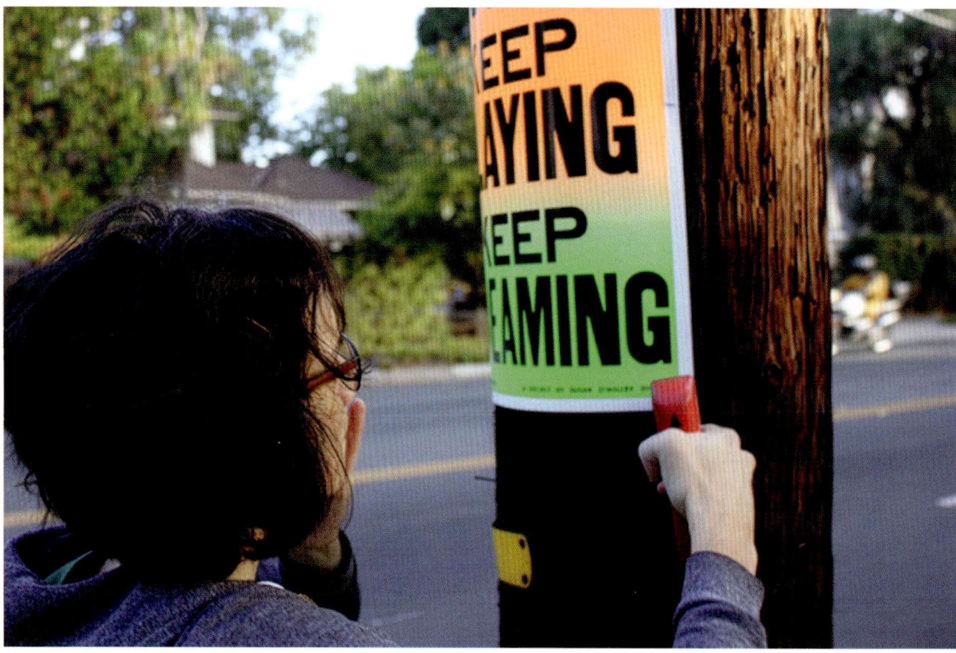

Pages 216–17: *It Gets More Fun* from *Community Advice*, 2012

Pages 218–19: *Love Is Everywhere Look for It* installation view, *Community Advice Revisited*, on view at the Palo Alto Art Center, October 2020–January 2021

Above: Susan O'Malley posting *Community Advice* posters, Palo Alto, California, 2012

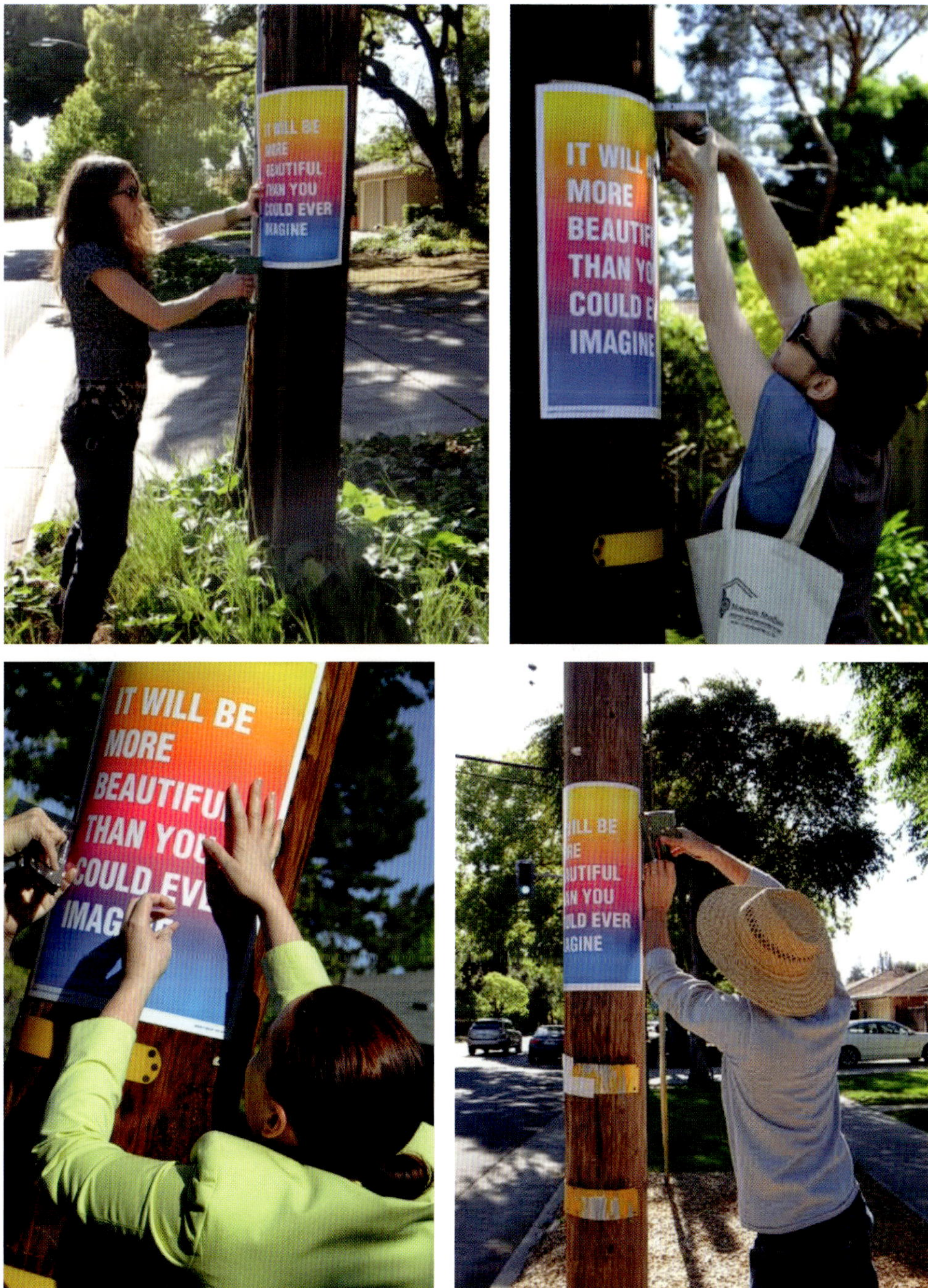

Staff members from Palo Alto Art Center posting memorial *It Will Be More Beautiful Than You Could Ever Imagine* posters, 2015

Advice from My 80-Year-Old Self

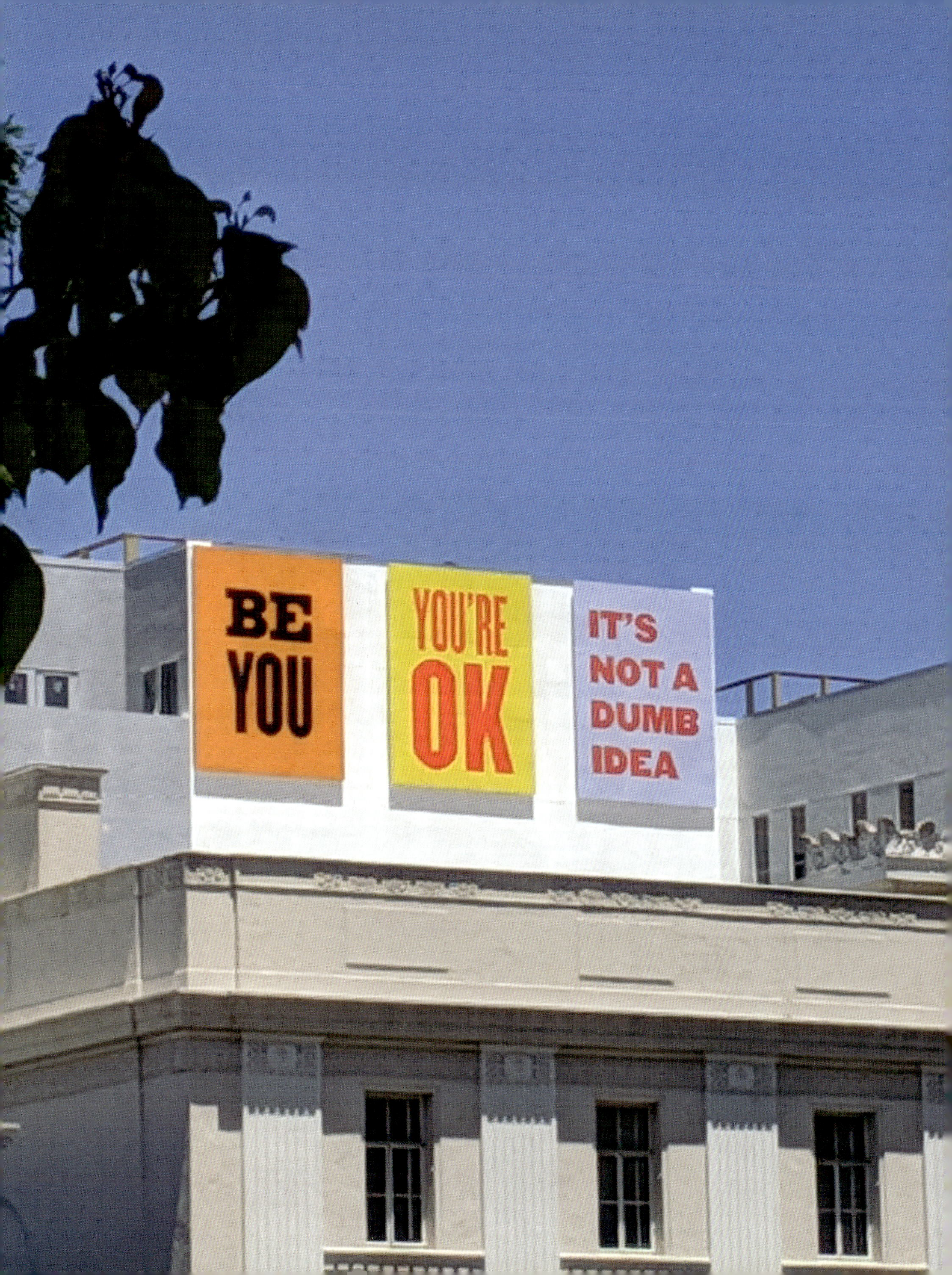
BE
YOU
YOU'RE
OK
IT'S
NOT A
DUMB
IDEA

Less Internet More Love

Amanda Curreri

Hi, I'm Susan O'Malley.

I'm reading this off a card that lives in my wallet.

The card was letterpress printed circa 2014, debossed with blue ink on white card stock. It's tucked into the back of a slim metal business card case.

These days the case and its contents are more memento than an active tool. In addition to Susan's card, the case holds several of my own. Susan and I printed these cards together during a calling card workshop taught by artist Carissa Potter. We gathered around one of the long worktables at the Kala Art Institute in Berkeley and tuned in to Carissa's ebullient frequency. The font on Susan's calling card isn't serif or sans serif. It's a rendering of Susan's own script, her handwriting.

Her use of direct address signals a key tenet in her artwork. Susan utilized vernacular forms like the calling card, conversations, broadsides, and billboards. Her artwork resonates with a friendly and inclusive voice. You can hear the inferred pause: . . . *and what's your name? Who are you? I want to know.*

The workshop marked the beginning of Susan's *Print Public* artist residency at Kala. Her public project, *Advice from My 80-Year-Old Self*, was developed during the two-year municipal artist residency that I facilitated as curator for that inaugural season. Susan and her then student project assistant, Julie Chau, interviewed neighbors along the historic San Pablo Avenue corridor, collecting hundreds of responses to the titular inquiry: What advice would your eighty-year-old self give you? Pulling quotes from these sidewalk conversations, Susan translated them graphically into a series of vibrant broadsides that have now traveled far, far beyond Berkeley.

A few of the earlier versions of the *Advice* prints hang on the wall of my office at the University of New Mexico. When my students see Susan's prints, something unequivocally shifts: "Enjoy your hair while you have it." "Take more chances, make more friends." The prints make eyebrows go up, they elicit smiles and nods, and a new camaraderie enters the room.

Page 223: *Be You; You're OK; It's Not a Dumb Idea* permanent installation, Berkeley, California, 2019

Pages 226–27: *Less Internet More Love*, from the *Print Public* project by Kala Art Institute, 2015

Susan had finished the *Advice* project ahead of schedule, so it was ready for installation when we at Kala got the news of Susan's death. We decided to carry out her plan, painting the words "Less internet, more love" on the storefront of Bob's Machining Company on San Pablo Avenue. Julie and I began with the yellow base layer and chalked in a grid for the black lettering. Family members and close friends gathered and shared food on the sidewalk, everyone trying their hand at collectively painting the letters. The installation became a real-time ritual of grieving and communion.

Susan didn't center her work in institutional spaces, but she traversed through them and beyond. A decade ago, her methodologies were framed within the discourse of San Francisco's Social Practice scene, yet they also fit today's decolonial praxis. Her legacy embodies an era of conversation as material practice and listening as a technology.

When was the last time you used a business card? Even emails feel passé today with DMs and video calls eliciting more immediacy yet less presence. Amidst these changing times, Susan's *Advice* series invokes the interpersonal stakes that affirm one's presence in this world. Hers is an art centered in optimism as a critical, collective practice.

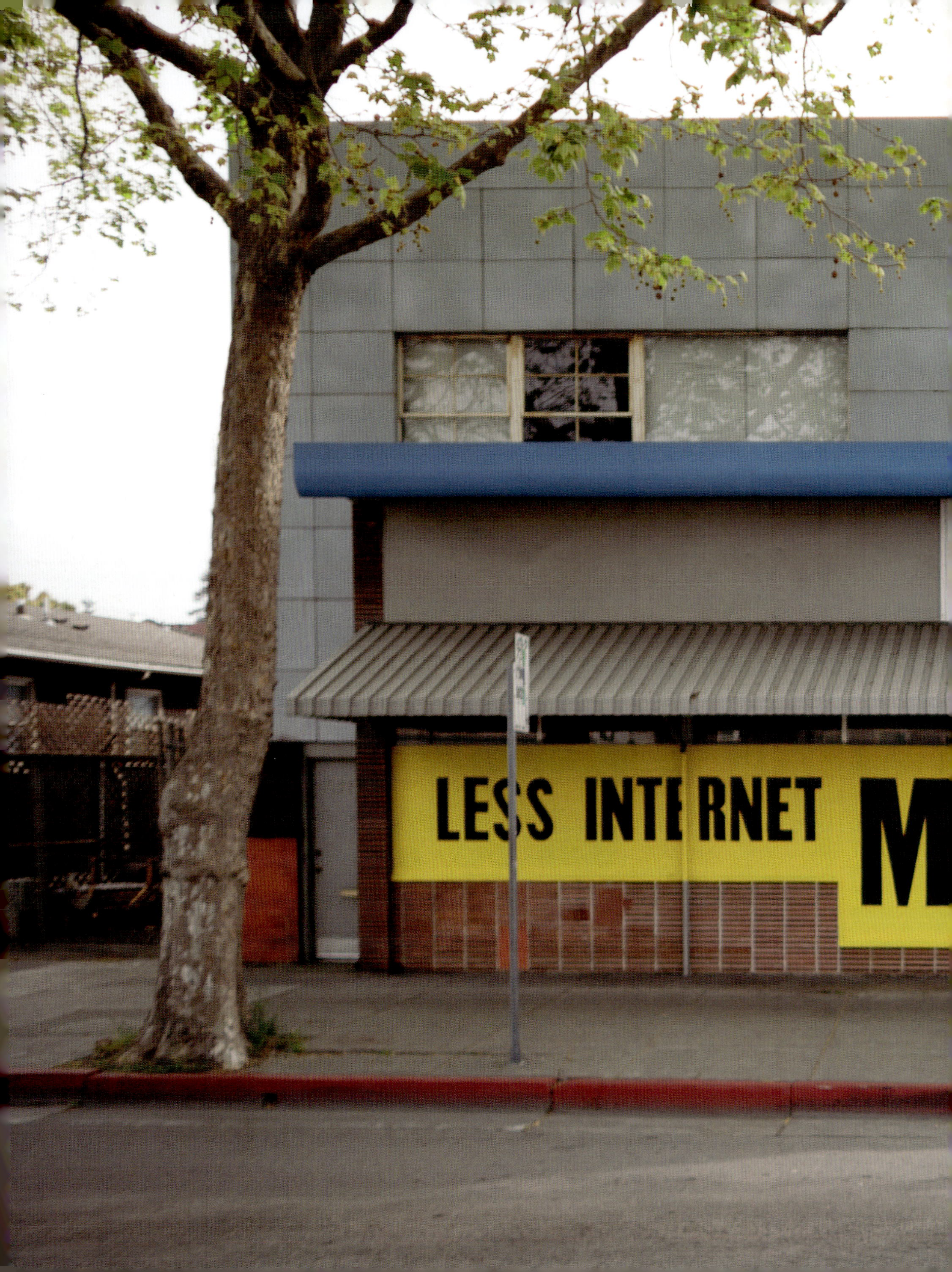
LESS INTERNET

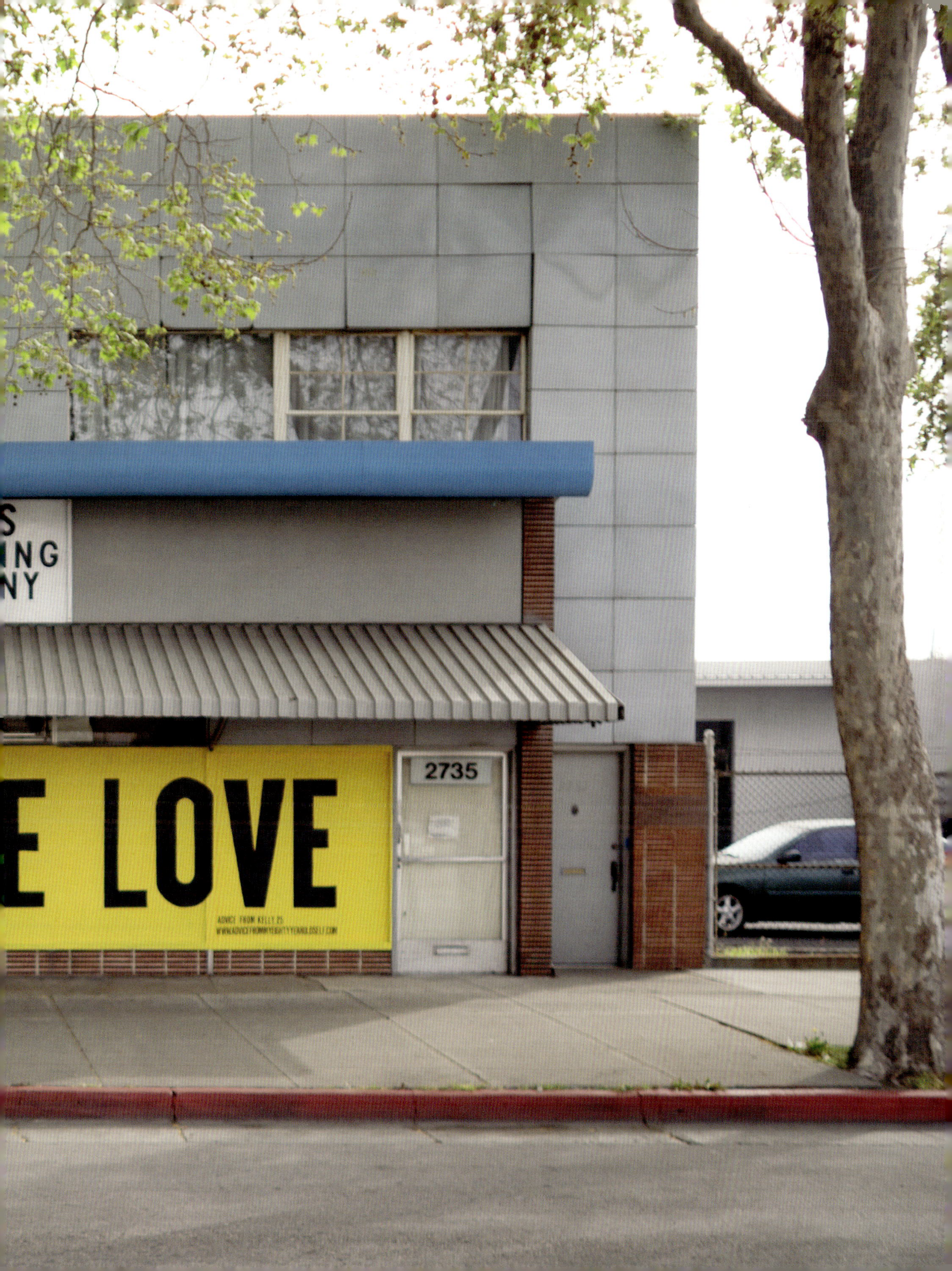
E LOVE
2735

Opposite: *Be You*, from the *Print Public* project by Kala Art Institute, 2015

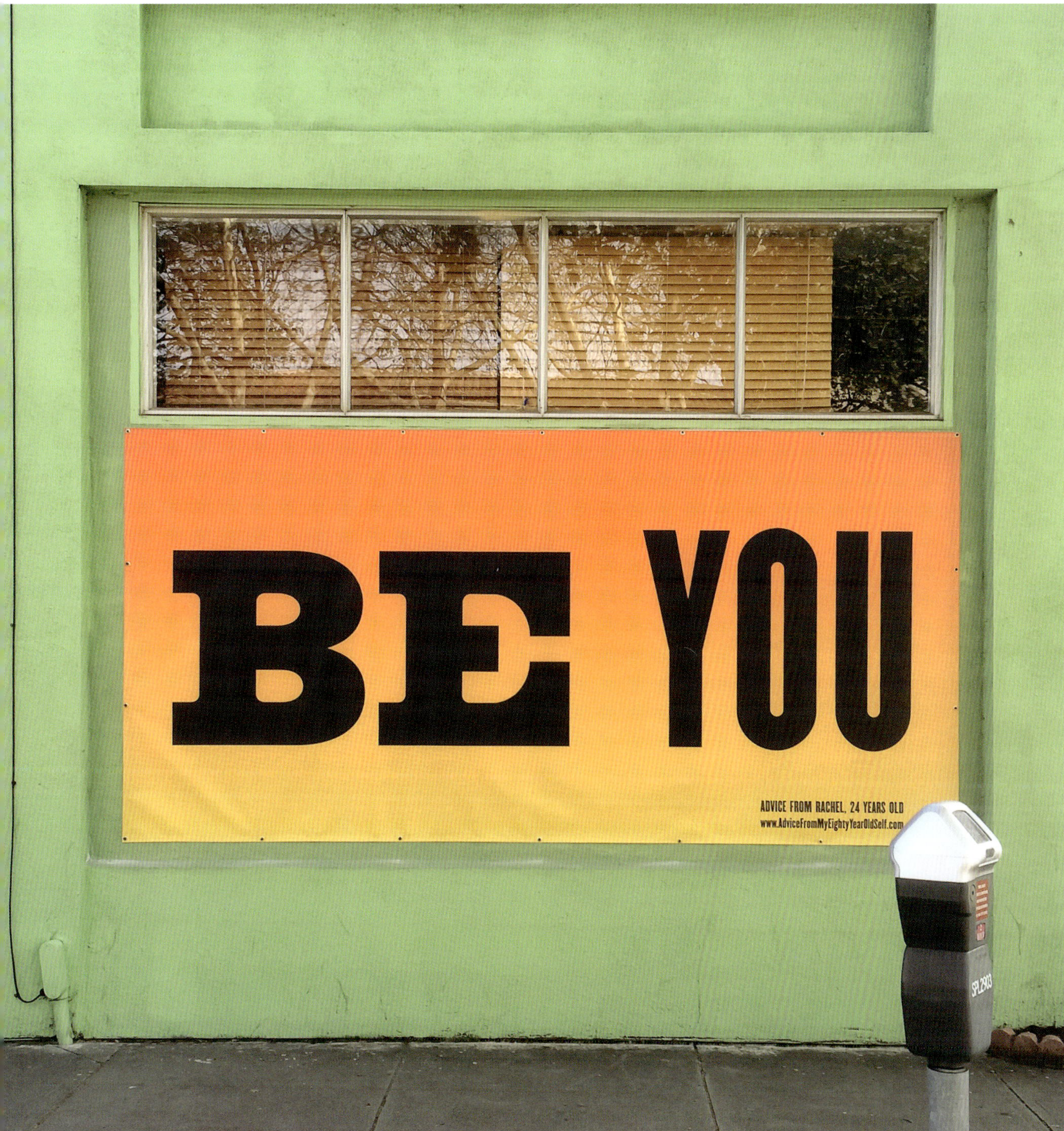
BE YOU
ADVICE FROM RACHEL, 24 YEARS OLD
www.AdviceFromMyEightyYearOldSelf.com

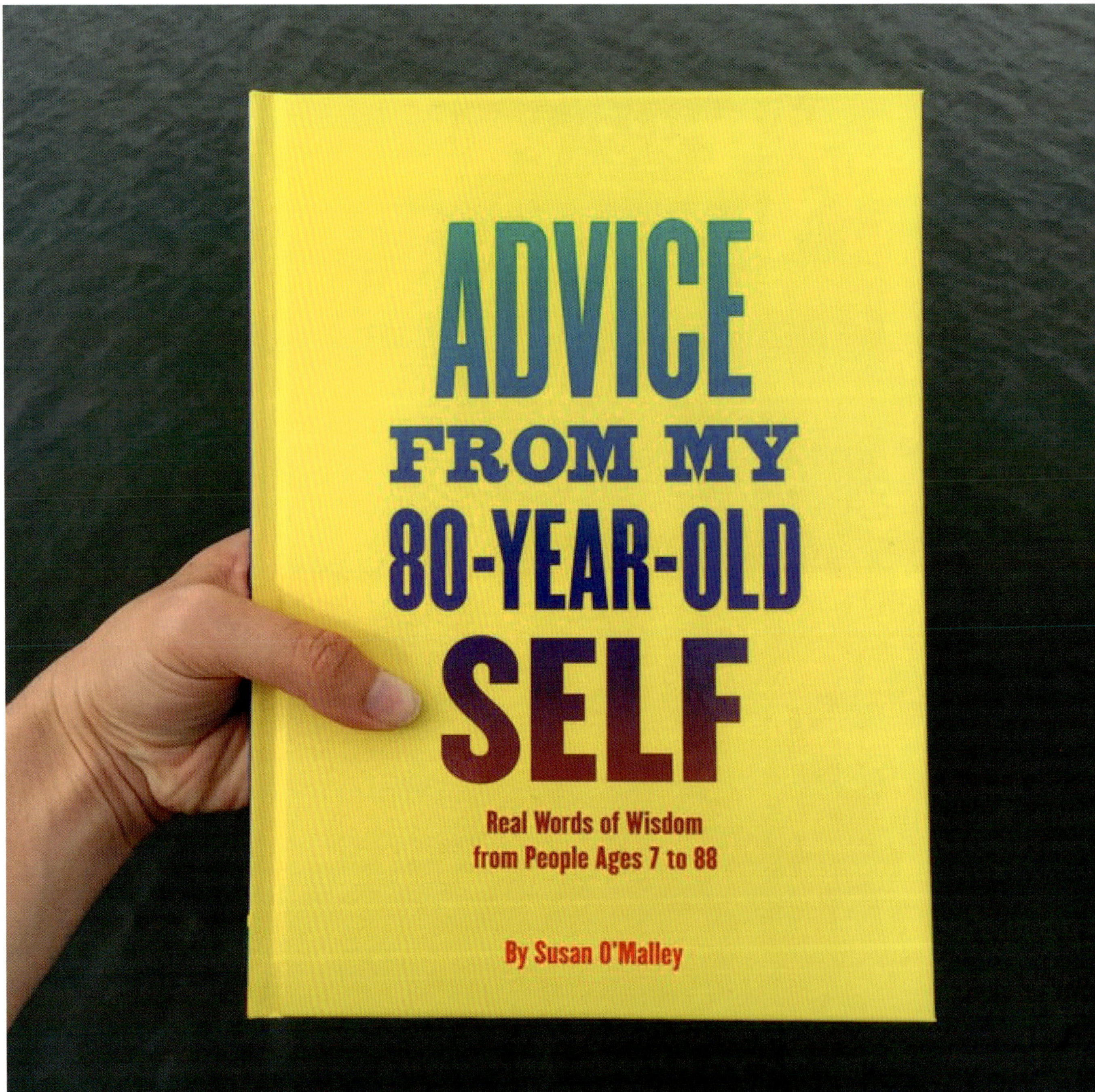

Above and opposite: Cover and pages from *Advice from My 80-Year-Old Self*, published by Chronicle Books in 2016

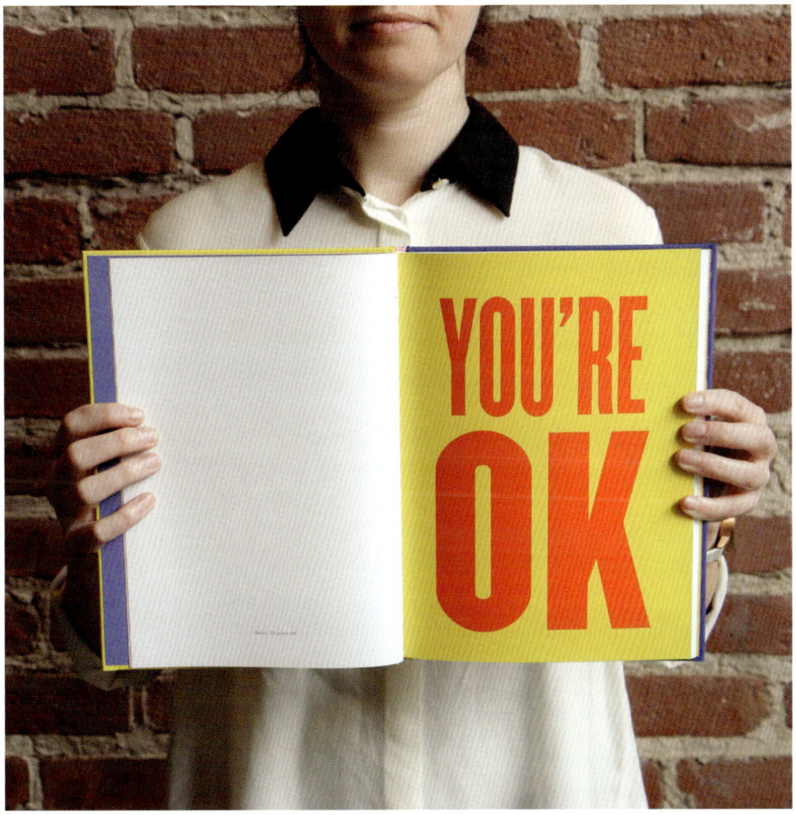
YOU'RE
OK

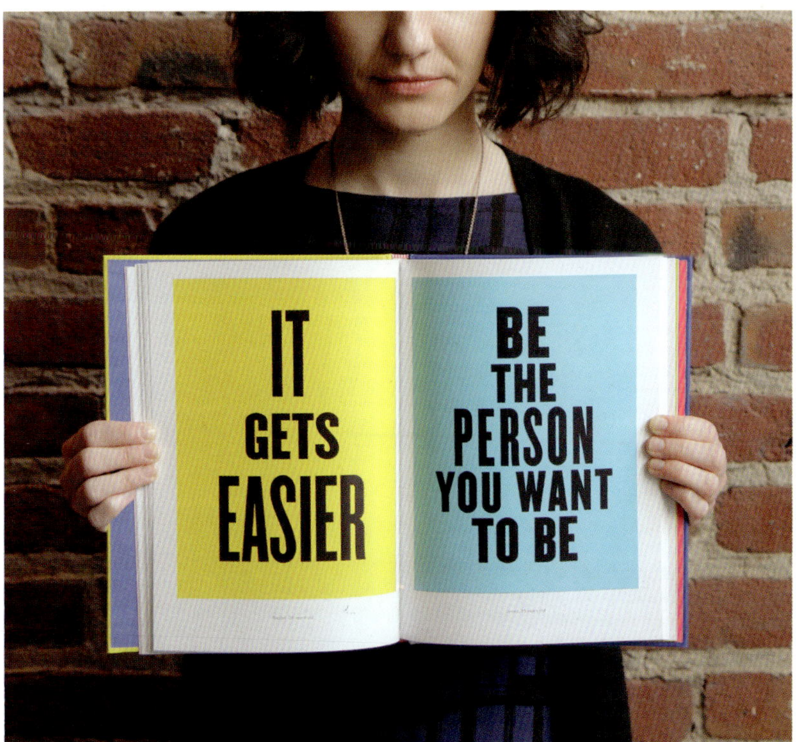
IT
GETS
EASIER
BE
THE
PERSON
YOU WANT
TO BE

IT'S
NOT A
DUMB
IDEA

IT'S
OK
TO HAVE SUGAR
IN YOUR
TEA

THIS
IS
A GOOD MOMENT
DON'T FORGET
THIS
MOMENT

ART
BEFORE
DISHES

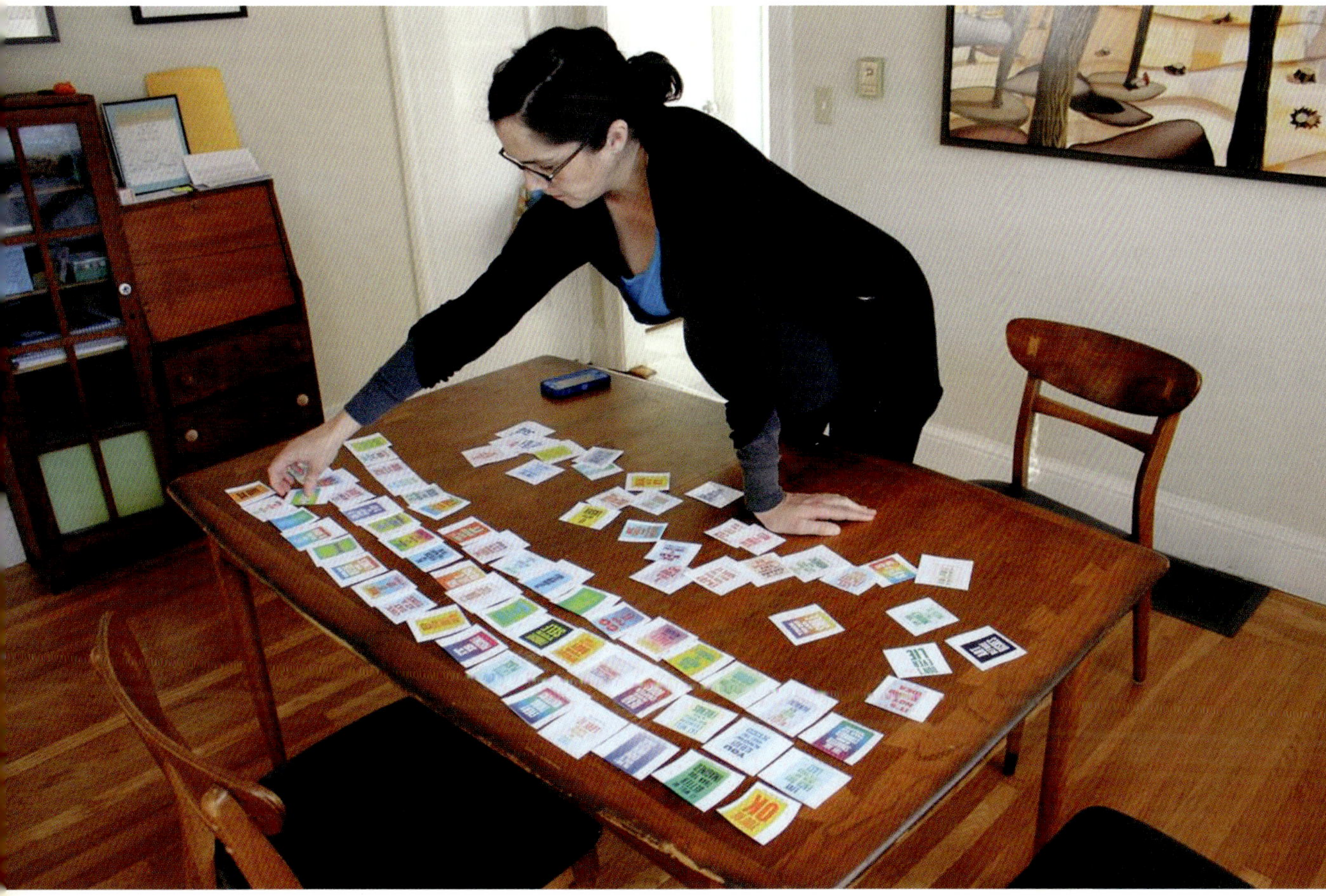

Opposite: Pages from *Advice from My 80-Year-Old Self*, published by Chronicle Books in 2016

Above: Susan O'Malley figuring out the page layout for the book *Advice from My 80-Year-Old Self*, 2015

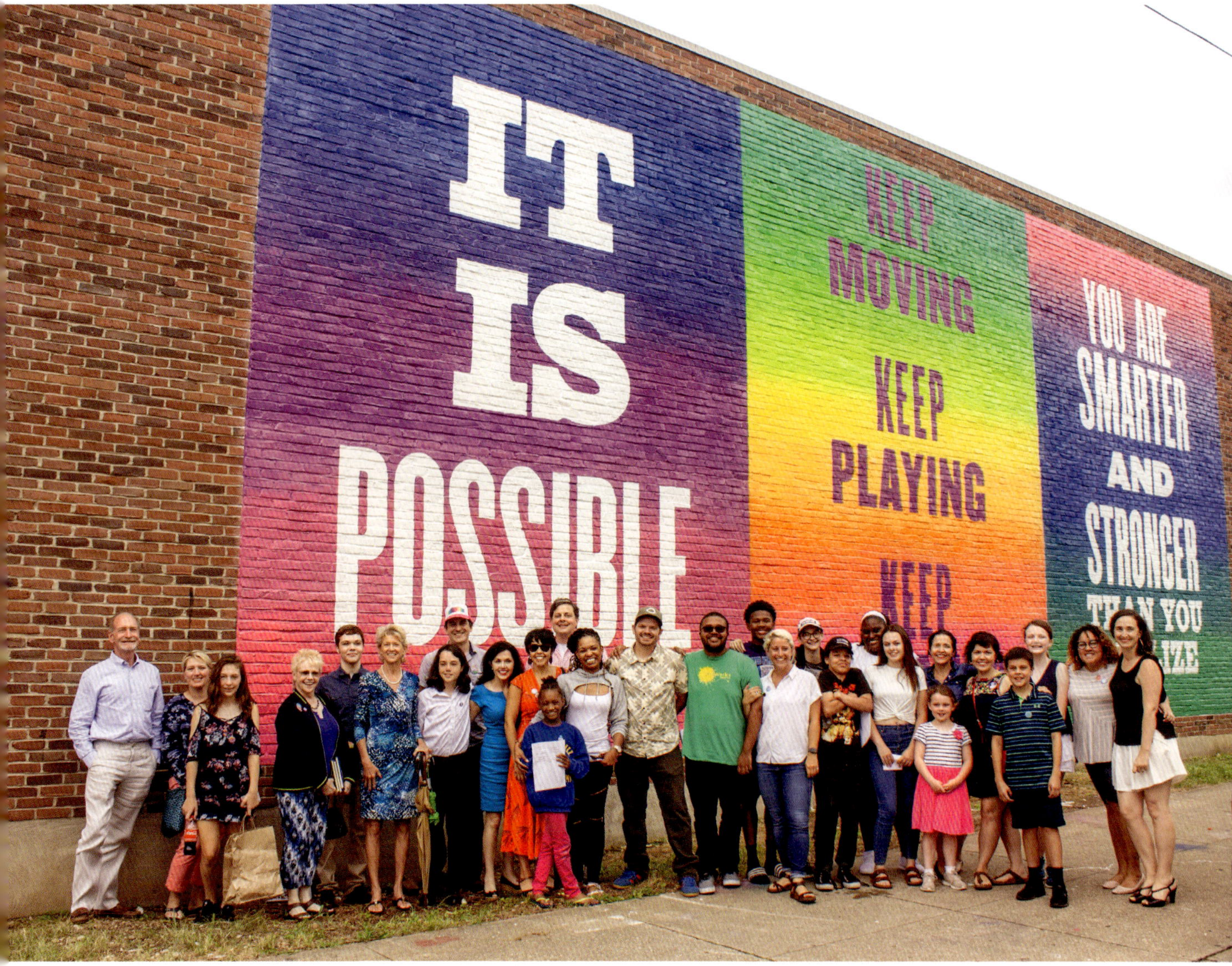

Above: This Susan O'Malley mural in the West End of Cincinnati was created through the partnership of the Seven Hills Neighborhood Houses and ArtWorks, a nonprofit that creates community-based public art providing career opportunities for artists of all ages. ArtWorks employed a team of eight local youth apprentices who worked under the direction of two local teaching artists to paint the large-scale mural and engage with the broader West End community with activities inspired by Susan O'Malley's work. The O'Malley family and artists are pictured here in front of the mural in 2018.

Opposite: Pages from *Advice from My 80-Year-Old Self,* published by Chronicle Books in 2016

Pages 236–37: *Be Here Now*; *You Are Exactly Where You Need to Be*; *Listen to Your Heart* billboard, Art Moves Festival, Toruń, Poland, 2010

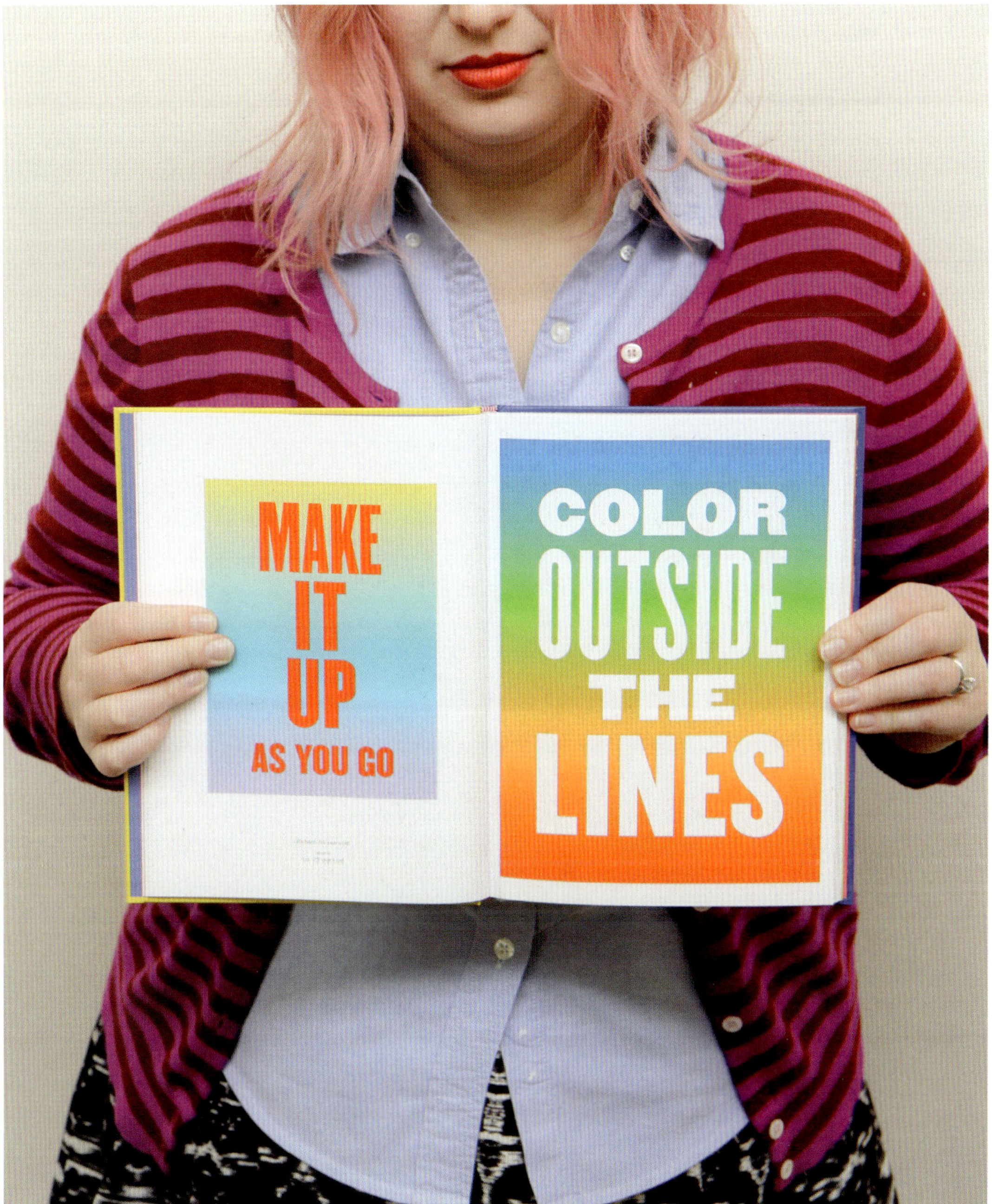
MAKE
IT
UP
AS YOU GO
COLOR
OUTSIDE
THE
LINES

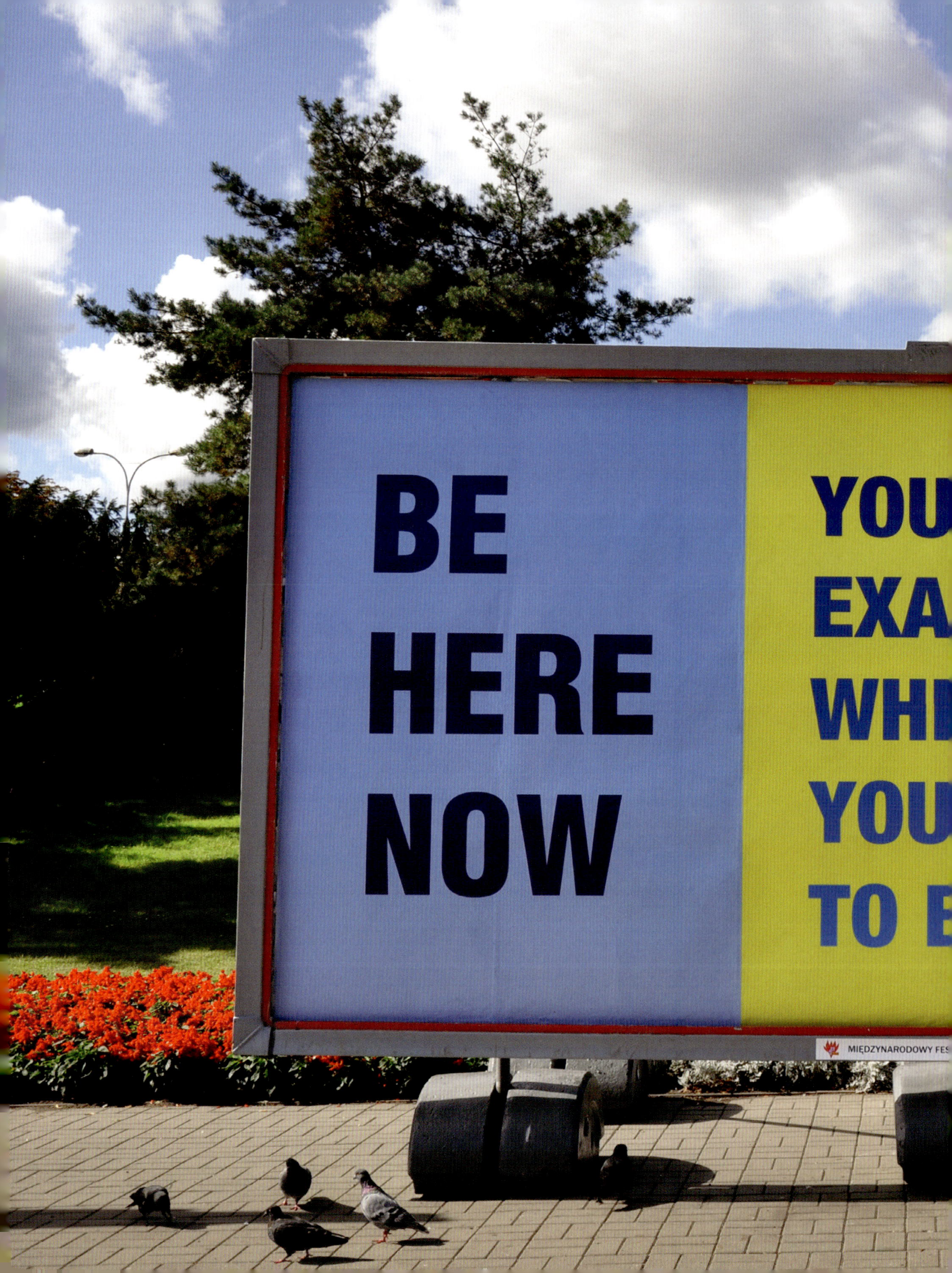
BE
HERE
NOW

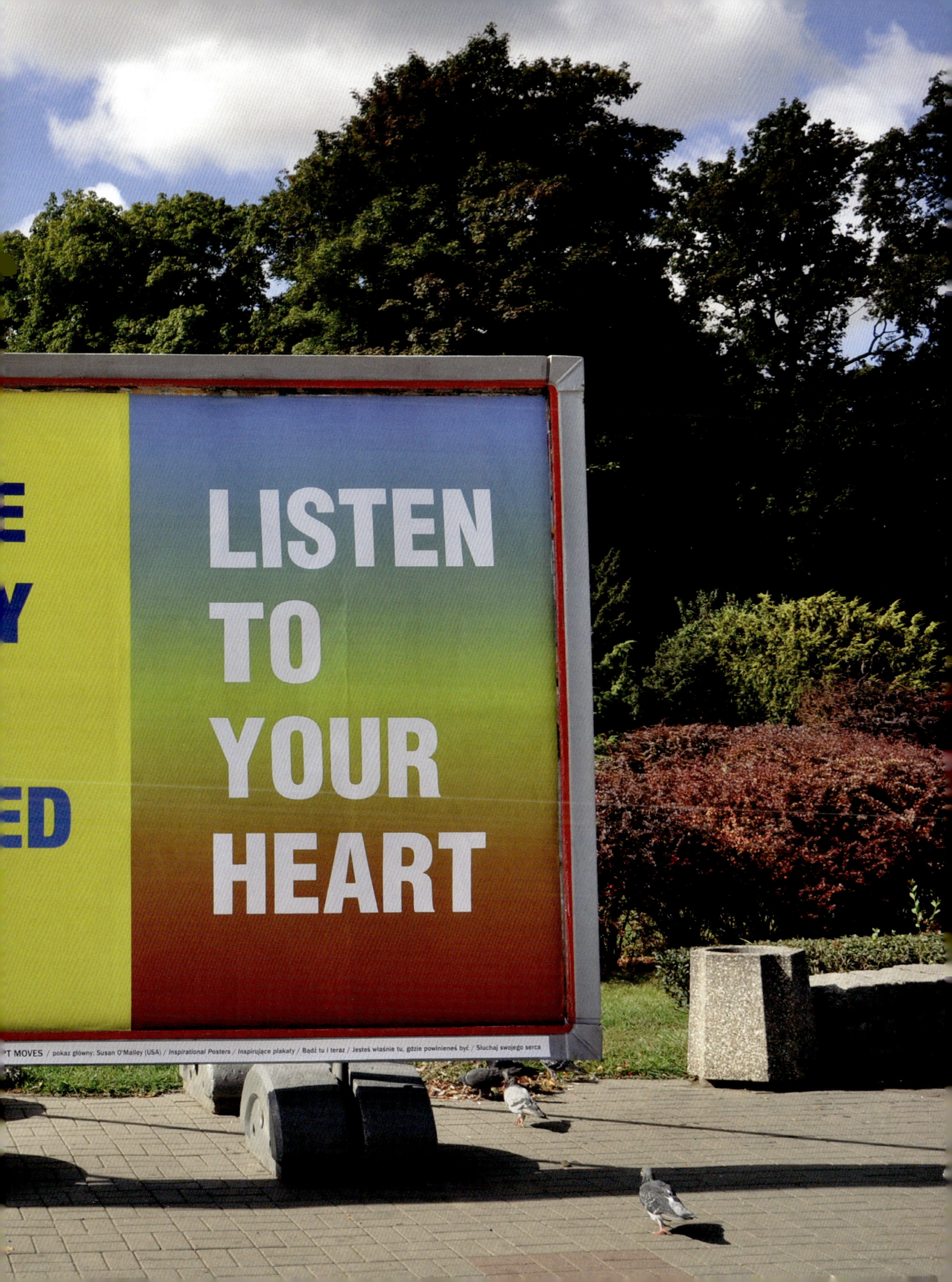
LISTEN
TO
YOUR
HEART
T MOVES / pokaz główny: Susan O'Malley (USA) / Inspirational Posters / Inspirujące plakaty / Bądź tu i teraz / Jesteś właśnie tu, gdzie powinieneś być / Słuchaj swojego serca

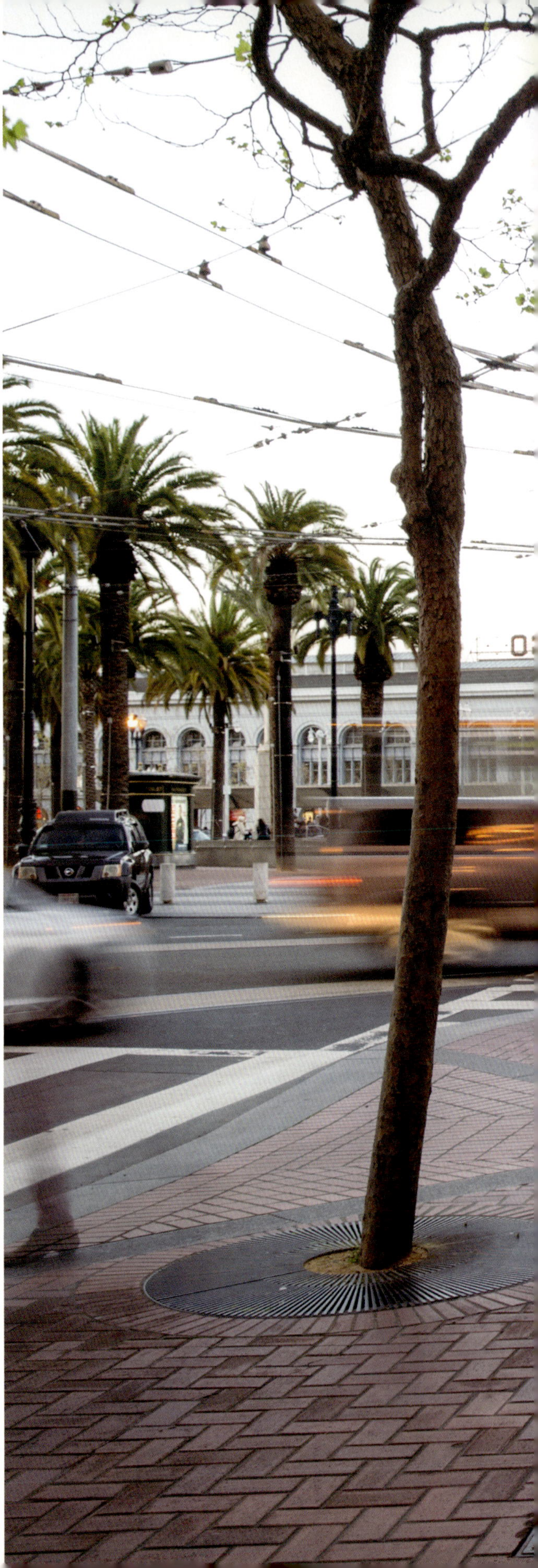

Pages 238–43: Art on Market Street posters from *Advice from My 80-Year-Old Self* series, San Francisco Arts Commission, 2016

Pages 244–45: *You Are Smarter and Stronger Than You Realize* from *Advice from My 80-Year-Old Self* series, San Diego airport, California, 2018

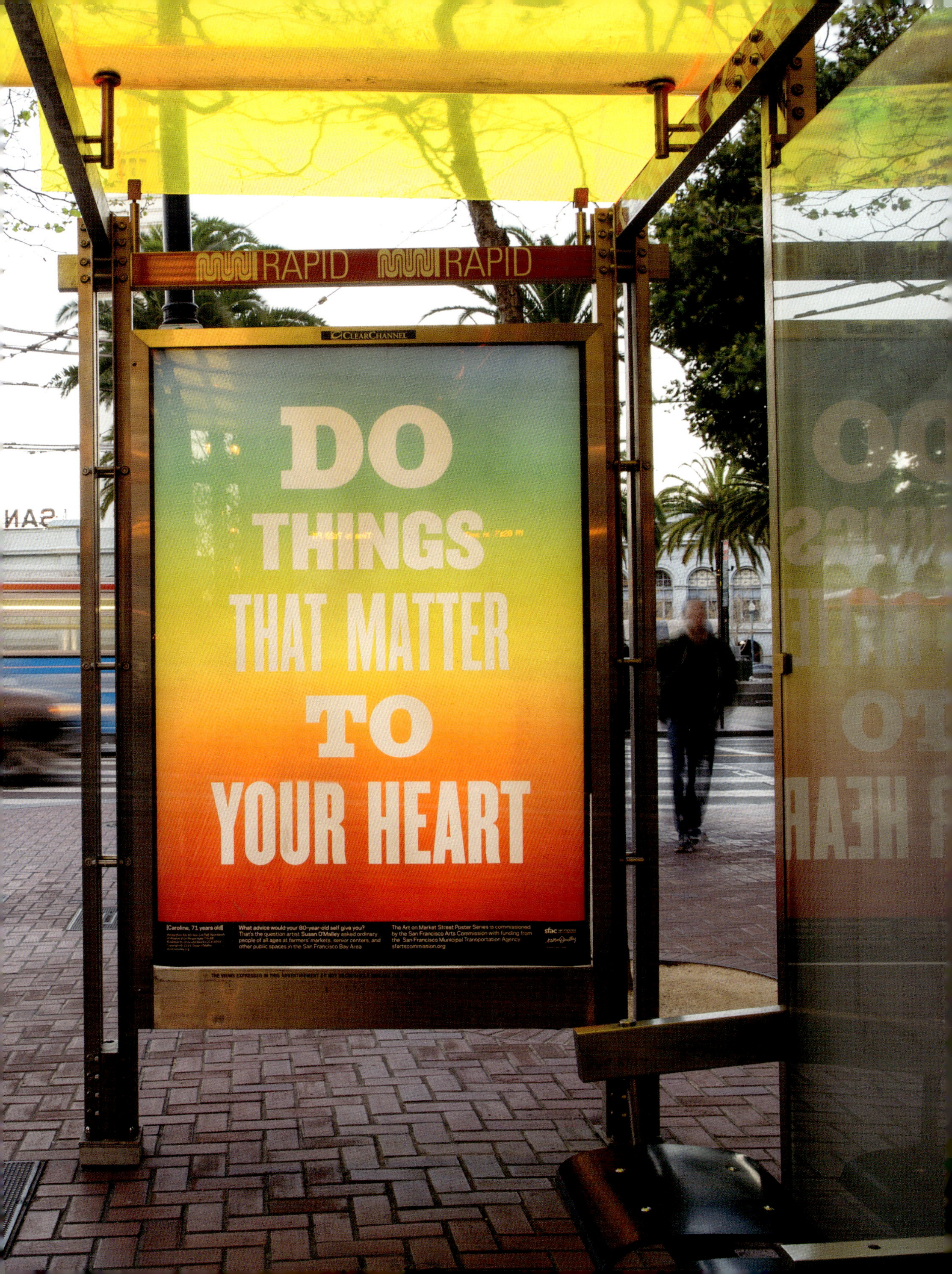
RAPID RAPID
CLEARCHANNEL
DO
THINGS
THAT MATTER
TO
YOUR HEART
[Caroline, 71 years old]
What advice would your 80-year-old self give you?
That's the question artist Susan O'Malley asked ordinary people of all ages at farmers' markets, senior centers, and other public spaces in the San Francisco Bay Area
The Art on Market Street Poster Series is commissioned by the San Francisco Arts Commission with funding from the San Francisco Municipal Transportation Agency
sfartscommission.org
sfac

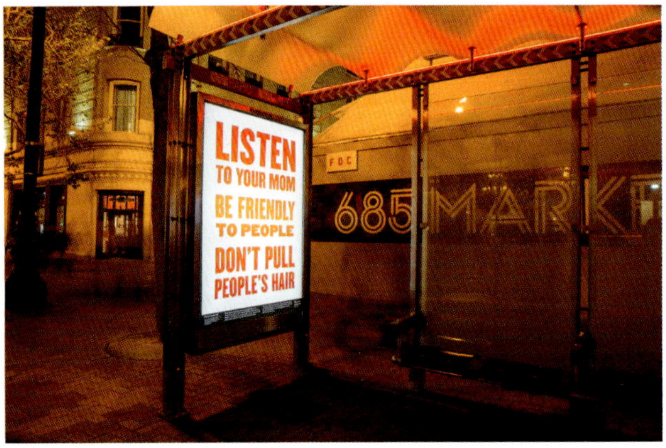
LISTEN
TO YOUR MOM
BE FRIENDLY
TO PEOPLE
DON'T PULL
PEOPLE'S HAIR

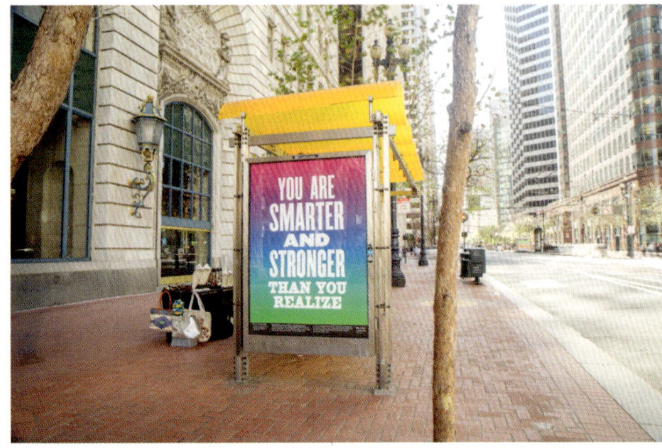
YOU ARE
SMARTER
AND
STRONGER
THAN YOU
REALIZE

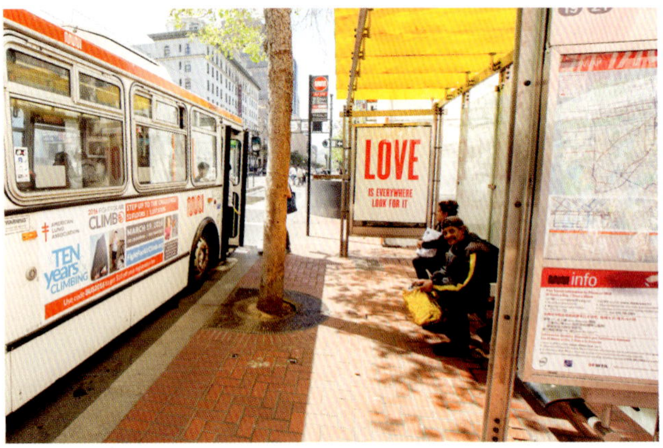
LOVE
IS EVERYWHERE
LOOK FOR IT

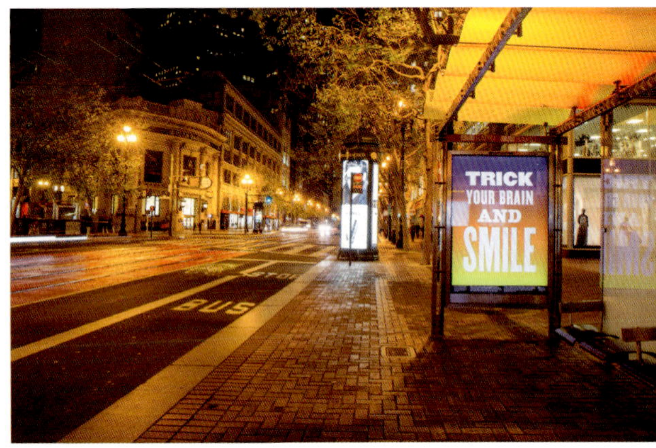
TRICK
YOUR BRAIN
AND
SMILE
BUS

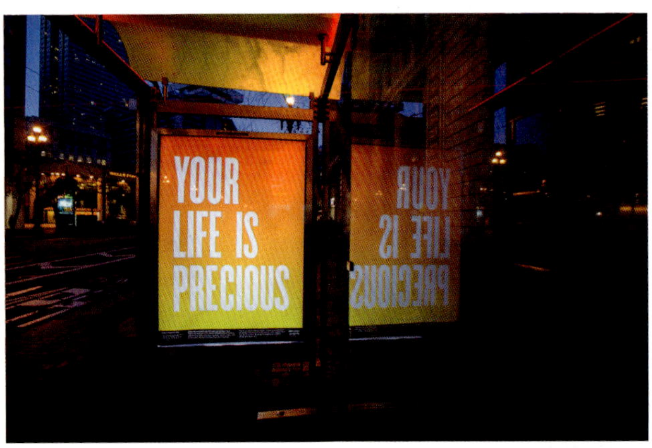
YOUR
LIFE IS
PRECIOUS

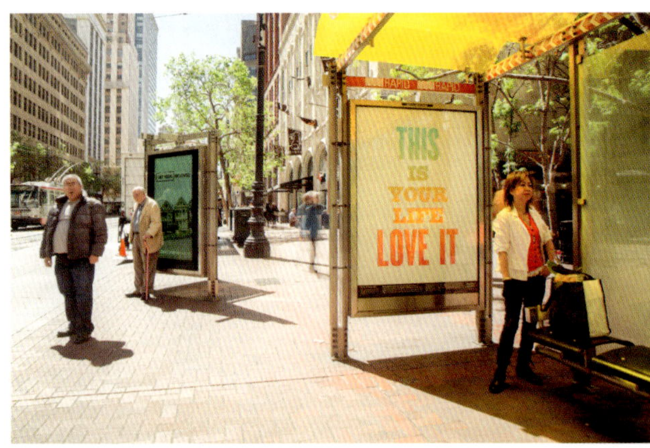
THIS
IS
YOUR
LIFE
LOVE IT

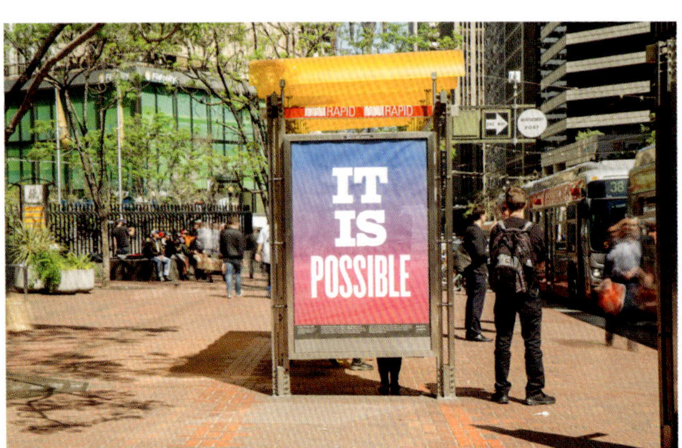
RAPID
IT
IS
POSSIBLE

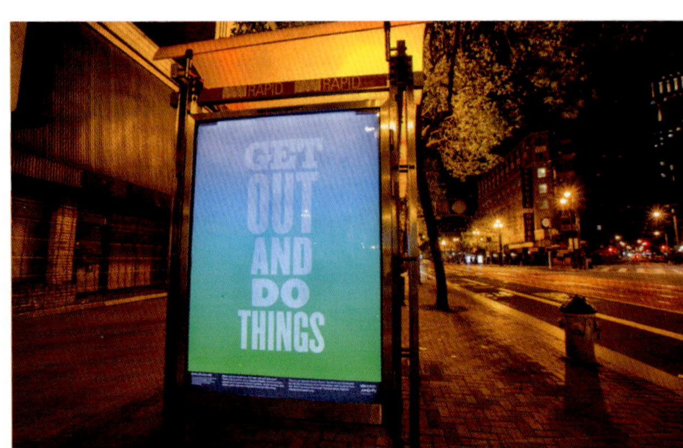
GET
OUT
AND
DO
THINGS

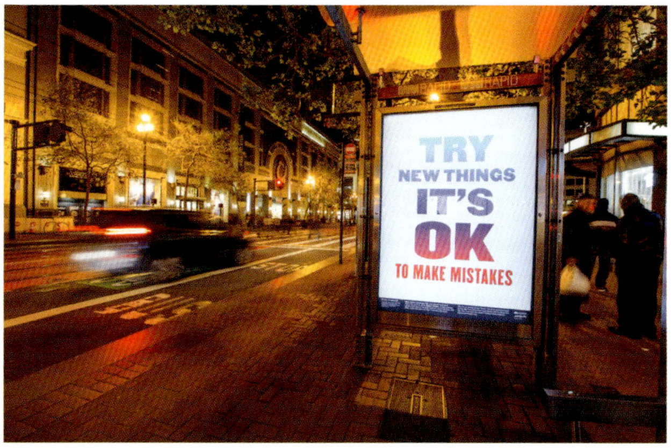
TRY
NEW THINGS
IT'S
OK
TO MAKE MISTAKES

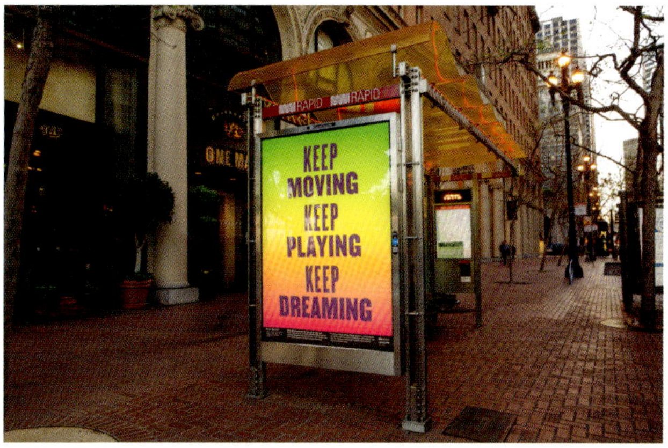
KEEP
MOVING
KEEP
PLAYING
KEEP
DREAMING

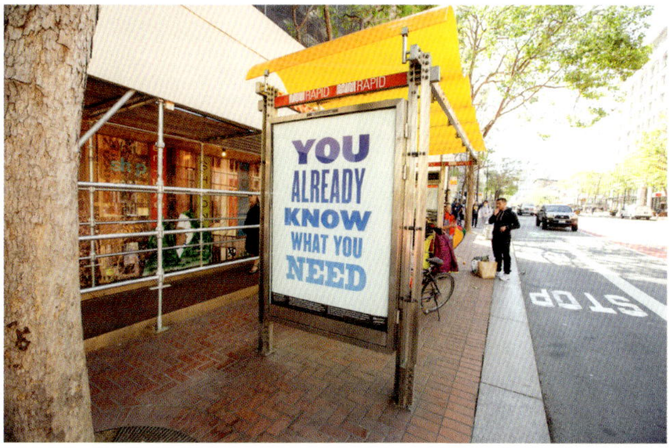
YOU
ALREADY
KNOW
WHAT YOU
NEED
STOP

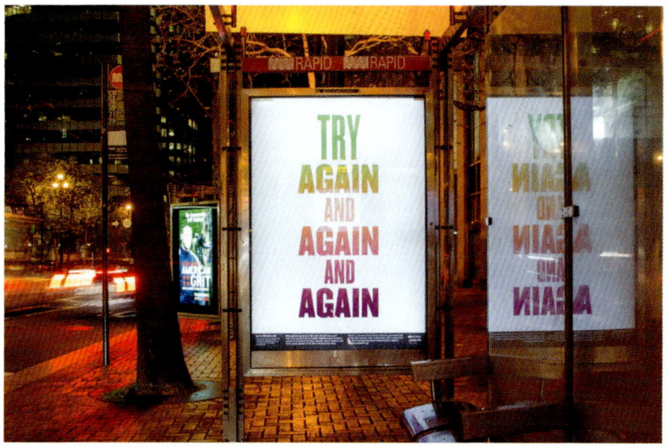
TRY
AGAIN
AND
AGAIN
AND
AGAIN

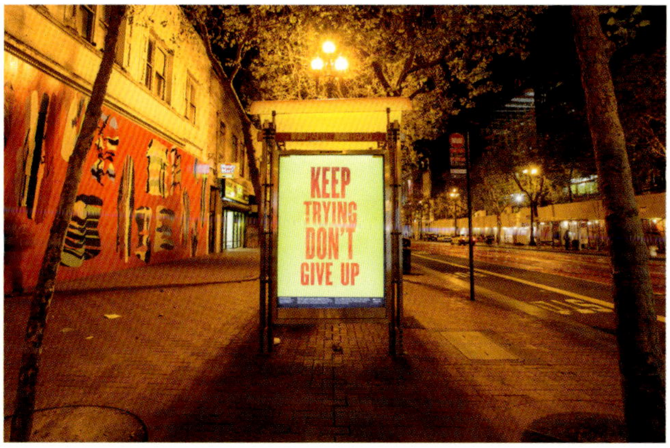
KEEP
TRYING
DON'T
GIVE UP

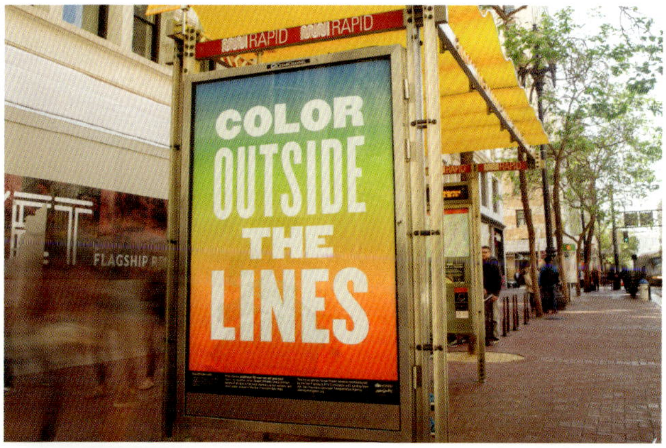
COLOR
OUTSIDE
THE
LINES

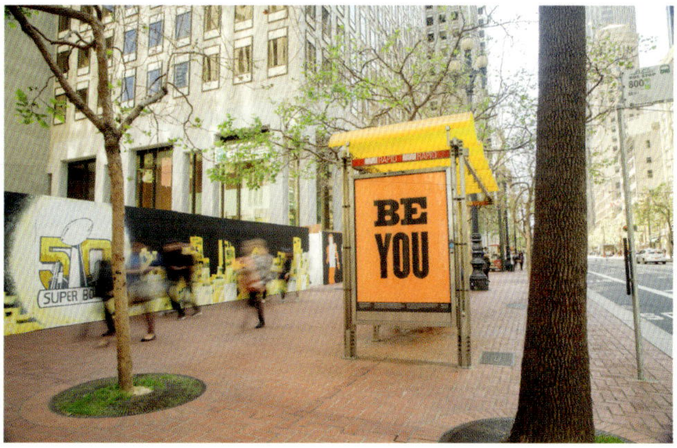
BE
YOU

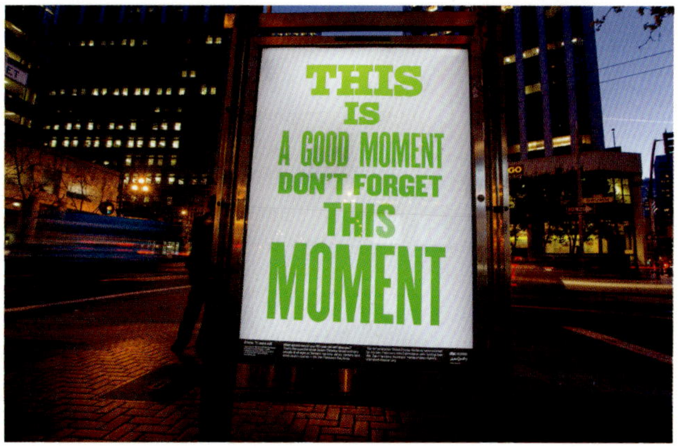
THIS
IS
A GOOD MOMENT
DON'T FORGET
THIS
MOMENT

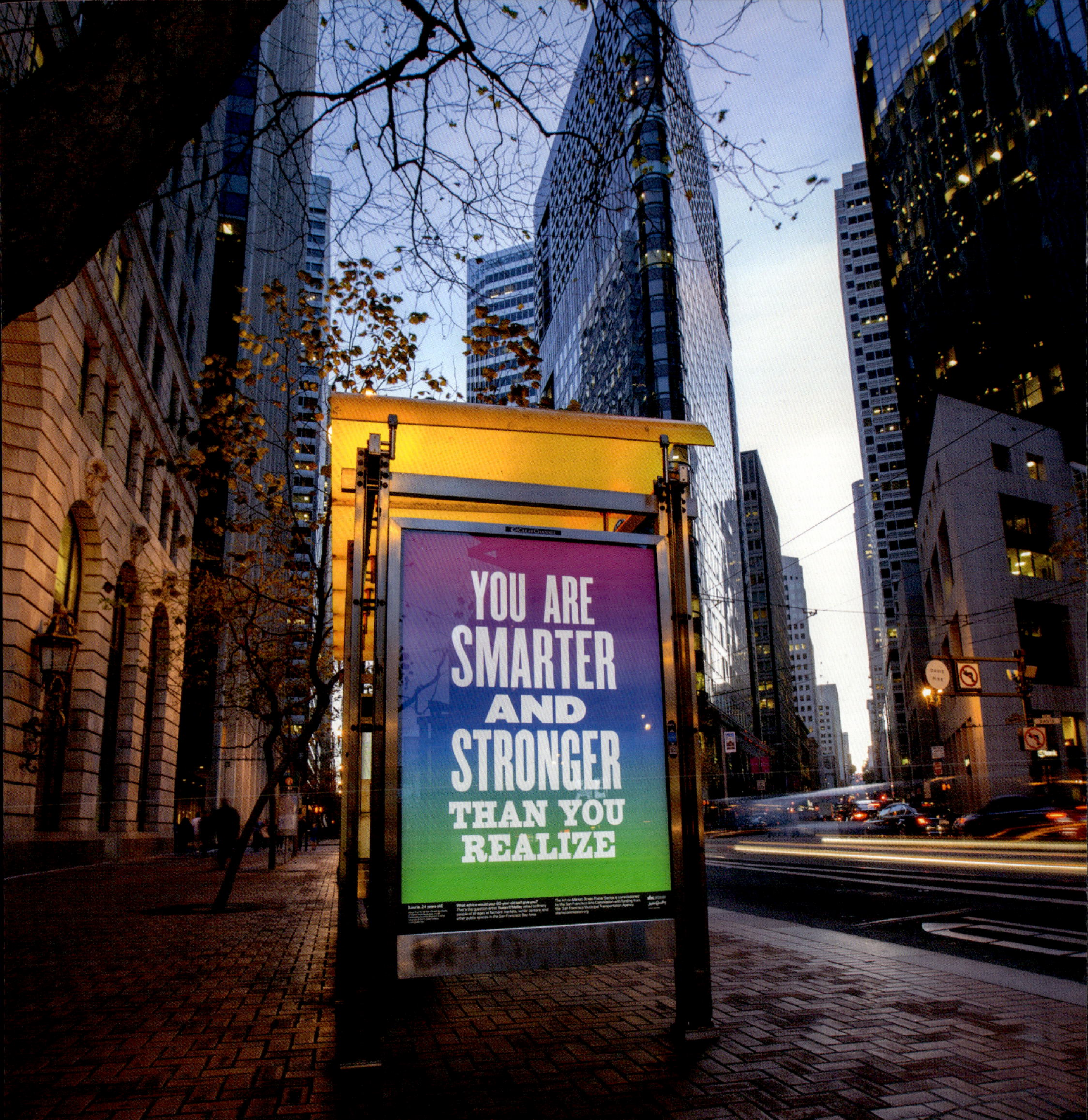
YOU ARE
SMARTER
AND
STRONGER
THAN YOU
REALIZE
Laurie, 24 years old
What advice would your 80-year-old self give you? That's the question artist Susan O'Malley asked ordinary people of all ages at farmers' markets, senior centers, and other public spaces in the San Francisco Bay Area.
The Art on Market Street Poster Series is commissioned by the San Francisco Arts Commission with funding from the San Francisco Municipal Transportation Agency.
sfartscommission.org

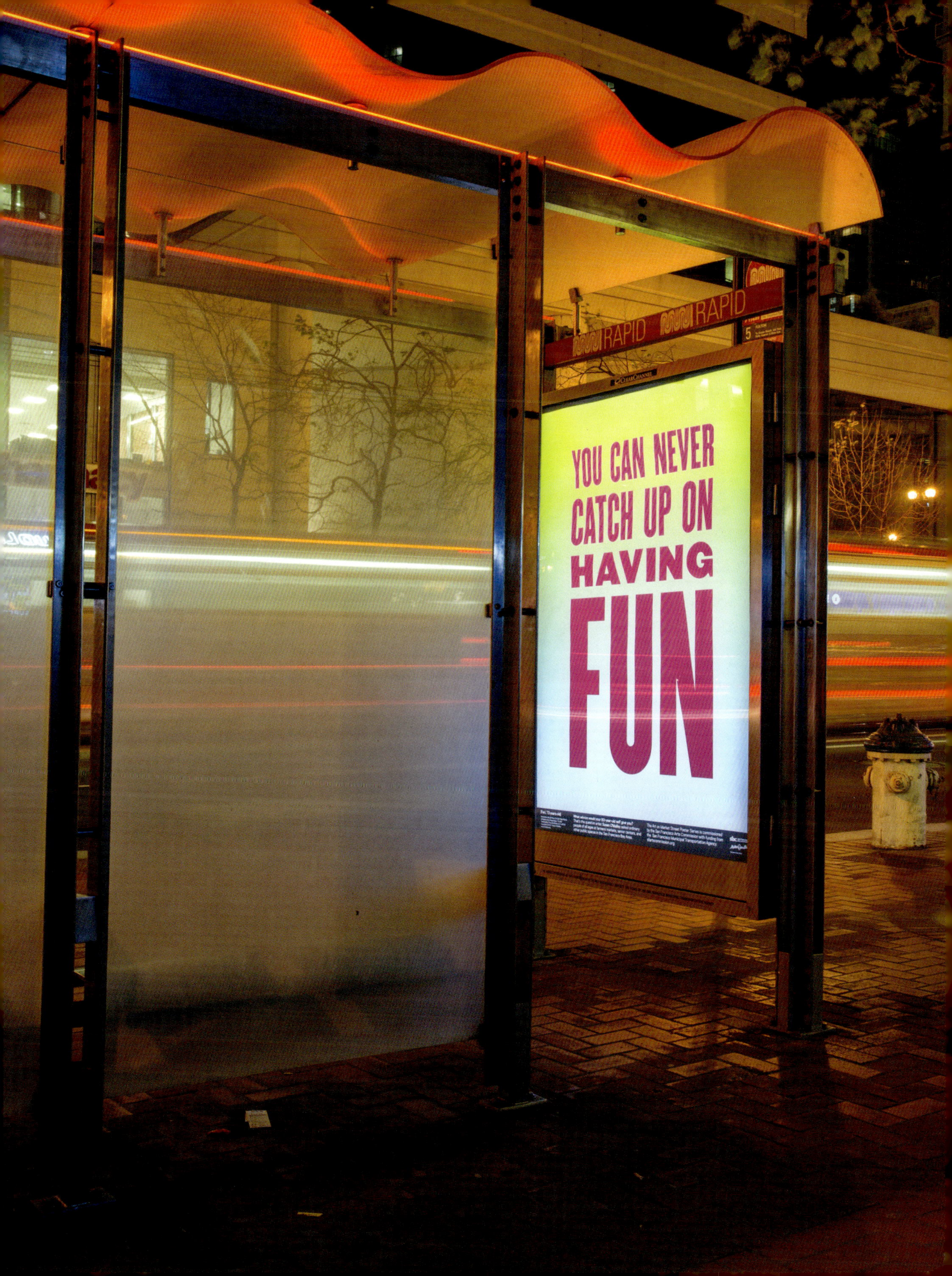

RAPID
RAPID
YOU CAN NEVER
CATCH UP ON
HAVING
FUN

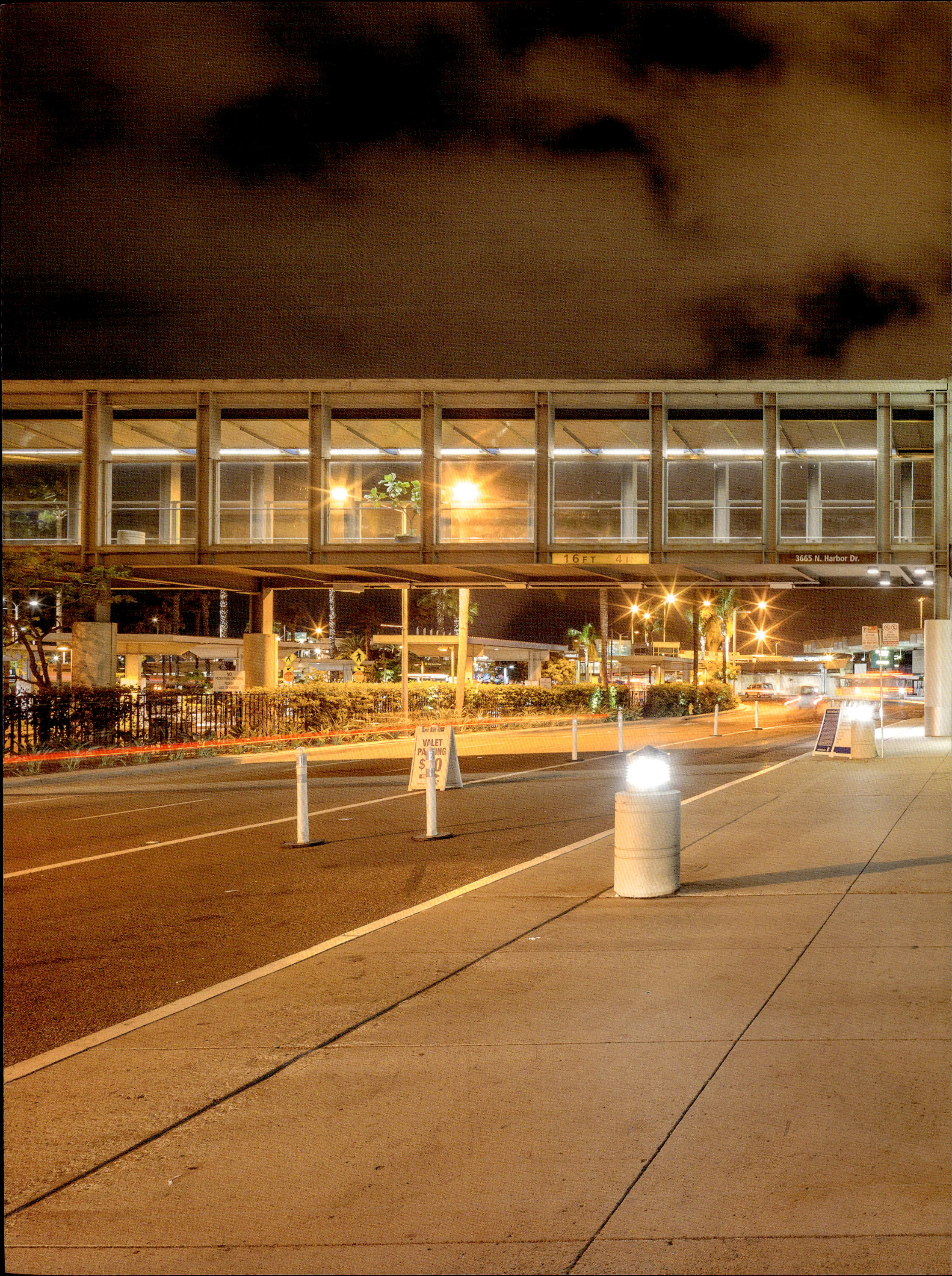
3665 N. Harbor Dr.
VALET

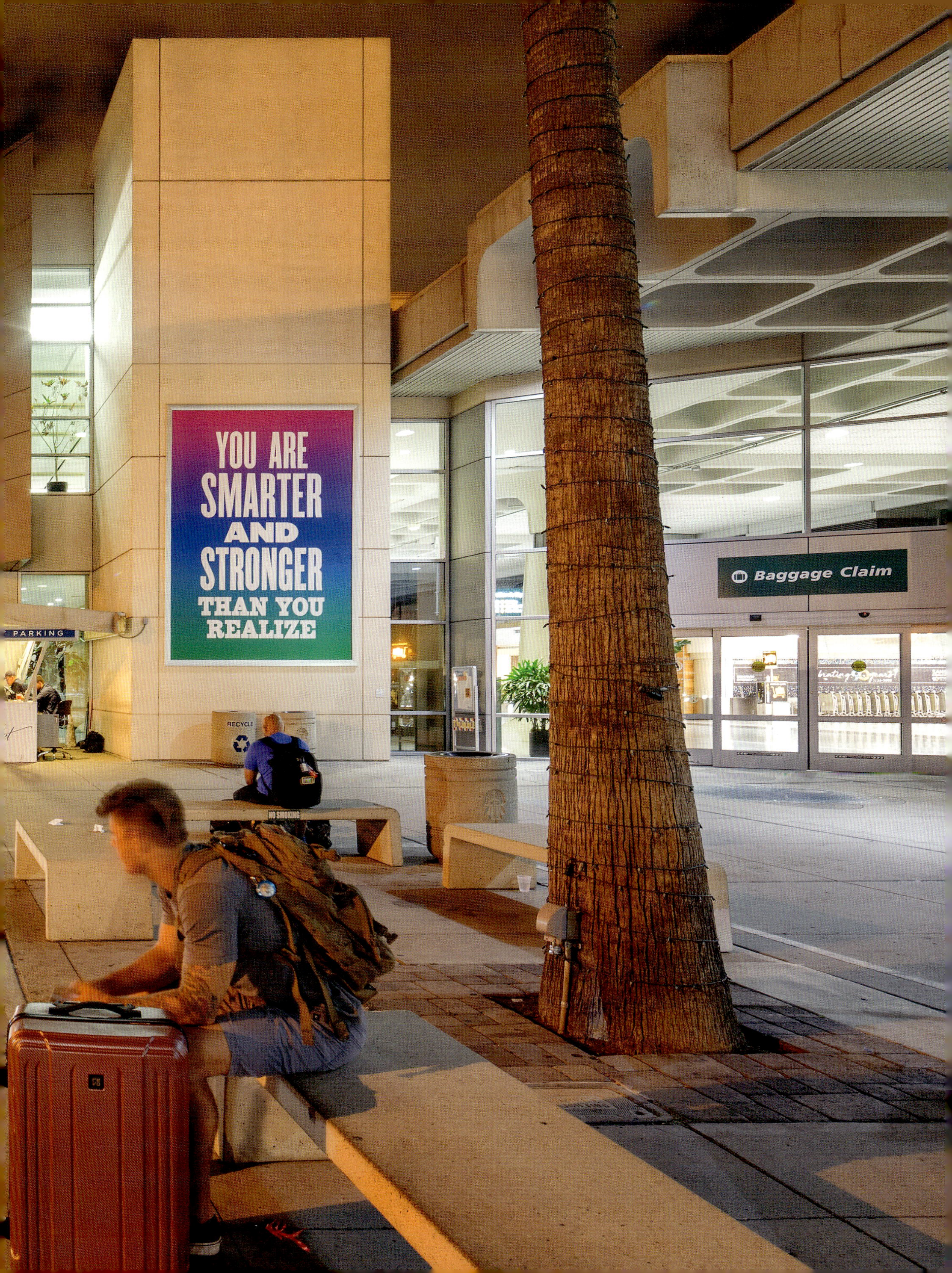
YOU ARE
SMARTER
AND
STRONGER
THAN YOU
REALIZE
Baggage Claim
PARKING
RECYCLE

Advice from My 80-Year-Old Self: The Murals at SFMOMA

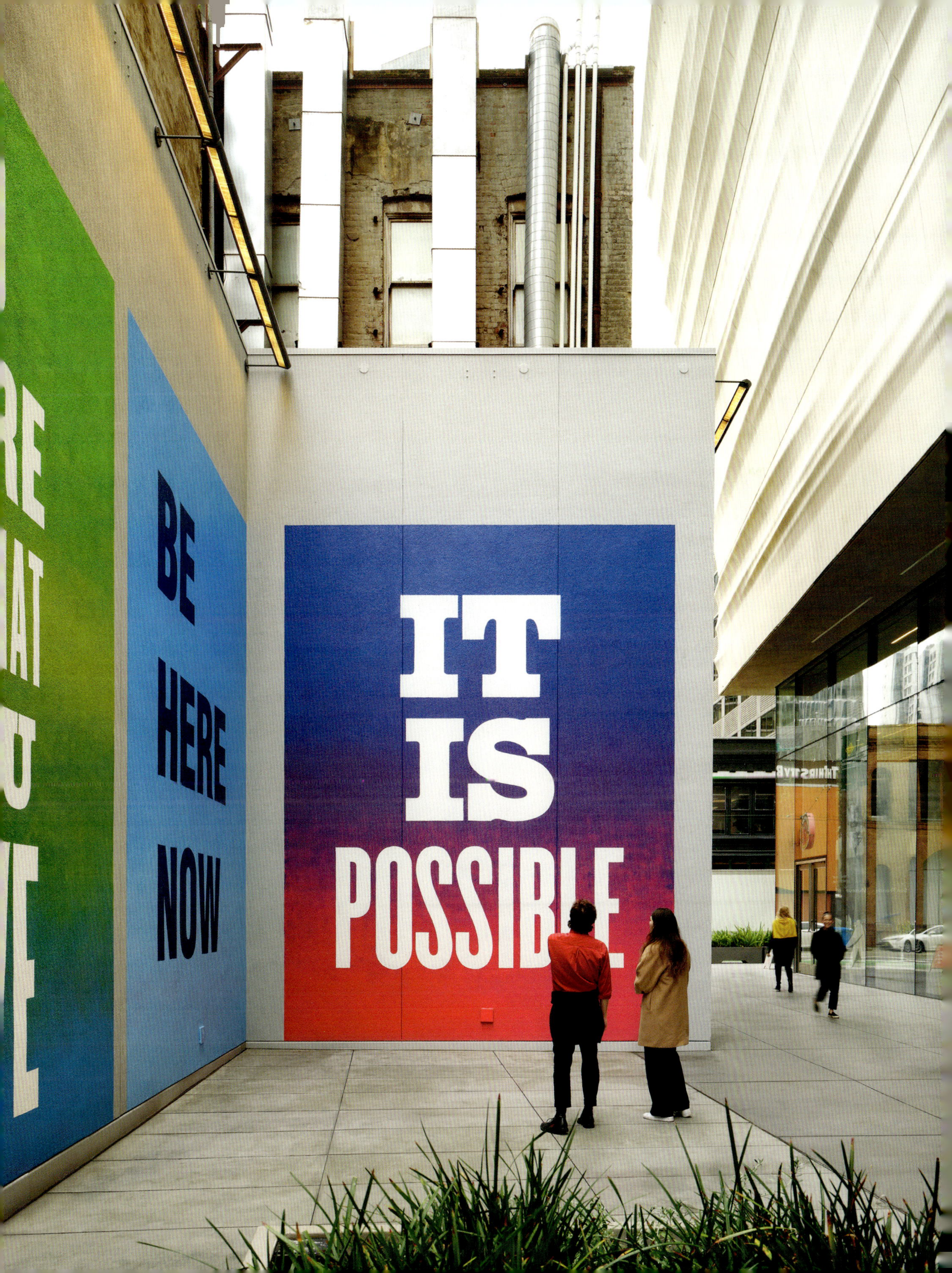
BE
HERE
NOW
IT
IS
POSSIBLE

Scaling Up: Susan O'Malley's *Advice* Murals at SFMOMA

Janet Bishop

When Christopher Bedford arrived from Baltimore to become the SFMOMA's eighth director in the spring of 2022, San Francisco was only very slowly recovering from the long tail of COVID-19. The tech-dominated downtown workforce remained largely remote. Retail was drastically diminished. So was tourism, historically a significant driver of the city's economy.

One of our energetic new leader's top priorities was to help fuel our South of Market neighborhood's return to life, with a focus on the experience of the museum at street level. Our goal was for the museum to embody a spirit of "radical hospitality," as he called it. By the end of the year we had opened a new restaurant on Third Street, engaged Jocelyn Tsaih to create new graphics to encourage visitors through our doors, sited Wu Tsang's *Of Whales* (2022) in our Botta Atrium, and installed a group of monumental murals by Susan O'Malley.

The museum had presented O'Malley's work twice before. In 2016 we acquired and installed *Advice from My 80-Year-Old Self* (2015), her brilliant suite of sixteen prints, each bearing a message collected in response to the question she posed to people of all ages and walks of life: "What advice would your eighty-year-old self give you?" O'Malley's friends Christina Amini and Christian L. Frock proposed that we accompany the installation with a giveaway. Before the works came down in 2017, more than fifty thousand *It Is Possible* buttons went off into the world, into button collections, and onto hats and bags and denim jackets.

Thanks to very generous gifts of art by Frock, in 2019, and Timothy Caro-Bruce, O'Malley's husband, in 2021, O'Malley is now among the artists of her generation represented in the greatest depth in the museum's collection. In 2021–22, SFMOMA featured an expanded selection of O'Malley's work—a full gallery's worth this time—alongside a room-size installation by her friend and sometime

---

Pages 247 and 250–51: Installation views of Susan O'Malley, *Do More of What You Love*, 2015; *Be Here Now*, 2009; *It Is Possible*, 2015; *Love Is Everywhere Look for It*, 2012; and *Make It Up As You Go*, 2015. San Francisco Museum of Modern Art, purchase, by exchange, through a gift of Michael D. Abrams, 2022. Howard Street breezeway, 2022. Photos by Matthew Millman.

Opposite: Janet Bishop with Alexis Pence and former San Francisco Giants outfielder Hunter Pence in the exhibition *One Day at a Time: Susan O'Malley and Leah Rosenberg*, San Francisco Museum of Modern Art, August 20, 2021. Photo by Katherine Du Tiel.

collaborator Leah Rosenberg. Rosenberg suggested titling the show *One Day at a Time*, a phrase originally collected by O'Malley in Berkeley that tapped into the inner wisdom of a twenty-one-year-old *Advice* project participant named Dionte.

For the 2022 transformation in and around SFMOMA's building, we could think of no artist whose work was better suited than O'Malley's for the massive walls near our Howard Street entrance. We selected five works from her *Advice* project: *Do More of What You Love* (2015), *Be Here Now* (2009), *It Is Possible* (2015), *Love Is Everywhere Look for It* (2012), and *Make It Up As You Go* (2015). Working closely with Joey Piziali of San Francisco's Romer Young Gallery, we stayed true to O'Malley's original files—her fonts, colors, and proportions. And we hired New Bohemia Signs to paint the designs at scale.

For a year and a half, starting in December 2022, O'Malley's larger-than-life murals were a gift to museum visitors, passersby, and the employees of nearby businesses—a bright spot within the downtown landscape that offered enduringly relevant, ever hopeful messages. People stopped, looked, and smiled. The murals could be seen from different vantage points—from the alley or exterior stairs at any time of day or night, or through the windows of the museum's Roberts Family Gallery, which then displayed a mural from a different era: Diego Rivera's *Pan American Unity* (1940). O'Malley's works remained on view until May 2024, at which point they were deinstalled to make way for another project. And while they are much missed, SFMOMA acquired the set of instructions needed to install them again in the future—a moment to look forward to.

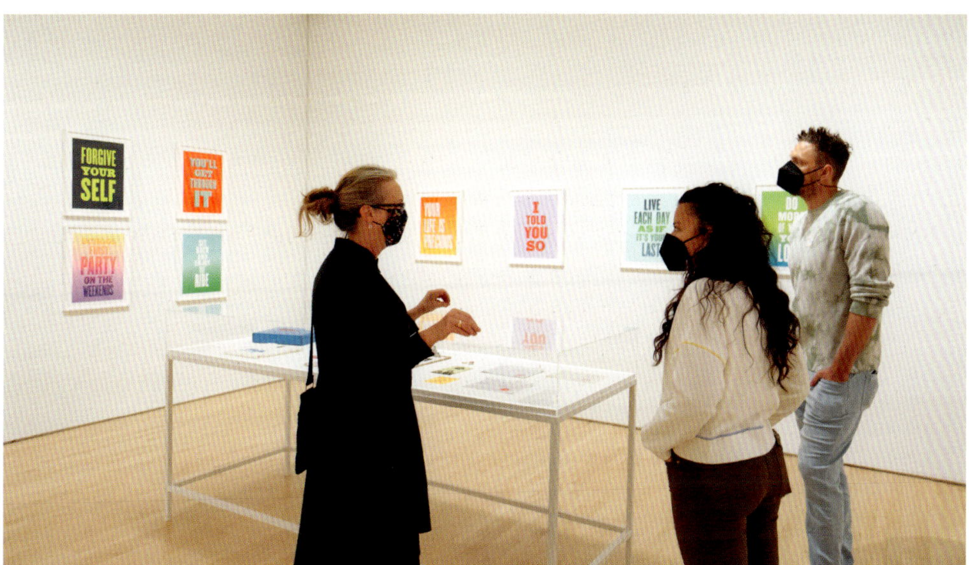

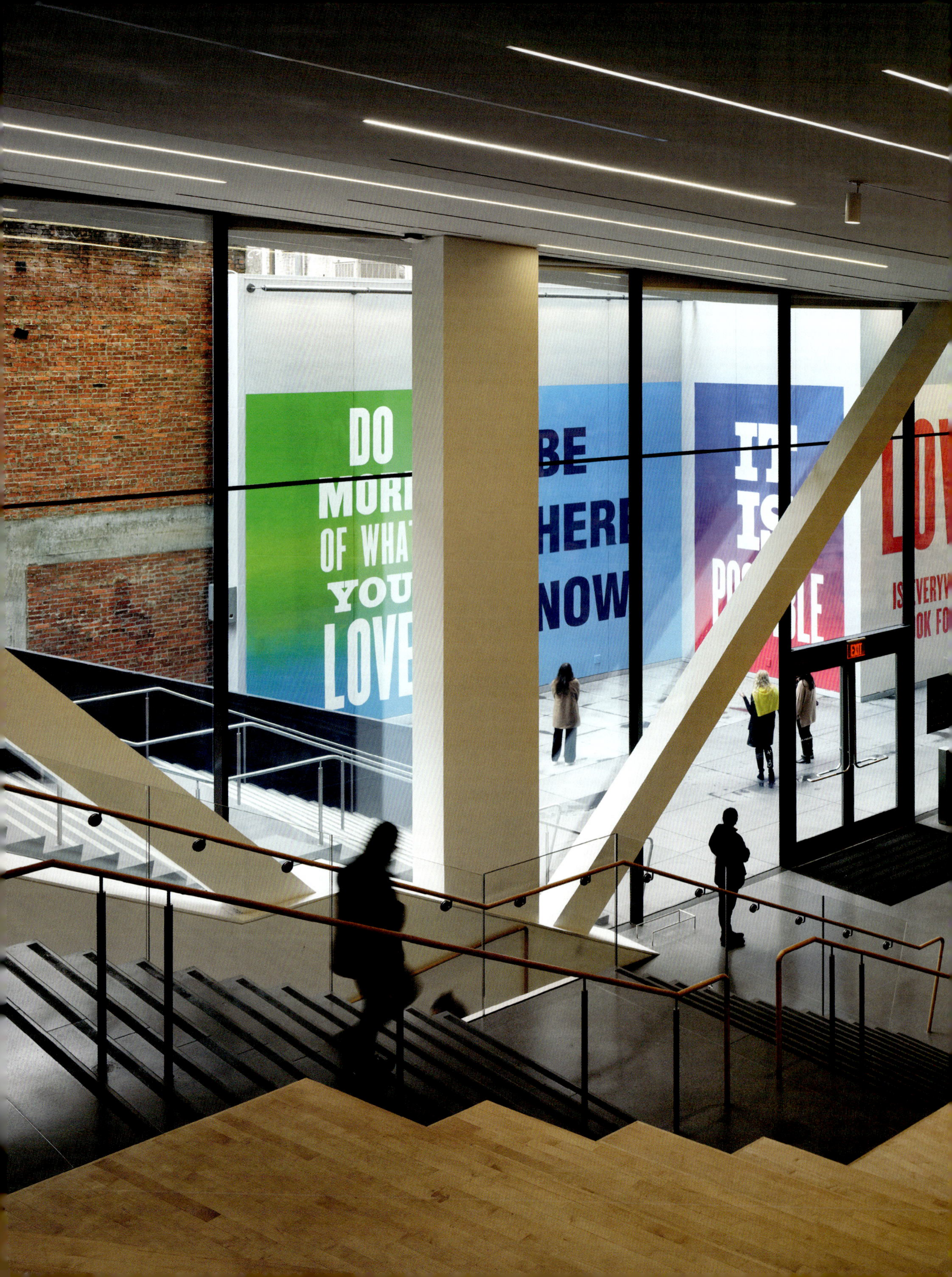
DO
YOU
BE
NOW
EXIT

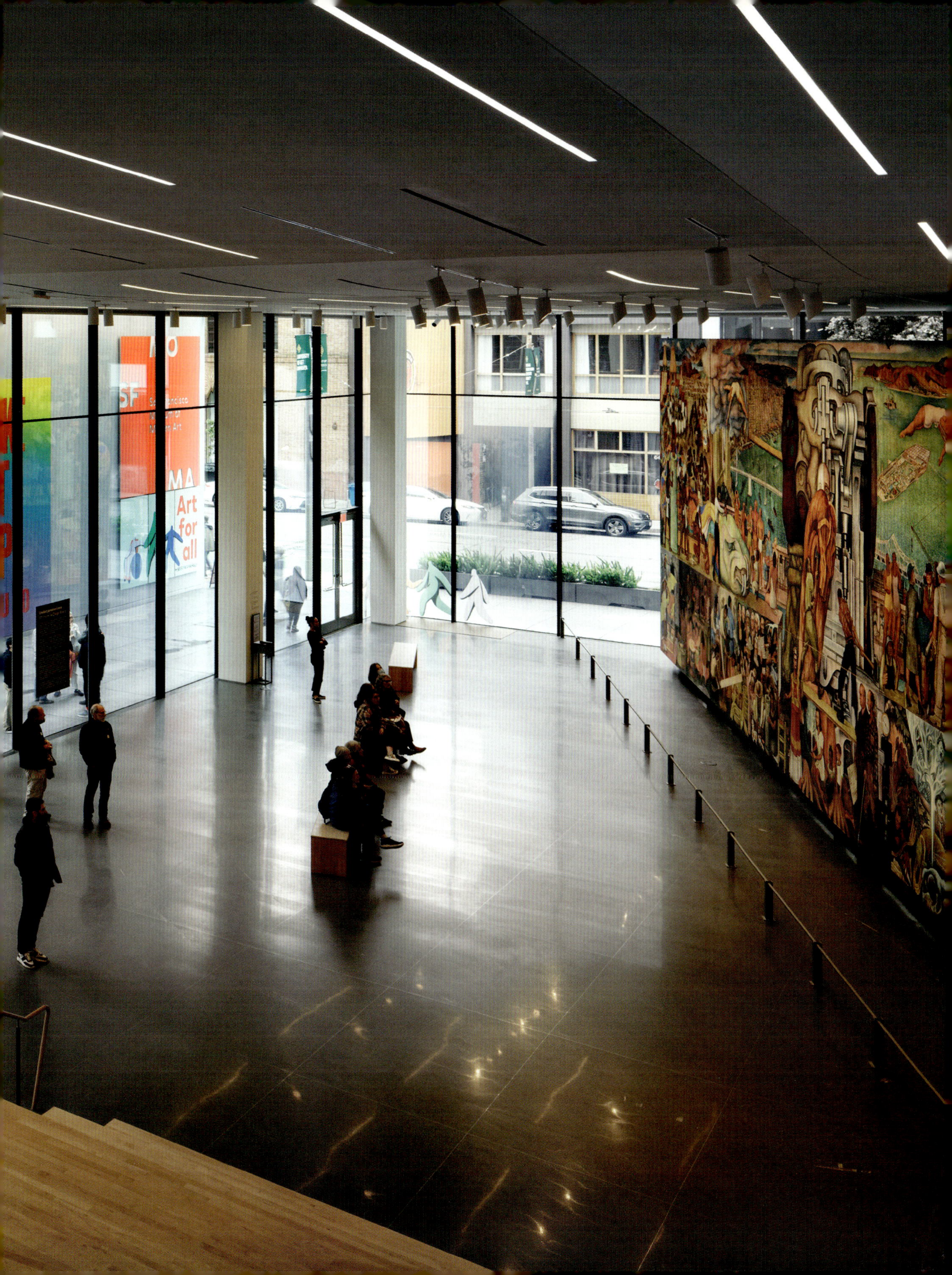
SF
MA
Art for all

On Influence

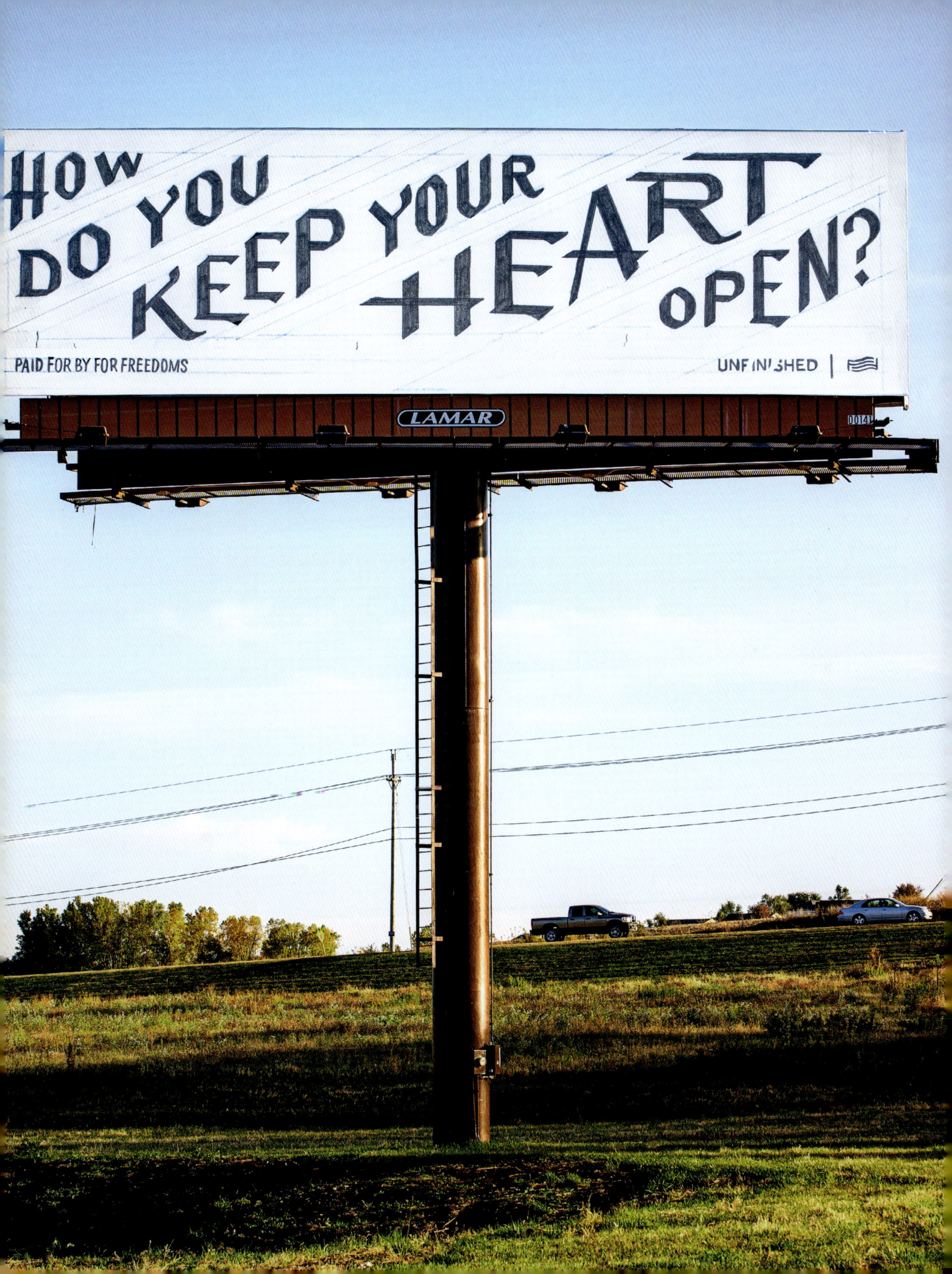

HOW DO YOU KEEP YOUR HEART OPEN?
PAID FOR BY FOR FREEDOMS
UNFINISHED
LAMAR

How Do You Keep Your Heart Open?

Christine Wong Yap

I met Susan O'Malley in California, but our friendship blossomed in Poland. We met in grad school in 2006 at California College of the Arts (CCA), and we remained friendly after I moved to New York City. We were both making text-based artworks with unabashedly optimistic statements. The artistic kinship I sensed between us was apparent to others, and our paths seemed destined to reconverge when we were curated into multiple group shows together starting in 2012. That September, Galeria Rusz invited us to Toruń, Poland, for Art Moves: A Festival of Billboard Art.

Susan's billboard featured three messages—"Be here now," "You are exactly where you need to be," and "Listen to your heart"—and was installed next to mine, which spelled out "Take charge of your happiness" in ribbons. Translations in Polish appeared on mobile billboards that were towed around the city. Eight years later I would create another billboard to honor Susan's life and influence on me.

In Toruń, Susan and I shared a room in the fifteenth-century Dwór Mieszczański (Burghers' Hall). One night, she enthusiastically recommended Cheryl Strayed's *Tiny Beautiful Things*, a collection of forceful candid essays. Susan, like Strayed, was being transformed by loss—another point of commonality that we would soon share.

Two weeks later, my dad passed away unexpectedly. In grief, my heart felt like it was cleaving itself from my chest. I felt isolated and lonely in my state of bewildered mourning. Few sources offered comfort; *Tiny Beautiful Things* was one. Gutted yet grateful, I thanked Susan for her prescient recommendation.

A few weeks later and still reeling with bereavement, I came back to California to create new work for *Happiness Is . . .*, a three-person exhibition curated by Donna Conwell at Montalvo Arts Center. It would feature Susan, our former classmate Leah Rosenberg, and me. When Susan led *One Minute Smile*, a participatory performance inspired by her mother's terminal illness, tears streamed down my face as our shared experience of losing a parent resonated in every fiber of my being.

In 2020, artist-run nonprofit organization For Freedoms asked me to create a billboard design posing a question for their 20/20 Awakening campaign. I sensed that the atmosphere of othering and divisiveness was connected to a baseline fear of the other—a distrust that prevented emotional vulnerability, connecting across

---

Page 253: Christine Wong Yap, *How Do You Keep Your Heart Open? (For Susan)* from For Freedoms 20/20 Awakening Campaign, Omaha, Nebraska, 2020. In partnership with McCourt Global. Photo by Jeff Scroggins.

differences, and finding common humanity. I created a pencil drawing, asking, "How do you keep your heart open?," and I dedicated it to Susan, explaining:

> "Keeping one's heart open" means experiencing setbacks, adversities, pain, loss, or grief—such as witnessing injustices and conflicts in the world—and responding not by becoming numb, cynical, or withdrawn, but by steadfastly remaining vulnerable and feeling, open to trusting others, choosing optimism, and staying engaged. It is to heal wounds with scar tissue alive with nerves, not hiding behind protective armor that desensitizes, distances, and diminishes the possibilities of humanization.
>
> To keep one's heart open is to embrace a mindset of abundance, rather than a mindset of scarcity; to opt for connection and generosity, rather than self-preservation; and to work toward belonging, rather than othering.[1]

I've thought a lot about Susan's courage over the years. In my practice, I've encountered the assumption that in order to be critical, one must be oppositional, be anti-something, point out problematic aspects, poke holes in arguments or artworks. This implies that being affirmative is uncritical. Likewise, earnestness and emotions can be associated with thoughtlessness. Susan's work is a testament that the opposite is true. Our insistence on the positive didn't arise from the ignorance of pain but in spite of it. Our approaches of vulnerability and affirmation are grounded in study, rigor, and intention.

Susan embraced the risks of being sentimental. She had faith that feeling self-conscious or ridiculous was a small trade-off for worthy, significant gains: By being vulnerable, we become more connected to each other. Art making, vulnerability, and connection went hand in hand for Susan. She wrote, "Making art gives me courage to be vulnerable—talk to strangers, put myself in awkward situations, meet new people etc."[2] Indeed, our practices share much in common with the three aspects of wholehearted living that Brené Brown has identified: vulnerability, love (a topic that appeared often in Susan's work), and belonging (which has become central to my practice).[3] For Susan, making art with vulnerability was "a practice of possibility and discovery,"[4] which is echoed in what keeping one's heart open means to me: "a continual process of exploration, feeling, risk-taking, and revising."[5]

Back in the mid-2000s I applied to CCA for grad school because I had enjoyed being an undergrad there. At the time, the fact that it was the home of the country's first Social Practice program wasn't a factor for me. But Ted Purves (1964–2017), who founded the program, became an important adviser to me, and the work of Susan and her fellow Social Practice majors expanded my understanding of what art could be and how artists could engage with the world. After grad school, I tentatively began making art that invited prescribed interactions. Now I embrace Social Practice and center relationships and contexts in my work. It turns out that Susan's and Ted's influences on me were like seeds that germinated under the surface before finally breaking through into the light.

And so "How do you keep your heart open?" was far from the only time I have experienced Susan's influence on my own work. Currently, I'm exhibiting projects about belonging at the Institute of Contemporary Art San José. My installation occupies the galleries that were once the print studio that Susan oversaw as curator and print director (2006–11). In one room I created an interactive activity with a hand-painted fifteen-part Venn diagram. Over the years, there have been many full-circle moments that reconnect me with Susan, like so many vibrant, overlapping loops.

In 2014, I received a fun assignment: Explain my work and artistic influences by way of proposing a dream group exhibition. Freed from constraints, who would you show alongside, and what would you show? I thought of Susan's *Community Advice* (2012), in which she created letterpress-printed posters based on responses to the questions, "What advice would you give your eight-year-old self? What advice would you give your eighty-year-old self?" Her project invited everyday people to take a long view of their lives, which I imagine prompted feelings of self-compassion. The results are humorous, tender, and wise. I loved the grassroots horizontality of the project, in which everyday people share their hard-won life lessons.

In the vein of *Community Advice*, I created *Life Lessons* (2022–present). Both projects present advice from everyday people as letterpress prints. Influenced by positive psychology and the role of reframing for resilience, I invite the public to write about adversity that they have faced, healthy ways they have coped, and advice they'd give to a friend in a similar situation. In exchange, contributors receive an existing print. I select and interpret phrases as hand-lettered designs, which I print on a letterpress printing press. Because I both give the print to the author of the original words and offer prints in exchange for writing from other new contributors, I imagine *Life Lessons* as a positive, upward spiral. Like Susan's life and work, the spiral originates with a spirit of generosity and humanism, and it appeals to the better angels of our nature to expand generatively outward.

---

[1] https://christinewongyap.com/work/2020/how-do-you-keep-billboard.html

[2] http://artmovesfestival.org/edition-2012/artists/

[3] Brené Brown, *The Gifts of Imperfection: Let Go of Who You Think You're Supposed to Be and Embrace Who You Are* (Hazelden Publishing, 2010).

[4] http://artmovesfestival.org/edition-2012/artists/

[5] https://christinewongyap.com/work/2020/how-do-you-keep-billboard.html

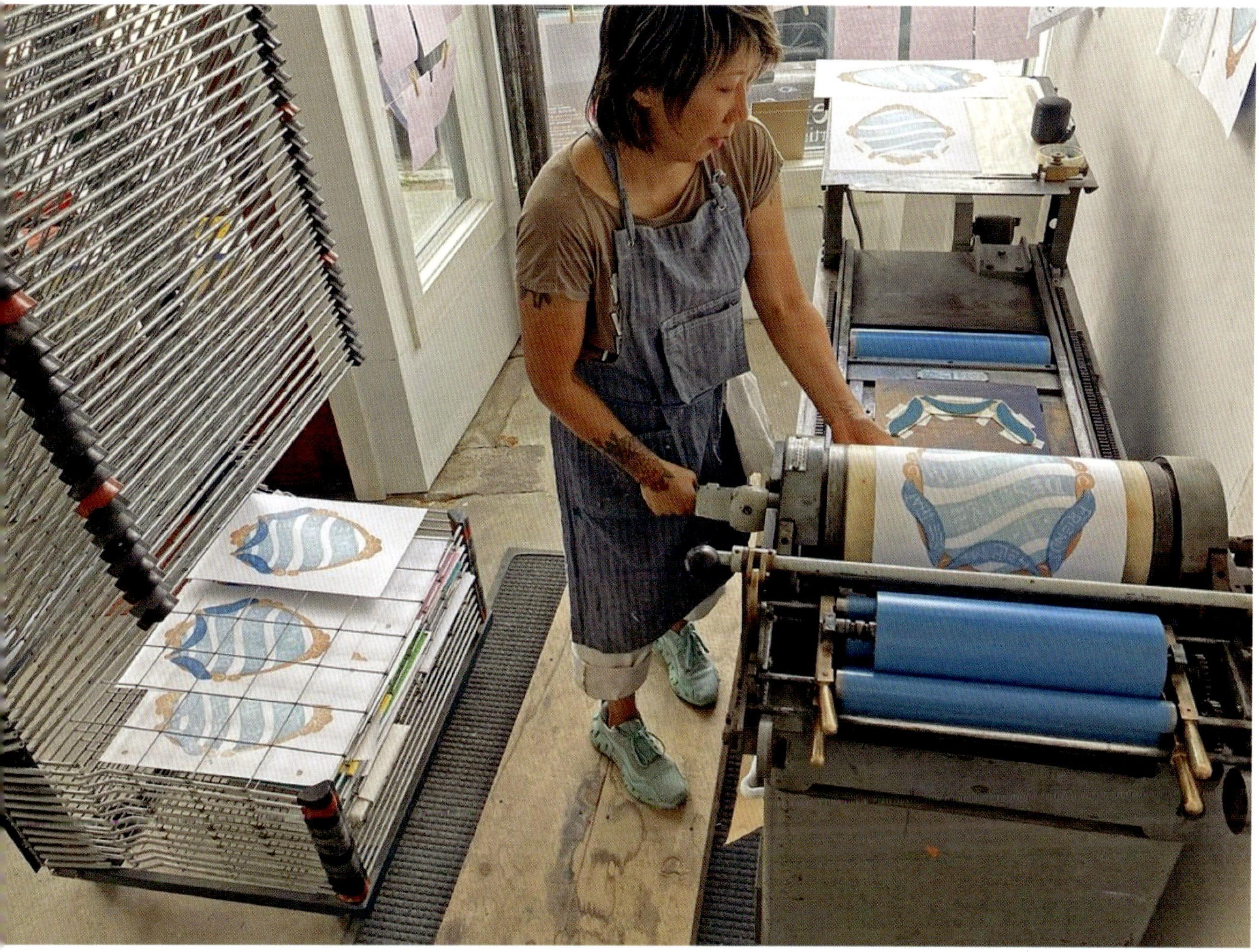

Above: Christine Wong Yap printing "Friends Help Me See I Deserve Comfort & Love" (inspired by Siraaj) in a residency at StudioWorks, a program of the Tides Institute & Museum of Art, a private not-for-profit organization in Eastport (Muselenk), Maine. Photo by Hugh French, courtesy of the Tides Institute & Museum of Art.

Pages 258–59: Christine Wong Yap with contributors, untitled interactive activity on fifteen qualities of belonging, hand-painted mural, fifteen reflection cards, art supplies; mural: 70 x 169 inches, cards: 5.5 x 4.25 inches each. In the exhibition *P L A C E: Reckonings by Asian American Artists*, Institute for Contemporary Art San José, 2024. The fifteen qualities of belonging were identified in collaboration with Evan Bissell. Photo by Glen Cheriton.

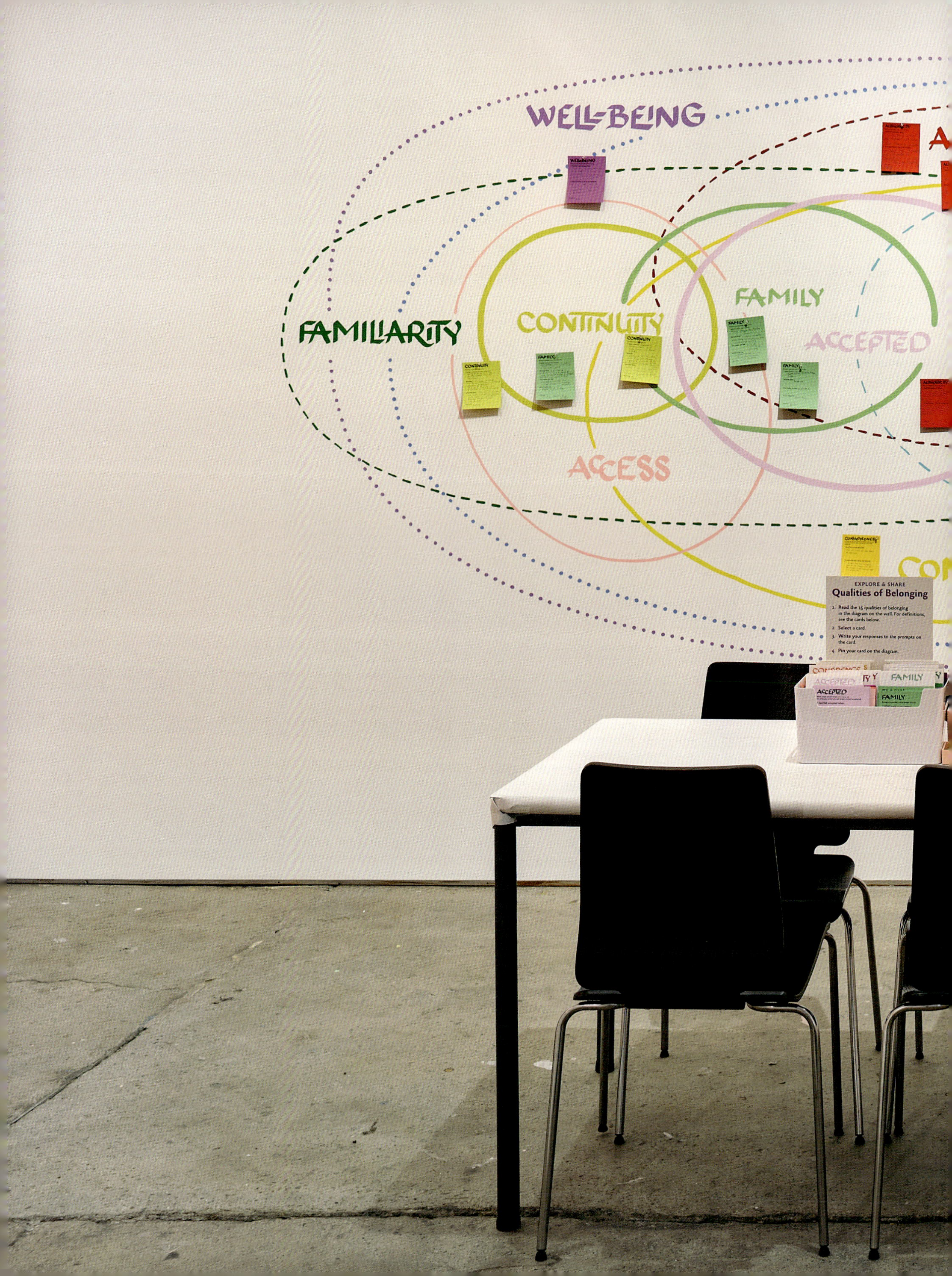
WELL-BEING
FAMILIARITY
CONTINUITY
FAMILY
ACCEPTED
ACCESS
EXPLORE & SHARE
Qualities of Belonging
1. Read the 15 qualities of belonging in the diagram on the wall. For definitions, see the cards below.
2. Select a card.
3. Write your responses to the prompts on the card.
4. Pin your card on the diagram.
FAMILY
ACCEPTED
FAMILY

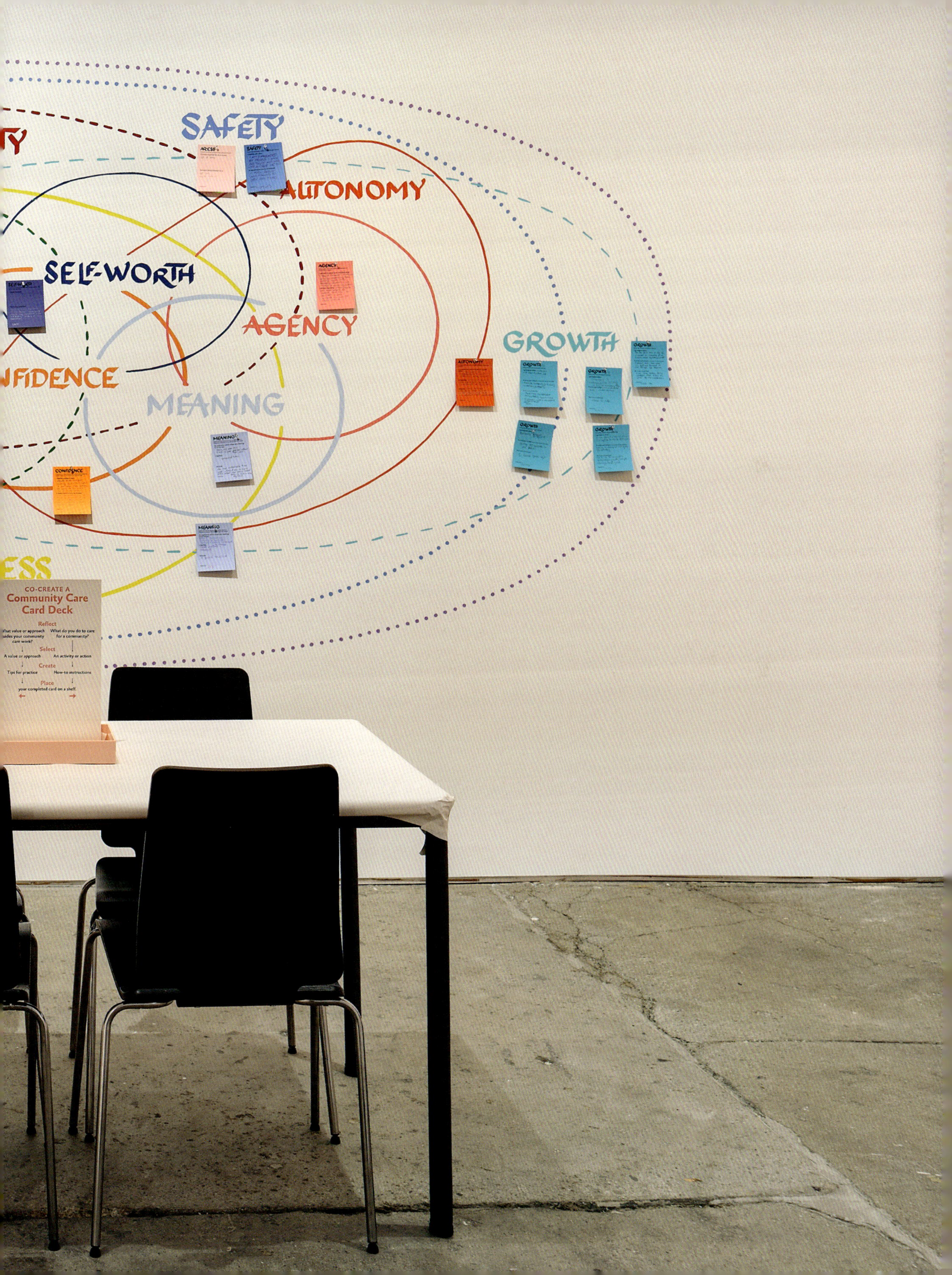
SAFETY
AUTONOMY
SELF-WORTH
AGENCY
MEANING
GROWTH
CO-CREATE A
Community Care Card Deck
Reflect
hat value or approach uides your community care work?
What do you do to care for a community?
Select
A value or approach
An activity or action
Create
Tips for practice
How-to instructions
Place
your completed card on a shelf.

Light and Hope

Kevin B. Chen

I first met Susan around 2006 or 2007. Whether you knew Susan for five years or five minutes, you were instantly connected and present with her, drawn in by her smile and especially her laugh. We collaborated on several projects over the years; I've curated her work into my exhibitions, and she's curated my work into hers. There was a wonderful mutual respect for the various roles we both played as artists and curators. I had numerous conversations with her about juggling these two practices, and I always appreciated her insights into how she balanced both. I was always humbled by her thoughtfulness and generosity: the handwritten note, the surprise gift, and the words of acknowledgment and appreciation.

I began teaching at the college level after Susan's passing. I've been fortunate to work with and learn from incredibly inspiring young people, many born in the late 1990s and early 2000s. When asked to share artwork that has deeply impacted them, numerous students have referenced Susan's *Advice* work in their class presentations. They encountered her work in the galleries at SFMOMA and the Oakland Museum of California; in murals on the side of Root Division, on Howard Street outside of SFMOMA, and in Martin Luther King Jr. Civic Center Park in downtown Berkeley; and through her postcards and posters. Susan believed in making her art accessible in public spaces. I find it remarkable that her work has provided so much inspiration and comfort to my students, who responded solely to the artwork without knowing Susan's life context. This truly shows the power of her *Advice* work.

My most recent group of students started college online in fall 2020. Besides facing a global pandemic that fostered feelings of social isolation, these young people also grew up negotiating the pervasive influence of social media, further heightening a sense of disconnectedness. Moreover, economic uncertainties, the specter of climate change, and escalating geopolitical tensions have all contributed to the overwhelming complexity of our world today. No matter one's age, to navigate through this, one needs strategies and tools for resilience and adaptability, a vision for a better future, and, most of all, a belief that there is light and hope beyond it all.

However, for students still learning about the world and themselves during a pandemic-impacted education, it's challenging to know where to find these strategies and tools. Many of the young people I work with are first-generation college students. In many families, especially immigrant families, open conversations about mental health are rare. For older generations, mental health issues have been heavily stigmatized and often misunderstood. Conditions like depression and anxiety were seen as personal weaknesses or moral failings. It is a significant cultural and generational shift that younger people now openly discuss the importance of mental health, not only for themselves but also for their families and communities.

The strength of Susan's *Advice* work lies in the economy of means in which she worked. She distilled life lessons and aspirations into accessible declarations and observations that, in her words, "remind me that we are different versions of each other trying to make our way through this life."[1] Her *Advice* works are like indispensable mantras urging us to become the best versions of ourselves, "not through some colossal effort at personal reinvention, but simply by slowing down. We just have to take a moment to pay attention and listen."

In overwhelming, isolating times, my students have found comfort in Susan's work, feeling seen and understood and finding hope and clarity. Fellow artist and friend Christine Wong Yap embraced a similar mindset in her 2020–21 project *How Do You Keep Your Heart Open? (For Susan)*, striving for connection and perspective with simple yet profound words of wisdom and love. These works have continued to provide a sense of light and hope, especially to a younger generation of college-age students.

---

[1] https://communityadvice.tumblr.com/statement

On Legacy

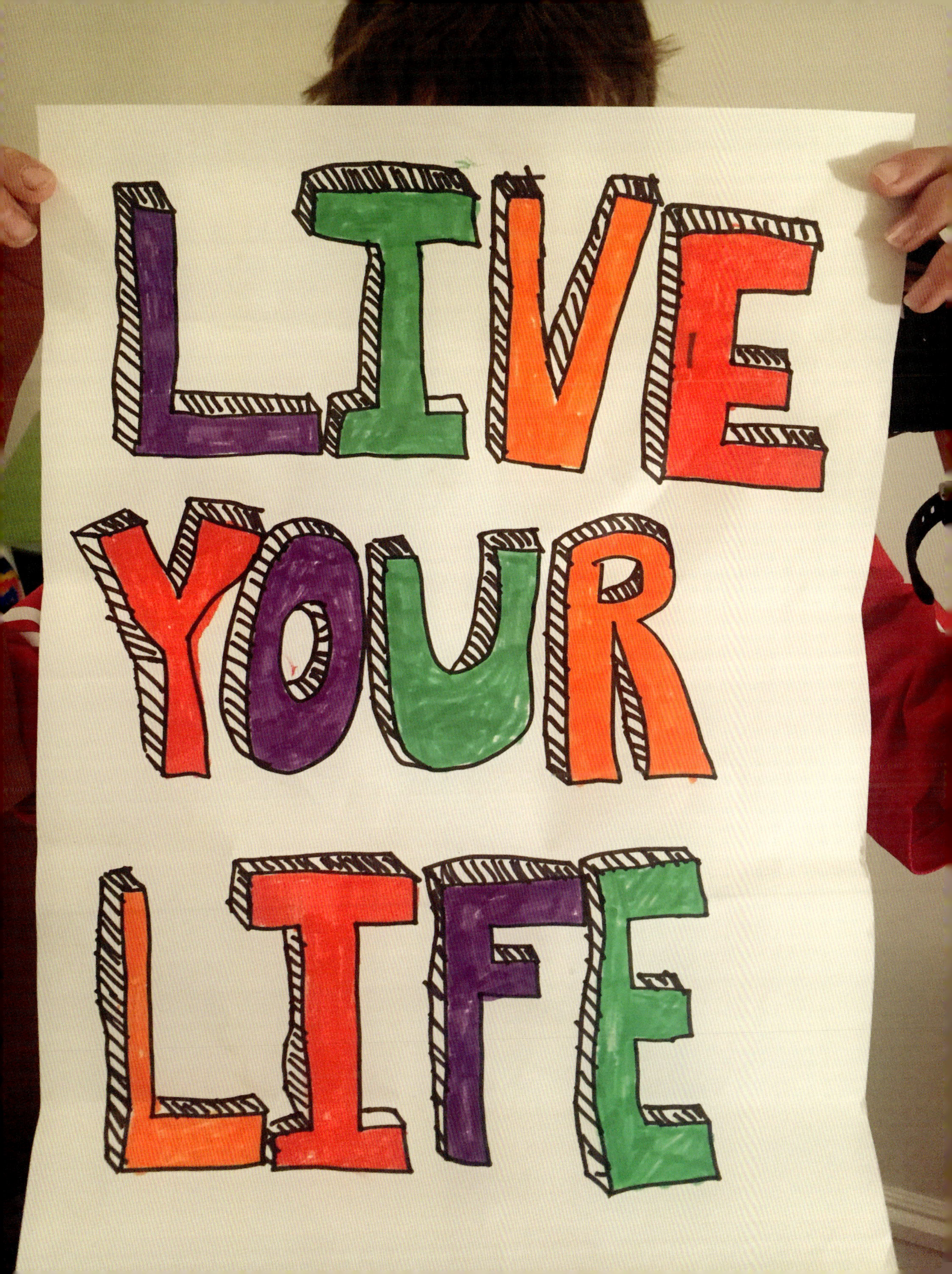
LIVE
YOUR
LIFE

Strategic and Necessary

Meg Shiffler

Staring down the camera with clenched fists at the ready, Susan O'Malley and Christina Amini pose for a photo promoting *Pep Talk Squad*, a collaborative performance-based public artwork launched in 2003. The prizefighter stances contrast with their open expressions and bright, friendly eyes. This image brings to mind the pivotal moment in the 2022 sci-fi film *Everything Everywhere All at Once*. As parallel universes are in chaos and face imminent destruction, Waymond Wang, deemed "silly" by his wife, delivers a heart-stopping monologue, a knockout punch that shatters her debilitating pessimism, heals their broken family, and restores balance to the multiverse.

> When I choose to see the good side of things, I'm not being naïve. It is strategic and necessary. It's how I learned to survive through everything. So, the only thing I do know is that we have to be kind. Please, be kind. Especially when we don't know what's going on. I know you see yourself as a fighter. Well, I see myself as one too. This is how I fight.

At another moment in the film, Waymond is asked how he shifted the mindset of a character hell-bent on landing a fatal financial blow. "I don't know. I just talked to her," he humbly responds, another testament to the power of connection and compassion. Understanding acts of empathy and kindness as deliberate survival tactics encourages an examination of Susan's work and her legacy through a lens of solidarity, responsibility, and impact.

As a graduate student at California College of the Arts in the nation's first Social Practice program, Susan asked her best friend and frequent collaborator Christina if she wanted to start a pep talk squad. Christina recalled thinking, "Sure. I'd do anything with Susan!" From 2003 to 2006 (with a short reprise in 2010), Susan and Christina offered pep talks to strangers in schools, galleries, and public spaces around the Bay Area. In each fifteen-minute session they listened compassionately, offered encouragement, and helped problem-solve.

In 2006, *Pep Talk Squad* was performed at Southern Exposure in San Francisco as a public program for the exhibition *Smart Ass*, curated by Kelsey Nicholson. At the event, Kelsey and her partner went into their Pep Talk thinking that it would be

---

Page 263: *Live Your Life*, elementary school student work inspired by Susan O'Malley, circa 2020

fun. They knew that Susan and Christina didn't have any formal training as counselors, and *Pep Talk Squad* was, by design, a little goofy, with matching red squad jackets and coordinated cheers. However, something unexpected occurred. Kelsey told me, "We were blown away by how deeply they listened and how insightful their feedback was. This totally magical thing happened, and in a way, it foretold the future of our relationship."

Scholar and author James Thompson has written extensively about the consideration of caregiving as an art practice and, conversely, the creation of artwork as an act of care. "Care Aesthetics is descriptive in analyzing and documenting the aesthetic experience of care in community, health and arts projects. But it is also normative—it is a proposal for change."[1] Thompson's framework uplifts and links the work of caregivers and artists as essential to vibrant, healthy, and sustainable communities as well as to more nourished and empowered lives.

Pep Talk Squad is a prime example of mutual aid, the act of community members voluntarily offering services or resources to each other, bypassing institutional support and systems of care within established structures. More than a decade after that project, democratizing care through mutual aid was in full swing during the COVID-19 pandemic. Neighbors, cultural communities, extended families, and friend circles mobilized to provide food distribution, childcare, mental and physical health support, transportation, and financial assistance. This multifaceted community-driven care was absolutely necessary for the survival and well-being of humankind across the globe. "Horrible in itself, disaster is sometimes a door back into paradise, the paradise at least in which we are who we hope to be, do the work we desire, and are each our sister's and brother's keeper. Many events plant seeds, imperceptible at the time, that bear fruit long afterward," writes Rebecca Solnit in her book *A Paradise Built in Hell*.

In 2022, an exhausting two years into the pandemic, artists Jessica Martin and Asherah Weiss bore such fruit as they collaborated with students at West Side Elementary in rural Healdsburg, California, to create *Peptoc*, a public art project inspired by *Pep Talk Squad* and Susan's *Advice from My 80-Year-Old Self*. The artists asked the students what they would say to "people having a bad day." *Peptoc* began with the display of posters designed by the students and continued with the activation of a call-in hotline offering the following menu of options: "If you're feeling mad, frustrated, or nervous, press one. If you need words of encouragement and life advice, press two. If you need a pep talk from kindergartners, press three. If you need to hear kids laughing with delight, press four. For encouragement in Spanish, press five."

Inspired by the personal nature and community scale of *Pep Talk Squad*, Asherah and Jessica anticipated a modest but impactful hometown response to *Peptoc*.

Instead, within days of launching, the hotline went viral. In a recent conversation, Jessica wondered if the massive ongoing response hinges on children's voices sparking the wisdom we all carry with us from our own childhood. *Peptoc* was not designed around adult perceptions of the naïve charm of children or a romanticization of their innocence. When a child tells you that you're going to be okay, it is a straightforward and powerful articulation of the interconnectedness of human experiences as well as an affirmation of our resiliency. Asherah affirms, "It's so deep because it's so simple."

The mutual aid provided by *Pep Talk Squad* was a customized, face-to-face, intimate experience between Social Practice artists and participant-collaborators in public spaces. In contrast, *Peptoc* was created through a meaningful engagement between teaching artists and students resulting in a heartfelt packaged gift to anyone in need of support. Yet the generous intent and transformative results of both projects were the same.

Has someone ever said something so kind to you that the words are embedded in a little lockbox in your psyche where paradigm-shifting sentiments live? The outcome of giving and receiving thoughtful and positive support ranges from momentary joy or relief to cataclysmic shifts that change the direction of the future by derailing us from one path to another or opening up an expanse that was closed before. A drop of water and all of its infinite ripples.

Susan O'Malley's portfolio is a collection of works that confront and challenge us to ward off cynicism and judgment in order to fearlessly embrace self-care and care for others. Jessica explains, "Susan systematically refused to hide behind the irony in art. She was just all heart and all love and all humanity." Community-engaged works like *Pep Talk Squad* and *Peptoc* are not humble, or quaint, or idealistic. They are exactly as described in *Everything Everywhere All at Once*—strategic and necessary.

---

[1] James Thompson. "Care Aesthetics, Coronavirus and Everyday Life." *Performance Research* 27, no. 6-7 (2022): 54-6.

Opposite: Part of the *PepToc* project, Jessica Martin's son, August, hangs his poster on a pole on a street in Healdsburg, California, 2022

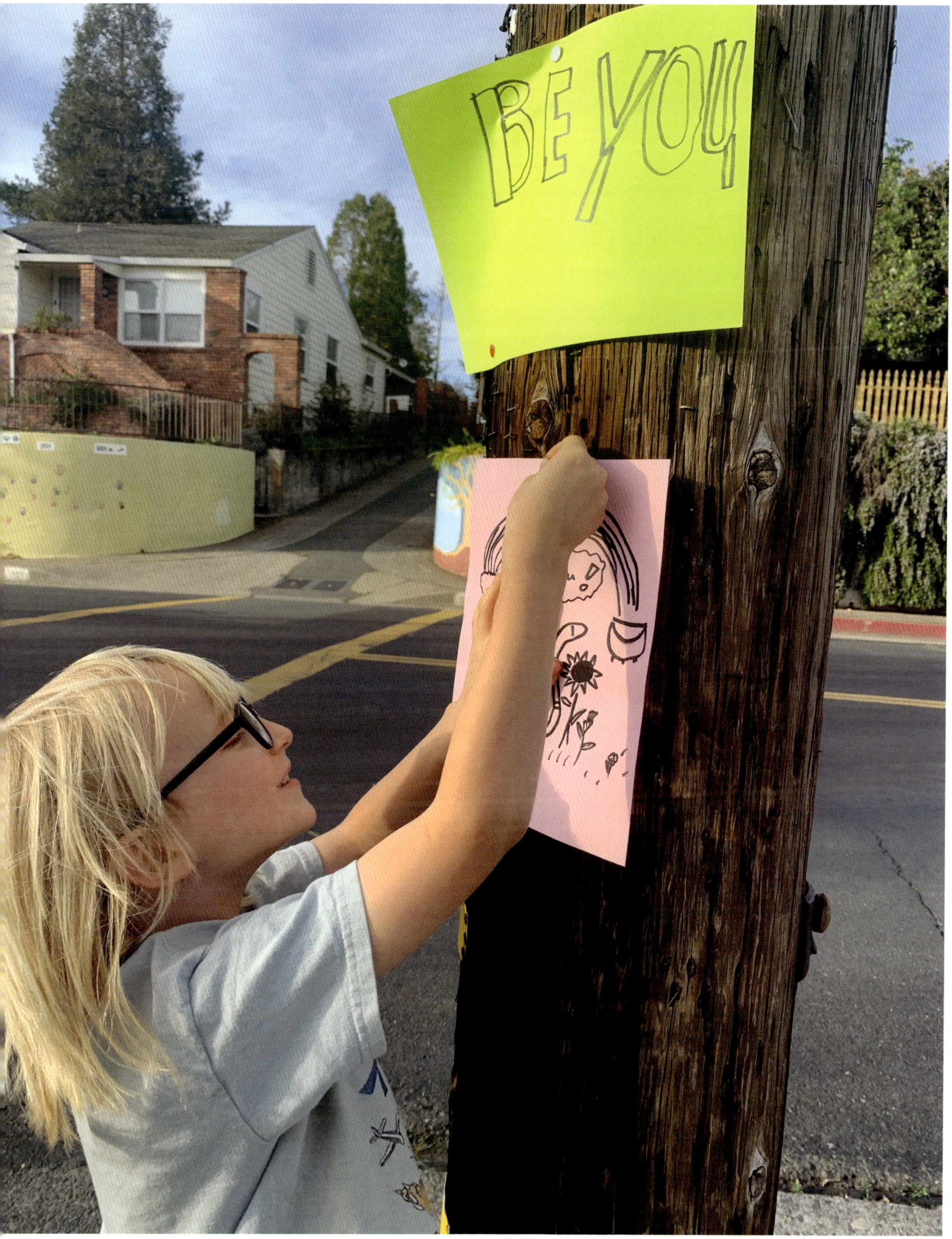
BE YOU

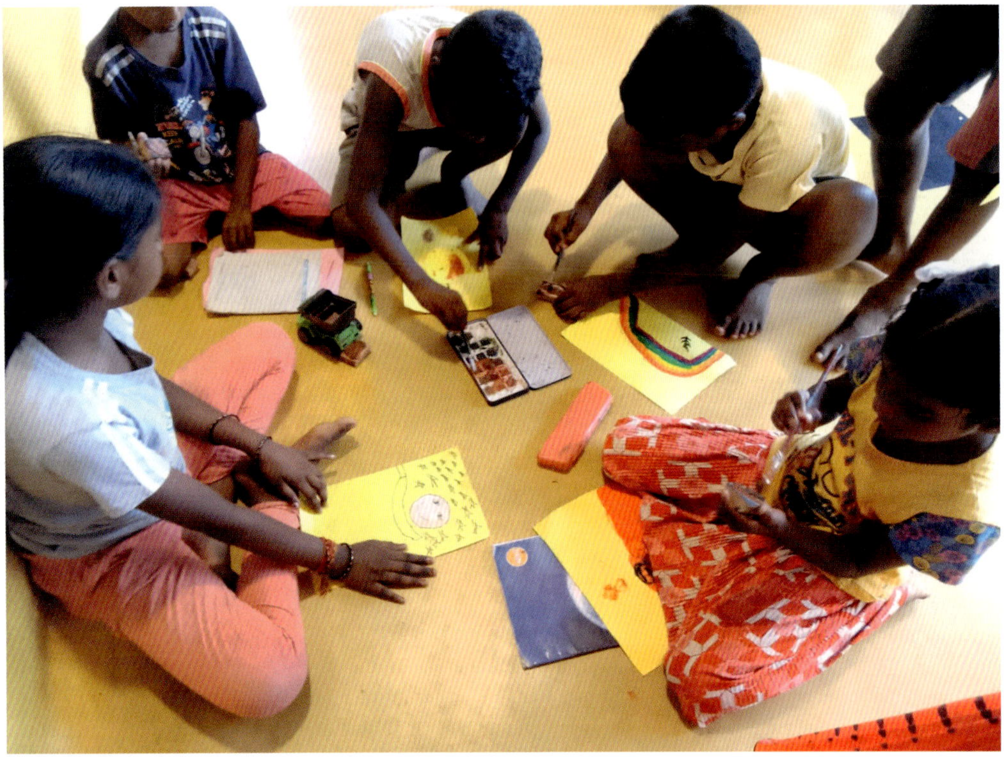

Above: Students in India working on their *PepToc* posters, 2022

Opposite: A child hangs up her *PepToc* poster in her community in San José, Costa Rica, 2022

Pages 270-71: *PepToc* posters from students in California, 2022

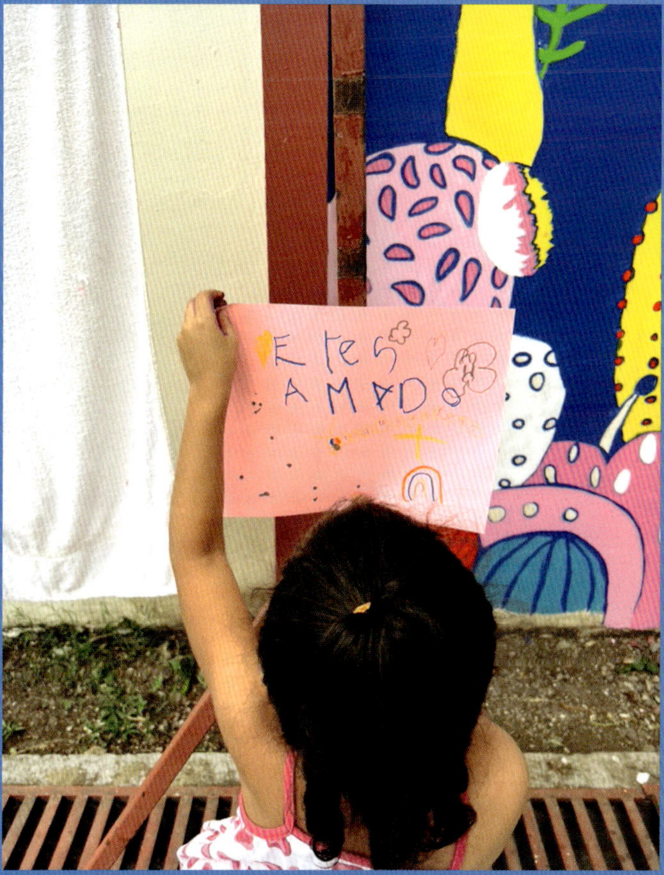
Eres
AMADO

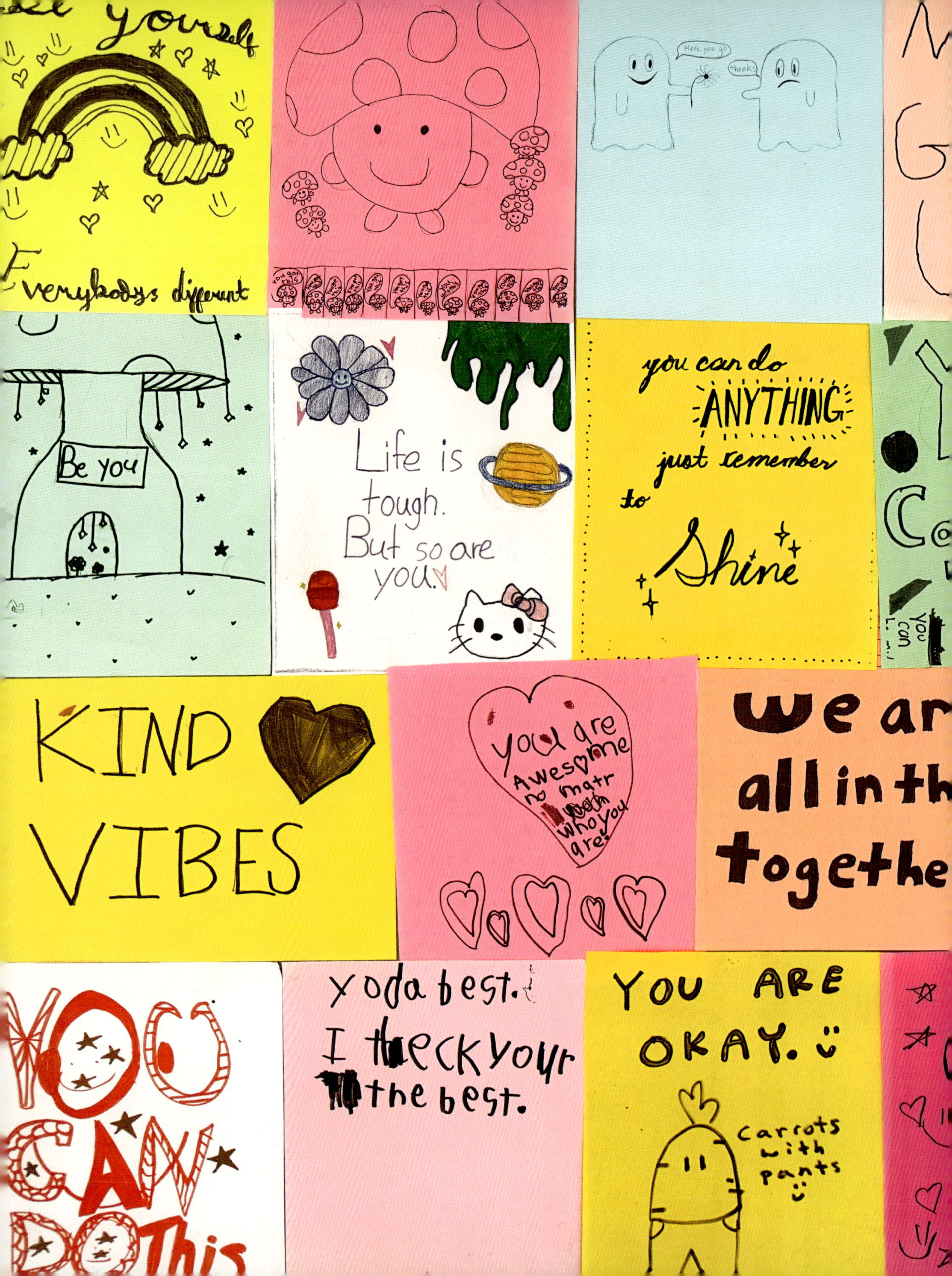
yourself
Everybodys different
Here you go
thanks
Be you
Life is tough. But so are you.
you can do ANYTHING just remember to Shine
KIND VIBES
you are Awesome no matr who you are
we ar
all in th
togethe
YOU CAN DO This
yoda best.
I check your the best.
YOU ARE OKAY.
carrots with pants

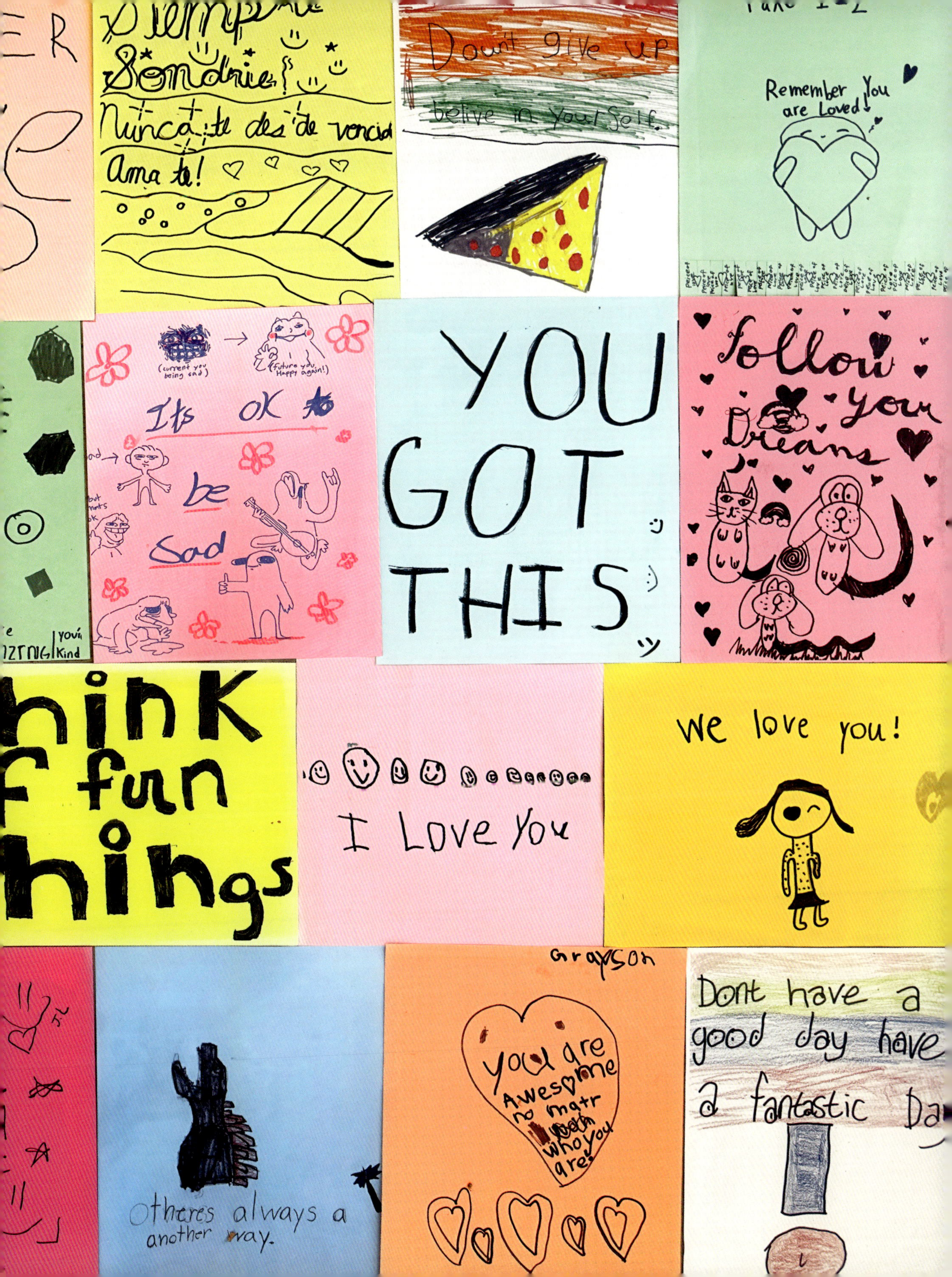
Sondrie!
Nunca te des de vencida
Ama te!
Don't give up
belive in yourself
Remember You are Loved!
It's OK to be Sad
(current you being sad)
(Future you Happy again!)
YOU GOT THIS
follow your Dreams
hink
f fun
hings
I Love You
we love you!
you're kind
Grayson
you are Awesome no matr who you are
Dont have a good day have a fantastic Day
theres always a another way.

Peptoc

Jessica Martin and Asherah Weiss

On a spring day in 2022, we went to West Side Elementary, a rural public school in Healdsburg, California, to work on our new community-based art project called *Peptoc*. In each class we started by asking, "What is something you could do or say that would help someone who is having a hard day?" All hands would immediately shoot up in the air. These kids had been through wildfires, a pandemic, and the challenges of growing up—they were fountains of wise and hilarious advice.

We invited them to collaborate with us in making posters out of their encouraging messages, which we would then post all around town for the local community. We also explained that Jessica would be creating a hotline featuring prerecorded pep talks by any student who wanted to contribute.

For inspiration to help get us started, we showed the students images from Susan O'Malley's *Advice from My 80-Year-Old Self* and her *Pep Talk Squad* with Christina Amini. As artists working in Social Practice, we wanted to teach the kids that art is much broader than just the typical drawing and painting class; it can be a conversation, a handmade poster hung on the street, or a simple act of generosity.

Little did we know, these students were also about to learn that a creative act can start a worldwide movement for joy. Three days after Jessica shared the completed hotline with the school community, it suddenly went viral, receiving sixty thousand calls an hour and media attention from all over the world. In the first two years of its existence, the hotline received a total of sixteen million calls, and it is still going strong to this day. Letters of thanks have been sent to the students from first responders, people suffering with anxiety, and other children. The hotline has been adopted as part of mental health programs for hospitals and schools. It has even saved lives.

We received numerous requests from around the world to participate in the project. In response, we invited anyone twenty-one or younger to create a poster in their home language, hang it up where they live, and send us a photo of it. We ended up receiving submissions from twenty-five different countries and all across the United States. We then turned a collection of these posters into a book, entitled *You Are Amazing Like a Rocket* (a phrase coined by a West Side fifth grader).

Susan O'Malley's legacy is deeply embedded in this project. Her spirit of generosity and playfulness and her belief in expansive approaches to art practice inform every aspect of our work with young people. Through her work and our project, we are reminded that creativity can span cultures, political affiliations, and age groups; and that creative practice gives us connection and support when we need it most. In addition, Susan's legacy lives on through a generation of children who have seen firsthand that their creativity and voice can make a life-shifting, positive impact on the world.

Do *you* need some encouragement? Call 707-8-PEPTOC.

Image Credits

Pages 2, 229, and 279: Photos by Christina Amini

Pages 60–61: Photos courtesy of Jon Rubin

Pages 91 and 94: Photos by Phil Yip

Page 109: Photo by Jake McConnell

Pages 143, 147–52, 158–61, and 179–81: Photos by Susan O'Malley, courtesy of Montalvo Arts Center, Saratoga, CA

Pages 154–57: Photos by Isaiah Plaza, © 2020 by Montalvo Arts Center, Saratoga, CA

Pages 172–75: Photos courtesy of Benjamin Laramie

Pages 177 and 195–97: Photos by Don Ross.

Page 186: Photo courtesy of Leah Rosenberg

Pages 189–93: Photos courtesy of Leah Rosenberg, Irving Street Projects, and Kelly Inouye

Pages 201–11: Photos courtesy of Jonn Herschend

Pages 213 and 218–19: Photos courtesy of Palo Alto Art Center, Palo Alto, CA

Page 215: Photo by Terry Acebo Davis

Page 221: Photos by Rebecca Barbee

Pages 239–43: Photos by Scott Chernis

Pages 258–59: Photo by Glen Cheriton, courtesy of the Institute of Contemporary Art San José, San Jose, CA

Pages 267 and 270–71: Photos by Jessica Martin

Page 268: Photo courtesy of Thamarai Educational Projects

Page 269: Photo by Zoe Holtermann

About the Contributors

CHRISTINA AMINI is the steward of the Estate of Susan O'Malley and a longtime collaborator of the artist. She is the Gift Publisher at Chronicle Books as well as an author and editor. Amini oversees O'Malley's art legacy, with an interest in sharing O'Malley's work with a wide audience. She lives in the Bay Area with her family.

JANET BISHOP is a Bay Area native and a longtime curator at the San Francisco Museum of Modern Art. Notable recent projects include traveling retrospectives of the work of Ruth Asawa, Joan Brown, and David Park.

VANESSA BLAIKIE and **JOEY PIZIALI** are the cofounders and codirectors of Romer Young Gallery, formerly Ping Pong Gallery. Their first solo exhibition with Susan O'Malley was in 2009, followed by her second solo exhibition, *My Healing Garden Is Green*, in 2012.

KEVIN B. CHEN has been an active presence in the Bay Area arts community for over three decades, working as a curator, visual artist, and educator.

DONNA CONWELL is a Bay Area–based curator who works with artists on the creation of new work, often in public spaces. She was a curator at the Lucas Artists Residency Program at Montalvo Arts Center from 2011 to 2024.

AMANDA CURRERI is an artist and educator living on the unceded territory of Tiwa and Pueblo Peoples, also known as Albuquerque, New Mexico. Her artwork is situated between textiles and painting characterized by an engagement with histories of social organizing and liberation.

HARRELL FLETCHER is the editor and copublisher of Some People Press, which supports and publishes the writing of formerly incarcerated writers (and others). He also volunteers at various animal welfare organizations in Oregon and goes on long walks every day.

LORI GORDON is a Bay Area–based artist whose work explores belief, coincidence, and humanity's relationship to the larger world. Through collaborative and experiential projects, she creates frameworks that invite unexpected interactions and make the ineffable visible.

JONN HERSCHEND is an award-winning filmmaker and experimental publisher who lives in Pasadena, California.

ELLEN KATO is one of Susan O'Malley's five siblings and was also, at times, her videographer and artistic collaborator. Ellen is a nurse practitioner focused on building and maintaining relationships with patients.

KAREN KIENZLE has been in the role of director of the Palo Alto Art Center since 2009. Her career has been dedicated to exploring the potential of art and museums as tools for communication, learning, personal expression, and community building.

BENJAMIN LARAMIE is a designer and craftsperson whose work focuses on materials, handcraft, and spatial design—emphasizing the integrity and enduring value of making by hand.

JESSICA MARTIN is a multidisciplinary artist based in Northern California. Her work is inspired by our sources of joy and the ways we experience meaningful connection to the world around us.

CARISSA POTTER is just a human trying (and sometimes failing) to connect. She makes art, writes books (like *Breathe Through It*), and runs the gift line People I've Loved while hosting *Bad at Keeping Secrets*, a newsletter about other humans doing fascinating things. She lives in Oakland with her partner and daughter and is practicing the messy art of loving people exactly as they are.

LAWRENCE RINDER is director emeritus of the UC Berkeley Art Museum and Pacific Film Archive. Formerly he was founding director of the Wattis Institute at California College of the Arts (CCA) and curator of Contemporary Art at the Whitney Museum of American Art. He has taught art and cultural history at Columbia University, UC Berkeley, CCA, and Deep Springs College.

LEAH ROSENBERG works across media—painting, installation, printmaking, sculpture, performance, and video—to spark new experiences of color. Her multisensory, multidimensional approach invites viewers to consider color's emotional and psychological impact in daily life, creating enriched encounters that deepen perception and connection.

JON RUBIN is an interdisciplinary artist who creates collaborative interventions into public life that reimagine individual, group, and institutional behavior. His socially engaged projects include running a barter-based nomadic art school, founding a national museum, operating a restaurant that produces a live talk show with its customers, and codirecting another that serves cuisine only from countries with which the United States is in conflict.

MEG SHIFFLER is a Bay Area–based curator, writer, and educator. She cocurated, with Kevin B. Chen, the solo exhibition *Do More of What You Love: Susan O'Malley* (January–May 2016) at the San Francisco Arts Commission Galleries, where Shiffler was the director and chief curator from 2005 to 2022. She is currently the inaugural director of Artist Space Trust, the nation's first community land trust for artists and culture bearers, and also the founder and curator of *Cities of Glass*, a ten-year independent project featuring commissioned works by global artists.

KELLY SICAT, director of the Lucas Artists Program at Montalvo Arts Center, supports the work of over one hundred artists each year; she sets vision and is responsible for the curation of annual thematic exhibitions, newly commissioned works, and development of strategic partnerships. She is the coeditor of *Hello Goodbye Hello*, a polyvocal reflection on the role of artist residencies in the life of an artist.

BONNIE TSUI is a journalist and author who lives in Berkeley, California.

ASHERAH WEISS is a community artist and educator based in Northern California. Her work encourages everyone to be creative through visual arts and improvisational play.

GRIFF WILLIAMS is an American painter, publisher, filmmaker, and gallerist. In 1993, he founded Gallery 16 in San Francisco. It was a prominent part of the art community for thirty-two years, working with artists including Lynn Hershman Leeson, William Kentridge, Jim Isermann, bell hooks, Rex Ray, Margaret Kilgallen, Mark Grotjahn, Paul Sietsema, Arturo Herrera, Michelle Grabner, and Ari Marcopoulos.

CHRISTINE WONG YAP is a visual artist and social practitioner who gathers and amplifies grassroots perspectives on belonging, resilience, and mental well-being through community engagement, drawing, printmaking, publishing, textiles, and public art.

Acknowledgments

Making a book is an act of love.

Thank you to all the contributors for your words and work. For saying "YES!" immediately.

Thank you to Team Susan Art, who, many years ago, helped me find my footing as the steward of Susan O'Malley's art estate. To Leah Rosenberg, thank you for being a sounding board and collaborator.

Thank you to the dear Chronicle Books team; to the entire company for the way you brought *Advice from My 80-Year-Old Self* to publication and expanded Susan's legacy in a way that only a book can. To the creative team on this book—Mirabelle Korn, Kristen Hewitt, Erin Thacker, Steve Kim, Michele Posner, Diane Levinson, and Karah Bengs—your attention, generosity of spirit, expertise, and collaboration is an extraordinary gift to me, to Susan, and to readers.

Thank you to editor and art enthusiast Bridget Watson Payne for being the first to imagine this book. My deep gratitude for you as a catalyst and comrade.

Thank you to the O'Malley family and to Tim Caro-Bruce for trusting me with Susan's legacy.

Thank you, Susan, for being an artist and a friend, always.

Opposite: Susan O'Malley in *Now Serving: Love*, San José Museum of Art, California, 2013

Page 280: *Love Is Everywhere Look for It* from *Community Advice* series, 2012

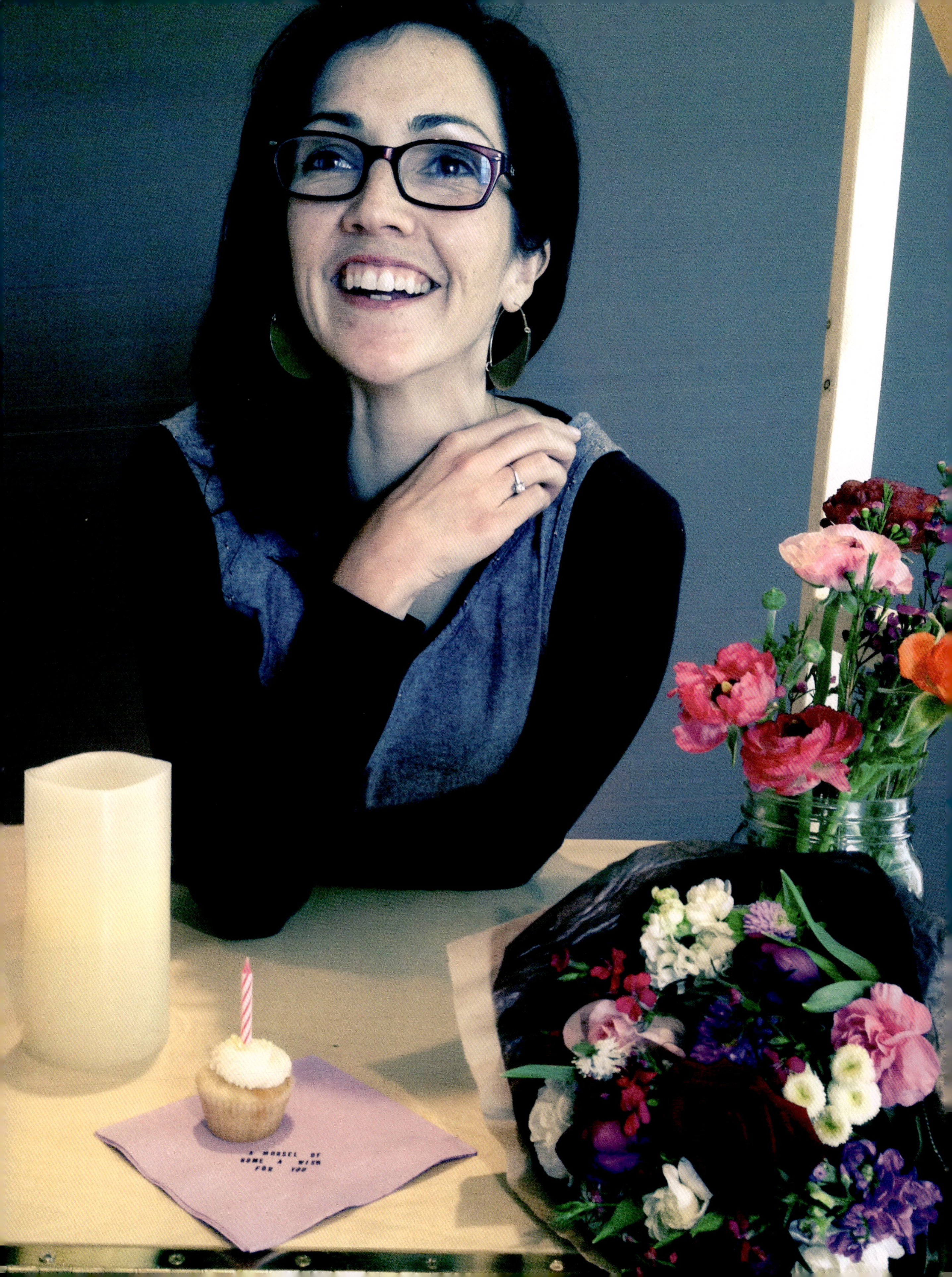
A MORSEL OF
HOME A WISH
FOR YOU

LOVE

IS EVERYWHERE
LOOK FOR IT